ARCHITECTURAL LIGHTING DESIGN

ARCHITECTURAL LIGHTING DESIGN

SECOND EDITION

GARY STEFFY

JOHN WILEY & SONS, INC.

Cover

The images on the cover are more thoroughly illustrated and discussed throughout the text. Clockwise from upper left, project locations and photo credits are: Michigan State Capitol in Lansing, ©Deitrich Floeter; University of Michigan Engineering Center in Ann Arbor, ©Stephen Graham; Frauenthal Theater in Muskegon, Michigan, ©Deitrich Floeter; St. Andrews Cathedral in Grand Rapids, Michigan, ©Gary Steffy Lighting Design Inc.; Penobscot Building in Detroit, Michigan, ©Glen Calvin Moon; Giorgio Beverly Hills in Beverly Hills, California, ©Stephen Graham.

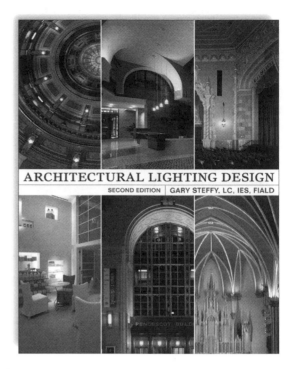

ARCHITECTURAL LIGHTING DESIGN

SECOND EDITION | GARY STEFFY, LC, IES, FIALD

This book was set in Univers 55 by Gary Steffy.

Library of Congress Cataloging–in–Publication Data

Steffy, Gary R.
    Architectural lighting design / Gary R. Steffy. —2nd ed.
      p. cm.
    Includes bibliographical references and index.
    ISBN 0–471–38638–3 (cloth)
    1. Lighting, Architectural and decorative. I. Title

TH7703 .S78 2001
621.32—dc21   2001023736

Printed in the United States of America
10 9 8 7 6 5 4 3 2 1

Contents

Contents

Preface

Yikes! In the first edition's preface, written in 1989, I indicated that the idea for a lighting design textbook came to me nearly ten years prior (so that's now long ago!). Certainly this book idea was not, and still is not, a unique one, but as both a practicing lighting designer and an educator (with stints at Michigan State University, The Pennsylvania State University, Wayne State University, and the University of Michigan since 1980), I thought I could bring a valuable perspective to the writing, reading, teaching, and learning of lighting design. The first edition was fun to write. Feedback on its readability was quite positive. Some universities adopted it as a class text, which was gratifying. But as I used the text myself, I saw shortcomings in its breadth. Further changes in technology since 1995 left much of the lamp, ballast, and luminaire discussions dated.

So, this second edition was encouraged by my editor at John Wiley & Sons, Inc., Margaret Cummins. Many thanks to her for the encouragement and for working through the enormous task of updating and renewing the text. Indeed, what started as an effort to inject some new material, update others, and leave nearly half of the text as it was, grew into a significant make-over. This is a second edition in title only. All new artwork, all new text and tables, and major additions of material constitute this second edition of *Architectural Lighting Design*.

Since 1990, priorities have changed in lighting design and in design practice. More is expected faster (by everyone of everyone else). Energy efficiency is growing in importance. Sustainability is now a priority. And yet, comfort in living and working environments, and productivity in work settings remain paramount to our present human condition. Lighting is in the thick of it—more than people realize. This text addresses lighting as the important, indeed critical, building system and design medium that it is.

Without good lighting, there is little reason to design such things as expensive granite lobby walls, or to detail beautiful millwork, or to break the bank on the best computers, or to spend millions on streetscapes. Without good lighting, we waste billions of dollars on salaries, benefits, and on energy—as folks are less comfortable and less productive. Good lighting does not mean expensive—except when compared to most of the lousy stuff passed off as "lighting" onto unsuspecting buyers and users every day.

This second edition more broadly covers lighting than its predecessor. An introductory chapter sets the stage for lighting as a medium and a business. The second chapter addresses lighting as the solution that it is to the biology of seeing. The remainder of the text essentially follows the phasing of most projects' design efforts—defining scope; programming; schematic design; design development (encompassed by several chapters—daylighting; lamps; luminaires; controls; design tools); contract documents; and construction administration. There was a lot of material left on the cutting room floor. Look for some of this to perhaps show up on the website www.ald2e.com. This is where updates will be posted and direct links are available to the online references cited herein.

Second edition.......

- Cited definitions throughout
- Light and health
- Environmental issues
- Programming
- Schematic design
- Daylighting
- Lamp technologies
- Cost magnitudes
- Contract documents
- Value engineering

Acknowledgments

There are many folks responsible in some way for my effort here. I specifically wish to thank Professor John Flynn for his devotion to lighting and architectural engineering during his tenure at Penn State. He taught me to appreciate light. Thanks also to Steve Squillace, David DiLaura, and Mark Rea.

Preface

Steve was my boss and mentor at Smith, Hinchman & Grylls in Detroit in the late 1970s and early 1980s. Steve was responsible for my career in lighting design. David, now at the University of Colorado, was (and still is) the provocateur—asking the tough questions about the vagaries of lighting design—and at the same time he was the illuminating engineer to whom many of us turned (and still do turn) for technically accurate answers to lighting quantity and performance questions. Mark, now with the Lighting Research Center at Rensselaer, was (and also still is) an even more direct (shall I say pushy?) provocateur. His questions were/are not only pointed, but less rhetorical and more practical. These folks help push my level of interest and professionalism in lighting, and for that I thank them immensely.

Mrs. John Flynn was instrumental in fulfilling my efforts to present some of Professor Flynn's work here in Chapter 4. Mrs. Flynn has kept much of John's work intact and available for review and, in this case, publication so that others may learn from his endeavors in the subjective aspects of lighting. Although running the Flynn clan is indeed Mrs. Flynn's priority, she has always been gracious in finding time to talk and meet with me about John's work. She was most gracious to offer the images that are Figures 4.22 through 4.27. Thank you, Iris.

Virginia North, now with Lawrence Technological University, took the time and trouble more than five years ago to review the first edition of *Architectural Lighting Design*, annotate her copy, and turn it over to me for consideration in development of this second edition. Her review served as a preliminary outline for updating the book. Many of her notes were literally interpreted and used in the writing of this second edition. Thank you, Virginia.

Bob Davis, now with the University of Colorado, was kind enough to critique the first four chapters. These were major rewrite efforts and set the tone for the rest of the book. I very much enjoyed Bob's critical approach that kept me, and the second edition, on track. Thank you, Bob.

Reviewers over the last decade have been most helpful in this rewrite effort. Some of these are indeed anonymous (as is typical in the book business, reviews are sought by potential users [in this case, university instructors] of both the first edition and of the proposed outline for revising the text—anonymity helps assure a sincere review). One reviewer whose effort was published and that helped shape the text in parts was Bob Marans, professor at the University of Michigan. A very insightful critique that I have attempted to address in this second edition. Thank you.

Thanks to my staff, Gary Woodall, LC, IES, IALD, and Damon Grimes for their help in artwork development, review, and keeping the practice going while I was writing. Thanks to my wife, Laura, and daughter, Heather, for what is becoming a biennial effort—allowing me to write away in quiet. Thanks to the manufacturers for permission to use their respective artwork throughout.

Finally, where would I be without copyeditors? Thanks very much to Diana Cisek and Liz Roles for such a thorough effort.

Practice and enjoy good lighting. Without it we have no environments worthy of the expense, trouble, and environmental havoc they incur.

Gary Steffy, LC, IES, FIALD
President
Gary Steffy Lighting Design Inc.
Ann Arbor, Michigan
gsteffy@ald2e.com

Background

D iving right into a discussion on **light** and lighting will inevitably result in discovery of previously unheard or at least undefined terms and techniques. Learning terminology out of context in a strictly glossary format is less than motivating, however. So, throughout the text, terms and phrases in boldface type are defined in sidebars along the outside margins. This allows quick reference without burdening the text discussion with verbose definitions.

In the United States, close to US$10 billion per year of lighting hardware is sold.[1] Lighting consumes nearly 25 percent of the electrical energy produced, or roughly half a trillion kilowatt hours (500 billion kwh) each year.[2] This results in expenditures approaching US$40 billion per year on electricity for lighting, not to mention the attendant charges for electricity to run air conditioners to cool such a load. More significantly, however, some of these lighting expenditures propel the working Americans who earn combined salaries of US$5.3 trillion.[3] These folks are then responsible for producing goods and services worth in excess of US$9.2 trillion per year.[4] Some of these lighting expenditures help Americans live in their homes and apartments. The challenge for the design team is to leverage the lighting operating and initial costs to get the most out of the built environment—more comfortable living environments and more productive work environments.

Architectural lighting design (also cited throughout as "lighting design") introduced here as an abstract theorem would be uninspiring and misleading. Lighting is a science *and* an art. Therefore, while many of the issues introduced here are grounded in science, much of the practical application discussed here is grounded in the art of practicing lighting design. So you will get a good dose of the author's perspective of what constitutes good lighting design practice—a perspective that has evolved and changed since the writing of the first edition ten years ago. Other lighting designers may practice differently—with different emphasis on different lighting criteria, on different lighting techniques, on different physiological aspects, and on different cultural aspects. Indeed, this is what makes lighting more an art and less a science.

Other lighting design branches or professions include automotive, television/studio, theater, exhibit/display, and concert. Some designers work in more than one branch, crossing from theater and/or concert to architectural, for example. This book deals with lighting design intended for permanent architectural applications, such as commercial (offices), institutional (healthcare, educational, and libraries, etc.), hospitality (restaurants, clubs, lounges, and hotels, etc.), governmental (government centers and courthouses, etc.), research (laboratories), and industrial. Residential and retail applications are also considered a part of architectural lighting design and are included here. However, these two applications rely heavily on theatrical techniques.

In the more than 100 years since the introduction of a commercially viable incandescent lamp, and no doubt accelerated with the introduction of the fluorescent lamp seventy years ago, shortcuts, rules of thumb, or **engineered approaches** solely addressing **illuminance** have evolved to shape lighting "design." Indeed, in an effort to make lighting a rote procedure. To save time (for the designers, engineers, distributors, manufacturers, and contractors). To such a point, that today energy legislation and light trespass

---

light

Visible radiation. Energy or electromagnetic waves operating at a frequency that stimulates photoreceptors in the eye. But think of our response to light as an "aftereffect." We see what happens after electromagnetic waves react to or interact with surfaces, objects, and materials. This reflected and/or transmitted light comprises our visual scene.

architectural lighting design

Lighting design dealing with more permanent applications associated with architecture and landscape architecture. Unlike the more transitory applications of theater lighting, concert lighting, trade show exhibit lighting, and the like. Throughout this text, architectural lighting design and architectural lighting designer (or lighting designer or designer) refer to the act of or the individual involved in the act of designing lighting for permanent architecture and/or landscape architecture.

Lighting.............................

- Hardware costs US$10 billion/year
- Consumes 25% of US electricity
- Electricity costs US$40 billion/year
- Influences sight for workers producing US$9.2 trillion/year in goods and services

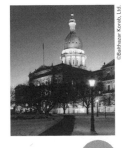

©Balthazar Korab, Ltd.

1

1.1 Background

engineered approaches

A reference to lighting solutions that are derived by specifying lighting layouts and hardware solely or almost solely on their ability to meet only illuminance criteria.

illuminance

The quantity of light falling on a given surface. Although important, illuminance is much too often the only criterion used to design a lighting solution. This is poor practice. US Customary: footcandles or fc. SI: lux or lx. About 10 lx = 1 fc.

soft (art) issues

Those aspects of lighting design that are not well grounded in scientific research, but based on anecdotal evidence (experience) and, perhaps, limited formal study(ies) and are believed to contribute to the success/failure of any given lighting design.

hard (science) issues

Those aspects of lighting design that are reasonably well grounded in scientific research and/or industry consensus as contributing to the success/failure of any given lighting design. Specific criteria targets can be established and then solutions derived via calculations to show compliance with criteria.

and light pollution ordinances are the excuses du jour for the sad lighting that is implemented every day in most every application in most every country around the world. This book, however, will help the reader realize the pitfalls of such limited design effort and explore the amazing potential that light (and, therefore, lighting) has on human comfort, productivity, visual "fabric" and architectural enhancement, and quality of life.

Right up front, it is important to know that the reference to "lighting designer" or "designer" throughout this text is to the individual or group of individuals responsible for the design, layout, and specification of the lighting recommended to achieve various lighting effects (qualities) and quantities on any given project. Lighting designers may have formal titles, such as architect, interior designer, electrical engineer and lighting designer. Indeed, on most projects worldwide, the architect, the interior designer, and/or the electrical engineer are the lighting designer.

So, like its predecessor, this second edition of *Architectural Lighting Design* is based on the author's lighting design experiences. Many of the issues covered here are "soft"—that is, anecdotal evidence suggests that their consideration is worthwhile, but you are likely to find that your own knowledge of these **soft issues** will grow and perhaps change with your design experiences. This growing experience base will then help to further enhance and shape your own design approach. Such refinement will continue as long as your design career continues if you are to remain a competitive, innovative designer.

Certainly, **hard issues** are addressed here, too. These include more engineering/scientific issues for which bodies of both empirical and anecdotal evidence exist. The successful lighting designer balances the soft and hard issues on every project. For residential projects, for example, soft issues are typically more important. Yet, for commercial projects, hard issues are typically more important. Nevertheless, tempering the hard issues with soft issues in commercial projects will generally lead to better work environments.

It is because of these soft and hard issues that lighting is often cited as both an art and a science. Lighting involves space, volume, form, texture, color, image (e.g., corporate image), and people—most of all, people. Lighting is both a **physiological** and **psychological** inducer. Above all else, regardless of the corporate image or the designer's ego, light (and, therefore, lighting) is about the people who are to use the space. Our task should be development of solutions that enhance people activities.

Design issues......
- Soft (art)
- Hard (science)
- Balancing the two

1.1 Conventions

Metrication has been accomplished throughout the world except in a few countries, the United States being the proverbial tail wagging the dog. Unfortunately, and increasingly, this requires a proficiency in both Système Internationale (SI) units and US Customary (aka, English, American or inch–pound) units. Table 1.1 outlines the more pertinent lighting metrics and respective units. Although both US Customary and SI units are referenced throughout the text, for precise, hard conversions, use Table 1.1. It is never

©Balthazar Korab, Ltd.

Background

wise, therefore, to speak of quantitative lighting criteria without attaching the intended unit of measure. For example, when one discusses the average illuminance in a parking lot, a responsible reference is to 5 lux. If one were to simply indicate that the lot illuminance is 5, the party hearing the information may, depending on his/her country of origin and educational background, mistake such a reference as 5 footcandles (which is about ten times the intensity of 5 lux).

Experience with any metric is important to understanding its significance and to appreciating degrees of variability and absolute quantities. In other words, look for opportunities to measure distance and to measure illuminance and luminance during educational exercises. This will allow greater ease of use of these metrics in a design career and will encourage greater rapport with the other design professionals on a project team and with peers.

more online @
http://physics.nist.gov/cuu/Units/index.html

1.2 Defining the problem—it's about vision

So, the problem for the lighting designer is not first and foremost a fashion problem—not an issue of selecting the most stylistically current **luminaire**. It is not primarily a problem of picking the most efficacious (see **efficacy** sidebar) **lamp** or the cheapest luminaire. The problem is about vision— helping end users to see comfortably and effectively. Seeing tasks well and offering sufficient comfort and pleasantness that people stay long enough to perform the task(s) expected of them in a reasonable timeframe. Not necessarily "work," but also typical living situations, such as reading the newspaper, shopping, strolling a downtown street with friends, enjoying a **son et lumière**, etc. Without light and/or the use of our eyes, we have neither visual architecture nor visual interior design. Engineering principles and artistic principles must be used together to address the physiological and psychological needs of the viewers—the people using the environments. Chapter 2 offers a more detailed discussion on the problem that lies ahead for any lighting designer and on every project. Then the remainder of the text is devoted to helping the designer establish a systematic approach for solving the problem on each project. This is an approach to identify issues and techniques for resolution, a framework for developing solution options, and a method for specifying the solution and following it through construction. Think about a lighting design approach this way. Three projects with identical uses, but three different clients need lighting design work. Depending on how each client prioritizes issues, the lighting design will and should be different. In one, emphasis might be on first cost. In another, emphasis might be on worker comfort/productivity. In the third, emphasis might be on sustainability. It is highly unlikely that the same lighting equipment laid out in the same way will meet these and other varying goals of all three projects while also meeting the users' physiological and psychological issues. The designer has to reserve these vision issues as foremost in any situation—otherwise what's the point of doing any construction project? Of course, this will, at times, conflict with the client's stated goals. Part of the design assignment, then, is to develop a lighting program, a lighting design, and a "sales pitch" to advance a lighting design appropriate for the users.

physiological

Pertaining to the human body's physical response. Lighting initiates vision through muscular, chemical, and neurological actions.

psychological

For purposes here, pertaining to the human mind's emotional or subjective response. In other words, the brain's reaction to physiological actions brought on by light. Light and color are believed to influence people's psychological reactions and influence their preferences for various architectural and/or landscape settings.

luminaire

The entire assembly of hardware components, including lamp(s), ballast(s), transformer(s), lens(es), reflector(s), socket(s), wiring and wiring connections, housing, etc., that result in a complete, operational (once installed and "hooked up") light source (aka, light fixture).

efficacy

The effectiveness of a lamp in producing light (**lumens**) relative to the power (watts) required to operate the lamp. Expressed as **lumens** per watt (LPW).

lumens

A measure of the amount of light emitted by a light source (lamp, sky, or sun) or falling onto a surface regardless of directionality.

©Balthazar Korab, Ltd.

1.3 Background

Table 1.1 Conventions

Metric	US Customary	Système Internationale (SI)	Conversion (US to SI)
Illuminance	footcandle (fc)	lux (lx)	multiply fc by 10.76
Length	inches (in)	millimeters (mm) [used for lighting hardware dimensions]	multiply in by 25.4
	feet (ft)	meters [used for architectural dimensions]	multiply ft by 0.3
Luminance	footLambert (fL)	candelas per square meter (cd/m^2)	multiply fL by 3.4
Power	watts (w)	watts (w)	NA
Power budget	watts per square feet (w/ft^2)	watts per square meter (w/m^2)	multiply w/ft^2 by 10.76
Temperature	°F	°K (re: visible radiation)[a]	°K = [(5/9)*T°F – 255.37][b]
		°C (re: thermal temperature)[c]	°C = (T°F – 32)*0.6

[a] Used in lighting as the metric of heat necessary to achieve visible radiation from "black body radiators," such as a hunk of iron.
[b] Where T represents the given temperature in degrees Fahrenheit. For the mathematically challenged, multiply the temperature in degrees Fahrenheit by 5, then divide by 9, and then subtract 255.37 to arrive at degrees Kelvin or °K.
[c] Used in architectural engineering as the metric for ambient or surface temperatures in the environment.

1.3 The industry

Lighting is about a US$10 billion dollar (annually) industry in the United States alone. It wasn't too long ago that anyone with a tin bending operation in a basement or garage could and did manufacture luminaires. As material and labor costs increased, though, and as code and industry standards demanded safer, better performing products, it became necessary to mass produce luminaires. And industry consolidation occurred. Decades ago, there were many lamp and **control**s manufacturers as well. Similarly, as production costs rose and standards were instituted and/or became sufficiently rigorous, consolidation occurred.

This consolidation has typically meant more choices of fewer styles of equipment. Worse, however, this consolidation has meant a greater increase in packaging of lighting equipment during both the specification and/or the purchase of lighting equipment for any given project. More on this in Chapter 12.

At this writing, General Electric (GE), Osram Sylvania, and Philips are the dominant lamp manufacturers (both in the United States and globally). In the US, luminaire conglomerates are Cooper Industries, Genlyte Thomas, Jac Jacobsen Industries, Lighting Corporation of America (LCA) and National Service Industries (NSI). Cooper includes Halo and Metalux. Genlyte Thomas includes Lightolier and DayBrite. JJI includes Alkco, Lam, and Nessen. LCA includes Columbia and Prescolite. NSI includes Lithonia.

more online @
http://www.nema.org/economics/factfig99/domship/div2.html
http://www.cooperindustries.com/
http://www.genlyte.com/
http://www.jjilightinggroup.com/about.htm
http://www.lca.net/
http://www.lithonia.com/

lamp

The device producing the visible energy (light). Light bulb is the more folksy reference.

son et lumière

French for "sound and light show." Sometimes may refer to just a light show or a light and water show. Typically involves carefully sequenced light, sound, and/or water effects.

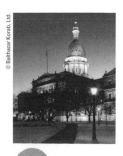

© Balthazar Korab, Ltd.

Background

1.4

1.4 Organizations

Worldwide, several organizations have taken the lead in the form of professional, technical, and trade associations, including **CIBSE**, **IALD**, and **IESNA**. The International Commission on Illumination (CIE or Commission Internationale de l'Eclairage) is the premier global organization on lighting technical matters. Constituent organizations of the CIE include many of the world's leading lighting organizations. The International Association for Energy–Efficient Lighting (IAEEL) is an information resource on efficient lighting products and techniques, and serves as a professional and technical network. All of these organizations solicit individual memberships.

The Rocky Mountain Institute (RMI) is a nonprofit organization promoting energy conservation and earth sustainability. Although individual memberships are not available, individual and corporate donations are used to partially fund the organization's efforts. RMI is not a standards setting body, but does help drive a continued interest in popular and scientific circles in energy effective use of earth's resources.

The IALD is an international professional society—engaged in activities promoting the profession of independent lighting design and promoting a corresponding code of ethical practice. This means practitioners operate in a mode independent from manufacturers, distributors, sales representatives, and electrical installers where conflicts of interest are likely. The IALD has about 500 members. The European Lighting Designers Association (ELDA) is advancing the interests of those in the various lighting professions in Europe—including manufacturing, distribution, and sales. ELDA has a membership base of about 70 people.

While all of the aforementioned organizations have the singular goal of maintaining or improving the human condition, there are certainly disputed means to that end. The designer needs to be familiar with the premises and/or criteria espoused by each organization, whether it be of technical, aesthetic, individual–level, societal–level, and/or ethical importance, and then help the client assimilate these criteria into priorities that best address immediate client needs without sacrificing longer term global needs.

Industry trade organizations also exist and contribute significantly to the transfer of information and/or the development of guidelines related to their specific mission. For example, the National Electrical Contractors Association (NECA) has a series of documents on the installation of lighting equipment for various applications, some of which have been approved as **ANSI** standards. The National Electrical Manufacturers Association (NEMA) develops technical standards, lobbies governmental agencies, and collects and disseminates industry data.

more online @

http://www.ansi.org
http://members.eunet.at/cie/
http://www.via-internet.com/elda/english/home.html
http://www.iaeel.org/
http://www.iald.org/
http://www.iesna.org/
http://www.lightforum.com/links/index.html
http://www.necanet.org/
http://www.nema.org/about/
http://www.rmi.org/

control

The electrical device(s) or mechanism(s) responsible for controlling the operation of the lighting in an environment. Could be simple toggle switches for on/off control, or programmable time machines that provide an elaborate son et lumière. Not to be confused with **optical control** (see below).

optical control

A reference to the method(s) used to control the intensity and distribution of light. Typically involving refractors (lensing), reflector(s), and/or louvers.

CIBSE

Chartered Institution of Building Services Engineers (Society of Light and Lighting).

IALD

International Association of Lighting Designers is a professional association devoted to the interests of independent lighting consultants.

IESNA

Illuminating Engineering Society of North America is the technical organization associated with lighting engineering and practice.

©Balthazar Korab, Ltd.

1.5 Background

ANSI

American National Standards Institute serves as administrator and coordinator of private sector voluntary standardization efforts in the United States. Documents may be submitted only by organizations meeting ANSI's accreditation standards. This assures that due process has been followed, that the document meets consensus opinion, and that the document is reviewed and revised in an open forum. ASHRAE, IESNA, NECA, and NEMA are accredited by ANSI.

ASHRAE

American Society of Heating, Refrigerating and Air–conditioning Engineers is the technical organization associated with mechanical (heating, ventilating, and air conditioning) engineering and practice.

EPA

The United States Environmental Protection Agency.

1.5 Codes, standards, and legislative actions

In the United States, lighting equipment for nearly all applications must comply with the National Electrical Code (NEC). As such, most lighting equipment must comply with Underwriters Laboratories (UL) standards. The NEC is intended to reduce the worldwide burden of fire and other hazards on the quality of life by providing a scientifically based consensus electrical code. UL standards establish safety requirements and parameters for testing of same for all kinds of products, including lighting and lighting–related components. Several testing facilities in the United States offer testing, listing, and labeling services for lighting equipment, including UL and ETL (ETL SEMKO). Products tested successfully can exhibit the UL or ETL labels. In Canada the Canadian Standards Association (CSA) offers standards similar to those UL espouses. In Germany, DIN Standards (Deutsches Institut für Normung) establish product and application performance requirements. Designers practicing in these and other areas need to specify equipment and performance standards according to the respective authoritative bodies.

On energy issues, in the United States, all states now have some form of energy code, as mandated by the 1992 Energy Policy Act (EPAct). The latest energy standard, **ASHRAE**/IESNA 90.1–1999 closely parallels the California Energy Commission's Title 24.6 code and is likely to become code for many states in the next few years. These standards and codes are intended to limit the electrical energy consumed by lighting and, thereby, limit the fuel consumption and subsequent pollutants necessary to make electricity.

Lamp disposal has been brought to the fore as both a health (toxicity) issue and as a sustainability issue (the "churn" of expending earth's resources and subsequent disposal of spent material). The **EPA** now requires that all lamps not meeting the toxicity characteristic leachate program (TCLP) be considered universal waste. In general, lamps that do not pass the EPA's TCLP need to be disposed in accordance with specific state or federal requirements or, preferably, recycled. Typically, for larger corporate sites for example, this means bulk quantities of lamps failing the TCLP must be disposed as a hazardous waste if not recycled. Where lamps are TCLP–compliant, then they may be disposed in landfills. However, recycling is still encouraged. Further, some states (i.e., Connecticut, Florida, Minnesota, and Vermont) do require that even TCLP–compliant lamps be disposed similarly to hazardous waste if not recycled.

Other regulations exist regarding lighting installations. Some municipalities now have local ordinances on parking lot lighting (typically establishing minimum requirements or maximum requirements or both), **light pollution**, and/or **light trespass**. The conundrum for the designer is in helping the client establish priorities—safety and security for users or the strong desire of a vocal minority to view more stars in the urban night sky. This has now become a lightning rod in the urban sprawl argument. What's unfortunate is that many in both groups can be accommodated with a significant moderation in the lighting intensities used in many exterior applications, and diligent selection, installation, and proper ongoing maintenance of lighting hardware.

more online @
http://www.ashrae.org/
http://www.bcap-energy.org/
http://www.bocai.org/book_building.asp
http://www.csa.ca/
http://www.cibse.org/
http://www.darksky.org/
http://www.din.de/

Background

```
http://www.energy.ca.gov/title24/index.html
http://www.eren.doe.gov/buildings/codes_standards/buildings/
http://etlwhidirectory.etlsemko.com/
http://www.iesna.org/
http://www.nema.org/government/environment/risk3296.html
http://www.nfpa.org/
http://www.sylvania.com/aboutus/pressrel/press/990716.html
http://www.ul.com/welcome.html
```

1.6 Certification—the NCQLP

Architects, engineers, and, more recently, interior designers in the building construction industry have been traditionally seen as the parties responsible for upholding life safety standards. As such, these individuals are required to hold licenses by states in which they practice (at this writing, not all states require licensing or registration of interior designers). As a means of egress during an emergency, lighting is a life safety building issue. As a complete building system, however, lighting has not been a serious component in the licensing of the design professionals. Indeed, lighting has been relegated status as a building commodity by some—as long as a minimal base standard of lighting is installed, folks living and working in the building will be well satisfied, or so the thought goes. However, in recent years, lighting efficiency has increasingly taken the brunt of the building energy codification. Lighting plays a prominent role in the sustainability story. Installation and maintenance of lighting plays a larger role in the application of energy efficient technologies on an ongoing basis. So, as society has demanded more from less with respect to lighting energy, a need arose to certify those people involved in all phases of lighting. Since 1990, an effort has been underway to develop industry–wide certification for the lighting professions—lighting designers (including architects, engineers, interior designers, and lighting consultants), lighting installers, lighting maintenance, lighting manufacturers, and the like. Thanks to seed funding from the IALD, significant program funding from the US EPA, support from the **DOE**, and major support from the IESNA, there now exists a certification body for lighting: National Council on Qualifications for the Lighting Professions. Based on educational background, career experience, and tested–standing, folks involved in lighting can be certified. Certification is then maintained on a three–year basis with **CEU**s or retesting.

This certification strengthens the common ties among the lighting disciplines or professions. If the designer is sufficiently engaged in specifying up–to–date technologies in a way that offers comfortable, productive, and aesthetically pleasing environments in an energy efficient way, then manufacturing and product distribution, installation, and maintenance personnel should be sufficiently competent to develop, make, sell, install, and maintain the lighting accordingly. Otherwise, much is lost in lighting system integrity and ultimately in user comfort and productivity. Further, energy savings and environmental progress are limited if not reversed.

There is optimism that such certification will become at least a voluntary requirement if not a legislated mandate. It is anticipated that corporate developers, facility managers, local, state, and federal governmental building agencies will eventually require that lighting design, manufacturing and distribution, installation, and maintenance functions are performed by NCQLP–certified (denoted by LC for Lighting Certified) professionals.

more online @
http://www.ncqlp.org/

light pollution
Overlighting that directly (through mis–aiming or poor luminaire design) or indirectly (reflected from ground planes or building surfaces) scatters in the night air to create a "haze of light" through which astronomy is difficult.

light trespass
Light from one property falling onto another property or glare visible from a neighboring or receiving property and that causes a nuisance to users of the receiving property.

DOE
The United States Department of Energy.

CEU
Continuing education units (CEUs) are credits awarded to designers who attend seminars, lectures, courses, tradeshows, and other events that are accredited by respective professional associations. CEUs help ensure one's knowledge on a particular topic or specialty is kept current. For example, to maintain one's NCQLP lighting certification (LC) status, a certain number of CEUs are required every three years.

©Balthazar Korab, Ltd.

Background

1.7 Education

Lighting education has advanced considerably in the past 10 years. While there are yet no degreed undergraduate lighting programs, there are several Master's programs in lighting. Further, many undergraduate programs offer lighting design classes. A complete listing of available lighting courses is published in *Lighting Listings*.[5] A search online is advisable for the most current options.

Because no formal degreed undergraduate programs in lighting exist, many lighting designers have educational backgrounds in related fields. Theater, electrical engineering, architecture, interior design, and architectural engineering are some typical degrees and/or careers leading to lighting design. Various universities have excellent lighting courses within the human ecology, architecture, fine arts, home economics, or engineering schools. Usually, though, one or two lighting courses are the extent of a student's exposure to lighting. With just these few classes and an intense interest, however, a career in lighting is practical and possible. Some schools offer additional independent study in lighting. For the student looking for more formal education in lighting, a Master's degree in lighting from a respected program is suggested. Perhaps a measure of the amount of student interest generated at any given lighting program is evident through IESNA student chapters and/or IALD student membership. Schools with IESNA student chapters and/or several IALD student members identify strong and/or storied programs.

One way to expand one's knowledge about lighting is to more deliberately observe the surrounding environment. Observation is such an obvious tool, yet so seldom used to educational advantage. Every waking hour of every day we see built environments. Many are poorly lighted, and many people even comment about the poor state of the lighting, yet we continue to design dreadful solutions. We should be more observant, identifying what is more successful or what is less successful. A working journal is one means of recording observations in both sketch and written word. An electronic camera also offers a reasonable record of existing environments. Here, however, written record needs to be made in a personal digital assistant or in the form of an oral recording with the image. The journal is a preferable option for the designer interested in developing and/or maintaining hand–drawn graphic skills. These sketches can, with some experience, be completed in about an hour and help the observer understand how light "renders" surfaces and spaces and can lead to better visualization of proposed designs. Included with the sketch should be a short description of the environment, the tasks, the technical aspects of the lighting (including sky conditions for daylight situations), whether or not the lighting seems appropriate, and how it might be improved.

more online @
http://www.lrc.rpi.edu/indexedu.html
http://www.lightsearch.com/cgi-bin/cosearch.pl?coproducts=college/university

1.8 Continuing education

The need for continuing education in lighting is growing. This is primarily due to the continuing education requirements of registration and/or certification. Several universities offer week–long seminars from time to time. The IESNA offers classes periodically through its section chapters

©Balthazar Korab, Ltd.

Background

and at its annual conference. The IESNA and the IALD offer seminars and workshops at the annual trade show LightFair. Technical and application papers presented at the IESNA annual conference are also excellent means of maintaining current techniques and practice. CIBSE also offers lighting seminars. In addition to LightFair, a host of lighting trade shows takes place annually or biannually around the globe, including Lighting, Luminaire Asia, Elec, Light, Euroluce, and Lighting Dimensions International (although more theatrical). The lamp manufacturers, GE, Osram Sylvania, and Philips, have regularly scheduled seminar programs at their respective lighting education centers around the globe. Several of the luminaire manufacturers also offer regular seminars. The Internet is likely to allow the offering of distant learning programs from many of these organizations and from universities. All of this activity may qualify for CEUs.

more online @

```
http://www.cibse.org/
http://www.cooperlighting.com/education/
http://www.gelighting.com/na/institute/about.html
http://www.iald.org/
http://www.iesna.org/
http://www.lightolier.com/html/techcenter.htm
http://www.lithonia.com/
http://www.lrc.rpi.edu/indexedu.html
http://www.lighting.philips.com/nam/education/
http://www.northwestlighting.com/calendar/ldlclass.htm
http://www.sylvania.com/lighting/educate/lp.htm
http://www.tsnn.com/cgi-bin/tsnn/iclass/
    iclass.show.schedule?iclass_id=64&client=1
```

1.9 Publications

Staying abreast of current technologies and design styles takes more than a week–long refresher course every few years. Many of the organizations cited in Section 1.4 published newsletters and/or magazines devoted to lighting issues. A number of paid–circulation magazines have established broad appeal by addressing architectural lighting design in whole or in part on a monthly or bimonthly basis. *Architectural Lighting* is published eight times each year and offers articles and reviews for those involved in designing and specifying architectural lighting. This magazine is available free to qualified industry members. *Architectural Record* publishes a special *Lighting* section on a periodic basis. *Lighting Design + Application* is the magazine the IESNA publishes monthly. *Lighting Dimensions* includes coverage of architectural lighting, as well as theatrical and studio lighting. Other periodicals include *Lighting, VIA, Professional Lighting*, and *Illuminotecnica Europe Light*. Some manufacturers, such as Philips, ERCO, and Zumtobel/Staff, also publish magazines on a regular basis (e.g., *International Lighting Review*).

Other lighting publications include research journals, newsletters, and papers (some presented in formal settings) by researchers and application specialists. The IESNA publishes the *Journal of the IES* biannually that documents papers selected for publication from those presented at the IESNA annual conference. The CIBSE publishes *Lighting Research & Technology* quarterly, documenting research work and results. The Lighting Research Center (LRC) at Rensselaer Polytechnic Institute offers information by hard–copy subscription publications and by online content. Consider the United States' Lawrence Berkeley National Laboratory (LBL) repository. Here, papers are available on lighting technologies, controls techniques, and

1.10   Background

lighting applications. The Electric Power Research Institute (EPRI) offers a quarterly journal with articles on a wide range of electric production, transmission, and application issues.

more online @

```
http://www.architecturalrecord.com/
http://eande.lbl.gov/BTP/pub/LGpub.html
http://www.epri.com/Journal.asp
http://www.etecnyc.net/default.html
http://www.eur.lighting.philips.com/ilr/
http://www.iesna.org/
http://www.illuminotecnica.com/base_menu_uk.htm
http://www.lighthouse.org/pubs_vresearch.htm
http://lightforum.com/archlight/index.html
http://lightingmag.com/
http://www.lightsearch.com/resources/magazines/index.html
http://www.lrc.rpi.edu/
http://www.musicandaudio.com/pl/contents.htm
```

1.10 The Internet

The Internet has revolutionized information exchange. Niche topics, such as lighting and vision (both taken for granted by the general public and, therefore, not garnering much topical publicity), can be readily researched in a timely manner. Search engines should be used on a periodic basis to review such topics as architectural lighting, architectural lighting design, lighting design, lighting research, and vision.

1.11 Endnotes

[1] NEMA, Domestic Shipment of Products within the Scope of NEMA's Lighting Systems Division (web page, 2000), http://www.nema.org/economics/factfig99/domship/div2.html. [Accessed October 15, 2000.]

[2] Ed Petrow, Lighting Research and Development (web page, 2000), http://www.eren.doe.gov/buildings/building_equipment/lighting.html. [Accessed September 17, 2000.]

[3] Infoplease, National Income by Type (web page, 2000), http://infoplease.lycos.com/ipa/A0104648.html. [Accessed September 17, 2000.]

[4] Infoplease, Gross Domestic Product or Expenditure (web page, 2000), http://infoplease.lycos.com/ipa/A0104575.html. [Accessed September 22, 2000.]

[5] Judith Block, *Lighting Listings: A Worldwide Guide to Lighting Publications, Research Organizations, Education Opportunities, and Associations* (York, PA: Visions Communications, 1995), pp. 62–96.

The Problem

Lighting is a problem revolving around how people feel in, react to, and function in various settings. Lighting is a biology or physiology problem as well as a psychology problem. To develop a successful lighting plan for any situation, the designer must be prepared to understand the problem as such. Defining it is, perhaps, the most crucial step in any lighting design. How well are people expected to function? How comfortable are people expected to be while they function? What is/are the function(s)? How can lighting best help with functionality and simultaneously influence people's emotional or subjective reactions in a positive way? Who are these people, and how do they feel, react, and function with their present lighting situation(s)? There are too many people with too many experiences in too many functional settings who are our clients. A better understanding of them and their needs is necessary before an answer can be proposed to meet their specific needs in a given architectural and social setting.

Vision is an amazing sense. It has a detection range of a million to one (sunlight to moonlight). It perceives things as "bright" when fully adapted under full moonlight, and yet perceives things as "dark" when fully adapted in the midst of a ferocious thunderstorm. It can identify an apple as red or an orange as orange under most light sources (regardless of the light source color) and under most intensities. It can ignore all of this if it is not tuned to "observe." Vision is under the control of the observer. Lighting designers can enhance or limit vision. So, the lighting issues that will be discussed here revolve around physiological and psychological issues.

2.1 Physiology

The eye responds to differences in specific reflected and transmitted **electromagnetic energy** (which we call "light")—the eye sees **chromatic** and **luminance contrasts**. Figure 2.1 outlines the electromagnetic spectrum and highlights the range of radiation to which typical, healthy eyes are sensitive. Daylight, moonlight, flame, and electric light characteristics interact with a given setting (architectural, landscape architectural, or native natural) creating reflections and transmissions of various wavelengths of visible energy for people to behold. Lighting designers can manipulate these reflections and transmissions to advantage—the charge of the lighting design team.

Because we see light reflecting from or transmitting through materials, the surface characteristics of these materials are critically important to the color and amount of reflected or transmitted light. Indeed, a good interior design plan can be rendered lifeless (read "ruined ") by bad lighting. Alternatively, a good lighting design plan can be ruined by bad interior design. These maxims hold for architecture and landscape architecture. So, a team effort is, indeed, a necessity if there is any hope of getting the most out of the lighting and out of the interiors, the architecture, and/or the landscape architecture.

> **more online @**
> http://imagine.gsfc.nasa.gov/docs/science/know_l1/emspectrum.html
> http://www.marine.rutgers.edu/mrs/class/josh/em_spec.html
> http://www.ccrs.nrcan.gc.ca/ccrs/eduref/tutorial/chap1/c1p3e.html#c1p3_i1

2.2 The eye

The eye is diagrammed in Figure 2.2. The cornea is a protective sheath over the lens that also provides much of the refractive (focusing) power. The iris is a thin, colored membrane (thus, one's eye color) that constricts (dilates) the pupil (located in the center of the iris) to control the amount of entering light.

electromagnetic energy

Electromagnetic energy or radiation is emitted when atomic particles vibrate. The frequency of the vibration determines the kind of radiation emitted. High frequency vibrations result in very short wavelength radiation, such as cosmic rays, gamma rays, and X-rays. Low frequency vibrations result in long wavelength radiation, such as microwaves, radio waves, and sound waves. Moderate frequency vibrations result in ultraviolet radiation, light, and infrared radiation. All of these varying wavelengths of radiation make up the electromagnetic spectrum. The metric for wavelengths is meters. Wavelengths of visible radiation are measured in billionths of a meter—10^{-9} meters or nanometers (nm). The shortest wavelengths of visible energy are about 380 nm (deep violet). The longest are about 770 nm (rich red).

chromatic contrast

Color contrast or color difference between two or more colors. Perceived by a typical, healthy eye. For example, a sunflower viewed against its green leaves.

luminance contrast

Measured brightness difference between two or more elements or details in the viewed scene as perceived by a typical, healthy eye. For example, when one looks through a window, one sees the luminance contrast between an overcast sky and the wall adjacent to the window.

Image ©Digital Vision

2.2 The Problem

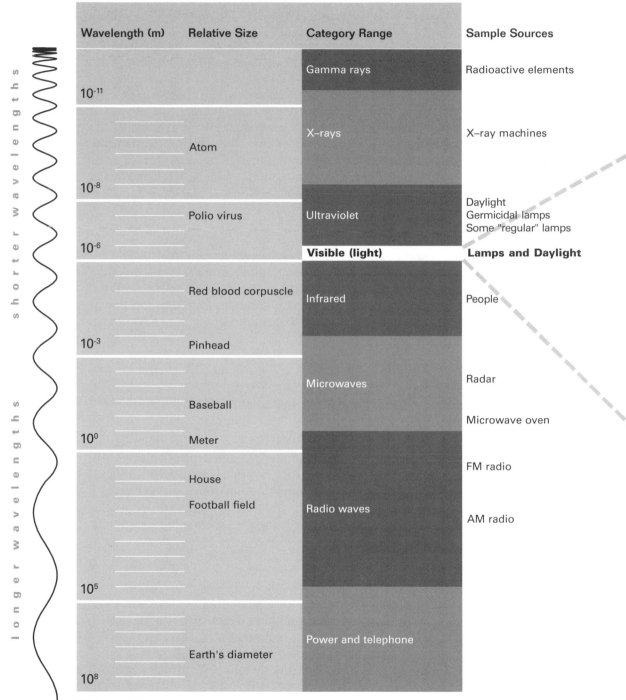

Wavelength (m)	Relative Size	Category Range	Sample Sources
		Gamma rays	Radioactive elements
10^{-11}		X–rays	X–ray machines
	Atom		
10^{-8}			
	Polio virus	Ultraviolet	Daylight Germicidal lamps Some "regular" lamps
10^{-6}		**Visible (light)**	**Lamps and Daylight**
	Red blood corpuscle	Infrared	People
10^{-3}	Pinhead		
		Microwaves	Radar
	Baseball		Microwave oven
10^{0}	Meter		FM radio
	House		
	Football field	Radio waves	AM radio
10^{5}			
		Power and telephone	
	Earth's diameter		
10^{8}			

shorter wavelengths

longer wavelengths

Image ©Digital Vision

Figure 2.1
Electromagnetic spectrum is diagrammatically represented here. A small but extremely significant portion is visible to humans. This is highlighted at 10^{-6} meters (visible radiation is typically reported in nanometers, or 10^{-9} meters—so 700 nm (deep red) is also 700 10^{-9} meters, or 0.7 10^{-6} meters, or 700 billionths of a meter).
Resource: Electromagnetic Spectrum Chart, The Exploratorium (http://www.exploratoriumstore.com/charandpos.html)

The Problem

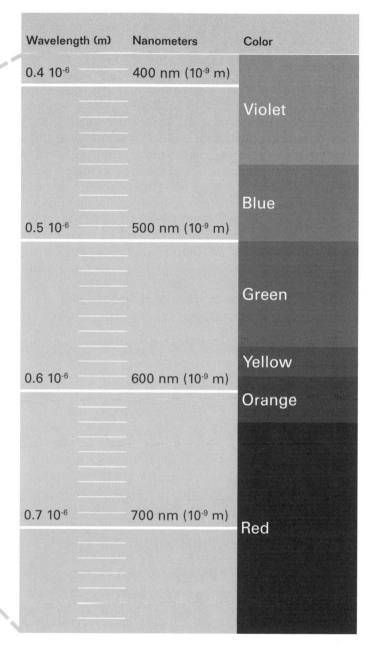

Wavelength (m)	Nanometers	Color
0.4 10⁻⁶	400 nm (10⁻⁹ m)	
		Violet
		Blue
0.5 10⁻⁶	500 nm (10⁻⁹ m)	
		Green
		Yellow
0.6 10⁻⁶	600 nm (10⁻⁹ m)	Orange
0.7 10⁻⁶	700 nm (10⁻⁹ m)	Red

visible radiation

Colors of visible electromagnetic energy or visible radiation are not as neatly categorized as shown. The visible spectrum is a continuum of colored light—a rainbow. There is not great unanimity in the scientific community about the short wave cutoff on visible radiation. Some references cite 400 nm as the shortest visible energy, while other references cite 380 nm. On the long wave cutoff, some references cite 700 nm, while others cite 770 nm as the cutoff. This graph shows 380 to 770 nm. Also, color categories here are for simple reference. Each color category can be further refined (e.g., blue–green and green–blue). For purposes of lighting design, it is reasonable to simply assign colored light the mid–value wavelength within the range shown here. So, for example, yellow light is 580 nm, blue light is 470 nm, and so forth.

speed of light

Light travels at about 186,000 miles per second (300,000 km per second).

speed of sound

Sound travels at about 750 miles per hour or 0.2 miles per second (1200 km per hour or 0.3 km per second).

This shutter–like adjustment works with photochemical changes in the eye's photoreceptors (rods and cones; discussed in depth under 2.3 Color vision) resulting in what's known as adaptation (see 2.4 Adaptation). At the same time, this shutter–like action works in conjunction with muscles to shape the lens for optimal focusing of the entering light.

After passing through the pupil, light then enters the lens. This is a crystalline diaphragm that focuses incoming light onto an imaginary point just behind the lens. Here, the focused light (which constitutes the image) inverts for a final "projection" onto the retina. The process of the lens focusing an image onto the retina is known as accommodation (see 2.5 Accommodation).

One or several structural defects in the eye can cause objects or scenes to appear out of focus. If the cornea is a bit too round or the entire eyeball a bit too long, the focal length of objects/tasks is too short and objects actually are

Image ©Digital Vision

2.3

The Problem

myopia

Nearsightedness. A condition, common to nearly 30% of the US population, where the eyeball is a bit too long or the cornea is a bit too round. Images are focused short (in front) of the retina. Near objects/tasks are clearly accommodated (focused), while distant objects/tasks are somewhat out of focus.[1]

hypermetropia (or hyperopia)

Farsightedness. The eyeball is a bit too short or the cornea is a bit too flat. Images are focused long (behind) the retina. Far objects/tasks are clearly accommodated, while closer objects/tasks are somewhat out of focus.[2]

20/20 vision

The customary standard in the United States for "reference" vision. This does not constitute perfect vision. The first value (always "20") represents the distance in feet at which the individual in question views objects/tasks clearly; the second value represents the distance in feet at which an individual with "normal reference" sight would view those same objects/tasks clearly. For example, 20/100 vision in an eye means that the tested eye must be within 20 feet of a visual target to see it as well as a normal reference eye would see at 100 feet from the same visual target! The metric equivalent is 6/6 vision.[3]

focused in front of the retina. This phenomenon is called **myopia**, or nearsightedness, as only nearer objects can be seen clearly.[1] If the cornea is a bit too flat or the entire eyeball a bit too short, then the focal length is too long and objects are focused behind the retina in a condition known as **hypermetropia** (or hyperopia), or farsightedness.[2]

Photoreceptors on the retina are activated by the focused light, and these, in turn, initiate signals or impulses through the optic nerve to the brain where image interpretation takes place. During relatively bright scenes, the cone photoreceptors are primarily active. Cones respond to higher luminance and detect color. These cells (of which there are about 4 million) are concentrated at the macula and are responsible for detail vision. Sharpest vision occurs in the fovea, which is located at the center of the macula. Rods (of which there are about 100 million) respond to lower brightness and do not detect color. Rods are absent in the fovea, but populate the rest of the retina and are, therefore, responsible for night vision. Since the cones populate the fovea exclusively, there can be no detailed vision in very low luminance (dim) situations. This explains why viewing of dim stars is accomplished with peripheral viewing and not by looking directly at a distant star or region of interest of the sky.

`more online @`
```
http://members.aol.com/MonT714/tutorial/the_eye/index.html
http://www.cim.mcgill.ca/~image529/TA529/Image529_99/projects97/25_Lacroix/
    WebSurfing.html
http://www.accessexcellence.com/AE/AEC/CC/vision_background.html
http://www-staff.lboro.ac.uk/~huph/
http://hyperphysics.phy-astr.gsu.edu/hbase/ligcon.html#c1
http://www.kellogg.umich.edu/conditions/search.html
http://www.nei.nih.gov/
```

2.3 Color vision

Color vision takes place under relatively high brightness conditions. Such vision is known as photopic. Under these conditions, the best detail vision is possible. For typical healthy eyes, corrected if necessary to **20/20 vision**, blue–green light (images) projects precisely onto the fovea. Violet–blue light (images), however, focuses slightly in front of the fovea. Hence, in an attempt to focus these images, the lens of the eye becomes slightly less convex and, therefore, the violet–blue image(s) appears to be slightly farther away. Red light (images), on the other hand, focuses slightly behind the fovea. Here, the lens becomes slightly more convex and, therefore, the red images appear to be slightly closer to the observer. These phenomena are sometimes used to advantage in design efforts—warm colors tend to advance, while cool colors tend to recede.

Color vision deficiency (color blindness) is typically hereditary. The deficiency may be minor, in which case distinguishing between several shades of the same color is difficult. In some cases, however, one color cannot be distinguished from another. About 8 percent of men and 1 percent of women have some form of color deficiency. Red–green deficiency, the inability to distinguish red from green, is most common. Blue–yellow deficiency is less common. Complete color blindness (being able to distinguish colors only as shades of black, gray, and white) is quite rare.[4] Some color vision deficiency does occur with age. As the lens clouds, there is less ability to distinguish color at lower light intensities and/or to distinguish between dark colors.[5] Generally, all colors are dulled, but blue is particularly muddied.

The Problem

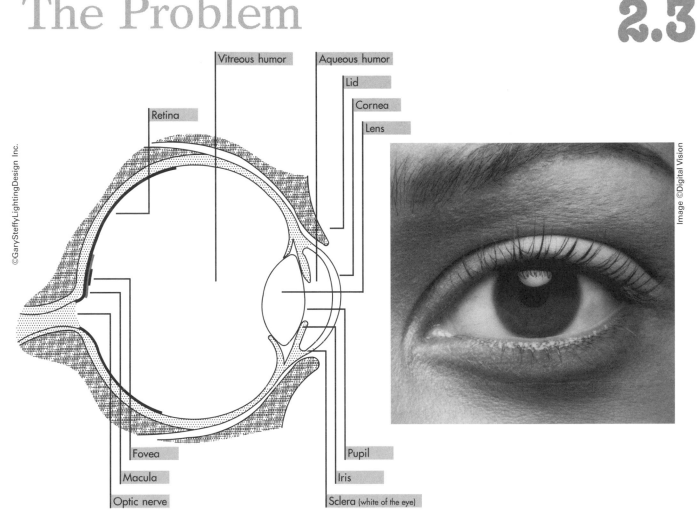

Figure 2.2
Diagrammatic vertical cross section of the human eye and photographic front elevation. Note: the fovea is actually indented into the macula, but is shown here as a graphic protrusion for clarity.

Color is not an inherent characteristic of surfaces. The color makeup of the light striking surfaces is as responsible for what color(s) healthy eyes see as the surface material itself. The upshot is this: the designer must carefully assess the light source(s) and the surface material(s) on projects to be assured that people see the intended color palette and that the most efficient use of light and color is achieved.

Color vision lessens with lower brightness settings. Mesopic vision refers to vision that occurs typically at dusk or dawn brightness settings, typified by environments lighted to perhaps 0.2 to 2 fc (2 to 20 lux). Here, both rods and cones are operating, but the detailed vision the cones offer is diminished by the relatively low brightnesses. Studies over the ten year period from 1990 to 2000 offer strong evidence that mesopic vision is enhanced somewhat by light that is richer in the bluer portion of the visible spectrum. This enhancement is most dramatic, however, under scotopic vision.

Scotopic vision takes place under very low brightness settings, typified by environments lighted to less than 0.2 fc (2 lux—full moonlight might offer 0.5 lux[6]). In such settings, blue–rich electric light sources offer significant **visual acuity** enhancement to eyesight over more yellow sources. For nightlighting of pedestrian paths and around residential areas, this is an important consideration. Studies show that using blue–rich sources to have an effect similar to that of doubling or nearly tripling light intensities using more

Color perception.........
- Depends on color makeup of light
- Depends on surface material
- Depends on health of eyes
- Depends on age

2.4 The Problem

visual acuity

Visual acuity refers to the effectiveness or accuracy of an individual's visual system.

::::::::::::::::::::::::::::::::

SPD

Spectral power distribution. A measure of the power or intensity of electromagnetic energy present in a given light source.[10] Typically reported in graph form showing the relative intensity of the various wavelengths of energy produced by a given light source (see Figure 2.3). Some light sources, like daylight on a sunny day, have a rather complete or full spectrum of visible energy (all colors of light are present to some degree). Other light sources, such as blacklights, have a very limited spectrum of light (mostly ultraviolet and deep violet electromagnetic energy is present in the SPD of blacklights). Recognize the implications, then, on how people perceive color. If a blacklight (rich in violet light) is aimed onto a red surface, the red surface will appear black since the red pigment is capable of reflecting only red light that strikes it, yet the blacklight only produces violet light. SPD is responsible, then, for how colors are rendered.

::::::::::::::::::::::::::::::::

Adaptation.....................

■ Depends on intensities
■ Depends on surface reflectances
■ Depends on duration of view
■ Depends on viewer's age

Image ©Digital Vision

yellow sources—a significant finding for safety and security and for the conservation of our resources.[7, 8, 9]

more online @
http://www.aoanet.org/
http://www.hazelwood.k12.mo.us/~grichert/optics/intro.html

2.4 Adaptation

Adaptation is a key process and one over which the lighting designer can have positive influence. Older eyes have longer adaptation periods than younger eyes because of the reduced elasticity of the iris and slowed photochemical process. The photochemical changes take place in the light sensing cells of the retina. So, when sighted people move from bright spaces to dark spaces and vice versa, adaptation occurs. The brighter the bright space and the longer the exposure to the bright setting, then the more dramatic the adaptation process when moving to a dark setting. Likewise, the darker the dark space and the longer the exposure to the dark setting, then the more dramatic the adaptation process when moving to a bright setting. However, adapting from bright to dark typically takes more time than adapting from dark to bright. So, when designing interior space adjacencies or exterior site lighting immediately adjacent to ingress/egress to buildings, this adaptation should be considered. For example, people walking from the bright outdoors into a theater will experience relatively long adaptation periods, readily leading to tripping or disorientation. This effect, from bright to dark is known as dark adaptation. Complete dark adaptation can take half an hour or longer. Because of this lag, and because of a momentary sense of blindness experienced when one first enters a darkened space, dark adaptation can be dangerous. This adaptation can be minimized by designing a space or series of spaces that act as both a time transition and a progressive dimness transition. Longer transition times and less harsh dimness transitions are appropriate for older users (typically over 40 years of age for purposes of vision/lighting issues).

Adapting from dark settings to bright settings may take just a few minutes. This is known as light adaptation. In extreme cases, say moving from dark theaters to daylit exteriors, some pain (typically referred to as glare) may be experienced as the eyes adapt.

Another form of adaptation is transient adaptation—experienced when the user is relatively stationary (so the overall environment is not changing as it does when walking from an outdoor setting at noon into a theater). As the user scans the scene, and if he/she is in a relatively dark zone but scanning to a bright luminaire or to an extraordinarily bright zone, then adaptation occurs. Adaptation also occurs with a converse situation—if the user is in a relatively bright zone but scanning to a dark zone, adaptation occurs. So, a person looking from a brightly lighted (read "overlit") parking lot into a nearby shrubbed area can experience this momentary or transient adaptation. Such a situation better allows muggers to hide. A more successful lighting solution may rely on a less bright parking area and some landscape lighting to keep the outlying or perimeter shrub area in some low level of brightness. So consistency or uniformity of brightness has a significant influence on adaptation and people's abilities to see a complete scene comfortably. Consider for a moment the effect of moonlight on a rural setting. Although the light level is very low (and, therefore, the brightnesses are very low)—a full moon on a clear night might provide 0.5 lux (0.05 fc)—the uniform light allows individuals to distinguish objects and movement in the

The Problem

landscape. Indeed, with sufficient time to adapt to such low brightnesses, most people can read newspaper headlines!

Some research indicates that in low vision situations, the **SPD** of the light source(s) can improve perceptions of brightness.[11, 12] Light sources with a high component of blue (known as "blue–rich" or "bluer") have the effect of reducing the size of the pupil (as would happen in higher light intensity settings), thereby providing the sensation of greater brightness. This can be used to benefit in various applications. In the situation of housing for the elderly, light sources relatively richer in blue than typical residential lighting (e.g., using fluorescent lamps of a minimum of 3000°K **color temperature** and preferably up to 5000°K instead of incandescent lamps) might be used in architectural details (e.g., coves, electric "skylights," etc.) in an effort to enhance impressions of brightness. In the situation of an open office area that houses both computer–aided design (CAD) operators (demanding very low intensities) and clerical staff (using local task lights for work light, but not wanting the impression of a cave as a work setting), light sources very rich in blue (e.g., 5000°K fluorescent lamps alone or even fitted with blue filter sleeves) might be used in an attempt to satisfy both sets of workers.

2.5 Accommodation

Accommodation is the process of focusing on an object or task. The ciliary muscle contracts to adjust the shape of the lens. Because accommodation is a muscular activity, a constant focus on a single object or task is tiresome. Indeed, eye breaks are recommended from time to time during the course of a work day so that focusing is not limited to static viewing situations. On the other hand, continually changing focus from one object/task (that is near, for example) to another object/task (that is somewhat farther, for example) fatigues the ciliary muscle from too much operation. This constant accommodation (as might occur when one views from very close task work to more distant task work) can result in visual fatigue. Particularly problematic with folks working on tasks involving computers and hard copies—alternately viewing close computer monitor and slightly more distant paper documents. Here, for example, the paper task should be positioned at the same distance and on the same plane as those of the computer screen position.

2.6 Aging

Aging affects the eye several ways, any one of which can reduce the effectiveness of one's vision. Together, however, these age related effects can have a significant negative impact on vision. Generally, it is important to remember that all functions tend to slow with age. The process of adaptation slows. This leads to a serious potential issue particularly when moving from bright settings to dim or dark settings. The designer is encouraged to minimize the degree of these changes by developing a series of transition spaces. Further, potential obstacles should be avoided—such as steps or quick and/or abrupt grade changes.

Accommodation also slows with age. Again, transitions from space–to–space or area–to–area should be gradual. Objects or tasks should be arranged so that accommodation is now limited. That is, the focal distances for the common and/or the more important visual items or tasks should be about the same. Hence, a designer might develop a sitting room in a home

---

color temperature

Also known as correlated color temperature (CCT) because all color temperature ratings are based on a standard reference approximating daylight—hence, the color temperature is correlated to a reference light source. Color temperature is a measure of the whiteness of light produced by a given lamp with 0°K as black. For example, imagine an iron ingot. At room temperature, the ingot produces (essentially) no radiation. It doesn't glow. It is black and, therefore, has a color temperature of 0°K (room temperature is actually more like 295°K, but on a relative scale, this can be considered very close to 0°K). If heat is applied to the ingot, it eventually glows red, then orange, then yellow, then white, then blue white, then blue (if we can assume it won't melt away). The absolute temperature of the ingot at these various colors is the metric for color temperature. So, a candle flame has a color temperature of about 2000°K. A standard, old, inefficient incandescent lamp has a color temperature of about 2700°K, while the new, crisp white halogen lamps typically have a color temperature of about 2900°K.

Image ©Digital Vision

2.6

The Problem

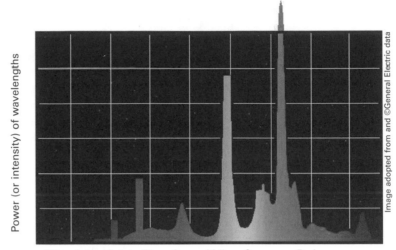

Power (or intensity) of wavelengths

Image adopted from and ©General Electric data

| Ultraviolet | Violet | Blue | Green | Yellow | Orange | | Red |

| 300 | 350 | 400 | 450 | 500 | 550 | 600 | 650 | 700 | 750 |

Wavelengths (in nm or 10⁻⁹ meters)

Figure 2.3

Spectral power distribution curve for GE's SPX30 fluorescent lamp. Note the strong spike of orange, a slightly weaker spike of yellow–green, and a weaker spike of blue. This is a triphosphor lamp—that is, a lamp composed of three phosphor layers. Each layer produces a specific color range of light (in this case, orange, yellow–green, and blue). The orange, yellow–green, and blue combine to make a relatively full spectrum white light. The strength of the orange results in a bias toward red, resulting in a warm white tone that renders skin tones quite well.

Aging impact.......

■ Slower adaptation
■ Slower accommodation
■ Presbyopia
■ Cataracts

Image ©Digital Vision

for an elderly client with the guests' chairs and/or sofa within a constant distance (diameter) from one another. Similarly, the television and favored objects and artwork might be kept within a constant distance from the likely preferred viewing position(s).

Presbyopia is an age–related phenomenon whereby the eye can no longer focus on near objects. The lens hardens and, hence, is less elastic as the eye ages. Focusing of near objects/tasks becomes more difficult. At the age of five, one has a near focus of perhaps 7 cm (3 in). By the age of 21, one has a near focus of perhaps 12 cm (5 in). By the age of 42, one has a near focus of about 25 cm (10 in). At the age of 46, near focus is about 32 cm (13 in), and that is considered a reasonable reading distance. But by the age of 55, near focus is now at arms' length reading distance which is about 55 cm (22 in)—hence holding the newspaper this far away becomes a practical, if tiresome, necessity without corrective eyewear.[14, 15] Presbyopia does not affect accommodation of far objects/tasks.

As the lens ages, it can become somewhat cloudy and yellow. By the age of 60, it may take twice as much light for an individual to see tasks as he/she required at 20 years of age. A sufficiently cloudy, yellow lens is known as a **cataract**. As the lens clouds, images become less focused and more blurred. The yellowing combined with the clouding reduces the overall image/scene brightness. Increased sensitivity to glare may also result from the increased scattering of light. So, while increased light intensities are desirable to overcome the dullness imposed by the clouding and yellowing, the locations and directionality of the light sources used are important—they should be kept out of the main line of sight or should be used to produce relatively uniform brightness. In general, fewer, high wattage luminaires should be avoided.

Constant exposure to ultraviolet (UV) radiation, cigarette smoke, and certain medications can lead to or accelerate cataract development.[13, 16] Heredity may also play a role. Diabetics tend to be more susceptible to cataracts. Some protective measures can be taken. In daylight situations, eyes should be shielded with sunglasses specifically designed to limit or eliminate UV radiation transmittance. In electric light situations, if eyes are likely to be exposed directly to nearby light sources for a period of time and/or light intensities are quite high, luminaires should be fitted with lensing that limits or eliminates UV radiation. Lensing for eyewear should be selected to limit or eliminate UV radiation transmittance.

The Problem

more online @

http://www.aoanet.org/
http://www.medem.com/MedLB/sub_detaillb.cfm?parent_id=30&act=disp
http://www.nlm.nih.gov/medlineplus/cataract.html

2.7 Astigmatism

Astigmatism is a refractive error caused by an irregularly shaped cornea. Normally, the cornea is essentially a portion of a sphere—with equal curvature in all directions. However, in some situations, the cornea is not quite spherical. As such, the cornea cannot then refract all of the light rays onto a single point or zone within the eye. Astigmatism is common and is not age related. It can be corrected with corrective lenses. Typical symptoms are blurred vision, headaches and visual fatigue (from the strain of attempting to focus), and/or squinting, eye discomfort, or irritation.[17, 18]

2.8 Seasonal affective disorder (SAD)

Seasonal affective disorder, SAD, affects perhaps 1 to 10 percent of the population, depending on which studies are referenced and in what region of the world the research was done. As its name indicates, SAD is a seasonal disorder attributed to the lack of light—either in duration and/or in intensity—during the winter months. It typically sets in between August and September and then ends the following March or April. Symptoms include lethargy, decreased concentration, and fatigue. Increased sleep, increased eating, and increased weight are common results of SAD. Studies show that between 60 and 90 percent of SAD patients can be treated successfully with light therapy. White light exceeding intensities of 2500 lux is necessary to have an impact. Most success appears to come from initial treatment consisting of 30 minutes of exposure to 10,000 lux in the morning. Light treatments are often made with fluorescent light boxes. Ultraviolet radiation is filtered from the treatment lamps to minimize the side effects of those wavelengths. It is important to reiterate that light therapy is based on white light of sufficient intensity. Indeed, intensity is more important than the spectral power distribution of the light source—so–called full spectrum lamps show no appreciable benefit in treatment compared to standard fluorescent lamps. In any event, people suspected of having SAD should undertake light treatment only under the care of a physician and/or an opthalmologist.

more online @

http://www.fhs.mcmaster.ca/direct/depress/sad.html
http://www.websciences.org/sltbr/jama.htm
http://www.websciences.org/sltbr/pubinfo.htm#SAD
http://www.geocities.com/HotSprings/7061/sadhome.html

2.9 Circadian rhythm

Circadian is of Latin origin and means "about a day." Circadian rhythm refers to the biological cycle of plants and animals. Recent research concludes that light absorption in the human eye sets and affects our circadian rhythms. As such, light therapy is seen as a method (if not the primary method) of adjusting circadian rhythms for jet–setters and night–shift workers. Doses of daylight or daylight–like intensities (thousands of lux) during the waking hours are important to setting or adjusting the circadian rhythm. Similarly, the absence of light (total darkness) during the sleeping hours is important. Designs can accommodate both of these conditions. Special "light rooms"

cataract

A clouding of the lens ultimately leading to hazy or blurred vision. Symptoms include: cloudy or filmy vision, increased glare sensitivity, halo around light sources when viewed directly, faded colors, poor night vision, multiple or double vision, and frequent changes in eyewear prescriptions.[13]

2.10 The Problem

where shift workers can take a "day break" might be designed into those facilities where two or three shifts are common. Residential settings (e.g., houses, apartments, hotels, etc.) can be designed with blackout shades (an absolute necessity for shift workers sleeping during daylight hours), as well as with carefully controlled exterior lighting at the minimum intensities of safety and security for the particular nighttime activity situation (to maximize the integrity of the normal sleeping period of darkness).

more online @
http://www.circadian.com/
http://www.nsf.gov/od/lpa/news/press/pr9611.htm

2.10 Psychology

Perceptions of lighted settings are the result of the brain's interpretation of physiological reactions to those lighted settings. These perceptions constitute the psychology of lighting and depend not only on the light intensities, patterns, and color, but also on the interpreter's previous experiences, culture, and mood. While many people might agree on the level of comfort; degree of attractiveness; spatial attributes, such as visual order, volume, simplicity; and the sense of personal space, such as intimate or public in a particular setting, these perceptions can vary mildly to wildly between people. Nor are these perceptions even held universally by all individuals. Hence, the psychology of light is less tangible with a less certain outcome than when encountered with the physiology of light. Nevertheless, a range of studies over the years does identify that lighting influences perceptions in a meaningful and somewhat predictable way.[19, 20] Flynn and colleagues concluded that the experience of lighted space is, at least to some extent, a shared experience.[21]

We like spaces that evoke a sense of pleasantness. Many people relate to the sense of relaxation, intimacy, apprehension, clarity, and so on. For sighted individuals, these responses are largely influenced by what they see. **Luminance**, then, is a significant factor in subjective responses. Luminance location (peripheral versus overhead) influences pleasantness and spaciousness. Luminance distribution (uniform versus nonuniform) influences spaciousness. Luminance intensities (bright versus dim) influence visual clarity. This can be used to assist in the success of a lighting design. Figures 2.3, 2.4, 2.5, and 2.6 illustrate how luminance location, distribution, and intensities influence perceptions. While illuminance on the tables can be held relatively constant, the luminances (or lack thereof), the smoothness (or harshness) of luminances, and luminance intensities throughout the room influence people's perception of the space. The acceptance of these luminance distributions has much to do with how they enhance or at least coordinate with the architecture and/or function. For instance, in the ballroom shown in Figure 2.3, if it is known that a video presentation will be made, then the lighting situation presented with just downlights might be quite acceptable to banquet attendees. Later discussion in Chapter 3 expands on the psychological or subjective aspects of lighting.

People appear to have luminance and illuminance preferences for work settings. So light can be used to help direct attention to tasks and make the setting comfortable from a brightness perspective for long term work. The lighting designer has immense influence and, therefore, immense responsibility in addressing luminance and illuminance not only on behalf of people's anticipated/desired physiological response, but on behalf of people's

Psychology.....................

- ■ Depends on the observer
- ■ Depends on luminance location
- ■ Depends on luminance distribution
- ■ Depends on luminance intensities

Image ©Digital Vision

The Problem

subjective or psychological response. Indeed, it makes little sense to establish light intensities that are considered appropriate for, say, reading, if people don't want to read in the resulting lighted setting. This is the ultimate waste of energy and earth resources.

more online @
http://www.nrc.ca/irc/bsi/92-5_E.html

2.11 Endnotes

[1] American Optometric Association, Common Vision Conditions: Myopia (web page, 1997), http://www.aoanet.org/. [Accessed September 24, 2000.]

[2] American Optometric Association, Common Vision Conditions: Hyperopia (web page, 1997), http://www.aoanet.org/. [Accessed September 24, 2000.]

[3] American Optometric Association, Common Vision Conditions: 20/20 Vision (web page, 1997), http://www.aoanet.org/. [Accessed September 24, 2000.]

[4] American Optometric Association, Common Vision Conditions: Color Deficiency (web page, 1997), http://www.aoanet.org/. [Accessed September 24, 2000.]

[5] Prevent Blindness America, FAQs about Color Blindness (web page, February, 26, 2000), http://www.preventblindness.org/eye_problems/colorvision.html. [Accessed September 24, 2000.]

[6] Peter Boyce, *Human Factors in Lighting* (New York: Macmillan Publishing Co., Inc., 1980), p. 8.

[7] Yunjian He, et. al., Evaluating Light Source Efficacy Under Mesopic Conditions Using Reaction Times, *Conference Proceedings—1996 IESNA Annual Conference* (New York: Illuminating Engineering Society of North America,1996), 236–257.

[8] Alan L. Lewis, "Equating Light Sources for Visual Performance at Low Luminances," *Journal of the Illuminating Engineering Society*, 1998, no. 1: 80–84.

[9] Alan L. Lewis, "Visual Performance as a Function of Spectral Power Distribution of Light Sources at Luminances Used for General Outdoor Lighting," *Journal of the Illuminating Engineering Society*, 1999, no. 1: 37–42.

[10] Carl Rod Nave, Spectral Power Distribution (web page, 2000), http://hyperphysics.phy-astr.gsu.edu/hbase/vision/spd.html. [Accessed October 1, 2000.]

[11] S. M. Berman, "Energy Efficiency Consequences of Scotopic Sensitivity," *Journal of the Illuminating Engineering Society*, 1992, no. 1: 3–14.

[12] S. M. Berman, et. al., "Spectral Determinants of Steady–State Pupil Size with Full Field of View," *Journal of the Illuminating Engineering Society*, 1992, no. 2: 3–13.

[13] National Eye Institute/National Institutes of Health, Information for Patients: Cataract (web page, April 2000; NIH Publication Number 99–201), http://www.nei.nih.gov/publications/cataracts.htm. [Accessed September 24, 2000.]

[14] Peter Howarth, This is Peter Howarth's Teaching Home Page, Loughborough University, Presbyopia (web page, 2000), http://www-staff.lboro.ac.uk/~huph/presby.htm. [Accessed September 24, 2000.]

[15] T. M. Montgomery, Optometric Physician, Anatomy, Physiology and Pathology of the Human Eye: The Crystalline Lens (web page, 2000), http://members.aol.com/MonT714/tutorial/the_eye/index.html. [Accessed September 24, 2000.]

[16] American Optometric Association, Eye Diseases: Cataract (web page, 1997), http://www.aoanet.org/. [Accessed September 24, 2000.]

[17] U-M Kellogg Eye Center Department of Ophthalmology and Visual Sciences, Eye Conditions/Astigmatism (web page, 2000), http://www.kellogg.umich.edu/conditions/refractive/astigmatism.html. [Accessed October 1, 2000.]

[18] Peter Howarth, This is Peter Howarth's Teaching Home Page, Loughborough University, Astigmatism (web page, 2000), http://www-staff.lboro.ac.uk/~huph/astig.htm. [Accessed October 1, 2000.]

[19] Dale Tiller, Lighting Quality, National Research Council of Canada, http://www.nrc.ca/irc/bsi/92-5_E.html [Accessed October 7, 2000.]

[20] Belinda Collins, *Evaluation of Subjective Response to Lighting Distributions: A Literature Review/NISTIR 5119* (Gaithersburg, MD: National Institute of Standards and Technology, 1993).

[21] John E. Flynn, et. al., "Interim Study of Procedures for Investigating the Effect of Light on Impression and Behavior," *Journal of the Illuminating Engineering Society*, 1973, no. 3: 94.

2.12 General References

IESNA Lighting for the Aged and Partially Sighted Committee. 1998. *Recommended Practice for Lighting and the Visual Environment for Senior Living.* New York: Illuminating Engineering Society of North America.

---

luminance
The amount of light reflected from or transmitted through a material. Measured in footLamberts (fL) (candelas/m²). Perceived as **brightness** (see below).

brightness
The subjective sensation caused by luminance(s). Recognize that this "sensation" not only depends on the luminance of the object and on the eyes doing the viewing and on the viewer's experience and mood, but also on the surrounding or environmental luminance conditions. For example, a car headlight energized during the day is not at all bright. However, the same car headlight at dusk does indeed have some "good" brightness. At night, the headlight has sufficient brightness to be considered bothersome. On a rainy night, the headlight has such intense brightness as to be glary. But the luminance of the headlight remains constant during each of these situations.

Image ©Digital Vision

2.12   The Problem

Figure 2.3 (top left)
Here in this large ballroom at a convention center, downlights alone are energized. Note the harsh contrast between table settings and background surfaces. This is a typical result of using downlights only. The perception might be of a dark, cavernous space.

Figure 2.4 (top right)
Luminous bowl pendents supplement the downlights. Note that the harshness of the contrast between table settings and background surfaces is diminished. Perception might be of a cavernous space since the ceiling height is emphasized and walls remain relatively dark.

Figure 2.5 (bottom left)
Downlights are supplemented with luminous bowl pendents and an upper–wall sconce element around the perimeter of the room. The sconces introduce brightness in the periphery. The sconces also help with room proportion and scale, providing some sense of intimacy even in such a voluminous space.

Figure 2.6 (bottom right)
All lights are energized, including a ceiling cove uplighting the large coffers. The cove lighting fills in ceiling shadows (caused by sconces— see Figure 2.5) and makes it appear as if the pendents are providing significant ceiling brightness. The diffuse light also offers better facial rendering for a social setting.

Lam, William M. C., Ripman, Christopher H., ed. 1992. *Perception and Lighting as Formgivers for Architecture*. New York: Van Nostrand Reinhold.

Moyer, Janet Lennox. 1992. *The Landscape Lighting Book*. New York: John Wiley & Sons, Inc.

Phillips, Derek. 1997. *Lighting Historic Buildings*. New York: McGraw–Hill.

Rea, Mark S., ed. and Thompson, Brian J., general ed. 1992. *Selected Papers on Architectural Lighting*. Bellingham, WA: SPIE Optical Engineering Press.

Rea, Mark S., ed. 2000. *The IESNA Lighting Handbook: Reference & Application*. New York: Illuminating Engineering Society of North America.

Rosenzweig, Mark R. 1999. "Vision: From Eye to Brain." In *Biological Psychology: An Introduction to Behavioral, Cognitive, and Clinical Neuroscience*, 2nd ed. Sunderland, MA: Sinauer Associates, Inc.

Project Scope

Perhaps obvious, but many times not clearly detailed, it must be understood what kind of project is to be undertaken; the extent of the work to be undertaken; the amount of compensation for time invested in the project according to some predetermined fee arrangement; and that the designer has reasonable access to the people who intend to use the planned space(s), or at least access to a competent, well–informed representative of the space users. Once such necessary formalities are dispensed, then lighting design can move forward.

The phases of lighting design typically parallel architectural design work and might include programming, schematic (or preliminary) design, design development, contract documents, and construction administration. Figure 3.1 shows the linear progression of a project from start to finish. Depending on the size of the project and/or the schedule, some of these activities may be merged with one another or even eliminated altogether from the designer's scope. Typically, the larger the project, the longer the schedule, and/or the more and distinct the phases, the greater the time requirements to complete the project, and the greater the fees necessary. So before starting work, the designer must understand what the work encompasses.

3.1 Project specifics

The size, extent, location, and type of the project and its schedule must be well understood before getting underway. Certainly, an office on the floor of an industrial plant may, but not necessarily will, be different than an office in the executive suite of a Fortune 500 company. Indeed, either of these offices will likely be different from that of a dot–com skunk–works. Further, few clients are willing to pay fees to perform the same analysis on a 100 ft² (10 m²) office as might be expected on a 250,000 ft² (25,000 m²) office. Understand the extent of the project.

The area of the project is important. This will offer some sense of the likely variety of space types involved. Additionally, larger projects typically enjoy the benefits of economies of scale—greater quantities of lighting hardware generally result in a lower per–unit cost. Further, the size of the project will offer clues to the depth of problem solving involved. Larger projects tend to have larger teams involved and, thereby, require greater time commitments to meetings to review design options and systems' integration issues. Larger projects tend to offer bigger challenges on dealing with expansive floor plans and mitigating sameness throughout. Finally, larger projects challenge the designer on specification and maintenance standards—minimizing the numbers and types of lamps, luminaires, ballasts, and lighting control devices involved.

The number of different space types involved is important information. Here, the designer will have an early sense on the diversity of the people and tasks that will need to be accommodated.

Understanding the schedule is critical to the timing and the degree of performance by the designer for the various stages of the design effort. Extraordinarily fast schedules tend to limit the designer to assessing hardware on which data is readily available, and limit the designer to the number of design scheme iterations that can be reviewed prior to settling on a preferred option.

Knowing the client and having access to the client influence the success of any given lighting design. Inevitably, and most times unintentional, information filtration occurs with every communicating party on a project.

Project specifics.........
- Size or area, number of spaces, and space types
- Schedule
- Client
- Team

Image ©Digital Vision

3.1 Project Scope

Project Scope

Depending on project economics, the team makeup, the schedule, and/or the client's level and breadth of concern about lighting, the scope may include an entire project, just a few rooms or areas, and just a few steps (e.g., 2nd, 3rd, and 4th). At times, just one step (typically the 4th) is undertaken. Abbreviated versions of the 2nd and 3rd steps are then appended to the 4th step (programming and schematic designing are still a necessity, just not formally recognized as full–blown steps).

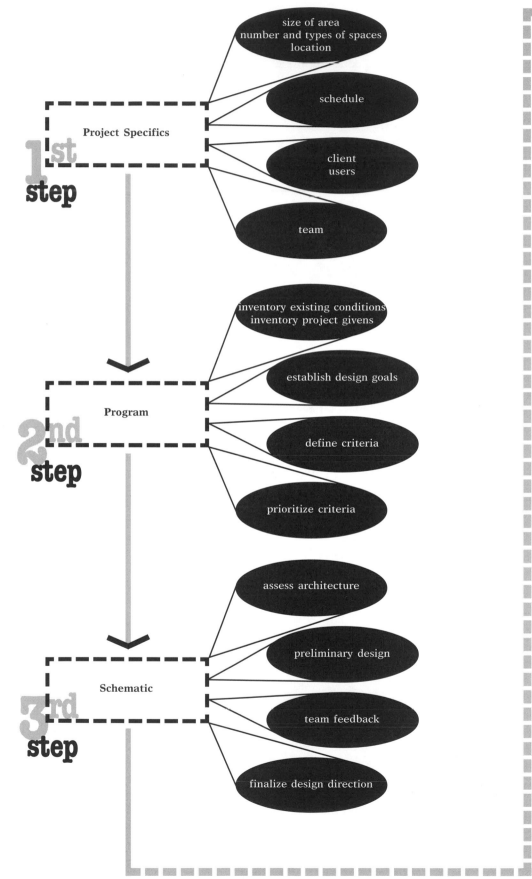

1st step — Project Specifics
- size of area / number and types of spaces / location
- schedule
- client / users
- team

2nd step — Program
- inventory existing conditions / inventory project givens
- establish design goals
- define criteria
- prioritize criteria

3rd step — Schematic
- assess architecture
- preliminary design
- team feedback
- finalize design direction

Project Scope

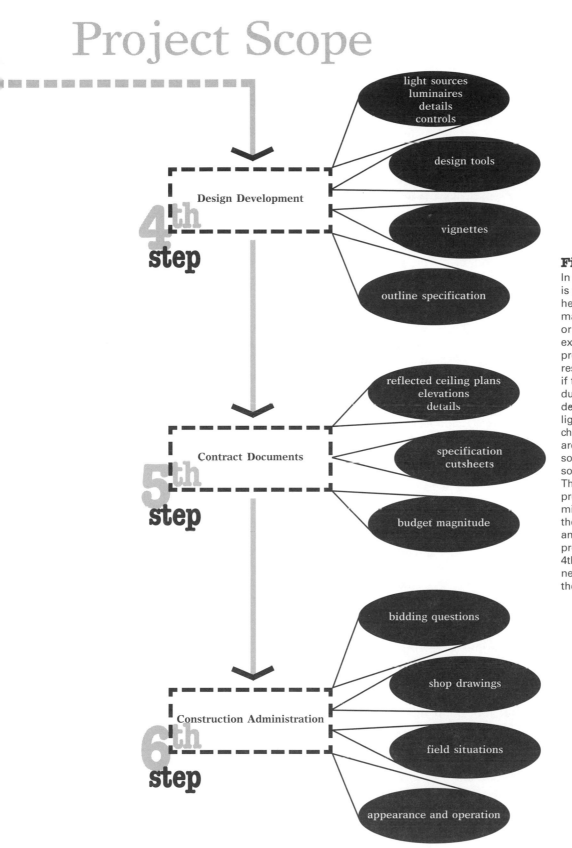

4th step

Design Development

- light sources
  luminaires
  details
  controls
- design tools
- vignettes
- outline specification

5th step

Contract Documents

- reflected ceiling plans
  elevations
  details
- specification
  cutsheets
- budget magnitude

6th step

Construction Administration

- bidding questions
- shop drawings
- field situations
- appearance and operation

Figure 3.1

In a typical project, the process is not strictly linear as depicted here. That is, several iterations may occur within some steps or even between steps. For example, in the 3rd step, the preliminary design needs to respond to the architecture—so if the architecture is evolving during the preliminary lighting design, then the preliminary lighting design will need to change or evolve with the architecture. Some design, some review, some revision, some more design, and so on. There are also times when the project so significantly changes midway through design that the process needs to begin anew. For example, if the project size doubles during the 4th step, then it may be necessary to start anew with the 2nd step.

3.1

Project Scope

HVAC

Heating, ventilating, and air-conditioning. Used as a reference to the professional (HVAC engineer) and/or to the system (HVAC). Pronounced as H–V–A–C or as H–Vac.

With ever-increasing communication speeds and where more work is to be accomplished in less time, there is a tendency to edit out information for brevity's sake. Much gets lost in translation between the actual users, the client, the client's representative, the architect, the engineer, and so on. Many times, users, particularly on large projects, are not representing themselves during the project design process. Sometimes, the client (the individual representing the entity paying the design fees) is far removed from the actual users of the building. The lighting designer's client might be an architect, an engineer, a developer, a facility engineer or a manager in the users' corporation, or the president or CEO of the users' corporation. The further removed from the users, the more care must be taken in interpreting lighting information provided by the client. Additionally, lighting decisions made by the client may not well represent the users' needs. For example, a developer may reject lighting options because they do not meet preconceived cost parameters, when, in fact, no lighting system at that cost point will meet the users' needs. Asking more pointed questions of the client and more carefully addressing programming may be necessary to better understand and address users' needs and convince the client of same.

On larger projects and those that are to be more successful, a team of design professionals is appropriate. Figure 3.2 outlines an organization chart of one possible team arrangement. This team is responsible for addressing the human (users) and the technical issues on the project. Additionally, and usually subliminally, the team must deal with ego(s). The team should then attempt to deal with these human, technical, and ego issues together. A team typically consists of a users' representative, an owner's representative, an architect, an electrical engineer, an interior designer, a mechanical (**HVAC**) engineer, a lighting designer, a fire-protection consultant, an acoustician, a landscape architect, a structural engineer, and a construction manager. Other possible team members may include a wayfinding consultant, a security consultant, and a code consultant. Depending on the scale and duration of the project, contractors play an important role on the team, reporting to the construction manager. Recognize that some of these team members may be one in the same. For example, an architect may elect to perform interior design, lighting design, fire protection, and acoustical services. Nevertheless, quite a few players are involved. Ignoring representatives of certain disciplines or attempting to work without their input may frustrate the design process and ultimately frustrate the owner, leading to unsatisfactory results. On the other hand, it is incumbent on all team members to share any specific requirements that they may have of other professionals on the team. For example, if the lighting designer has no knowledge that the HVAC engineer intends to return air through ceiling luminaires, then there is a great likelihood that the ceiling luminaires will not be specified with this air-return capability; indeed, there may not even be any ceiling-recessed luminaires planned for the project.

Fine examples of teamwork are often found on historic restoration projects. On these projects, additional team members, beyond those cited above, might include art conservator, materials and painting conservators, an historian, and, most importantly, a lead restoration architect. Further, contractors are key members of the team on such projects—where exploration of existing physical conditions is necessary to appreciate what, how, and if lighting can be integrated into details or architecture, or mounted on the architecture in a way that is reminiscent of what might have been

Image ©Digital Vision

Project Scope

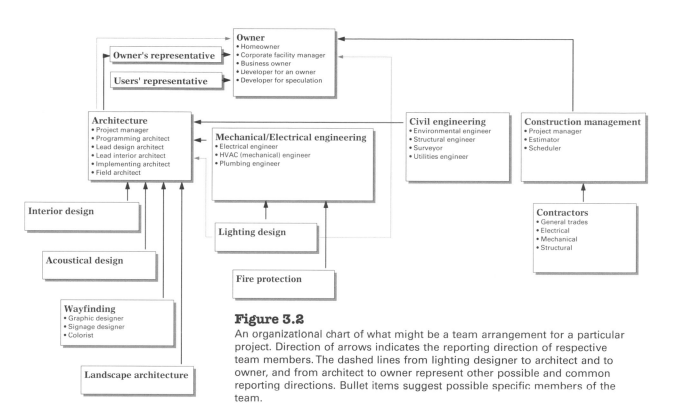

Figure 3.2
An organizational chart of what might be a team arrangement for a particular project. Direction of arrows indicates the reporting direction of respective team members. The dashed lines from lighting designer to architect and to owner, and from architect to owner represent other possible and common reporting directions. Bullet items suggest possible specific members of the team.

authentic to the original architecture or to discretely locate modern equipment. Figures 3.3, 3.4, and 3.5 illustrate a portion of the results of such an effort by a full complement of team members. It cannot be overemphasized that the work by all of the team members was crucial to the final result's success. This includes the owner's representative (for the project shown in Figures 3.2, 3.3, and 3.4, several owner's representatives were involved). The give and take, the breadth of ideas discussed and explored, and the robustness of the resolution greatly depend on this team approach. Unfortunately, many clients today believe such a team approach takes too much time and too much money. However, no shortcuts offer the same degree and success of results as a full team.

3.2 Programming

Programming a project is critical to understanding the kinds of living and working functions that are going to occur or at least are expected to occur on a given project. Programming may be nothing more than a survey of existing conditions (where do the users or owners now live or work and what kinds of living or working are done there) with a critical eye toward future desires or needs for their living and working. For example, if a client has workers using standard computer monitors with a few plasma screens interspersed as a test situation, then some detective work is in order. Are these plasma screen monitors (which for this example are flatter, are more matte, and exhibit better contrast than the standard computer monitor) being considered for mass implementation in the near future? Do users find these screens better or worse and why? Will the use of these screens coincide with more or less work on the computer by the users? Will users keep the old monitors in addition to the new and use both?

Programming...........
- ■ Understand space functions
- ■ Understand users
- ■ Inventory existing conditions
- ■ Establish design goals
- ■ Propose lighting criteria
- ■ Prioritize criteria

Project Scope

In addition to understanding the intended living and/or working functions and an understanding of the people doing the living/working, programming includes an inventory of existing conditions and project givens, establishing design goals, proposing lighting design criteria, and prioritizing that criteria. Programming is discussed in Chapter 4.

3.3 Schematic design

After sufficient programming has occurred, the designer is in a position to begin thinking about how lighting can best meet the programming require-ments of the project and recording those thoughts for team consideration. A schematic indicates that the design has progressed from nothing to at least space adjacencies, potential enclosure ideas, spatial volume, and preliminary space layouts. Schematic lighting design typically results in an understanding and agreement among the team members of lighting criteria, general lighting approaches (e.g., if architectural coves are an important ceiling element, then lighting of these coves would be a schematic lighting approach—with an idea toward lamping [fluorescent, for example]), and styling of luminaires (e.g., simple and clean, simple and industrial, or highly detailed and Victorian, etc.).

In the best situation, work between the architectural schematic design and the lighting schematic design is iterative. That is, some preliminary thoughts on architecture are posed and lighting thoughts based on the program requirements *and* the newly conceived architectural thoughts are then posed. Here, there may be discussion regarding the lighting outcome *if* the architecture can be reconfigured in various ways, or the lighting may well work with the architecture as schematically proposed. Alternatively, it is not unreasonable for lighting thoughts based on the program to be posed first, with preliminary architectural thoughts then following. In any event, however, there is and must be a back and forth exchange of thoughts on architecture and lighting in order to advance a plan to the client that has the best intentions of the program in mind. Otherwise, the architecture may be beautiful, but the lighting may render it ugly. Worse, the architecture may support the work, but the lighting may not (or vice versa). Generally, good architecture cannot overcome the flaws of lousy lighting. However, good lighting typically can compensate for flaws of bad architecture. Most users are experts in seeing; few are experts in architectural design.

Think about this another way. If the architecture includes dark, polished granite walls in a small elevator lobby, but the lighting is downlights and the walls are, therefore, dark, then will the money be well spent on the dark, polished granite? The lighting concept should include lighting of the granite walls (which, by the way, will provide a more pleasing, comfortable visual environment than will downlights alone). Alternatively, if the lobby walls are painted drywall, is wall lighting a bad idea? The wall lighting will accentuate bad tape joints or nail pops. The team must decide, however, if the experience of the space as a brighter, more spacious elevator lobby isn't more important than avoiding the lighting of a poor drywall installation. Not lighting the walls will result in a dull, darker, more cave–like elevator lobby.

Once a schematic design(s) has been established, then feedback from the entire team is necessary—unless this feedback has occurred during the iterative process throughout schematic design. The other professionals must have a chance to understand the preliminary lighting design and respond to it, particularly if the lighting schematic poses a problem or problems with

Schematic design...

- Assess architecture
- Preliminary design
- Team feedback
- Finalize design direction

Image ©Digital Vision

Project Scope

other systems' functions and/or their success. If feedback is significant, then additional lighting design iterations will be necessary to refine the scheme to a point where other disciplines are not negatively affected or have had a chance to modify their respective systems' schemes to work with the lighting scheme. Unless the physically impossible is being asked of the lighting scheme (e.g., no lights in or hanging from the ceiling of a 100,000 ft² [10,000 m²] department store) to accommodate other disciplines, then back and forth design ideas should be readily exchanged in an effort to hone in on a viable, collaborative lighting scheme.

Once feedback has been received and addressed, the lighting scheme is finalized. This yields preliminary lighting plans illustrating the scope of various lighting strategies throughout the project and documenting preliminary light sources and some luminaire types. As the scheme is advanced for client review and hopeful approval, the stage is set for design development. Major changes in schematic approach after this point may wreak havoc on the team's efforts, perhaps resulting in a requirement for additional fees to develop a new schematic, and resulting in a longer project schedule. Schematic Design is discussed further in Chapter 5.

Design development....
- Use design tools to assess design
- Select lamps
- Select luminaires
- Develop details
- Develop vignettes
- Develop outline specifications

3.4 Design development

When a scheme is approved, the next step is to review and propose specific equipment alternatives and layouts to meet the intent of the scheme. So, if a design scheme calls for uplighting of vaulted ceilings, then the design development phase will be the time to establish how to accomplish this uplighting.

Light sources are the engines that propel any lighting solution. Before specific luminaires are selected, the lighting designer should establish the most suitable lamping for a given scheme. Once light sources are reviewed and a selection is narrowed, luminaires can be reviewed and a selection of these narrowed for design team consideration. Light sources are covered in Chapter 6 (Daylight) and in Chapter 7 (Electric Light). Chapter 8 covers luminaires.

Where architectural details are part of the design scheme, these need to be further refined in the design development phase. This is not to be a final, construction detail, but should illustrate the size of the detail necessary to hold the lighting hardware and to permit its appropriate optical performance, its orientation, and required finishes for successful operation. Details are discussed throughout the text in appropriate related chapters, such as Daylight, Lamps, and Luminaires.

Controls (how lights are switched or dimmed on/off) should then be developed to illustrate how the various luminaires and details are to be switched and/or dimmed. Automation should play a significant role in controlling lighting to avoid energy waste during unoccupied conditions. Special controls may be necessary in more functionally complicated spaces, such as presentation rooms, auditoriums, boardrooms, conference rooms, home theaters and the like. Controls are discussed further in Chapter 9.

Design tools are necessary in the design development phase, or perhaps even in the schematic design that help illustrate the lighting ideas and offer some quantitative analyses of the proposed lighting. These tools range from the labor intensive model building, hand sketching, and airbrushing techniques, to the computer rendering and calculation techniques. The charge is to convince you and your team members that the proposed lighting will,

Contract documents..
- Reflected ceiling plans
- Elevations
- Details
- Specifications
- Cutsheets
- Budget magnitude

Image ©Digital Vision

3.5 Project Scope

Team/Michigan Capitol

Project: Rotunda and upper corridors, and façade and site
Owner: State of Michigan
Restoration architect: Richard Frank, FAIA
Implementing architects: Architects Four (now SmithGroup), Quinn Evans Architects, and Wigen Tincknell Meyer & Associates
Lighting designer: Gary Steffy Lighting Design Inc.
Mechanical engineer: Shreve Weber Stellwagen
Electrical engineer: Shreve Weber Stellwagen
Structural engineer: Robert Darvas & Associates
Historian: William Seale
Art conservator: Detroit Institute of Arts
Stone conservator: Norman Weiss
Materials conservation and reconstruction: Washington University Technology Associates
Painting conservator: Darla Olson
Wayfinding: Corbin Design
Landscape architect: William Johnson & Associates
Construction manager: The Christman Company
Electrical contractors: F.D. Hayes Electric Co. and Quality Electrical, Inc.

charrette

A short, intensive design or planning activity. Typically, a half– or full–day session when design team members engage in an intensive design meeting to sort through various design issues and assess the likely impact of various design options. The result is, typically, NOT a design, but a direction of one or several potential design options that are to be pursued further with pros/cons presented at a later session.

Figure 3.3
Restoration of the 1879 Michigan State Capitol was completed in 1992. Introducing modern systems and infrastructure was a significant task—one that could not and would not have been so successful without the diligent **team**work of many professionals. Here, the interior of the dome is viewed from the main floor. Such lighting is the result of design **charrettes** to review and develop options on the many systems involved and ultimately of the architect's ability to coordinate and integrate the various systems. The decorative ceiling around the perimeter is lighted by floor–integrated uplights. See Figures 3.4 and 3.5.

indeed, offer an aesthetically pleasing appearance and also meet the programmed needs of users. Chapter 10 discusses design tools.

Development of at least **vignette** layouts and an outline specification is the result of this phase. This helps to consolidate the lighting ideas and clarify the proposed lighting for all team members. This also permits the registered professionals on the project to assess systems' integration issues and request clarifications or revisions by respective team members.

3.5 Contract documents

In order to formalize the lighting design, the lighting designer must pull together documents that finalize the lighting and provide a clear indication of where and what kind of lighting equipment is necessary to meet the needs of the users. Unless registered to practice architecture or electrical engineering, the lighting designer cannot offer sealed or stamped documents. However, the lighting designer should provide finished and complete reflected ceiling plans, clarification documents (such as lighting details and elevations illustrating wall–mounted lighting equipment), and lighting specifications. Part of the specification (an appendix) should include cutsheets for clarity of luminaire, lamp, and/or detail selection. The contractor can use cutsheets to procure more accurate **shop drawings** and installation instructions.

At the contract document phase, there is sufficient information to provide a complete cost magnitude. For lighting, this should include hardware cost magnitude and some sense of installation cost magnitude. Further, life cycle cost magnitude may be necessary in order to justify the use of more expensive (initially), longer life, and/or more efficient lighting equipment.

All of the material the lighting designer generates in this phase must then be qualified and compiled by the registered professionals and issued as part of their respective contract documentation to contractors for pricing and/or bidding. Chapter 11 discusses the various aspects of contract documents.

Project Scope

©Balthazar Korab

Figure 3.4

Floor–integrated uplights at the balconies were certainly not original to the 1879 building. Programming of the rotunda, however, called for a brighter appearance (more surface luminance). In addition to the near–original and relatively dim historic lighting, this meant introducing more period lighting (hanging from the balconies or walls) or discretely using modern lighting (uplighting was one of several methods reviewed). After deliberation by the team, and after a mockup in situ, it was agreed that the uplights were least obtrusive to introduce more overall luminance. The uplights accent specific architectural elements—the pilasters and the balcony armatures—thereby enhancing the effect of the lanterns on each armature.

vignette

An abbreviated portion of a lighting layout that expresses the typical characteristics (such as dimensions, locations, orientations, and type of luminaires) of the lighting plan without developing a complete, entire plan(s).

::::::::::::::::::::::::::::::::

shop drawings

Detailed luminaire drawings provided by the luminaire manufacturers and submitted through the contractor for the team's review and recommended disposition (e.g., rejected, accepted with changes, accepted). These shop drawings typically show detailed dimensional and material characteristics of the lighting equipment. Shop drawing review is considered a "check step" that helps the design team confirm that the contractor has indeed ordered the equipment as specified to meet the users' needs.

::::::::::::::::::::::::::::::::

3.6 Construction administration

Once a project has been issued to a contractor (or to several contractors) for pricing and/or bidding, another phase of work begins for the lighting designer. Here, there may be a need for clarifications during the bidding process. As questions arise from bidding contractors, electrical distributors, or lighting equipment manufacturers' representatives, the lighting designer may be asked to provide answers or clarifications.

After bidding is complete and the project has been awarded to a contractor, additional questions may arise during the procurement of materials and/or as construction progresses. At some point (hopefully well in advance of lighting installation), the contractor submits shop drawings of the lighting equipment to the team for review and recommended disposition. These are typically more detailed drawings of the lighting equipment—showing precise dimensions, lamping configuration, intended operational orientation, and any mounting hardware, aiming, and/or rotational hardware and locking devices.

There may be times during construction when it becomes apparent that there are conflicts between lighting equipment and other systems. Depending on installation sequences, any field changes resulting from other systems' integration issues, and depending on the level with which the registered professionals compiled the documents, it may be necessary for site visits to assess the field situation(s) and address these as they develop.

As the project nears completion, the lighting designer visits the project to assess the lighting effects and to assess the visual aesthetic of the exposed lighting hardware. Incorrect lamping, luminaire finishes, aiming, lensing, and the like can lead to poor lighting effects—too little light, too much light, too narrow a light pattern, too broad a light pattern, and so on. Construction administration is discussed in more detail in Chapter 12.

Construction ....

- ■ Address bidding questions
- ■ Review shop drawings
- ■ Address field situations
- ■ Assess appearance and operation

Image ©Digital Vision

Programming

Getting a handle on the problem involves assessment of the users' existing conditions and intended future living and/or work conditions. In other words, what is the program for the people in the to–be–designed space. Programming a project does not necessarily take much time, although, large, rather unusual projects generally require a substantial amount of programming time. Lighting programming does require a concerned and committed lighting designer interested in the kinds of criteria that make a space successful for the people who use it. The quality of the programming effort affects the quality and success of the lighting design. If the design is for speculative construction, then its prospective occupants may not be available, but it is reasonable to assume occupants' characteristics, their existing working conditions, potential tasks, and so on. The programming phase consists of inventorying conditions of existing space(s), inventorying givens for the planned space(s), establishing design goals, and defining and prioritizing criteria.

4.1 Inventorying conditions of existing space(s)

Taking inventory of the existing conditions of any project is critical in assessing vision, perception, and subsequently lighting needs of users. It is preferable for the lighting designer to have knowledge of a variety of characteristics of the existing architecture. The process of getting to know the architecture, as well as the perceptions of the users, the owner, and the other designers, prepares the lighting designer for making rational, appropriate decisions as the project progresses. A checklist shown in Table 4.1 can be used as a guide for taking inventory of the conditions of existing space(s) on a project. This can be gathered from a variety of sources. The architect and/or interior designer undoubtedly has made programming progress of his/her own. A memo, report, sketches, and/or drawings may exist that detail the existing conditions. Where such information is unavailable from other sources, the lighting designer will need to investigate the users' existing situation first hand. Even where information is available from others, the lighting designer should investigate the existing conditions first hand. This entails visits to the facility or facilities in which the users are now living/working. A record can then be made of many of the items outlined in Table 4.1. To better understand the views of the owner and other designers on the conditions of the existing space(s), meetings or at least voice conversations should occur.

Some of the inventory information is a matter of observation and measurement taking. Some information, however, requires interaction with users. Questions regarding users' opinions of existing lighting conditions will help in assessing the strengths and weaknesses of the existing environment and begin to direct the designer toward solutions to meet any shortcomings when planning the new construction or the renovation of the existing facility. A few points of etiquette, however. First, clear all site visits and any lines of questioning with the owner or owner's representative and/or with your client. Second, work up just a few simple, short, and unambiguous survey questions that relate to lighting (see Table 4.2).[1] Third, don't make a scene (don't get caught up in an employee rally of opinion; don't express disrespect of past designers' efforts or of owners). Although lighting is an important issue and although some information from the owner/user is better than none, the programming task is to survey the existing situation and not to incite users with undue frustration or consternation.

Image ©Digitalvision

4.1.1 Programming

Table 4.1 Inventorying existing conditions

Status (✔)	Parameter	Existing Condition
▭	Space dimensions	• lengths • widths • heights
▭	Spatial form	• rectilinear • curvilinear • long/narrow and tall/short • short/wide and tall/short
▭	Space activities	• primary (may be several) • secondary (may be several)
▭	Visual tasks	• prioritize by importance • prioritize by time spent on each
▭	Occupants' ages (by group)	• 20 to 40 years old • 40 to 60 years old • 60 or more years old
▭	Furnishings	• low and open • low and closed • high and open • high and closed
▭	Surface finishes	• degree of gloss • colors • reflectances (percentage)
▭	Lighting	• illuminances • luminances • luminaire types, layouts, and lamping • daylighting (view/no view)
▭	Users' feedback	• prior complaints about environment or work • on–site feedback
▭	Owner's feedback	• present image • perceived quality of existing environment • present operating costs
▭	Designers' impressions	• monument to prior design team • monument to owner • improves human condition

4.1.1 Space dimensions

The size of the space has an impact on a variety of lighting issues in the existing space(s). Quantitative aspects are affected by space geometry. If ceilings are low and luminaires are spaced far apart, nonuniformity occurs typically resulting in complaints about either too much light (if an individual is seated directly under a luminaire) or too little light (if an individual is seated between luminaires). Space dimensions also allow for some quick "**takeoffs**" of area (ft^2 or m^2) and budget associated with present lighting configurations. That is, the lighting designer could do some quick estimates about how much the original lighting system cost. This can provide a benchmark for discussing better lighting in the planned spaces.

Image ©digitalvision

Programming

takeoffs

Related to quantities, as in the takeoff of each area, the number of each type of luminaire, or other elements necessary for establishing budgets. Usually taken off of plans or in situ.

4.1.2 Spatial form

The geometry of the space affects the success of a variety of lighting techniques. Quantitative aspects, such as lighting efficiency, are greatly influenced with space shape and geometry. Generally, larger, moderate ceiling spaces (10 to 12′ in height) offer a more efficient use of daylight and electric light. In existing situations with narrow, low–ceiling spaces, light efficiency is relatively low. Subjective aspects, such as spatial comprehension are also influenced by spatial form. Long, narrow spaces with low ceilings promote a sense of enclosure or confinement particularly when downlit and with no wall lighting.

4.1.3 Space activities

Understanding activities in existing situations can greatly help the lighting designer develop more appropriate lighting criteria. For example, in a retirement center, if the lobby is currently used for short–term socializing (greetings and good-byes) and for long–term socializing where users take up knitting, card playing, philately, or other hobbies in the lobby, then simply addressing the newly planned space as a lobby and lighting it accordingly will result in serious underlighting.

4.1.4 Visual tasks

One way to get to know the kinds of task that are likely to be involved in the planned spaces is to know the kinds of tasks performed in the existing spaces. Space users should be observed and queried regarding the kinds of tasks they typically perform and the importance and duration of these tasks. Users and/or the owner should be asked to confirm that these kinds of tasks, in this priority of importance, and in these durations, are anticipated in the planned spaces. If not, then the lighting designer should ask for specifics about the kinds of tasks, their priorities, and duration of such tasks in the planned spaces.

4.1.5 Occupants' ages

Lighting requirements change with age. Generally, 60–year–old eyes need at least twice as much light as 20–year–old eyes to perform a task at the same degree of accuracy and timeliness. Some assessment, then, of the ages of people using the existing space is important in evaluating any comments these people may make about the success or failure of the lighting in the existing space. By observation, the lighting designer should attempt to categorize users' ages by percentage of population.

Aging eyes are also more sensitive to glare than young eyes. General lighting and task lighting may elicit complaints of glare depending on the age of the population and on the degree (or lack) of optical control (e.g., lensing, louvering) or on the optical distribution of light (e.g., indirect versus direct).

4.1.6 Furnishings

Lighting system efficiency is greatly influenced by furnishings. Further, shadows that can result in complaints of dimness or too little light are a result of furniture configurations and room geometry. Tall workstation partitions (e.g., greater than 4′–6″ in height) and low ceilings (e.g., a ceiling height at or less than 3′–0″ higher than the height of the typical workstation partitions) along with the ubiquitous binder bins or shelves all combine to reduce

Image ©digitalvision

4.1.7 Programming

Table 4.2 Existing conditions' survey questions

Status (✔)	Parameter	Questions
▬	Space activities	• How is this space used? • What do you consider the primary tasks here? • Are there any secondary tasks?
▬	Visual tasks	• What is the most important task? • Are there any other tasks of similar importance? • What are the visual aspects of your work?[a] • How much time do you spend in this room each day? • How much time do you spend on each task or activity?
▬	Users' feedback[b, 1]	• The lighting is comfortable. [agree/disagree] • The lighting is too bright. [agree/disagree] • The lighting is too dim. [agree/disagree] • The lighting causes serious shadows. [agree/disagree] • The lighting is functional. [agree/disagree]

[a] If you encounter a task that is unusual or you're simply unfamiliar with it, ask a question like this one in order to gain more information about the seeing portion of the task.
[b] See endnote 1 for additional tips and questions when surveying users. Most questions cited here under "Users' feedback" are attributable to endnote 1.

lighting effectiveness and introduce strong shadowing. So, an assessment of existing conditions can offer insight into what may be proposed for the planned spaces or may offer support for changing workstation configurations, ceiling heights, or both.

The furnishing configurations also influence subjective impressions. Greater density of workstations and/or taller partitions introduce a sense of confinement. This may influence, then, subjective reactions from users of the existing spaces.

4.1.7 Surface finishes

Surface finishes affect both the quantitative aspects of light and the subjective aspects of light. In the existing facility, reviewing the reflectance (percentage of light reflectance) and the gloss (degree of specularity or matteness) of surfaces will help in understanding glare (or lack thereof) and degree of overall brightness impressions (or lack thereof). Additionally, surface reflectances greatly influence transient adaptation as users switch views between paper tasks, computer tasks, and background surfaces. Low reflectance surfaces are likely to create transient adaptation problems—tired eyes and/or headaches may result during the course of a day.

4.1.8 Lighting

Humans are, indeed, creatures of habit. Regardless of their merit, there are certain postures, rituals, events, foods, and places of which people become accustomed, even desirous. A living or working environment may be quite inappropriate and ill–equipped to meet a user's needs, yet because it has been "home" or "the office" for a period of time, the user has adapted to it. To avoid negative reactions and complaints when users move into new environments, designers must either "account" or "educate." Illuminance measurements should be made both on horizontal work surfaces (or floors or laps) and on vertical work surfaces (computer screens, writing boards, and tack boards). Luminance measurements should be made of typical room surfaces and tasks. A record should be made of the types of luminaires and lamps in use and their layout. Notes should be made of typical control settings (are lights energized or

Image ©digitalvision

Programming

off when people are using the space[s]?). A record of daylight–admitting openings should be made as well. This allows for later comparison to proposed planned daylighting and for assessment of the importance of view. All of this survey information should be used to develop new proposed lighting and to avoid faux pas in the development of that lighting. Indeed, the most problematic solution would be one that is nearly identical to the users' existing situation and that the users have identified as problematic!

By accounting for the features exhibited by the user's old environment, the designer may be able to avoid harsh differences between the old and new environments, or may see the need to educate the client about proposed changes. In a classic example, users move from an office lighted with glary, lensed luminaires to one lighted with low–brightness parabolic louver luminaires. Although the parabolic lighting system exhibits less direct glare than the lensed lighting system, the parabolic lights produce more directional (and, therefore, harsher) downlighting. Further, because the parabolic luminaires concentrate the light downward, whereas the lensed luminaires distribute light more diffusely throughout a space, the parabolic lighting creates a "darker" look since the walls receive less light. Compounding this effect is the relatively great amount of light directed onto the horizontal surfaces (work surfaces and floors) from the parabolic luminaires. So the work surface may be perceived as overlit while the room is perceived as underlit. The lighting designer could account for the greater room brightnesses experienced in the lensed–luminaire environment by using higher reflectance, matte surface finishes, by introducing some uplighting onto the ceiling, or by introducing wall lighting to increase the perception of brightness. These techniques of increasing spatial brightnesses are particularly important when folks are moved from a space lighted to 30–year–old lighting criteria to a space lighted to our present–day lighting criteria.

Educating users, though a noble goal, is a difficult process, as the designer usually cannot get an audience with all of the users of a new environment. If one–on–one discussion is possible, or if educational material (e.g., a project website) can be developed, then user education may be an effective means of presenting new concepts, thereby avoiding or minimizing complaints.

4.1.9 Users' feedback
Most owners of larger and more commercial space types (e.g., offices, libraries, apartment buildings, retirement communities, and so on) are not users of those spaces. Getting user feedback on existing conditions requires the designer to survey the users and/or to review any file of previous complaints about the workplace. Table 4.2 suggests some questions for surveying users. This information can be used both to assess the existing environment's lighting and to develop more successful lighting solutions for the proposed spaces.

4.1.10 Owner's feedback
Although, as noted above, most owners are not the users of the planned spaces, the designer should take stock of how the owner perceives the existing environment. Is it considered comfortable and pleasant? If a work environment, is it considered state of the art and productive? Does it promote the kind of image the owner wishes to promote? As with previously accrued information, this can be used to help develop design solutions for the newly planned spaces.

4.1.11 Programming

4.1.11 Designers' impressions
Designers on the project will likely have opinions about the owner's existing space(s). These should be heard—helping the lighting designer understand potential biases of the other designers, and, in turn, this will assist in developing lighting ideas for the planned spaces. Opinions alone, however, are insufficient information. An understanding of the issue(s) surrounding the opinion will help unravel the real reason behind designers' likes and dislikes. For example, many design team members may hate fluorescent lighting. Typically, this hatred comes from past experiences with lousy color, cool–toned fluorescent lamps that flickered throughout the day. Further, much of the old fluorescent lighting equipment simply had poor glare control.

4.1.12 Summary of inventory of existing conditions
A short report or journal record of the users' existing conditions should be made. The designer hopefully learns from both the bad and good aspects of the existing conditions. Further, as the designer develops design goals, he/she should realize those aspect of the existing conditions that don't or won't support comfortable, productive, living or working and thus be prepared to educate users on these aspects during the remainder of the design process.

4.2 Inventorying givens for planned space(s)
At the same time that an inventory of conditions of the existing facility(ies) is being made, there are likely to be "givens" about the new project that may significantly influence lighting design, or alternatively that the lighting designer should influence. These "givens" are related to the owner's, the users', and the designers' perspectives on the specific project. The reference to "designers" is intended to be all–inclusive (indeed, including the lighting designer). Table 4.3, which is similar to yet different from Table 4.1, outlines the kinds of information that might be available about the planned space(s).

4.2.1 Space dimensions
The size(s) of the planned space(s) has an impact on a variety of lighting criteria. Quantitative aspects are affected by space geometry. Generally, larger, open spaces offer more efficient use of daylight and electric light than smaller spaces. Narrow, low–ceiling spaces offer the least efficient use of light. Subjective aspects are also influenced by space geometry. Light can be used to enhance or to limit some of these subjective influences. For example, a narrow space can be made to feel wider by using light colored walls and then lighting the walls. Ceiling height influences general lighting approach. Ceiling heights less than 9'–0" are unlikely candidates for ceiling–suspended **indirect**, **semi–indirect**, or **direct/indirect** lighting systems.

4.2.2 Spatial form
The spatial form of the newly planned spaces will ultimately affect lighting system efficiency and the users' perceptions of the space. Further, lighting can be used to enhance architectural elements. For example, where curvilinear forms are developed architecturally, lighting can and should be used to enhance these forms. Figure 4.1 illustrates how a lighting detail was used to accentuate a series of asymmetric ceiling vaults. Where geometry is forced by other programming requirements (e.g., long corridors), lighting and color can help minimize the apparent length and/or maximize the apparent width.

Programming

4.2.3 Space activities

Space activities in the planned project may be different from those that occur in the owner's existing spaces. Hence, it is important to know how spaces are intended to be used and what kinds of visual activities may be involved. For example, perhaps the existing lobby in a retirement center that is now used for hobby activities may be replaced with two spaces—a new lobby and a new activity room. So, the new lobby may be solely intended as the short term meet/ greet space. As such, lighting criteria are much different than if the planned lobby was to have the dual role of meet/greet and as a hobby activity center.

4.2.4 Visual tasks

Getting a detailed list of specific tasks for the planned spaces is necessary to understanding the kinds of visual activities that are anticipated. Prioritizing these tasks by importance and by time spent on each will help the designer to establish lighting criteria appropriate to address these tasks. For example, if working on computers ultimately takes just half an hour each day, then it may not make much sense to develop lighting criteria and lighting solutions to address users working on computers. On the other hand, if the computer task is linked to life/death situations (e.g., monitoring a patient's vital signs), then lighting should be developed to permit users easy, convenient, and accurate viewing of the computer screen.

For this exercise, the designer must be quite specific in analyzing the visual tasks. For example, it is not sufficient to visit the users' existing facility, observe an accounting function, and simply jot down that the task is accounting. Are the users reading and writing hard copy? If so, what is the medium(s) (e.g., black pen on white paper, hard pencil on green ledger, etc.)? Are the users reading and writing with a computer? What are the screen characteristics? Is the screen internally illuminated, or is room light needed for viewing of the screen?

4.2.5 Occupants' ages

A review of the occupants' ages established when inventorying conditions of existing spaces is necessary here. More than likely, the occupants in the newly planned spaces will be of similar demographics. Lighting criteria should be developed based on these age groupings. To some extent, some arbitrary priorities will need to be made. Do the older people constitute the greatest percentage of the population in the newly planned spaces? How susceptible are their tasks to light intensity? For example, if much of the visual work involves reading large–text, boldfaced labels of a repetitive nature, then light intensities will not likely be a factor in accurate task perfor- mance—experience and alertness are the more important factors in task performance.

4.2.6 Furnishings

An understanding of the nature of furnishings is important to establish how light will be absorbed or redirected in a space and what kinds of tasks may take place at specific locations. Furniture layouts are used to assess such conditions in the newly planned space(s). Not only are plan layouts neces- sary, but furniture elevations are required to understand how/if shadows will be detrimental to the use of the space(s).

indirect lighting

Architectural lighting achieved with luminaires exhibiting an indirect light distribution—90 to 100% of the light exits the luminaire upward; 0 to 10% of the light exits the luminaire downward. NOTE: this is not to be confused with currently popular self– contained luminaires where lamps may be hidden from view, yet produce significant luminaire luminance due to close proximity of lamp to reflector.

semi–indirect lighting

Architectural lighting achieved with luminaires exhibiting a semi– indirect light distribution—60 to 90% of the light exits the luminaire upward;10 to 40% of the light exits the luminaire downward. NOTE: this is not to be confused with currently popular self–contained luminaires where lamps may be hidden from view, yet produce significant luminaire luminance due to close proximity of lamp to reflector.

direct/indirect lighting

Architectural lighting achieved with luminaires exhibiting an indirect/ direct light distribution—40 to 60% of the light exits the luminaire upward; 40 to 60% of the light exits the luminaire downward. NOTE: this is not to be confused with currently popular self–contained luminaires where lamps may be hidden from view, yet produce significant luminaire luminance due to close proximity of lamp to reflector.

Image ©digitalvision

4.2.7 Programming

Table 4.3 Inventorying planned project's givens

Status (✔)	Parameter	Givens on Planned Project
▬	Space dimensions	• lengths • widths • heights
▬	Spatial form	• rectilinear • curvilinear • long/narrow and tall/short • short/wide and tall/short
▬	Space activities	• primary (may be several) • secondary (may be several)
▬	Visual tasks	• prioritize by importance • prioritize by time spent on each
▬	Occupants' ages (by group)	• 20 to 40 years old • 40 to 60 years old • 60 or more years old
▬	Furnishings	• low and open • low and closed • high and open • high and closed
▬	Surface finishes	• degree of gloss • colors • reflectances (percentage)
▬	Daylighting	• daylighting (view/no view)
▬	Owner's expectations	• image • perceived quality of planned environment • initial costs and planned operating costs
▬	Designers' expectations	• monument to design team • monument to owner • improve human condition

4.2.7 Surface finishes

The designer should also take note of the proposed wall, ceiling, and floor finishes. He/she should consider enhancing the texture, grain, or sheen of these materials with light. Since color values (reflectances) of these surfaces greatly affect lighting efficiency, their selection should be made with great care (see 4.5.3 for more on value). The lighting designer should advise other team members of selections that pose great inefficiencies for the lighting system and/or pose luminance problems. Knowing materials' colors will help the designer select an appropriate lamp. Alternatively, the designer should select the lamp and then select materials under this lamp.

Programming

fenestration
The opening(s) or aperture(s) in a building that permit the entry of daylight.

Figure 4.1
Understanding spatial form is important for applying lighting solutions that are not only appropriate to meet the quantifiable lighting criteria, but also enhance the architecture. Spending money on such architectural forms and then not accentuating these forms with light tends to be a waste of money. Here, even the detail holding the uplight is itself detailed to allow some light to "leak" out the bottom dentil work.

4.2.8 Daylighting

Where daylighting is intended to be a significant factor in the lighting of the space(s), the architecture should follow the dictates of daylighting geometry. For example, narrow, and high–ceiling geometry are best with daylight apertures (**fenestration**) on the long walls. Alternatively, and particularly in retrofit or renovation projects where the architecture already exists, daylighting opportunities should be explored based on fenestration and space geometry. Clarification from the users and/or owner should be sought regarding daylighting versus view. Daylighting as a means to providing illuminance and/or luminance throughout the day is one application known as "daylighting." Most users are most concerned about view aspects—hence another application of "daylighting." Still a third application of "daylighting" is related to physiological well–being, including most notably seasonal affective disorder (SAD).

4.2.9 Owner's expectations

The designer should take stock of what the owner expects of the newly planned environment. Issues of environmental quality and budget should be addressed early in the programming phase to avoid later surprises and disasters in both the planning and the financing of the project. Are there image requirements that need to be conveyed by the architecture, interior design, and lighting to users and/or visitors? Are there quality expectations that the owner has seen or experienced in other facilities and expects to see incorporated into the new space(s)? Finally, what ego issues, if any, need to be addressed? Is the owner

4.2.10 Programming

after the largest structure, the tallest building, the highest–tech facility, etc., to achieve some notoriety?

Budget matters need to be defined. The owner should be educated on the costs/benefits or lack of benefits of various approaches. For example, an owner may indicate initially that the setting is to have "no frills," which to him/her probably means no decorative lighting. Yet decorative lighting is responsible for the human–scale aspects of an environment, providing a more homey, pleasing atmosphere. It also is responsible for establishing an image and alleviates the blandness of general lighting techniques.

4.2.10 Designers' expectations

To avoid surprises and difficulties in the design goals and design concept phases, the designer(s) should clearly state any personal expectations. Ego considerations are an inherent part of the design process and should be openly discussed with the owner. Some designers have "signatures" that are exhibited in nearly all of their projects, which may be responsible for the client's selection of the designer for a given project. Lighting can play an important role in expressing this signature. For example, it is desirable to use rich materials (e.g., marble, granite, or wood) in speculative–building lobbies. Such an upgrade in materials can play a profound role in developers' abilities to sign and retain lessees. Often, however, these expensive materials are left unaccented—visually expressing a lack of commitment and concern for quality, detail, and comfort—the very attributes for which designers hope to be recognized, and the very characteristics that landlords wish to promote! The lighting designer should express and address his/her own expectations early and follow through with lighting concepts and details that promote those expectations and those of others on the team.

4.2.11 Summary of inventory of givens for planned spaces

A short report or journal record of the planned spaces' givens should be used as a reference. The impact of these givens on the lighting design should be outlined for the record and shared with the team. The designer should make every effort to accommodate and address these givens. This may entail education of the users on various aspects of the proposed lighting and how that lighting has been developed to address the givens of the planned spaces. Alternatively, the designer may need to educate other team members and/or the users on how revising some of the givens of the planned spaces can result in better lighting.

4.3 Establishing design goals

With a clear understanding of the users' existing conditions and of the givens for planned spaces, the designer is now in a position to develop specific lighting design goals. Design goals are those attributes, both soft (art) and hard (science), that the lighting system is designed to address. So, prior to designing, these goals need to be established. The programming discussed to this point is the basis for defining the design goals. Design goals are criteria. It is important to note, however, that these design goals are not steadfast, finite requirements. These are goals toward which the design team should strive. For various reasons, these goals may not ultimately be attainable on a project. For example, at the last minute, the owner may experience financial problems that result in difficult but necessary cost cuts that will

Image ©digitalvision

Programming

negatively affect design goals. Other circumstances beyond the design team's control include owners' and users' opinions, change in staff, corporate takeovers, homeowners' divorces, and the like.

Seldom are design goals conveniently straightforward and easily stated. Perhaps this is why many designers today elect simply to place a uniform array of downlights or rectilinear luminaires on a reflected ceiling plan in order to generate "enough light." This approach permits the designer to meet the legal requirements of a project without expending much time and money. In fact, it is ironic that as design has become more and more demanding, as the service sector of the economy has increased—requiring more attention to the human–scale aspects of design—designers have been discounting fees, thereby eliminating the time and money available to properly review the lighting and other systems needed for appropriate function and behavior. Providing only "enough light" may, in fact, create occupant complaints and dissatisfaction and ultimately lead to a reduction in performance, less time spent in the offending environment, and an overall morale problem. A comprehensive list of lighting design goals is categorized in Table 4.4 and discussed in Sections 4.4, 4.5, and 4.6. Some goals are straightforward (e.g., codes), but others may require considerable research and thought prior to their resolution (e.g., daylighting). This list should be used as a guide to expand the designer's perspective on appropriate vision and related lighting aspects.

4.4 Spatial factors

Design goals associated with spatial factors relate to the architecture of the building, the interior architecture of the spaces, the impact of lighting on other building systems, and the integration of lighting with other building systems. The designer must address physical issues of architectural form, surfaces, and integration. For example, how can the lighting enhance the architectural philosophy? How can lighting enhance the order and pleasant appeal of the architecture? How can lighting enhance the 3–dimensional aspects of the architectural form? How can lighting be integrated with the architecture and building systems to best meet the programming needs without encumbering the space with out–of–scale hardware or hardware that is stylistically inappropriate for the architecture and interior furnishings?

Defining these spatial factor goals is the only reasonable means of developing lighting solutions that are sympathetic to the architecture and interiors. Nevertheless, with the exception of code requirements, these goals should never supersede the psychological and physiological factors, nor the task factors. It is paramount that lighting goals strive to best accommodate those users' needs discovered during the inventorying of both existing conditions and the planned project's givens.

4.4.1 Visual environment pleasantness

Visual environment pleasantness is the appropriate marriage of light and architecture toward a common goal of pleasantness—a very subjective, often attainable end. Pleasantness is achieved when the architecture, interiors and/or landscaping, and their support systems reinforce the visual setting. However, pleasantness is not blandness. In a poetic sense, pleasantness is the harmony of all things in the built condition. Typically, pleasantness is achieved when team interaction is high—in other words, if team members work in isolation, then there will likely be less harmony in architectural

4.4.1 Programming

detailing, finishes, and systems' integration. A few examples best illustrate what is commonly considered visually pleasant. Figures 4.2, 4.3, and 4.4 show a classic, highly integrated interiors solution that a team of engineers and designers developed. Figures 4.5, 4.6, and 4.7 exemplify urban planning with a high sense of pleasantness achieved with architectural scale, planning, and urban systems' integration. Finally, Figures 4.8 and 4.9 illustrate the pleasantness aspect in an interior architectural situation.

The lighting system is likely to remain in place for many years prior to any move or renovation. The environment is built to support people over that period of time. People are an expensive asset—pleasantness would seem an important issue.

Lighting techniques that help with pleasantness include lighting hardware scale and shape; lighting hardware spacing and relationships to architectural elements and other building systems; and resulting luminance patterns, intensities, and uniformities.

▶ *Lighting hardware scale and shape*: Where luminaires are intended to regress or disappear into the architecture, smaller sizes and simpler geometries are best. A rule–of–thumb on size: where ceilings are within 10′ (3 m) of the floor plane, where luminaires are exposed (not hidden in details), and where the luminaires are not contributing to spatial character, consider luminaires of less than 7″ (175 mm) in diameter or in width. Where these luminaires are exposed (not recessed), the height or depth of the luminaire should also be less than 7″ (175 mm). For every 2 feet of ceiling height, another 1″ (25 mm) can be added to diameter, width, and/or height. Smaller is better, however, in those situations where the lighting hardware is intended to be a background, unimposing element and not to contribute to spatial character. Where luminaires are recessed into ceilings or walls, the geometry of the face should be round, square, or rectangular. Where luminaires are exposed (and, therefore, 3–dimensional), cylinders, cubes, or soft, curvilinear shapes are best if lighting hardware is to remain unnoticed. Figure 4.10 illustrates a scale problem with lighting hardware.

When situations arise where lighting hardware is to contribute character to the architecture and is intended to offer significant presence, the scale of luminaires needs to relate to the architectural scale. Indeed, luminaires may need to be quite large. Luminaire styling and detailing need much more attention where people are intended to take notice of the lighting hardware. Figure 4.11 illustrates lighting hardware of appropriate scale when using lighting hardware as part of the architectural character. Such luminaires are significant visual cues even when unlighted. The streetlight in Figures 4.5, 4.6, and 4.7 shows the importance of scale when attempting to have an impact with lighting hardware in developing a sense of place and character. Figures 4.8 and 4.9 exemplify scale for sconce and valance elements when these are also important architectural elements.

▶ *Lighting hardware spacing and relationships to architectural elements and other building systems*: The spacing of luminaires should relate in some way to architectural or landscape components, such as structural bays, pilasters, beams, joists, trees, planters, pavement patterns, flooring patterns, and the like. Recognize the importance of this spacing relationship characteristic from Figures 4.2 through 4.9. Where lighting hardware is "sharing" space or surfaces with other systems, such as mechanical (HVAC) diffusers, sprinklers, speakers, and construction joints,

Image ©digitalvision

Programming

Table 4.4 Lighting Design Goals

Category	Status (✔)	Lighting Design Goal
Spatial factors		▶ visual environment pleasantness
		▶ spatial definition
		▶ spatial order (3–D vs. 2–D planning)
		▶ circulation
		▶ flexibility
		▶ controls
		▶ acoustics
		▶ HVAC
		▶ ceiling systems
		▶ codes
		▶ ordinances
		▶ sustainability
Psychological and physiological factors		▶ sensory responses
		▶ visual hierarchies and focal centers
		▶ visual attraction
		▶ subjective impressions
		▶ daylighting
		▶ nightlighting
		▶ health
Task factors		▶ visual tasks
		▶ luminances
		▶ surface reflectances
		▶ surface transmittances
		▶ illuminances

or street furniture, such as drains, benches, planters, and the like, the proximity to these elements and consistent spacing and position with respect to these repeating elements are important for minimizing visual clutter or visual noise.

▶ *Luminance patterns, intensities, and uniformities:* The previous few paragraphs deal with the visual impact of the lighting hardware on, in, and with the architecture and/or landscape. Just as important toward maintaining a pleasant visual setting is how the lighting effects—the luminances—influence the view of the setting. The luminance patterns

Image ©digitalvision

4.4.2 Programming

Figures 4.2 (top), 4.3 (bottom left), and 4.4 (bottom right)
Visual environment pleasantness: Lighting is well integrated with the interior architecture. All but task lights are hidden from view in details that appear "natural" or "seamless" with the architecture. Luminaire detail modules are relatively small to maintain some human scale and to minimize the sense of overall length that would otherwise be present with simple continuous cove and wallwash details. The luminance patterns enhance the architectural elements, softly highlighting edges. The consistent, peripheral luminances contribute to a sense of spaciousness. Task lights are clustered and of small size to relate to users' scale and locations. Aircraft is an Airbus 320–series. [Note: Gary Steffy Lighting Design Inc. did not provide any lighting consultation on this project.]

should support the architectural setting, not introduce harsh, discontinuous luminances that literally destroy the view of an entire setting. For example, in Figure 4.8, note how the downlights are spaced to prevent harsh scallop patterns (sharp luminance patterns) on the upper member of the deep wood trusses (at the ceiling plane) and on the bottom cord of the trusses spanning below the ceiling. Hence, in the total view of Figure 4.9, the luminance patterns enhance the architectural elements presented by the cathedral wood ceiling rather than introduce harsh, distracting streaks or patterns. Luminance patterns can be visualized only with extensive experience, or alternatively with extensive calculations to assess light patterns and distributions within given settings.

4.4.2 Spatial definition

Walls and ceilings are used to define space physically. Lighting key surfaces or portions of surfaces can enhance the spatial definition intended by the architecture of walls and ceilings. This is not to say all walls and/or ceilings should be lighted. Indeed, very selective lighting can offer distinct, interesting, and visually complete spatial definition. The key, then, is to develop patterns of light that support the architecture, rather than work against the architecture or leave it sufficiently unlighted to prevent its expression. Figure 4.12 exemplifies lighting supporting spatial definition.

Programming

©Gary Steffy Lighting Design Inc.

Image ©digitalvision

Figures 4.5 (top left), 4.6 (top right), and 4.7 (bottom)

Visual environment pleasantness: The lighted composition of Les Champs Elysées Avenue, Paris, is elegantly spectacular. The highlighted monument of Arc de Triomphe is bordered by an allay of trees fitted with light strings. The avenue vehicular pavement and sidewalk are lighted with straightforward roadway lights hidden in the tree canopies and camouflaged by the light strings. Pedestrian postlights enhance the night stroll, but are also quite important as a daytime cue marking the avenue's elegance and history. Figures 4.5 and 4.6 offer a better clue as to the scale of the postlights. Each lantern head is likely 3′ (1 m) in overall height. [Note: Gary Steffy Lighting Design Inc. did not provide any lighting consultation on this project.]

4.4.3 Spatial order

Architecture generally promotes some sense of order through structure, pattern, and aperture arrangement. Lighting can enhance this order. Using lighting hardware in layouts and spacings that are sympathetic to the architecture will help strengthen the architectural order. In its 2–dimensional plan view, a particular lighting layout may look appropriate, but in 3–dimensional space, the lighting hardware and/or the luminance patterns may not support the order and hierarchy of the architecture. Luminance patterns can also be used to promote architectural order. Figures 4.13 and 4.14 illustrate how lighting detracts from the spatial definition and order attempted by the architecture. Figures 4.15 and 4.16 illustrate a similar application (hotel) where lighting was intentionally planned to support the spatial definition and order of the architectural and focal elements.

Lighting can also enhance architecture of a deconstructive style. Lighting hardware and/or luminance patterns can be used to accentuate the varied planar and/or compound curvilinear elements that form the architectural space envelope. Indeed, lighting these elements in a nonuniform fashion can itself promote the style of deconstructive architecture.

4.4.4 Circulation

Lighting can be used to help direct people from one zone to another. Greater luminances (typically at walls and/or the ceiling as opposed to the

Image ©digitalvision

4.4.5

Programming

Figures 4.8 (left) and 4.9 (right)

Visual environment pleasantness: There is no recess depth in the ceiling. A field of the ubiquitous suspended "trash can" downlights would introduce visual clutter. So, surface mounted downlights of a relatively small rectangular shape (1′ [300 mm] footprint by 1′–6″ [450 mm] height) were painted out to match the ceiling. Luminaire spacings were based on the joist and rafter spacings, and located to avoid harsh luminance patterns on joists. To provide sufficient light around the perimeter of the pool and to hide extensive mechanical ductwork, a large–scale valance was created (nearly 6′ [1.8 m] in height). The valance provides a "glow" of light onto the nearby pool deck and introduces uplight to accentuate the wood ceiling. Large–scale sconces (nearly 5′ [1.5 m] in height with the bottom mounted at 8′ [2.4 m]) are proportionally appropriate to the architectural envelope.

©C.M. Korab

©C.M. Korab

floor) will attract attention. A single zone or area of high luminance or a series of high luminance zones can then lead people through a space or from one space or area to another. This technique can be used in open areas even where architecture does not define "the path." See Section 4.5.3.

4.4.5 Flexibility

Flexibility has many meanings. So, the design team must agree on what kind of flexibility, if any, the lighting system is to have for a specific project. For example, flexibility may mean that:
- all or most luminaires are readily moveable
- lighting quantities and quality remain constant (people can be moved around with no change in lighting)
- lighting quantities and qualities are changed by addressing (controlling) luminaires

4.4.6 Controls

Spatial factors and the success with which lighting addresses them are dependent on controls. Switching lighting effects on/off and/or dimming lighting over the course of a day can change the impact of the architecture. Further, **temporal control** or dynamic control can itself help establish some of the spatial factors previously discussed (e.g., visual hierarchy, circulation, and focal centers). Task factors, discussed later in this chapter, can significantly influence the need for controls as well. Also, there will always be some sort of lighting control (to control both electric lighting and daylighting quantities and qualities) in built environments. Simple wall switches are the bare minimum required by code. Controls make sense in terms of economics, global environment protection, and occupant protection and satisfaction. For electric lighting, controls may include: switches, dimming, time–of–day

temporal control

Dynamic control over time. Involves a time machine or programmed computer program to control light intensity, color, motion (e.g., chasing effects), flashing, and the like. Static control or the traditional definition of "control" is the simple act of turning a light or series of lights on and off, or dimming them from one steady state to another.

Image ©digitalvision

Programming

Figure 4.10
Here, the lighting hardware does not lend character to the architecture. The scale of the luminaires is too great—large, heavy elements looming overhead and cantilevered from what appears to be a relatively thin (insubstantial) curvilinear fascia. The fact that the luminaires are not level contributes to the sense of overwhelming scale and a lack of architectural order. [Note: Gary Steffy Lighting Design Inc. did not provide any lighting consultation on this project.]

Figure 4.11
Here, the lighting hardware lends character to the architecture and offers significant visual cueing toward the entry. As such, the scale of the luminaires must relate to the scale of the building façade. Further, the luminaires have a translucent medium on at least three sides that helps to visually reduce scale (the more transparent the lighting hardware, generally the larger it must be to have a significant presence). [Note: Gary Steffy Lighting Design Inc. did not provide any lighting consultation on this project.]

control, occupancy sensors, photocell sensors, and centralized building energy management. For daylighting, controls may include photocell sensors and local manual switches or devices for control of window treatment. This is discussed further in Chapter 9.

4.4.7 Acoustics

Lighting can have a negative impact on spatial acoustics. The lighting designer should be in a position to address goals the acoustician establishes. Nevertheless, it is incumbent on the acoustician or on the architect (as the design leader and coordinator) to relay any lighting–related acoustics goals to the lighting designer as early as possible—during the programming of the project—so that informed lighting design can proceed in the schematic design phase.

Luminaire ballasts and transformers can introduce noise into spaces and/or into audio amplification systems. Chokes are available to minimize this noise. Using remote ballasts or transformers can reduce noise, but this is providing the remote equipment is sound isolated from noise–sensitive spaces. Further, remote equipment needs to be easily accessible and well ventilated as determined by the registered professionals on the project. Electromagnetic ballasts and transformers are notorious noise generators; however, certain versions of electronic ballasts and transformers may also cause problems. Electronic components operating above 20,000 **Hz** are not audible.

Hz
Hertz. The SI metric for frequency of wavelengths of energy. 1 Hz represents one wavelength cycle per second. Audible sound ranges from 20 to 20,000 Hz.[2]

4.4.8 Programming

A reference to ceiling tile edge conditions. A tegular edge is a notched right–angle corner.

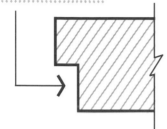

©Robert Eovaldi

Figure 4.12
Spatial definition: The curvilinear walls of this cylindrical stairwell are accented with a slot detail (a continuous opening in the ceiling along the juncture of the ceiling and wall). Light coming from the slot provides a soft line of light that enhances the curve of the cylindrical stairwell.

The makeup of the lighting hardware can also have a negative influence on architectural acoustics. For example, in open plan offices, ceiling–recessed lensed luminaires, ceiling–recessed small cell (paracube) louver luminaires, and large, flat–bottomed pendent indirect luminaires all of which exhibit a width of at least 1′ (0.3 m) can easily reflect sound from one workstation or area to another. In these office situations, consider narrow profile luminaires (less than 8″ in width), or in the case of pendent lights, consider round profiles (to avoid a flat bottom).

4.4.8 HVAC
Heating, ventilating, and air–conditioning can be influenced by lighting—both by lighting loads or power budgets (total wattage of lights) and lighting equipment air–handling capabilities. As with acoustics, the responsibility for HVAC lies with the mechanical engineer. The lighting designer, however, needs to be in a position to meet the goals the mechanical engineer establishes. It is incumbent on the mechanical engineer to convey these goals as early in a project as possible—during the programming of the project—so that informed lighting design can proceed in the schematic design phase.

Lighting power budgets are particularly important to the mechanical engineer in establishing cooling loads and in sizing air–conditioning and heating equipment.

Some recessed luminaires have the capability to extract air (return air through the luminaire housing into ductwork or plenum spaces and ultimately back to the central conditioning units) and/or to supply conditioned air into the environment. Although such a feature may be convenient for the mechanical engineer, it should never be the sole or primary reason for selecting a particular lighting solution.

4.4.9 Ceiling systems
The architect establishes the ceiling system or systems to be used in a particular project. These ceiling systems establish other design goals for the lighting designer. Here, however, the lighting designer should work to

Image ©digitalvision

Programming

Figures 4.13 (top) and 4.14 (bottom)

Spatial definition: Linear, angular forms are the architectural "edges" defining space in both figures. In both situations, however, lighting is not enhancing the architectural envelope. Indeed, the harsh scallops in both settings are detracting from spatial definition. In the top figure (4.13), downlights too close to the wall strongly accent portions of the wall, thereby not accentuating the wall's linearity. Arguably, these scallops define the elevator doors, but even for this "task" they are located much too close to the wall. Finally, the downlight is oddly lighted by an "errant" downlight. Nevertheless, lighting is unsupportive in defining the elevator lobby, so there are just a few elevators over there along a wall.

In the bottom figure (4.14), the lighting effects do not enhance the area sufficiently to demark this as the registration desk for a large hotel. The back wall is dark, and only the right end of the reception desk receives enough light to attract some attention. Worse, the angular bulkhead is inconsistently lighted with odd scallop patterns that do not accentuate the shape, size, or location of the bulkhead.

Spatial order: The lighting in both installations fails to contribute to spatial order in a meaningful fashion. Other than the brute force nature of the scallops above elevator doors in Figure 4.13 (top), the lighting in both installations apparently has been laid out in 2–dimensional plan view (on paper) with little regard for the 3–dimensional character of the architecture. This actually leads to visual chaos or visual noise, thereby detracting from spatial order. Alternatively, look at the reception desk in Figure 4.15 to better appreciate how light can be used to assist with spatial definition and spatial order. [Note: Gary Steffy Lighting Design Inc. did not provide any lighting consultation on this project.]

influence the architect on establishing ceiling surface reflectance characteristics—as these can significantly affect the efficiency of the lighting system (higher reflectance finishes are more efficient) and the glare potential of the lighting system (more specular surfaces are prone to glaring reflections). Matte, white ceiling surfaces are best. If recessed lighting is used, then the type of recessed luminaire trim and mounting version will be influenced by the ceiling system.

Ceiling systems can be categorized as suspended, drywall, and structural. Each of these ceiling systems typically requires that the lighting equipment has specific trim/mounting configurations to fit into or onto the respective ceiling type. In more typical construction, drywall or gypsum panels are attached to structure to provide a ceiling plane. Where cost, future flexibility, acoustics, and/or accessibility are key criteria, ceilings are likely to be suspended. In these situations, a grid system of metal runners or inverted Tees (Ts) is suspended from the building structure. These Ts, depending on their exact cross–section, are either exposed or concealed. Exposed Ts include the common T grid and the slot grid. In any event, the grid work can then accept panels to create a finished look and to provide some acoustic capability. Ceiling panels or tiles may have a right–angle edge to simply fit or lay into the inverted T grid. Alternatively, ceiling tiles may have a **tegular edge** to allow the bottom face of the panel to float about ¼ to ½" below the grid line in the case of standard inverted Ts, or to allow the bottom face of the panel to flush out to the same elevation as the bottom of a slot–T (see Figures 4.17 and 4.18).

Drywall ceilings are also known as gypsumboard, Sheetrock®, wallboard, plasterboard, or plaster ceilings. In construction prior to the mid–20th century or even in some new construction where more ceiling character and mass

4.4.9 Programming

©C.M. Korab

Figure 4.15
Spatial definition and order: In this hotel reception lobby, architectural elements were delineated with light and important focal features highlighted to enhance definition and order. The inset shows a closeup view of the relief sculpture and the highlight necessary to achieve the primary visual focus. Note how all of the lighting effects combine to enhance the 2– and 3–dimensional aspects of the architecture.

©C.M. Korab

Figure 4.16
This is the view from the hotel entry into the reception lounge. From the front door, the highlighting of the fireplace sculpture and the brightness surrounding the custom chandelier offer the focal destination to the visitor. Once in this transition zone, the front desk is off to the right (see Figure 4.15).

Image ©digitalvision

are desired, plaster is common. Drywall has a more traditional appearance and is certainly more monolithic than lay–in ceilings (see Figures 4.19 and 4.20). As such, it is considered a higher–end treatment. Because of drywall's good sound–reflection characteristics, it is not considered appropriate in large, open office areas.

Structural ceilings are typically exposed wood, metal, or concrete decks of the floor or roof above. Many times, the depth between the bottom of the structural ceiling plane and the next floor surface or the roof surface is sufficiently shallow so lights cannot be recessed into these ceilings. Hence, lights are surface mounted or suspended from these ceilings.

more online @
http://www.armstrong.com/armstrong_home.jsp
http://www.celotex.com/products/commercial/ceilings/ceilings.htm
http://www.usg.com/Product_Index/1_0_product_index.asp?vFamily=2

Programming

Figure 4.17

Ceiling systems: This office installation is fitted with a suspended, exposed slot–T grid system arranged in a 2 by 2' pattern (600 by 600 mm). The acoustic ceiling tile consists of a fabric cloth facing painted high reflectance matte white and backed by fiberglass. The edges of the tiles are tegular to slip over the corner of the slot–T. Given its very narrow width (just over ½" [12 mm]), the slot–T creates a soft reveal rather than a harsh shadow line that can be created with wider T systems and tegular tile.

4.4.10 Codes

Codes, of course, are law. The registered professional (the architect or engineer) on every project must assure that all codes are met prior to a project's completion. If the lighting designer is not also acting in the capacity of one of these registered professionals, then the architect or engineer must address lighting–related code issues and direct the lighting designer as or if necessary. Ultimately, the registered professionals must check the work of the lighting designer and that of any non–registered consulting specialty. Some of the more typical and universal code requirements include egress lighting, luminaire thermal protection requirements, ADA–compliance, and power limits.

Egress lighting relates to providing a lighted path of egress during emergency conditions. Lighting requirements typically range from 1 to 3 fc (10 to 30 lx) minimum, maintained on the path of egress, as well as exit signs of appropriate size, luminance, and color located at paths and egress ways indicating the direction of exit and the actual exit point. In the past decade, many codes have evolved to require signage to be mounted low to the floor to account for smoke buildup and the ultimate obscuration of those exit signs mounted high on walls and/or above exits. Registered professionals should select egress lighting hardware and establish its quantities and locations on plans in accordance with current federal, state, and local codes.

Thermal protection of all luminaires is a necessity for those lights recessed into ceiling and wall construction with cavity voids where insulation may be present or close proximity to construction materials will occur. The thermal protector acts much like a small circuit breaker. The thermal protector "trips" or disengages if the luminaire overheats due to improper lamping or because

4.4.10 Programming

©2001, Steelcase Inc. Reprinted with permission.

Figure 4.18

Ceiling systems: This installation is fitted with a suspended, exposed T grid system arranged in a 2 by 2' pattern (600 by 600 mm). The acoustic ceiling tile consists of a fabric cloth facing painted high reflectance matte white and backed by fiberglass. The edges of the tiles are tegular to slip over the corner of the T. This creates a stronger shadow line compared to the slot–T version (see Figure 4.17). Also, note that the wider T element (see inset) reflects light differently than the ceiling tile—the T is metal painted in a semi–gloss white finish that is not as matte as the face of the ceiling tile itself. This is particularly noticeable with indirect lighting systems.

IC–rated

A reference to a luminaire rated for insulation contact. IC–rated luminaires are typically required in residential construction where lots of insulation is used in most all walls and ceilings. Non–IC–rated indicates that the ceiling or wall recessed luminaire is not rated for insulation contact— more common in commercial installations.

ADA

Americans with Disabilities Act, passed by the U.S. Congress and signed into law by the president in 1990, establishes guidelines for accessibility to public and commercial facilities by people with disabilities.

Image ©digitalvision

the luminaire is surrounded by inappropriately positioned insulation that does not allow for proper heat dissipation.

In nearly all residential construction, the luminaires are likely to come in contact with or to be surrounded by insulation, so most municipalities require that residential lighting be suitably thermally protected to withstand the effects of the insulation. However, such luminaires often exhibit some deficiencies. The lower–cost models are not nearly as durable or rugged as many commercial luminaires. Their height and width may preclude their use in certain construction types (e.g., the stud spacings and heights may prohibit use of all but the lowest wattage—and, therefore, smallest—**IC–rated** luminaires. The higher quality versions have a wide variety of finish, lamping, and aperture options. Further, the higher quality luminaires tend to exhibit better glare control and better aiming and locking mechanisms (important for adjustable accents aimed onto artwork or features).

In some instances, commercial grade luminaires are deemed appropriate for their lighting effects, yet are to be installed in insulation–filled walls or ceilings. Here, the local inspector and electrician must be consulted to determine if the construction of "thermal breaks" around the luminaires designed to keep insulation at least 3" (75 mm) from any component of the luminaire will meet with approval.

The Americans with Disabilities Act (**ADA**) of 1990 requires, among other things, that lighting equipment not impede the movement of people. Obvious, perhaps, but not well observed by designers prior to this act's signing. Wall sconces may not protrude more than 4" (100 mm) beyond the face of the wall or, alternatively, they need to be mounted so that the bottom of the wall sconce is at least 6'–8" (2 m) **AFF**. Where torchieres are used, elements may not protrude more than 1'–0" (0.3 m) from the torchiere post. As noted in the discussion on controls, the ADA also has requirements for the mounting of wall switches. An illuminance of 5 fc (50 lx) is required at elevator thresholds.

Programming

Figure 4.19
Ceiling systems: This installation is fitted with a drywall ceiling trimmed out in millwork elements on roughly 4 by 4' (1.2 by 1.2 m) spacings. In support of other spatial factors previously discussed, note that the wall/ceiling juncture is uniformly lighted to enhance the spatial definition (even when the room is darkened for AV presentations). Artwork is softly highlighted to further enhance spatial definition, yet remain a backdrop to room activities.

Power–limit codes (or energy budget codes or just simply energy codes) were initially established as a direct result of the oil embargoes of 1973 and 1979. These power limits were intended to simply reduce connected load (watts) and, thereby, reduce energy consumption. These codes have evolved to be more holistic in their approach and result. Although connected loads are still limited, controls requirements and daylighting requirements also need to be addressed. As such, these codes are now better targeting energy use and sustainability. For example, automatic controls are mandatory for many lighting applications. Table 4.5 cites a few space types and typical respective power limits as defined by ASHRAE/IESNA 90.1/1999. The ASHRAE/IESNA standard is considered the current "model code" on energy use, and most states are likely to adopt it in the near future. California's Title 24/Section 6 is similar and was itself the model for ASHRAE/IESNA 90.1/1999.

Regulations are in place by the US Environmental Protection Agency (EPA) on disposal of lamps containing mercury and other hazardous materials. This includes fluorescent, high pressure sodium, and metal halide lamps, as well as cold cathode and neon lamps and mercury vapor lamps. Users handling bulk quantities of these lamps are now required to recycle them or dispose of them in hazardous waste landfills. Lamp manufacturers are introducing low mercury lamps that are TCLP–compliant. That is, these lamps meet the EPAs toxicity characteristic leaching procedure and, therefore, are exempt from the regulations. Nevertheless, users of these TCLP–compliant lamps are still encouraged to either recycle them (preferably) or to dispose of them in hazardous waste landfills. Handling any of these lamps should be done with great care and only by professional maintenance personnel or licensed electricians. During the programming phase, then, it is important to determine what the client's position is or will be on lamp disposal and target lamp criteria that address that position.

`more online @`
```
http://www.lrc.rpi.edu/Futures/
http://www.solstice.crest.org/index.shtml
http://www.eren.doe.gov/buildings/codes_standards/buildings/
```

AFF

Above finished floor. The distance from the finished floor plane to the imaginary or real plane of interest. For example, work surfaces are typically 2'–6" (0.75 m) AFF. Typically used to reference interior dimensions. Not to be confused with **AFG** (see below).

AFG

Above finished grade. The distance from the finished grade plane to the imaginary or real plane of interest. For example, an exterior wall sconce might be mounted so that its bottom is 6'–8" (2 m) AFG. Typically used to reference exterior dimensions.

4.4.11 Programming

4.4.11 Ordinances

Ordinances are statutes or regulations typically enacted by local governments. As with codes, the registered professional (the architect or engineer) on every project must assure that all ordinances are met prior to a project's completion. If the lighting designer is also not acting in the capacity of one of these registered professionals, then it is imperative that the architect or engineer address lighting–related ordinance issues and direct the lighting designer as necessary. Ultimately, the registered professionals must check the work of the lighting designer and that of any nonregistered consulting specialty. Some of the more typical ordinance requirements are exterior lighting related and include light pollution and light trespass.

Light pollution (not to be confused with light trespass—see below) relates to light being dispersed in the air. Water vapor and air pollution offer sufficient light refraction and light reflection characteristics to adversely interact with exterior electric lighting at night. Common sense, if practiced, would be sufficient to limit light pollution. First, overlighting exterior areas does not effectively reduce crime or improve nighttime seeing. Hence, lighting intensities (illuminances) should be limited to criteria espoused by the Illuminating Engineering Society of North America or other recognized lighting authority. Further, the application of light should be carefully established and limited. For example, lighting a façade should depend on the materials with which the façade is made. Vision–glass walls (clear glass) will simply redirect any accenting or floodlighting up to the sky! These surfaces act like mirrors and should simply not be lighted. Even opaque–surface facades (e.g., brick, stone, and wood, etc.), need not be wholly flooded with light. Many times, this is ineffectual in highlighting any architectural character or features. High wattage floodlights with wide beam spreads are most likely to cause light pollution. Using white light at IESNA–proposed intensities is much more effective than using yellow light at higher intensities (more on this below).

Light trespass occurs where light is perceived to trespass, if not actually does trespass onto adjoining property and/or into nearby buildings, and is found to be annoying. To some extent, common sense application of light can help mitigate light trespass. However, there will generally be problems with exterior nightlighting since some folks will simply be offended that any lighting that they can detect is used after their bedtime. As such, this can be a highly charged issue, particularly in urban areas. Light trespass can be divided into two categories—light source glare and light spill. Light source glare occurs when lights are either designed in such a way that the light source is then directly visible from nearby property(ies), and/or are of high intensity causing bright surfaces and objects to reflect too brightly to neighboring properties. Light spill occurs when some measurable amount of light (illuminance) falls onto adjoining or nearby property(ies).

Making serious sacrifices of the nighttime users' vision and function in order to alleviate light pollution is not a reasonable method of addressing this problem. Monochromatic light sources, such as high pressure sodium and low pressure sodium, are preferred by astronomers, for example. However, these light sources create impressions of dim, dingy lighting and promote a sense of unsafe, insecure nighttime settings. Indeed, to counteract such dim appearances, shopping centers, service stations, toll road ticket plazas, and the like have resorted to increasing illuminances above recommended intensities in an attempt to offer users a brighter, cheerier, and

Programming

©C.M. Korab

©GarySteffyLightingDesign Inc.

Figure 4.20

Ceiling systems: This installation features an oculus between the first and second floors. Above the oculus on the ceiling of the second floor is a cove detail. To provide additional visual interest to the coved ceiling, the architect developed a plan of progressively smaller slabs or sheets of drywall. The edge of each sheet then catches the light from the cove. The inset shows a view through the oculus (the photographer was on the first floor) to the second floor coved ceiling detail.

safer–feeling environment. So, this overlighting exacerbates light pollution and uses more energy (thereby creating more industrial air pollution) than lighting solutions with white light sources meeting reasonable lighting intensities for nighttime viewing situations.

Aggressive salesmanship by retailers (aka one–up–manship) has, unfortunately, seriously and negatively affected light pollution and light trespass. As retailers look for methods of differentiating their locale, many have resorted to increasing exterior parking lot and building lighting to ridiculous levels. Parking lots are lighted to between 5 and 10 fc (50 and 100 lx), literally two to five times the intensities recommended for even the busiest of parking lots. Building façades are now flooded with 1000 watt floodlights, causing reflected glare and direct glare problems—not to mention all of the wasted light flooding into the night sky. Service station fueling islands, in a misguided attempt to address security issues, are lighted to more than 50 fc (500 lx). Car lots are lighted to more than 20 fc (200 lx) in an attempt to attract attention (and so they have). These practices are foolish, environmentally unfriendly, and plain garish. See Section 4.6 for more discussion about appropriate illuminances for various applications.

more online @

http://www.municode.com/
http://www.bpcnet.com/codes.htm

Image ©digitalvision

4.4.12 Programming

Table 4.5 Typical Power Budget Standards

Space Type	Power Budget[a]	Qualified Adder[b]
Classroom	1.6 w/ft² (17.2 w/m²)	plus 0.35 w/ft² (3.77 w/m²)
Conference room	1.5 w/ft² (16.1 w/m²)	plus 0.35 w/ft² (3.77 w/m²)
Corridor	0.7 w/ft² (7.5 w/m²)	
Lobby	1.8 w/ft² (19.4 w/m²)	plus 1.0 w/ft² (10.8 w/m²)
Open office	1.3 w/ft² (14.0 w/m²)	plus 0.35 w/ft² (3.77 w/m²)
Retail	2.1 w/ft² (22.6 w/m²)	plus 1.6 w/ft² (17.2 w/m²)

[a] Only "typical" values cited. See ASHRAE/IESNA 90.1/1999 for complete list of application spaces, space types, and complete instructions for compliance.
[b] Those spaces where VDTs are primary tasks may have an additional power budget as cited under "Classroom," "Conference room," and "Open office"; those spaces where special decorative lights (e.g., chandeliers and/or sconces) are required for special decorative appearance may have an additional power budget as cited under "Lobby"; and those retail areas where lighting that can be specifically directed (aimed) onto merchandise may have an additional power budget as cited under "Retail."

4.4.12 Sustainability

Sustainability is a relatively new term in the construction industry. Although power budgets or energy codes have a similar end, their interest is limited to the use of energy. Sustainability is a movement whereby the design, construction, and maintenance of any installation are to use as few, and preferably all–natural, nontoxic, resources as practical and/or to use recycled resources. The intent is to minimize the amount of energy and pollution expended in extracting resources from the earth and making products. Further, the intent is to minimize the damage of throwing away spent materials. For lighting, this is an emerging issue. For lighting applications, attempt to use highest efficacy, longest life, white–light–producing lamps. If any toxic materials need be used, they should be limited in application and should yield maximum benefits.

4.5 Psychological and physiological factors

The previous section defined lighting design goals relative to the architectural setting within which users live and work. Another set of lighting design goals revolves around the users' biological need for light and reaction to light. The way in which an environment is presented to its users is at least partly responsible for the way they perceive and react to it; thus, lighting can play a significant role in people's psychological and physiological responses to an environment. The distribution of luminances in a space can influence perceptions of the space's intended functions, level of comfort, and apparent spatial volume. Luminance levels and ratios are responsible for visual comfort. Exterior views appear to be related to satisfaction and motivation.

4.5.1 Sensory responses

While no definitive links are known to exist between light and other sensory responses, a few studies and/or some experience indicate light can influence other sensory responses. For example, very low and nonuniform brightnesses, particularly when coupled with some intermittent accent lighting on perimeter objects (e.g., wall art), seem to promote quieter settings. Alternatively, high uniform brightnesses seem to promote louder settings. The auditory senses are, it seems, affected by light intensities.

Programming

The thermal sense may be affected by the color of visual experience. A study in the mid–1970s indicated that people in warm–tone settings lighted with warm–tone light tended to feel 2 to 3°F warmer than the actual room ambient temperature.[3] Likewise, people in cool–tone settings lighted with cool–tone light tended to feel 2 to 3°F cooler than the actual room ambient temperature. Regardless of a designer's intent, then, light and color can have an impact on other senses. These affects should be considered during the design process to avoid disappointment upon project completion. For example, when a designer plans a retirement community, if interior finishes are cool–toned, it may not be advisable to enhance this palette with cool–toned light sources. This may exacerbate the elderly populations' sensitivity to cold.

4.5.2 Visual hierarchies and focal centers

Visual hierarchies are quite appropriate to signify varying degrees of importance among various areas, surfaces, and objects. Using light to help identify the visual hierarchy intended by the owner and/or other team members is crucial to the effectiveness of these hierarchies. Figures 4.15 and 4.16 illustrates one such application of visual hierarchy with light to help direct users' attention into and around a space.

Focal centers are specific objects or elements (e.g., artwork, floor medallions, and ceiling domes, etc.) that are a special feature of the environmental setting. Enhancing these focal centers with light is almost always a must, and this can contribute to several design goals already discussed: spatial order, visual hierarchy, and circulation. There are times, however, when a focal center is developed specifically for visual interest, visual identity, and/or eye muscle relaxation (which is particularly important in work–related settings). As a design goal, those focal centers that are important and necessary to add interest or identity to an area should be identified. It is worth noting, however, that the 3–dimensional aspects of space and light interaction must be carefully reviewed as well. Otherwise, light patterns may not properly enhance the focal centers and may inadvertently create distracting luminance patterns. This is a common issue. If artwork is planned for a wall, for example, and the exact location is not established during the lighting planning process, then it is likely that the lighting equipment won't be in the right place to best highlight the artwork upon project completion. This results in odd–angled luminance patterns as lights are aimed toward artwork. Figure 4.21 illustrates a focal center being used to help direct people through a large public space.

4.5.3 Visual attraction

Over the past thirty years, there have been a number of studies and assessments on people's reactions to various lighting situations. Much of this work shows that luminance patterns, intensities, contrasts, and locations (horizontal versus vertical planes) can influence how people perceive a given space and respond to it. Table 4.6 outlines the attraction power associated with luminance contrasts regardless of their location and size. These contrasts can be used to help attract attention and develop visual hierarchies in the built environment. Luminance contrasts can be used to guide people to objects or spaces and can lead people through spaces. This requires careful planning of both illuminance and surface/material finish. Luminance is a result—actually the product—of illuminance and surface reflectance or of illuminance and

4.5.3 Programming

additive color

This is a phenomenon of light—the mixing or adding of various colors (wavelengths) of light. Wavelengths work in an additive fashion, combining or adding together to form a different color of light. For this discussion, the primary colors of light are red, green, and blue. When at least two of these specific wavelengths are combined, in varying degrees (or intensities), they create other colors. If all three primary colors of light are added together, the result is white light.

subtractive color

This is a phenomenon of pigments (inks, paints, and dyes)—the mixing of various colors of pigments. Pigments react to light by absorbing (subtracting) some wavelengths and reflecting others. When pigments combine, they subtract more and more wavelengths from the white light striking them. For this discussion, the primary colors of subtractive color are cyan, magenta, and yellow. When at least two of these specific pigments are mixed, in varying degrees, they create other colors. If all three primary subtractive colors are mixed together, the result is technically a black pigment.

©C.M. Korab

Figure 4.21
Focal centers: To the immediate left of the transition space shown in Figure 4.16, a relatively long and large public corridor connects the reception lounge to the dining room, the conference center, and, ultimately, to the casino. To help direct people along this corridor, accented architectural features and art are used. This photo illustrates the first of these features—a highlighted, life-sized sculpture. Figure 4.20 is a long view back from beyond this highlighted sculpture and reinforces the significance of the focal center established by lighting the sculptural–relief at the front desk (shown in Figure 4.15).

surface transmittance. So, for example, the surface/material reflectance of the background versus the surface/material reflectance of the focal element is as critical to establishing luminance contrast as the illuminance on the background versus the illuminance on the focal element. Think of it this way: To make an object barely stand out against a wall when the illuminance on both the object and wall is the same, the wall will need to be painted half the reflectance value of the object (then the luminance contrast from the object to the wall would be 2 to 1). Alternatively, if the object and wall have the same reflectance value, then the object will need to be lighted to twice the illuminance of the wall in order to achieve a 2 to 1 luminance contrast from the object to the wall. So, the designer must decide where visual attraction requirements need to occur on a project and to what degree or attraction power. Then surface finishes and illuminances must be planned accordingly.

Chromatic contrast can also be used to advantage in establishing visual attraction and visual hierarchy. Surface color and/or colored light offer great, largely untapped resources for visual attraction. Table 4.7 outlines approximations of the effect of color on visual attraction.[5] However, the mixture of colored light onto colored surfaces can result in disaster if not carefully understood and planned. Alternatively, when carefully studied, some visually powerful effects result with colored light on colored surfaces. This is achieved through tests and mockups.

To understand these effects, the designer needs to appreciate the difference between **additive color** and **subtractive color**. Additive color occurs with visible energy or light. Colors of light add together to create more colors of light or, when all colors are combined, white light. Subtractive color occurs with pigments, dyes, inks—surface material coloration. Pigments, when lighted, actually subtract out (absorb) some colors of light and selectively reflect others. So, a pure red surface material will appear red (or at least reddest) only when lighted with a source (lamp) that has some red energy present in it. Hence, a blue light on a red surface will result in a gray or near–black surface appearance.

Image ©digitalvision

Programming

Herein lies a common problem. In many installations, the selector of the architectural/interior finishes does not fully appreciate the impact of the lighting on these surfaces. Finishes are selected under one light source (typically high–level incandescent or daylight), while the lighting design is ultimately based on fluorescent lamps with SPD properties different from the incandescent or daylight references used for surface finish selection. Colors end up drab and dingy or overly intense in appearance. For lighting design, **hue**, **value**, and **chroma** of surfaces and objects are either important lighting design parameters or should be selected based on the lighting design. Hue should depend on, or affect, the lamp SPD (i.e., the wavelength makeup of light will influence what surface color is perceived). Value should depend on, or affect, lighting system efficiency (i.e., higher values more efficiently reflect light than lower values). Chroma should depend on, or affect, the light intensities on various surfaces (i.e., duller color may require more light than saturated color to be appropriately visible as something other than a gray tone).

> `more online @`
> http://www.adobe.com/support/techguides/color/colormodels/munsell.html

hue

Based on the Munsell Color System, hue refers to the color family (e.g., red) and is reported by color abbreviation of which there are ten (R=red; YR=yellow–red; Y=yellow; GY=green–yellow; G=green; BG=blue–green; B=blue; PB=purple–blue; P=purple; and RP=red–purple).

value

Based on the Munsell Color System, value refers to color lightness and is reported on a scale of 0 (black) to 10 (white). The Munsell value is roughly the square root of the color's reflectance.

chroma

Based on the Munsell Color System, chroma refers to color saturation (e.g., intense red or dull red).

4.5.4 Subjective impressions

Over the past thirty years, research has resulted in some understanding of the relationships between luminances and luminance patterns and people's preferences, sense of visual clarity, and sense of spatial volume.[6,7,8,9] Figures 4.22, 4.23, 4.24, 4.25, 4.26, and 4.27 exemplify the kinds of light settings that people evaluated (this particular study was done in the early 1970s) and that ultimately led to the definition of five specific impressions influenced by various luminance aspects.

Table 4.6 Luminance Contrasts for Attraction[4]

Attraction Power	Effect	Potential Applications	Luminance Contrast[a]
Negligible	barely recognizable focal	• museum displays • office artwork • retail sales racks	2 to 1
Marginal	minimum meaningful focal	• fine dining artwork • office lobby artwork • residential artwork • retail select feature displays	10 to 1
Dominant	strong significant focal	• retail high–end display	approaching 100 to 1

[a] Focus–to–background luminance ratio

Ultimately, five impressions were identified that appeared related to luminances. These five impressions are visual clarity, spaciousness, preference, relaxation, and privacy. Thus, the designer now has some guidance on luminance aspects necessary to elicit several subjective impressions. Where people are expected to live and/or work for extended periods, then, subjective impressions should be identified that will enhance life and/or work within the given architectural envelope. The luminance influences derived from these studies can be categorized by uniformity, location, and intensity. Luminance uniformity is an indication of how smoothly or uniformly luminance is distributed over surfaces or objects throughout the room. Location is an indication of the primary plane(s) of luminance application—horizontal (work surfaces and/or floor surface) or vertical (peripheral wall surfaces).

4.5.4 Programming

horizontal activity plane

An attempt to generally identify the work plane or floor plane. In work settings, the work plane, desktop, or tabletop qualifies as the horizontal activity plane. In transition and circulation spaces, the floor qualifies as the work plane. In classroom settings, desktops qualify as the work plane. In churches or auditoriums, laps qualify as the horizontal activity plane. Referring to any one of these as simply a work plane would imply that the situation is indeed one of concentrated, long-term work, which is not always the case. Hence, the more generic reference to horizontal activity plane.

Table 4.7 Chromatic Contrasts (of transmitted light) for Attraction[5]

Color[a]	Relative Luminance[b]	Relative Brightness[c]
Warm white	1.0	1.0
Gold	0.6	0.7
Red	0.1	0.2
Green	1.4	2.0
Blue	0.4	0.6

[a] Color of transmitted light. Modeled with fluorescent lamps exhibiting named color of light commonly available in the 1970s (the time of the study cited).[3]
[b] Photometric luminance (as measured in laboratory setting).
[c] Brightness as judged by most observers. Recognize that blue appears to be about 60% of the brightness of white, whereas blue light measures about 40% of the luminance of white. In other words, the color of light has a significant influence on people's perceptions of the brightness of the light.

Intensity is an indication of the degree of luminance at the **horizontal activity plane** (work plane or floor plane)—relatively low or dim versus relatively strong or bright.

Ignoring the subjective impressions does not mean subjective reactions won't be present or prominent in the finished project. Indeed, many projects where little emphasis is placed on anything other than illuminance criteria result in spaces that are likely to elicit negative reactions. Because these are subjective impressions, there may not be any overt or recognized reaction by users. Negative impressions of the visual environment may simply result in users wishing to spend less time in the setting, but not knowing why or even realizing a causal relationship exists. Or perhaps negative impressions result in poorer attitudes. In any event, such negative impressions are a further waste of energy and resources—minimizing the value of the installed hardware and the energy used. The point is this: subjective impressions are a fact of human use. Lighting should be developed that attempts to promote or evoke more positive attributes.

The following subjective impressions are key criteria in developing lighting solutions for many types of spaces. In fact, the impressions deemed appropriate to a given project should establish the basis for the lighting solution on that project. The specific luminance uniformity, location, and intensity offer explicit guidance on how light should be applied in the space and, therefore, what kind of lighting solutions should be considered.

▶ *Visual clarity*: Visual clarity refers to the users' perceived abilities to distinguish architectural and interior detail, features, objects, and other people's features. Scalar descriptors are clear versus hazy. The crisper and more distinct are architectural and other people's features, the greater the clarity perception rating. Flat, shadow–free lighting yielding low–to–moderate luminances (particularly of the horizontal activity plane) tends to elicit a perception of haziness. Figures 4.28 and 4.29 illustrate the concept of visual clarity in the exterior environment. Figures 4.30 and 4.31 use two of the comparative images from the lighting study previously discussed to illustrate the difference between the hazy and clear scalars. Visual clarity is believed to be an important subjective impression for work settings. It is best enhanced with higher luminance of the horizontal activity plane in the central area of a workspace. Some peripheral luminance is helpful in eliciting visual clarity. Luminance uniformity does not seem to be a particularly strong determinant.

Image ©digitalVision

Programming

Several lessons here. First, relatively low levels of general lighting and/or relatively dark surfaces will, if used alone, result in impressions of haziness. Regardless of the use of direct, indirect, or indirect/direct lighting systems for general lighting then, emphasis is necessary at the work surface and, to a lesser extent, in the periphery. Three lighting layers need attention—the ambient layer, task layer, and accent/architectural layer. Further, attention must be given to the impact of surface finishes—with a need to consider higher reflectance work surfaces and wall surfaces required to enhance the subjective impression of visual clarity while minimizing energy consumed.

▶ *Spaciousness*: Spaciousness refers to the users' perception of spatial volume. A lack of peripheral luminance apparently elicits a sense of confinement from many people. Scalar descriptors are spacious versus cramped. Higher (greater) peripheral luminance applied rather uniformly (to all or most of the peripheral surfaces) enhances the sense of spaciousness. Figures 4.32 and 4.33 use two of the comparative images from the lighting study previously discussed to illustrate the difference between the cramped and spacious scalars. Spaciousness is believed to be an important subjective impression for high occupancy areas, such as circulation spaces, transition spaces, assembly halls, and the like. It is best enhanced with higher or greater luminance of the periphery (walls). Luminance uniformity does seem to be a particularly strong determinant—the more uniform the wall luminances, the stronger the impression of spaciousness.

Several lessons here. First, downlighting alone typically evokes a sense of cramped space or confinement. Second, dark wall finishes exacerbate this impression of confinement. Third, the application of peripheral lighting can also serve to assist with architectural definition.

▶ *Preference*: Preference refers to the users' general evaluation of lighted space—their preference (or lack thereof) of a space. Typically, the more uniform the luminances in the central portion of a space, and simultaneously the lower the luminances of the periphery, the less preference for the space. Scalar descriptors are like versus dislike. Relatively nonuniform luminances throughout a space, along with peripheral luminances, enhance preference. Figures 4.34 and 4.35 use two of the comparative images from the lighting study previously discussed to illustrate the difference between the like and dislike scalars. Preference is believed to be an important subjective impression for any space where users are expected to live and/or work for extended time periods. Preference is best enhanced with higher or greater luminance of the periphery (walls). Luminance nonuniformity does seem to be a particularly strong determinant—the less uniform the luminances throughout the space, the stronger the preference.

Several lessons here. First, downlighting alone typically evokes a sense of dislike. Second, dark wall finishes mixed with lighter wall finishes can assist in eliciting preference. Third, the application of peripheral lighting, particularly in conjunction with varied wall finishes, can also serve to address preference.

▶ *Relaxation*: Relaxation refers to the users' perceived degree of work intensity. Nonuniform peripheral luminances elicit a sense of relaxation. Uniform, central luminances elicit a sense of tenseness. Scalar descriptors are relaxed versus tense. Figures 4.36 and 4.37 use two of the comparative

4.5.4 Programming

Condition 1 Ratings Summary
- Neutral evaluative ratings
- Generally promoting a hazy, quiet impression
- Strongly promoting impression of confinement

Condition 2 Ratings Summary
- Somewhat neutral evaluative ratings tending toward more pleasant impression
- Neutral clarity ratings
- Promoting impression of spaciousness

Condition 3 Ratings Summary
- Relatively strong negative evaluative ratings
- Strongly promoting a hazy, quiet impression
- Neutral spaciousness ratings

Figure 4.22
Condition 1: Overhead/direct low illuminance (10 fc [100 lx] on table) setting (incandescent downlights).

Figure 4.23
Condition 2: Peripheral/indirect low illuminance (10 fc [100 lx] on table) setting (fluorescent lighting on long walls and incandescent lighting on short walls).

Figure 4.24
Condition 3: Overhead/indirect low intensity (10 fc [100 lx] on table) setting (indirect fluorescent lighting).

evaluative ratings

These are people's ratings of general evaluation or feelings about the setting. Scalars are:
▶ friendly vs. hostile
▶ pleasant vs. unpleasant
▶ like vs. dislike
▶ harmony vs. discord
▶ satisfying vs. frustrating
▶ beautiful vs. ugly
▶ sociable vs. unsociable
▶ relaxed vs. tense
▶ interesting vs. monotonous

perceptual clarity ratings

These are people's ratings of the degree of distinctiveness of objects, architecture, detail, and other people in the setting. Scalars are:
▶ clear vs. hazy
▶ bright vs. dim
▶ faces clear vs. faces obscure
▶ distinct vs. vague
▶ focused vs. unfocused
▶ radiant vs. dull
▶ noisy vs. quiet

spaciousness ratings

These are people's ratings of the degree of spaciousness experienced in the setting. Scalars are:
▶ large vs. small
▶ long vs. short
▶ spacious vs. cramped

Programming

Condition 4 Ratings Summary
- Relatively strong positive evaluative ratings
- Neutral clarity ratings
- Relatively neutral spaciousness ratings with some strength in rating of impression of room length

Condition 5 Ratings Summary
- Relatively strong negative evaluative ratings
- Strongly promoting clarity ratings
- Somewhat promoting spaciousness ratings

Condition 6 Ratings Summary
- Strong positive evaluative ratings
- Strongly promoting clarity ratings
- Strongly promoting spaciousness ratings

Figure 4.25
Condition 4: Overhead/direct and selected peripheral/indirect low intensity (10 fc [100 lx] on table) setting (incandescent downlighting [like Condition 1 in Figure 4.22] and incandescent lighting on short walls).

Figure 4.26
Condition 5: Overhead/indirect high intensity (100 fc [1000 lx] on table) setting (indirect fluorescent lighting [like Condition 3 in Figure 4.24] but greatly increased illuminance).

Figure 4.27
Condition 6: Overhead/direct, overhead/indirect, and peripheral/indirect moderate intensity (30 fc [300 lx] on table) setting (combination of Conditions 1, 2, and 3).

images from the lighting study previously discussed to illustrate the difference between the tense and relaxed scalars. Relaxation is believed to be an important subjective impression for more casual spaces, such as waiting rooms, lounges, many dining establishments, and conference spaces. Recognize that this attribute is considered important then for hospitality–type spaces and, therefore, is an acceptable technique in commercial facilities where these kinds of spaces exist. Relaxation is best enhanced with nonuniform luminance of the periphery (walls). Luminance intensity does not seem to be a particularly strong determinant.

Several lessons here. First, downlighting alone typically elicits a sense of tenseness not of relaxation. This should signal that uniform, direct lighting for any setting, including workspaces, is typically undesirable if it is the only lighting technique used. Second, the intermittent need for peripheral luminance means that art accenting and/or wall sconces alone are reinforcing lighting techniques where a sense of relaxation is desired.

4.5.4 Programming

©GarySteffyLightingDesign Inc.

©GarySteffyLightingDesign Inc.

Figures 4.28 (left) and 4.29 (right)

Visual clarity: The impression of visual clarity (or lack thereof) can be experienced in the exterior environment as well as the interior environment. The overcast condition on the left results in flat, featureless detail in the environment—a visually hazy situation. Contrasts (from lighter elements to darker elements) are muted compared to those exhibited in the sunny condition on the right (see the white building in the middle–right of each image; see the white window frames in the lower–right house of each image). The sunny condition offers better edge definitions, higher contrasts, and, therefore, better clarity—a visually clear situation. A similar comparative situation is shown in Figures 4.30 and 4.31 at right.

▶ *Intimacy*: Intimacy refers to the users' perception of private or intimate space. Relatively uniform and high (great) luminances in the zone of the user elicit a sense of public space. Scalar descriptors are private versus public. Higher (greater) peripheral luminance applied nonuniformly (intermittently around the periphery) enhances the sense of intimacy or privacy. Intimacy is believed to be an important subjective impression for more intimate casual spaces, such as some lounges, clubs, restaurants, and residential living spaces. It is best enhanced with relatively higher or greater luminance of the periphery (walls), but in a nonuniform manner, and is further enhanced with relatively low luminance in the zone of the users. Luminance nonuniformity does seem to be a particularly strong determinant—the more nonuniform the wall luminances, the stronger the impression of intimacy.

Several lessons here. First, downlighting alone typically elicits a sense of more public space—the users are highlighted. Second, wall finishes are ultimately not as significant here as with the other four subjective impressions. Indeed, darker wall finishes intermittently lighted enhance the sense of intimacy. Third, low luminance in the zone of the user is critical to the sense of intimacy. Overly bright casual settings will be perceived as public and less inviting to those seeking an intimate setting.

Color rendering and color temperature also appear to be factors influencing subjective impressions. Color rendering is an indication of how well colors are rendered under a given light source and depends on the lamps' spectral power distributions. A system of measuring color rendering exists. Lamps are rated on a color rendering index (CRI) scale up to 100. There is no bottom end to the scale. Indeed, some lamps have negative color rendering indices—an indication that these lamps actually skew color perception quite significantly and quite negatively. For most applications, high color rendering lamps are suggested. A high CRI (greater than 80) results in crisper color appearance to materials and objects and provides better skintone appearance than a low CRI. This is especially important in low light environments. Here the color contrast boost offered by high color rendering lamps can help, to some extent, make up for the loss in luminance contrast of the lower illuminances.

Image ©digitalvision

Programming

How subjects rated visual clarity in each condition

Condition 3 Ratings Summary
- Relatively strong negative evaluative ratings
- **Strongly promoting a hazy, quiet impression**
- Neutral spaciousness ratings

Condition 6 Ratings Summary
- Strong positive evaluative ratings
- **Strongly promoting clarity ratings**
- Strongly promoting spaciousness ratings

visual clarity applications
▶ Work settings

visual clarity luminances
▶ Luminance uniformity: not a key factor
▶ Luminance intensity: higher rather than lower
▶ Luminance location: at central, horizontal activity plane and some peripheral (wall) surfaces

visual clarity design directions
▶ Higher (greater) luminance of horizontal activity plane, and higher (greater) luminance in central area
  - select light finishes for activity planes (e.g., light-colored desktop—30 to 40% reflectance)
  - illuminate work surface(s) to greater intensity than adjacent areas (e.g., use task-oriented direct lighting that could include task lights or some ceiling-integrated direct lighting)
▶ Some peripheral luminance
  - select light finishes for wall surfaces (e.g., 30 to 50% reflectance)
  - illuminate walls (e.g., wallwashing, accenting on artwork, or sconces)

©GarySteffyLightingDesign Inc.—a gift of the John E. Flynn Estate

Figure 4.30
Condition 3: Overhead/indirect low intensity (10 fc [100 lx] on table) setting (indirect fluorescent lighting). [See Figures 4.22 through 4.27 for complete set of lighting conditions. The above figure is originally Figure 4.24.]

©GarySteffyLightingDesign Inc.—a gift of the John E. Flynn Estate

Figure 4.31
Condition 6: Overhead/direct, overhead/indirect, and peripheral/indirect moderate intensity (30 fc [300 lx] on table) setting (combination of Conditions 1, 2, and 3). [See Figures 4.22 through 4.27 for complete set of lighting conditions. The above figure is originally Figure 4.27.]

Poor color rendering lamps (e.g., CRI less than 65) should be limited to zones where few people are anticipated to occupy the area and/or occupancy is limited to very short time periods, and tasks are not color sensitive.

Color temperature is an indication of the whiteness of the light produced by a lamp. There is some indication that warmer-toned lamps (also known as lower color temperature lamps—color temperature less than 3500°K) have several influences. First, for equal illuminance, the lighted space may appear somewhat dimmer to many users. Second, and probably because this color temperature range approximates that of incandescent light, many users consider this color of whiteness to yield a more homelike and comfortable setting.

4.5.5 Daylighting

Programming of daylighting involves several distinct strategies—view, health, illuminance, and sustainability. It is reasonable to develop a daylighting approach on any project based on any one of these strategies, several of

Image ©digitalvision

4.5.6 Programming

▶ Circulation spaces
▶ Assembly spaces

spaciousness luminances

▶ Luminance uniformity: uniform
▶ Luminance intensity: somewhat greater
▶ Luminance location: peripheral (wall) surfaces

spaciousness design directions

▶ Uniform wall luminances
  • uniformly light walls (e.g., wallwashers, wallslots, or consistent accent lighting)
▶ Somewhat higher (greater) luminance of walls
  • select light finishes for walls (e.g., 30 to 50% reflectance)
  • illuminate wall(s) to greater intensity than horizontal activity plane
▶ Peripheral luminance
  • select light finishes for wall surfaces (e.g., 30 to 50% reflectance)
  • illuminate walls

How subjects rated spaciousness in each condition

Condition 1 Ratings Summary
• Neutral evaluative ratings
• Generally promoting a hazy, quiet impression
• **Strongly promoting impression of confinement**

Condition 2 Ratings Summary
• Somewhat neutral evaluative ratings tending toward more pleasant impression
• Neutral clarity ratings
• **Promoting impression of spaciousness**

©GarySteffyLightingDesign Inc.—a gift of the John E. Flynn Estate

©GarySteffyLightingDesign Inc.—a gift of the John E. Flynn Estate

Figure 4.32
Condition 1: Overhead/direct low illuminance (10 fc [100 lx] on table) setting (incandescent downlights). [See Figures 4.22 through 4.27 for complete set of lighting conditions. The above figure is originally Figure 4.22.]

Figure 4.33
Condition 2: Peripheral/indirect low illuminance (10 fc [100 lx] on table) setting (fluorescent lighting on long walls and incandescent lighting on short walls). [See Figures 4.22 through 4.27 for complete set of lighting conditions. The above figure is originally Figure 4.23.]

these strategies, or all of these strategies. However, daylighting can succeed only with complete team effort. Further, development of daylighting inevitably demands that the design team address daylighting luminances. Since daylight is such a strong source, some form of glare or veiling reflections will result unless the team has meticulously addressed daylighting. For example, if the architect and lighting designer develop daylighting, but the interior designer is not part of the design process, then potential errors in interiors planning will include use of low (dark) reflectance surfaces, specular (shiny or polished) surfaces, misorientation of workstations and computer screens, and/or selection of improper shading treatments, to name a few. This is discussed further in Chapter 6.

4.5.6 Nightlighting

As reported in Section 2.3 (Color Vision), our ability to detect detail and color depends both on our eyes and on the lighting situation. In the recent past,

Image ©digitalvision

Programming

How subjects rated preference in each condition

Condition 5 Ratings Summary
- **Relatively strong negative evaluative ratings**
- Strongly promoting clarity ratings
- Somewhat promoting spaciousness ratings

Condition 6 Ratings Summary
- **Strong positive evaluative ratings**
- Strongly promoting clarity ratings
- Strongly promoting spaciousness ratings

preference applications
▶ Most occupied spaces

preference luminances
▶ Luminance uniformity: nonuniform
▶ Luminance intensity: not a key factor
▶ Luminance location: some emphasis of peripheral (wall) surfaces

preference design directions
▶ Nonuniform luminances
  • light walls selectively and/or somewhat dramatically (e.g., wallslots and accent lighting)
  • light ceiling areas selectively and/or somewhat dramatically
▶ Peripheral luminance
  • mix some dark finishes (e.g., 10 to 20%) with some light finishes for wall surfaces (e.g., 30 to 50% reflectance)
  • illuminate walls somewhat dramatically

Figure 4.34
Condition 5: Overhead/indirect high intensity (100 fc [1000 lx] on table) setting (indirect fluorescent lighting [like Condition 3 in Figure 4.24] but greatly increased illuminance). [See Figures 4.22 through 4.27 for complete set of lighting conditions. The above figure is originally Figure 4.26.]

Figure 4.35
Condition 6: Overhead/direct, overhead/indirect, and peripheral/indirect moderate intensity (30 fc [300 lx] on table) setting (combination of Conditions 1, 2, and 3). [See Figures 4.22 through 4.27 for complete set of lighting conditions. The above figure is originally Figure 4.27.]

lamps were tested and evaluated based on laboratory reference standards that presumed the users' eyes would be photopically adapted—operating under relatively high light intensity situations (greater than 2 fc [20 lx]). Recent research shows that the spectral power distribution of the light source significantly influences most people's visual acuity under scotopic and mesopic vision—low light intensities (less than 2 fc [20 lx]). Where scotopic vision is anticipated (e.g., intensities less than 0.2 fc [2 lx]), bluer, whiter light sources may offer more than a twofold improvement in visual acuity. As light intensities increase to the threshold for photopic vision, this improvement diminishes. So, for night situations, particularly exterior environments where light intensities are quite low and where people are interacting socially or where security is of concern, the use of monochromatic light sources, such as high pressure sodium or low pressure sodium, are discouraged.

4.5.7 Programming

relaxation applications

▶ Waiting rooms
▶ Lounges
▶ Sit-down restaurants
▶ Conference rooms
▶ Casual areas

relaxation luminances

▶ Luminance uniformity: nonuniform
▶ Luminance intensity: not a key factor
▶ Luminance location: peripheral (wall) surfaces

relaxation design directions

▶ Nonuniform luminances
  • accent selective walls (e.g., wallwashers, wallslots, and consistent accent lighting)
  • accent artwork
  • accent selective activity planes
▶ Peripheral luminance
  • use light finishes for selective wall surfaces (e.g., 30 to 50% reflectance)
  • illuminate walls selectively
  • accent artwork
  • use sconces

How subjects rated relaxation in each condition

Condition 3 Ratings Summary
• Relatively strong negative evaluative ratings (considered tense)
• Strongly promoting a hazy, quiet impression
• Neutral spaciousness ratings

Condition 4 Ratings Summary
• Relatively strong positive evaluative ratings (considered relaxed)
• Neutral clarity ratings
• Relatively neutral spaciousness ratings with some strength in rating of impression of room length

Figure 4.36
Condition 3: Overhead/indirect low intensity (10 fc [100 lx] on table) setting (indirect fluorescent lighting). [See Figures 4.22 through 4.27 for complete set of lighting conditions. The above figure is originally Figure 4.24.]

Figure 4.37
Condition 4: Overhead/direct and selected peripheral/indirect low intensity (10 fc [100 lx] on table) setting (incandescent downlighting [like Condition 1 in Figure 4.22] and incandescent lighting on short walls). [See Figures 4.22 through 4.27 for complete set of lighting conditions. The above figure is originally Figure 4.25.]

4.5.7 Health

Over the past 40 years, there has been much ado about light and health. As noted in Section 4.5.4, and previously in Chapter 2, light does, indeed, affect health profoundly. However, many so-called studies have been espousing the spectral power distribution (the wavelength makeup) of light as significantly altering physiological behavior. Perhaps the most common myth is the "fact" that so-called full-spectrum light significantly improves academic achievement, mood, health in general, and work productivity. It is reasonable to conclude that there is no panacea—indeed, so-called full-spectrum electric light has no substantive impact (positive or negative) on people.[10] While there is certainly evidence of health effects of specific intensities of light (e.g., relatively high illuminance intensities to set circadian rhythm), little evidence of health effects related to spectral quality of light exists, except that

Programming

ultraviolet (UV) radiation helps the skin produce vitamin D. However, it is also clear that too much UV exposure will result in sunburn and, ultimately, in melanoma. So, introducing electric light (or even daylight) in living and working environments with significant amounts of UV radiation is inappropriate. Hence, programming the other physiological and psychological factors cited in Section 4.5 will, when combined with the spatial factors (Section 4.4) and task factors (Section 4.6), result in comfortable, healthy, and productive lighting for living and/or working environments. In the absence of any new research or of corroboration of previous research by independent researchers and reviewers, there is no need to heed the hype surrounding "full–spectrum" lighting.

As noted, light affects the circadian rhythm. As such, light can be used to benefit when/if the circadian rhythm is upset. For example, shift workers may experience upset circadian rhythms. Here, high doses of light at the beginning of the shift can help with resetting circadian rhythms.[11] This might be done at the shift workers' homes with light treatment from localized light boxes or at work in light rooms. Similarly, folks experiencing SAD can be treated with localized light boxes or light rooms. The programming phase should establish if such treatment is necessary, and, if so, if it should be treated with localized light boxes (a specified, purchased item) or by light rooms (an architectural lighting design and specification item).

4.6 Task factors

It is no secret: programming and designing toward many of the lighting design goals outlined as Spatial Factors (Section 4.4) and Psychological and Physiological Factors (Section 4.5) involve architectural and interior design and, thus, are fun to think about and resolve for most designers—and more time–consuming compared to Task Factors. Task factors, while perhaps not as much fun, are considered easy (although this perception is based on a false assumption that lighting calculations are straightforward or, when done by computer, are infallible). This, no doubt, explains why most lighting design today revolves exclusively around task factors. Define a few tasks, establish (look up in a reference) some illuminance criteria, perhaps address some luminance criteria (and in the process look at surface reflectances), and voilà, this results in easily quantifiable criteria that can be solved with a regular array of lights in or on a ceiling. Next project, please! This is unfortunate. Designing just for task factors usually results in visually uninteresting, less people–oriented solutions (look at Figure 4.14 versus Figure 4.15). The challenge is to convince the owner, users, or both that the project will be in place for 10, 20, 30, or more years—is an easy, convenient, and lower–cost resolution best in the long run for business or for living? Hence, task factors as discussed here are intended to be only one part of the programming of a project—to be included along with spatial factors and psychological and physiological factors.

Programming appropriately for task factors involves a review of visual tasks, luminances (and, therefore, surface reflectances and transmittances), and illuminances. Making a full analysis of the kinds of visual tasks that are likely to occur is the best means of preparing the designer to solve unique lighting challenges. A complete review of tasks is likely to lead to a comprehensive lighting solution that will meet users' requirements for most all tasks most or all of the time.

4.6.1 Programming

vertical illuminance

Light falling onto a vertical plane (e.g., walls or partitions) or, where facial recognition, or teleconferencing, or viewing computer or television monitors are an issue, light falling onto an imaginary vertical plane.

ambient lighting

Referring to the general background lighting in a space. Typically considered as one of three layers of light—task lighting, ambient lighting, and architectural feature or accent lighting. Because ambient lighting is the background lighting, it will likely affect all people in a space.

VDT

Video display terminal, computer screen, or computer monitor.

4.6.1 Visual tasks

Solutions for lighting the visual tasks can only be as good as the programming. Sections 4.1.4 and 4.2.4 outline such programming of visual tasks. This programming needs to be all–inclusive. Tasks, such as facial recognition, tend to be overlooked or ignored, but such tasks require sufficient **vertical illuminance**. This is particularly important for corridor and sidewalk lighting.

Establishing the amount of time that users spend on given visual tasks may help the designer determine the **ambient lighting** requirements for a space. For example, if **VDT** tasks are performed for less than an hour a day, and if handwritten paper tasks are performed most of the day, then it may not be reasonable to design an ambient lighting system for the VDT task operation. Generally, the tasks people perform most of the time are the tasks that the lighting should accommodate. An exception is when a critically important task is performed for only a short period of time. Then it is reasonable to design the lighting to accommodate the very important task(s).

As noted previously in Sections 4.1.5 and 4.2.5, users' ages have an impact on lighting requirements. Typically, older eyes require more light than younger eyes to see a task equally as well. Further, older eyes tend to require some sort of lens correction—resulting in eyewear. The frames and lenses can exacerbate glary lighting situations and shadows that are predominate with downlighting solutions.

4.6.2 Luminances

Luminances and the resulting contrasts or differences between them, as well as chromatic contrasts, are the external or environmental effects responsible for our sight. Luminances play a significant role in how we see, react, and accomplish tasks. For purposes of general comfort, absolute luminances of any surface, window or daylight element, or luminaire should be limited. To what degree, however, remains a tough question. Our response to luminance depends on several key factors, including the background luminance (the overall luminance to which the eyes are adapted), the luminance of the area or source in question, the size of the area or source in question, the color of the area or source in question, and the condition of the eyes doing the observing. A classic example of the dilemma that luminances pose is to ponder if car headlights are glary. During the night, when the background luminance is very low, and if the headlights are near the line of sight, then most folks will judge them to be glary. However, if the headlights are well out of the line of sight, they pose less of a **disability glare** problem and, perhaps, pose only a **discomfort glare** problem. Further, during daytime conditions, the headlights are not judged as glary (the background is quite bright) even when directly in the line of sight. Less extreme situations are downlights in an office setting. When are they glary? Perhaps a more important issue is when do surface luminances (particularly wall luminances, window luminances, and luminaire luminances) become significant enough to create **reflected glare** or **veiling reflection** problems for users of VDT screens.

If and how people judge glare depends on the luminance of the source or area of concern, the size of the source or area of concern, the luminance of the surrounding visual field, the position of the source or area of concern in the visual field, the number of sources or areas of concern in the visual field, and the configuration (layout) of the sources or areas of concern.[12] The luminance of the source is a function of the source itself—is this a lamp or a

Programming

Table 4.8 Luminance Limits to Consider for Visual Comfort

Source[a]	Application[b]	Suggested Luminance Limit[c]
Luminaire[d]	• Classroom	250 fL (850 cd/m²)
	• High–tech industrial	250 fL (850 cd/m²)
	• Industrial	750 fL (2250 cd/m²)
	• Medical lab	250 fL (850 cd/m²)
	• Office	250 fL (850 cd/m²)
	• Transitional[e]	500 fL (1700 cd/m²)
Surfaces[f]	• Classroom	250 fL (850 cd/m²)
	• High–tech industrial	250 fL (850 cd/m²)
	• Industrial	250 fL (850 cd/m²)
	• Medical lab	250 fL (850 cd/m²)
	• Office	250 fL (850 cd/m²)
	• Transitional[e]	500 fL (1700 cd/m²)
Daylight media[g]	• Classroom	250 fL (850 cd/m²)
	• High–tech industrial	250 fL (850 cd/m²)
	• Industrial	750 fL (2250 cd/m²)
	• Medical lab	250 fL (850 cd/m²)
	• Office	250 fL (850 cd/m²)
	• Transitional[e]	1000 fL (3400 cd/m²)

[a] The source of luminance.
[b] Luminance is somewhat application specific. In recent years, however, tasks performed in many such applications include reading of electronic media and/or reviewing fine 2– and 3–dimensional detail. Hence, luminance limits are similar for various applications.
[c] These values are based on data from a variety of reference sources, some of which are consensus based.[16, 17, 18] Some data (noted by an asterisk [*]), lacking any reference sources, are solely the author's judgment.
[d] Luminaire luminances are more annoying and, therefore, more serious as the luminaire is viewed directly—luminaire is near line of sight. Hence, 55°, 65°, and 75° (angles above vertical—vertical is considered 0° and called nadir) are considered most important. Values cited are an average luminance at 55°. Luminaire candlepower data have been found more indicative of the glare potential of a given luminaire. Look for the IESNA to offer glare limits based on candlepower data in the near future.
[e] Spaces where task performance is limited to either casual or intermittent work and where room surfaces are light in color and/or washed with light to maintain balanced luminances.
[f] Opaque wall and ceiling surfaces reflecting light and presumed to have a matte finish (so that reflections are diffuse). Values cited are maximums.
[g] Light transmitting wall and ceiling surfaces. Values cited are maximums.

luminaire, is it an area of wall or ceiling, or is it a window during daylight hours. Typically, people will tolerate high source luminance if the source is relatively quite small. Alternatively, people are likely to accept a window of high luminance more readily than a luminaire of high luminance—since the window offers significant perceived benefit over "an ordinary light fixture." Sources in the periphery can typically exhibit greater luminances without being considered offensively glary than sources near the line of sight.

Given all of the variables influencing glare, luminance limits or guidelines for luminaires and room surfaces are elusive. Further, glare is dependent on the condition of the viewer's eyes and on the viewer's experiences and cultural background. In other words, seldom will the condition arise where no people find a given situation glary. However, based on consensus opinion over the past half century, based on some research, and based on experience,

disability glare

Glare sensation experienced as a result of viewing a light source or reflection of such great luminance as to be visually disabling—the observer cannot see or can see in only such a limited capacity that his/her vision is essentially disabled.

discomfort glare

Glare sensation experienced as a result of viewing a light source or reflection of sufficient luminance to cause discomfort, but the observer is still capable of seeing.

reflected glare

Considered a misnomer, but used by many people to identify light reflections that interfere with vision. See veiling reflection below.

veiling reflection

Reflection(s) of light(s) from task surfaces (e.g., computer monitors, TV screens, glossy paper, glass–enclosed artwork, and wet roadways, etc.) that veil some or all of the task from view.

4.6.3 Programming

Table 4.9 Luminance Ratio Suggestions[12, 13, 14]

Intent	Ratio of Interest	Suggested Luminance Ratio
Maintain task attention	• Paper task to computer monitor	3:1 or 1:3
	• Task to immediate background surfaces[a]	3:1
	• Task to darker distant background surfaces	10:1
	• Task to lighter distant background surfaces	1:10
Minimize discomfort glare	• Task to daylight media	40:1
	• Task to luminaires	40:1
	• Daylight media to adjacent surfaces	20:1
	• Luminaires to adjacent surfaces	20:1
Minimize veiling reflections	• Adjacent ceiling zones (intensive computer use)	4:1[b]
	• Adjacent wall zones (intensive computer use)	4:1[b]
	• Adjacent ceiling zones (limited computer use)	8:1[c]
	• Adjacent wall zones (limited computer use)	8:1[c]

[a] From paper to desk; from paper to tack surface; from computer monitor to desk; from computer monitor to tack surface.
[b] Where computers use monitors that have a glossy finish and/or where detailed viewing is critical (e.g., CAD work, scientific modeling).
[c] Where computers use monitors that have a matte finish and/or negative contrast screen (full color).

some guidance can be offered for luminance limits for general situations. Table 4.8 outlines luminance limits that might be considered for a variety of applications and a variety of luminance sources.

Luminance limits are helpful in avoiding discomfort glare situations and limiting the extent of veiling reflections for many tasks. However, for people viewing computer and TV monitors, and digital readout displays, luminance ratios are critically important. These are the ratios of the luminance of one source or area as compared to a nearby source or area. For direct lighting systems, this means that the luminaires themselves need to be relatively dim or low–brightness in order to not create harsh contrasts or ratios with the surrounding darker ceiling. For indirect lighting systems, this means that the ceiling luminance directly above the luminaires must be of similar intensity as the area between luminaires. Further, with indirect luminaires, the bottom of the luminaire either needs to be relatively small (less than a several inches), needs to be rounded (to capture and reflect a bit of the light from the ceiling), or needs to have some soft transmitted light through it so that the luminaire is not harshly contrasted against the lighted ceiling. Table 4.9 outlines luminance ratios to consider in various applications.

4.6.3 Surface reflectances

Luminances are the result of reflected light or transmitted light. Reflected light is a result of illuminances (light quantities) and surface reflectances interacting. Therefore, surface reflectances need to be a conscious design goal. They have a direct bearing on energy use. Lighter surfaces reflect more light and can yield energy savings by as much as 20 percent.[15]

Generally, matte surface finishes are better for work environments than specular surface finishes. This eliminates the harsh, glary reflections that are problematic when electric light or daylight reflects from specular or polished

Programming

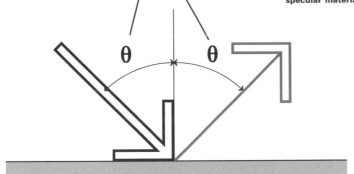

This is the angle of incidence —

This is the angle of reflectance (which is equal to the angle of incidence for specular materials)

θ   θ

Figure 4.38
Specular reflection: The reflected light may be so concentrated as to cause veiling reflections and/or reflected glare. In work environments, specular surfaces can be a distraction as light reflects harshly in specific directions. Specular materials are known as glossy, polished, or shiny, and can be light, medium, or dark in value or tone.

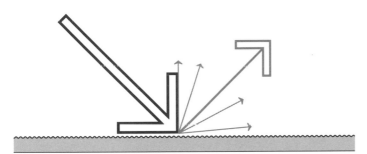

Figure 4.39
Semi–specular (or spread) reflection: The reflected light may be concentrated enough to cause veiling reflections. In work environments, semi–specular surfaces can be a distraction because light reflections veil surface materials. Semi–specular materials are known as etched, honed, or brushed, and can be light, medium, or dark in value or tone.

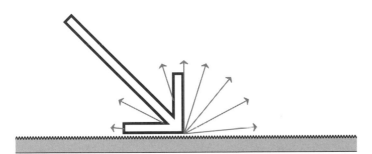

Figure 4.40
Diffuse reflection: The reflected light is equally distributed in many directions, resulting in a general, soft glow. In work environments, diffuse surfaces best provide a comfortable setting for users. Diffuse materials are known as matte or textured, and can be light, medium, or dark in value or tone.

surfaces at a specific angle (the angle at which people happen to view the task or areas). Figure 4.38 illustrates the concept of specular reflection; Figure 4.39 illustrates the concept of semi–specular or spread reflection; and Figure 4.40 illustrates the concept of diffuse reflection.

For most office furniture, 20 percent reflectance should be a minimum and 40 percent, or so, a maximum. This can be achieved with some light woods and most medium–to–light laminates. Table 4.10 outlines guidelines for typical surface reflectances in work environments. These guidelines are based on realistically attainable reflectances.

There is a common misbelief that changing a given surface finish from matte to specular will increase total reflectance. In some cases, for example, kitchen countertops have been specified as honed (matte) black granite. When the designers are reminded that this countertop will appear dark, the specifications are changed from honed granite to polished (specular) granite

4.6.3 Programming

Table 4.10 Surface Reflectance Guidelines for Work Environments

Surface	Suggested Reflectance (matte[a])	Complying Material[b]
Worksurfaces	20 to 40%	• Light woods
		• Medium and light laminates
		• Medium and light ink blotters
Window treatments opaque[c]	30 to 50%	• Medium to light blinds
		• Frit pattern glass[d]
Window treatments image preserving[e]	3 to 5%	• Frit pattern glass[d]
		• Mesh shade
Floors	10 to 20%	• Medium to light carpet
		• Medium to light wood
		• Medium tile
Ceilings	85% or greater	• Premium white tile
		• Ultra–white tile
		• White white paint
Walls	30 to 50%	• Light fabric
		• Medium to light vinyl wall covering
		• Medium to light paint
		• Very light wood
		• Very light stone
Open office partitions	20 to 50%	• Medium to light fabrics
		• Medium to light laminates[f]

[a] Some specular trim materials can provide visual interest. Contiguous and larger surfaces should be matte finish. Values intended for commercial spaces.
[b] See Table 4.12 for a selected list of building materials, some of which comply with these suggested reflectances.
[c] Opaque window treatments should be relatively light in color on the interior surface.
[d] Frit coatings are unique—they can be opaque and yet light in color (typically requires a double coat of frit), and when applied in a perforated–appearance pattern they permit view through (also known as image preserving).
[e] For residential applications, sheer fabrics of high reflectance (30 to 50%) are appropriate to introduce diffuse daylight. In commercial applications, however, such high reflectance window treatments cause luminance ratio problems with users of VDTs.
[f] Generally not appropriate acoustically.

in the belief that this will reflect more light! This is incorrect—the total visible light reflectance is unchanged from honed to polished. Instead, what little light is reflected from the black granite, will, in the case of polished granite, all reflect in one very specific direction—usually toward the user standing at the countertop attempting to prepare food. This harsh reflection causes veiling reflections and, perhaps, even reflected glare. If the user's eyes happen to be located in the same direction as the reflected light is directed, he/she will see a relatively large amount of light in a small area (veiling reflection and/or reflected glare). If the user's eyes are not located in the direction of reflected light, he/she will see no reflected light (hence, a black countertop will look dark). The point is this: unless the user is made aware of the issue in advance and still wishes for dark countertops or work surfaces, the designer should not specify dark honed or polished countertops or work surfaces.

Reflectances of typical surfaces are reported in Table 4.11. This list is intended to illustrate the reflectance values of surfaces that are commonly considered for many applications. However, final selections for the majority of the large surfaces in most environments should follow the guidelines in Table 4.10.

Image ©digitalvision

Programming

Table 4.11 Reflectance Values for Some Typical Materials

Category	Material	Typical Reflectance (%)[a]
Specular Luminaire reflectors	• Aluminum	
	Alzak® polished	85
	Coilzak® polished	90
	Polished	60 to 70
	• Chromium	63 to 66
	• Silver	90 to 99
	• Stainless steel	55 to 65
Specular Building materials	• Clear vision glass (high transmittance)[b]	5 to 10
	• Stainless steel	55 to 65
Semi–specular Luminaire reflectors	• Aluminum	
	Alzak® semi–specular	70 to 80
	Coilzak® semi–specular	75 to 85
Semi–specular Building materials	• Aluminum	
	Brushed	55 to 60
	Paint	60 to 70
Diffuse Luminaire reflectors	• White paint	75 to 90
	• White porcelain enamel	65 to 90
Diffuse Masonry and finish materials	• Brick	
	Light buff	40 to 45
	Dark buff	35 to 40
	Red	10 to 20
	• Granite	20 to 25
	• Gray cement	20 to 30
	• Limestone	35 to 60
	• Marble	30 to 70
	• Sandstone	20 to 40
	• White paint	75 to 90
	• White plaster	90 to 92
	• White terra–cotta	65 to 80
	• Wood	
	Birch, light	35 to 50
	Mahogany	6 to 12
	Oak, dark	10 to 15
	Oak, light	25 to 35
	Walnut	5 to 10

® Alzak is a registered tradename of Alcoa. ® Coilzak is a registered tradename of Alcoa.
[a] Values are approximate.[16] Check with product manufacturer for data.
[b] Value is percent reflected light from the inside surface of the glass. From a survey of glass manufacturers' literature.

4.6.4 Surface transmittances

Although luminance can be a result of light being reflected from surfaces, they also can result from light being transmitted through various surface types. Surface transmittances as a design goal will depend on the luminance and luminance ratio goals established. Surfaces with high transmission are likely to result in luminance ratios greater than the 1:10 limit between task and distant lighter surfaces (such as windows and bright door sidelights). Even relatively low transmission surfaces, if backlighted by intense sources (e.g., daylight) can result in exceeding the luminance ratio of 4:1 from one zone to another (e.g., wall area to window area). Hence, some sort of trans-mission reduction or light source intensity reduction (the light source behind the transmitting surface) is necessary. If an image–preserving transmitting

4.6.4 Programming

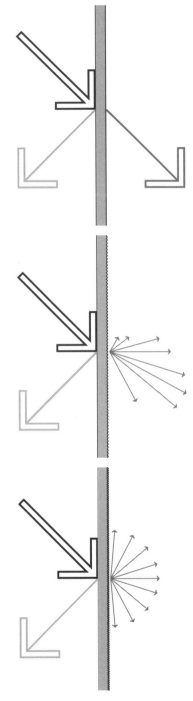

Figure 4.41

Direct transmission: The transmitted light may be so concentrated as to cause discomfort and/or disability glare. If the light source is quite directional and concentrated, the zone of glare may be quite small since the transmitted light continues in a very specific direction. In work environments, direct transmission surfaces can be a distraction because light transmits harshly in specific directions. Direct transmission materials are known as image–preserving and can be high, medium, or low in transmission capability.

Figure 4.42

Spread transmission: The transmitted light may be concentrated enough to cause discomfort glare and/or veiling reflections (once the transmitted light hits other surfaces or tasks and reflects back to the user). In work environments, spread transmission surfaces can be a distraction because light transmissions are of sufficient intensity to draw attention. Spread transmission materials are known as ribbed or patterned, and can be high, medium, or low in transmission capability.

Figure 4.43

Diffuse transmission: The transmitted light is equally distributed in many directions, resulting in a general, soft glow, unless the incoming light is too intense, in which case the result is discomfort glare and/or veiling reflections (once the transmitted light hits other surfaces or tasks and reflects back to the user). In work environments, diffuse transmission can be extraordinarily uncomfortable if it is associated with daylight. Not only does the user have no view, but experiences high degrees of discomfort glare and/or veiling reflections. Diffuse transmission materials are known as matte, textured, heavily etched, or opal, and can be high, medium, or low in transmission capability.

surface has a high transmission, then changing the surface to a non–image–preserving surface will not necessarily decrease luminance. Since non–image–preserving materials exhibit either spread or diffuse transmission characteristics, the transmitted light is directed in many directions and, therefore, creates an overall glow or luminance. In fact, luminance may increase, on average, across the entire transmitting surface. This action also negates view benefit through the transmitting surface (which may or may not have been the design intention—for example, a privacy screen may be a non–image–preserving surface to permit some room light to pass through, but preventing identification of the people in the adjoining space and/or

Programming

preventing identification of their facial expressions. Figures 4.41, 4.42, and 4.43 illustrate the concepts of direct transmission, spread transmission, and diffuse transmission respectively. The resulting luminance issue is dependent on both the light source hitting the transmitting surface and the transmission character of the surface.

4.6.5 Interior illuminances

Illuminances are partly responsible for luminances. As illuminance interacts with surface reflectance or surface transmission, the result is reflected or transmitted light—luminance. As a design goal, then, illuminances are important. Illuminance requirements depend on the task or tasks to be performed, on the criticality of the task, and on the users' ages.

Tasks themselves are reflective and/or transmissive in nature. The degree of reflectances and/or transmissions involved help to determine the illuminance necessary for accurate, timely assessment by users. For example, if office workers are decoding special forms that have black dots on dark gray paper (considered a low contrast task), a fair amount of illuminance will be required just so the workers can detect the black dots against the gray background and identify their location on the form. Alternatively, if the black dots are on white paper (considered a high contrast task), less illuminance will be necessary to detect the black dots and identify their location on the form.

Indeed, quite a few visual tasks have been reviewed over the years by the Illuminating Engineering Society of North America (IESNA) and for which illuminance criteria are suggested.[17] These listings of visual tasks need to be scrutinized carefully. Footnotes describe special circumstances or conditions surrounding various tasks. Some tasks may sound identical to other visual tasks, but occur in different situations (e.g., health care versus office) or have a different relationship to the user (e.g., intensive task work or intermittent task work). Illuminance requirements are known to vary depending on task criticality (task importance) and users' ages (see Section 2.6). Previous editions of the *IESNA Handbook* addressed these issues by providing illuminance ranges—lower ends of the ranges were considered appropriate for tasks where criticality was not an issue and/or where users were typically under 40 years of age; middle values of the ranges were considered appropriate for most typical commercial environment situations where task criticality deems some attention and users' ages might typically range from 40 to 55 years of age; higher ends of the ranges were considered appropriate for tasks where criticality was a serious consideration (e.g., pharmacist reading a doctor's prescription and/or reading drug vial labels) and/or where users were over 55 years of age.[18] IESNA documentation as of this publication date no longer provides definitive direction on modifying illuminance values to address issues of task criticality and users' ages. However, based on the previous editions of the *IESNA Handbook* and on research cited previously in Section 2.6, consideration should be given to the scaling of illuminance values. Table 4.12 outlines basic horizontal illuminance guidelines the IESNA has proposed over the last decade and offers suggestions on scaling illuminances. Figure 4.44 illustrates zones of various illuminance needs.

Horizontal illuminances are important where visual assessment is of things relatively horizontal in orientation, such as small objects on a floor, irregularities in a floor, or a paper on a table or desk. A fair number of visual tasks, however, are oriented vertically or near–vertical. A significant example is the task of conversation that includes the visual task of facial assessment.

Lighting layers....

■ Ambient
■ Task
■ Accent (or fill)

4.6.5 Programming

Image ©digitalvision

porte cochère

A feature of large, French homes is an entrance, typically of two large wooden carved doors, through which a wheeled carriage or vehicle can pass to an interior, open court. The term is commonly used in America to identify a canopy under which vehicles may pass to disembark passengers. For example, many large hotels have porte cochères.

Table 4.12 Horizontal Illuminance Targets

IESNA Category[17]	IESNA Description[17]	Discussion	Examples[a]

A	Public spaces	Areas of casual passage and/or where very short and very basic/repetitive visual tasks are prominent and/or where tasks are internally lighted, such as some:	• Atriums[e]
			 • Auditoriums[e]
			 • Backlighted tasks
			   • Exclusively microfiche work
			   • Exclusively VDT work
			 • Corridors
			 • Dance clubs
			 • Lobbies[e]
			 • **Porte cochères**
			 • Residential areas

B	Simple orientation for short visits	Areas of deliberate and necessary passage and/or of conversational activity and/or of limited casual reading (materials held horizontally), such as some:	• Atriums • Auditoriums • Ballrooms • Corridors • Elevators • Lobbies • Residential areas • Stairs
C	Working spaces where simple visual tasks are performed	Areas of casual and/or recreational reading or where periodic task performance is required, such as some:	• Banking lobbies • CAD work • Casino gaming • Church naves • Copyrooms • Corridors • Restrooms • Stairs

D	Performance of visual tasks of high contrast and large size	Areas of prolonged casual and/or recreational reading or where visual work is consistently easy to read, or where paperwork is intermittent, such as some:	• Backlighted tasks
			   • Intensive microfiche work
			   • Typical VDT work
			 • Cashier checkouts
			 • Casino gaming
			 • Conference rooms
			 • Libraries
			 • Merchandising
			 • Paperwork tasks
			 • Reading lounges
			 • Residential areas

E	Performance of visual tasks of high contrast and small size, or visual tasks of low contrast and large size	Areas of prolonged assessment of consistently difficult to read documents or detailed 3–dimensional tasks	• Accounting ledgers (handwritten) • Bank tellers' stations • Casino gaming • Commercial kithens • Hair styling studios • Healthcare spaces • Laboratories • Merchandising • Poor quality copies • Video conferencing
F	Performance of visual tasks of low contrast and small size	Areas of prolonged assessment of highly intricate or significant work, or work requiring high degree of eye/hand coordination	• Basketball gyms • Educational demonstrations • Healthcare spaces • Merchandise feature displays • Workbenches
G	Performance of visual tasks near threshold[f]	Areas of exceedingly small, intricate, and detailed work and/or requiring a very high degree of eye/hand coordination	• Baby delivery beds • Surgical tables

^a Where circulation spaces are listed, targets are intended to apply to floor plane. Where workspaces are listed, targets are intended to apply to horizontal work surface. Where tasks are listed, targets are intended to apply to horizontal work surface on which task is located. Reference cites more definitive tasks and more expansive list.[17]
^b All values cited are guidelines for consideration and intended to be average, maintained targets achieved on the task area.
^c Where tasks are rather important to the function of an individual, other people, or an organization, or where users' ages might be typically 40 to 55 years, consideration should be given to increasing base illuminance targets by about 50% as represented here.

Programming

IESNA Guideline[b,17]	Important Task or Users of 40 to 55 Years of Age[b,c]	Critical Task or Users of 55 Years of Age or Greater[b,d]
3 fc (30 lx)	4.5 fc (40 lx)	6 fc (50 lx)
5 fc (50 lx)	7.5 fc (75 lx)	10 fc (100 lx)
10 fc (100 lx)	15 fc (150 lx)	20 fc (200 lx)
30 fc (300 lx)	45 fc (400 lx)	60 fc (500 lx)
50 fc (500 lx)	75 fc (750 lx)	100 fc (1000 lx)
100 fc (1000 lx)	150 fc (1500 lx)	200 fc (2000 lx)
300 fc (3000 lx) to 1000 fc (10,000 lx)	450 fc (4500 lx) to 1500 fc (15,000 lx)	600 fc (6000 lx) to 2000 fc (20,000 lx)

Image ©digitalvision

[d] Where tasks are critically important to the function of an individual, other people or an organization or where users' ages might be typically 55 years or greater, consideration should be given to increasing base illuminance targets by about 100% as represented here.

[e] Particularly appropriate for more historic settings and/or public monuments.

[f] Threshold indicates tasks that are difficult to discern because of their very small size and/or very poor contrast.

4.6.5 Programming

Table 4.13 Vertical Illuminance Targets

IESNA Category[17]	IESNA Description[17]	Discussion	Examples[a]

A	Public spaces	Areas of casual conversation (facial recognition is important) and/or large congregations of people (facial recognition) and/or where light–sensitive materials are displayed and/or where tasks are internally lighted, such as some:	• Artwork (museum quality)
			 • Atriums[e]
			 • Auditoriums[e]
			 • Backlighted tasks
			    • Exclusively microfiche work
			    • Exclusively VDT work[g]
			 • Cafes
			 • Casino gaming
			 • Corridors
			 • Dance clubs
			 • Dining
			 • Elevators
			 • Lobbies[e]
			 • Lounges
			 • Porte cochères
			 • Residential areas

B	Simple orientation for short visits	Areas of deliberate conversational activity and/or of limited casual reading (materials held vertically), such as some:	• Artwork (museum quality)
			 • Atriums
			 • Backlighted tasks[h]
			    • Intensive microfiche work
			    • Intensive VDT work
			 • Casino gaming
			 • Conferring/meeting
			 • Grooming
			 • Residential areas
			 • White boards

C	Working spaces where simple visual tasks are performed	Areas of scrutinized assessment and/or eye/hand coordination, such as some:	• Filing rooms (highly active) • General merchandising shelves • Healthcare spaces • Machine rooms (servicing) • Supermarket shelves
D	Performance of visual tasks of high contrast and large size	Areas of prolonged assessment of consistently difficult to read documents or detailed 3–dimensional tasks	• Art studios • Basketball gyms • Hair styling studios • Healthcare spaces • Laboratories • Library stacks • Merchandising feature displays • Videoconferencing • Workbenches
E	Performance of visual tasks of high contrast and small size, or visual tasks of low contrast and large size	Areas of prolonged assessment of highly intricate or significant 3–dimensional work, or work requiring high degree of eye/hand coordination	• Baby delivery beds • Educational demonstrations • Merchandise feature displays • Surgical tables • Workbenches
F	Performance of visual tasks of low contrast and small size	No citations	No citations
G	Performance of visual tasks near threshold[f]	No citations	No citations

[a] Where circulation spaces are listed or where people are likely to be standing, targets are intended to apply to imaginary points (four cardinal viewing directions of north, east, south, and west) at about 5'–6" AFF. Where meeting spaces are listed or where people are likely to be sitting, targets are intended to apply to imaginary points (four cardinal viewing directions of north, east, south, and west) at about 4' AFF. Where work spaces are listed, targets are intended to apply to the center of the task (roughly). For example, for VDTs, targets are intended to apply to imaginary points (four cardinal viewing directions of north, east, south, and west) at about 4' AFF. Reference cites more definitive tasks and more expansive list.[17]
[b] Except for backlighted or internally lighted tasks such as VDTs, all values cited are guidelines for consideration and intended to be average, maintained targets achieved on the task area. For backlighted tasks, use IESNA Guideline as a maximum, maintained target achieved on the task area.

Programming

IESNA Guideline[b, 17]	Important Task or Users of 40 to 55 Years of Age[b,c]	Critical Task or Users of 55 Years of Age or Greater[b,d]
3 fc (30 lx)	4.5 fc (40 lx)	6 fc (50 lx)
5 fc (50 lx)	7.5 fc (75 lx)	10 fc (100 lx)
10 fc (100 lx)	15 fc (150 lx)	20 fc (200 lx)
30 fc (300 lx)	45 fc (400 lx)	60 fc (500 lx)
50 fc (500 lx)	75 fc (750 lx)	100 fc (1000 lx)
100 fc (1000 lx)	150 fc (1500 lx)	200 fc (2000 lx)
300 fc (3000 lx) to 1000 fc (10,000 lx)	450 fc (4500 lx) to 1500 fc (15,000 lx)	600 fc (6000 lx) to 2000 fc (20,000 lx)

[c] Where tasks are rather important to the function of an individual, other people, or an organization or where users' ages might be typically 40 to 55 years, consideration should be given to increasing base illuminance targets by about 50% as represented here. For backlighted tasks, use IESNA Guideline as a maximum, maintained target achieved on the task area.
[d] Where tasks are critically important to the function of an individual, other people, or an organization or where users' ages might be typically 55 years or greater, consideration should be given to increasing base illuminance targets by about 100% as represented here. For backlighted tasks, use IESNA Guideline as a maximum, maintained target achieved on the task area.
[e] Particularly appropriate for more historic settings and/or public monuments.
[f] Threshold indicates tasks that are difficult to discern because of their very small size and/or very poor contrast.
[g] For backlighted tasks performed exclusively over a relatively long duration, lower vertical illuminances are best—use the IESNA guideline as a maximum.
[h] Special note: with the advent of flat and matte VDT screens, the maximum vertical illuminance on VDTs can be as great as 20 fc (200 lx), providing that intensities are uniform and that ceiling luminance ratios meet criteria outlined in Table 4.10.

4.6.6 Programming

©Stephen Graham

Figure 4.44
Illuminance criteria are intended to apply to very specific task zones or areas in any given space. It is inappropriate to simply design a general horizontal illuminance level throughout a space—this is not energy efficient and is not a sustainable practice. In this retail lounge area, vertical illuminance applies to the casual seating area (in this situation deemed to be IESNA Category A—casual conversation) as noted by pointer **1**; and to the feature merchandise areas (in this situation deemed to be IESNA Category D—feature displays) as noted by pointer **2**. Horizontal illuminance applies to the floor area (in this situation deemed to be IESNA Category A—to provide sufficient light for casual circulation) as noted by pointer **3**.

Another significant example is in a work environment—the VDT screen. Here, too much light on the screen can wash out text and graphics, so vertical illuminance should be relatively low. Where people use VDTs exclusively, vertical illuminance should be near zero on VDT screens. Where VDTs are used intensively (e.g., typical office situation), vertical illuminances should be moderate. Table 4.13 outlines basic vertical illuminance guidelines proposed by the IESNA and offers suggestions on scaling illuminances. Here, however, you can see that for such internally lighted tasks as VDT screens (where the contrast of the text and graphics on screen are critical to the successful viewing of the task), as people age, and/or as task criticality increases, vertical illuminance should be held constant or decreased, *not* increased as is the case with tasks that are not internally illuminated.

To minimize energy use and to maximize visual interest in any environment, it is recommended that several layers of lighting be used to achieve all of the appropriate horizontal and vertical illuminances for a given situation. The three layers of light are typically labeled ambient, task, and accent (or fill). Ambient or general lighting is intended to be a base level of general light throughout an area or space. Task light is intended to augment the ambient light so that appropriate illuminances are achieved on task areas. Accent light is used to provide illuminance on elements of visual interest, such as special architectural details or artwork. This accent light also serves to help balance luminances in a space (see Table 4.9).

4.6.6 Exterior illuminances
Illuminances are partially responsible for luminances. The illuminance targets outlined in Tables 4.12 and 4.13 are for interior spaces and tasks or, in the case of porte cochères, interior–to–exterior transition spaces. Most exterior

Image ©digitalvision

Programming

Table 4.14 Selected Roadway Illuminance Guidelines

IESNA Roadway Class[19]	Abutting Land Use[19]	Discussion	Example	IESNA Guideline[a]	Illuminance[b]	Uniformity[c]
Major roadway	Heavy volume of nighttime vehicular and pedestrian traffic (IESNA classifies this land use as "commercial")	A route of through traffic flow, connecting areas of primary traffic generation in densely developed business areas with important rural highways or expressways.	A roadway passing through a downtown or near–downtown shopping district.	• concrete pavement:	1.2 fc (12 lx)	3:1
				• asphalt pavement:	1.7 fc (17 lx)	
Major roadway	Relatively few nighttime pedestrians (IESNA classifies this land use as "residential")	A route of through traffic flow, connecting areas of primary traffic generation in densely developed business areas with important rural highways or expressways.	A roadway passing through a residential neighborhood that connects a business district to a rural highway.	• concrete pavement:	0.6 fc (6 lx)	3:1
				• asphalt pavement:	0.9 fc (9 lx)	
Local roadway	Moderate volume of nighttime pedestrian traffic (IESNA classifies this land use as "intermediate")	A route of local traffic intended for direct access to destinations. Local roadways connect to collector roadways that themselves feed to major roadways.	A street passing by municipal facilities such as libraries and rec centers, and/or passing by apartment complexes and corner convenience stores.	• concrete pavement:	0.5 fc (5 lx)	6:1
				• asphalt pavement:	0.7 fc (7 lx)	
Local roadway	Relatively few nighttime pedestrians (IESNA classifies this land use as "residential")	A route of local traffic intended for direct access to destinations. Local roadways connect to collector roadways that themselves feed to major roadways.	A street passing by residences and/or apartment complexes.	• concrete pavement:	0.3 fc (3 lx)	6:1
				• asphalt pavement:	0.4 fc (4 lx)	

[a] Pavement designations are typical for US (concrete pavement is Type R1 and asphalt pavement is Type R3).[19]
[b] Values cited are horizontal, average, and maintained on pavement.
[c] Ratios cited are average–to–minimum.

applications have much different requirements—for two reasons. First, outdoor applications of electric light are important for nighttime situations. Here, the eyes are essentially dark–adapted, and not much illuminance is necessary to elicit a response. Second, most nighttime outdoor tasks involve relatively large objects and relatively gross assessments (e.g., are there obstacles on the sidewalk, are there pedestrians in the street, etc.). The single largest issue with exterior lighting is the preponderance of overlighted applications. Unfortunately, particularly in the United States, an attitude of "more is better" is pervasive. Competition among retailers, particularly fueling stations and auto dealerships, has resulted in ratcheting of illuminances to absurd levels. Some exterior lighting guidelines are outlined in Tables 4.14, 4.15, and 4.16. These are intended as maintained targets—see the discussion below on targets. Overdesigning is not an option—this results in energy waste and exacerbates light pollution and light trespass.

With the exception of egress lighting requirements and some parking lot lighting requirements, illuminance targets are intended to be just that—the target to which the designer should design the lighting system. Even where minimums are cited, the designer should attempt to design a lighting system that meets the minimum criteria, rather than overlight to some higher arbitrary level. Although calculational inaccuracies, as well as in situ voltage and construction fluctuations (e.g., actual paint reflectance), affect final illuminance outcomes, designs are generally considered to be in compliance

4.6.6 Programming

Table 4.15 Selected Pedestrian Path Illuminance Guidelines

Walkway Type[19]	Abutting Land Use[19]	Discussion	Example	IESNA Guideline[a] Horizontal Illuminance[c]	Uniformity[d]	Vertical (areas prone to crime)[b] Illuminance[e]	Uniformity[d]
Roadside sidewalks	Heavy volume of nighttime vehicular and pedestrian traffic (IESNA classifies this land use as "commercial")	A sidewalk with heavy nighttime pedestrian traffic adjacent to a roadway with heavy nighttime vehicular traffic.	A sidewalk adjacent to a major roadway passing through a downtown shopping district.	1 fc (10 lx)	4:1	2.2 fc (22 lx)	4:1
Roadside sidewalks	Relatively few nighttime pedestrians (IESNA classifies this land use as "residential")	A sidewalk with very little nighttime pedestrian traffic adjacent to a roadway.	A sidewalk adjacent to a roadway passing through a residential neighborhood.	0.2 fc (2 lx)	4:1	0.5 fc (5 lx)	5:1
Paths and stairs distant from roads	Irrespective of pedestrian activity levels, although some level of activity is anticipated throughout the night	A finished path or stairs distant from roadways with very little nighttime pedestrian traffic to a moderate amount of nighttime pedestrian traffic.	A pedestrian path passing through a central–city park or campus of a 24–hour complex or university.	0.5 fc (5 lx)	10:1	0.5 fc (5 lx)	5:1

[a] Pavement designations are typical for US (concrete pavement is Type R1 and asphalt pavement is Type R3).[19]
[b] Particularly careful scrutiny with the users/client is necessary to determine the need for vertical illuminance. Vertical illuminance is intended to be applied to those areas that are prone to criminal activity. This may require a review of police records for historical data or may require a determination by users/client if the site may harbor future criminal activity given its location and/or likely nighttime activity level.
[c] Values cited are horizontal, average, and maintained on pavement.
[d] Ratios cited are average–to–minimum.
[e] Values cited are vertical, average, and maintained at points 5'–6" AFG (above finished grade) in the four cardinal viewing directions (north, east, south, and west).

with target criteria when calculations show illuminances to be within a variation of a maximum of 20 percent, and preferably 10 percent or less.

The ninth edition of the *IESNA Handbook* reports sufficiently detailed and robust guidelines for roadways and pedestrian pathways.[19] However, for parking lot lighting, the eighth edition of the *Handbook* offers much more useful and restrained guidance by reporting criteria for various parking lot types.[20] Here again, and it cannot be overstated, minimum illuminances are intended to be the design targets. Overdesigning has no known advantage.

For roadway lighting, criteria are based on pavement types, abutting land use, and roadway class. Pavements in the United States are essentially concrete (known as Type R1 pavement) or asphalt (known as Type R3 pavement), although some experimentation is underway with varying road pavements to maximize pavement life and minimize slippage. Pavement type influences how light reflects and how much light reflects to drivers. Abutting land use is important in order to assess likely nighttime pedestrian and vehicular activity. Finally, roadway class identifies likely vehicular speed and volume of traffic. Each of these factors influences illuminance criteria. Table 4.14 outlines a select few roadway illuminance guidelines. Roadway lighting and car headlights are intended to assist drivers in identifying obstacles on the roadway, lane markings, and other vehicles. Roadway lighting does not especially assist drivers in sufficiently and readily identifying pedestrians. For ready identification of pedestrians, vertical illuminance is key.

Pedestrian path lighting is intended to address personal safety and security. Note the distinction. Personal safety involves minimizing or eliminating the risk of being hit by vehicles, bicycles, rollerbladers, and the like. Personal security involves instilling or enhancing a sense that one is safe from personal crime. There are no highly reliable statistics showing that

Programming

Table 4.16 Selected Open Parking Lot Illuminance Guidelines

| | | Optional Guideline[a] | | | |
| | | Horizontal | | Vertical | |
Lot Type[20]	Discussion	Illuminance[b]	Uniformity[c]	Illuminance[e]	Uniformity[d]
High activity level	A parking lot where high levels of nighttime activity occur, such as sporting events, cultural or civic events, and malls.	1 fc (10 lx)	4:1	none cited	none cited
Medium activity level	A parking lot where moderate levels of nighttime activity occur, such as community shopping centers, office parks, airport and commuter lots, recreational centers, and residential complexes.	0.6 fc (2 lx)	4:1	none cited	none cited
Low activity level	A parking lot where little nighttime activity occurs, such as corner stores, industrial and educational facilities, and churches.	0.2 fc (2 lx)	4:1	none cited	none cited

[a] These guidelines are based on previous editions of IESNA Guidelines[20]. Latest IESNA Guidelines offer little practical guidance on parking lot lighting.[19]
[b] Values cited are horizontal, minimum, and maintained on pavement.
[c] Ratios cited are average–to–minimum.

illuminance reduces or eliminates crime. However, appropriate vertical illuminance offers pedestrians an ability to better detect peripheral movement (and, thereby, take precautionary action to a perceived threat) and, should a crime occur, permits greater potential for more accurate identification of the perpetrator(s). As unpopular as it is, particularly to environmentalists and dark–sky advocates, vertical illuminance generated by white light sources offers the best lighting for personal safety and sense of security. Indeed, studies show that whiter light is more than twice as efficient for many exterior nighttime visual tasks.[21, 22, 23] Indeed, if the designer uses monochromatic yellow sources, such as high pressure sodium or low pressure sodium lamps, a doubling or tripling of the suggested lighting criteria will be appropriate to achieve visual performance similar to that achieved under the bluer, whiter sources such as metal halide. Table 4.15 offers illuminance guidelines for selected pedestrian paths.

Parking lot lighting is intended to provide both safety and a sense of security. Because of the very nature of parking lots—potentially great numbers of stationary objects and yet potentially low activity levels given the great expanses involved—illuminance guidelines are limited to minimum horizontal criteria. Great care should be taken to achieve uniformity criteria, otherwise serious shadowing is likely with parked vehicles. Further, consideration might be given to making calculations at both vehicle roof heights and at ground plane to assess horizontal illuminance and uniformity at each plane, thereby offering improved uniformity throughout. Table 4.16 offers suggested guidelines for selected parking lot types. These guidelines are based on the eighth edition of the *IESNA Handbook*. Values cited in the ninth edition are ridiculously low base levels with footnotes encouraging ridiculously high design levels. Such wide swings essentially offer the reader little guidance.

For parking decks, the enclosed nature of the facility requires illuminances that are consistently higher than those necessary for open parking lots.

4.7 Programming

Further, given the limited daylight penetration, electric lighting illuminance is typically required in the interior zones. Finally, because of limited sightlines, tight lanes, and corner conditions, vertical illuminances are necessary for pedestrian safety. Various criteria are found in the most recent (ninth edition) and the preceding (eighth edition) editions of the *IESNA Handbook*.[19,20]

4.7 Lighting criteria and priorities

This chapter has attempted to cover all lighting issues that should be considered on every project. Some issues will easily be dismissed, given the project at hand. Others will be important issues in the development of a successful lighting solution. In any event, the material outlined here should serve as a checklist. Review the checklist, and establish which design goals are appropriate to your specific project. Be honest and be fair to the client. If you establish just one or two criteria, you are shortchanging the client and users. Where criteria is deemed important or essential, specific data should be recorded in the checklist or in report fashion. This allows easy future reference and helps with presentation of the various criteria to the users and/or client. Sharing such a checklist with other team members can help solidify a design and/or act as a catalyst for discussion about various criteria. This checklist can also help identify priorities.

4.8 Programming statement

A project is only as good as its programming. Without appropriate programming, the project is likely to fail, perhaps not entirely, but in some aspect. Indeed, many clients admit that their previous installation initially was deemed a success by all involved, including users, until time to downsize or upsize—in which case, perhaps, lighting flexibility was insufficient, or until a certain season (e.g., during winter, southern exposures exhibit greater glare potential). These are issues that could have been addressed with comprehensive programming. One final note: programming can only be as good as the information the users/client allow designers to collect—this may be a function of fees, project schedule, and/or user accessibility.

The program should then be conveyed to the client. For most projects this may be nothing more than an oral presentation of "the facts" as defined by the team and based on a review of various issues. For other projects, this may necessitate a brief report—see Figure 5.2 for a sample schematic design brief that includes programmatic statements and very preliminary guidance on achieving the programmed needs. Recognize that this is not a complete criteria statement or a complete design statement. This should provide the client with a salient overview of the project's needs and likely ways to deal with those needs.

4.9 Endnotes

[1] Neil H. Eklund and Peter R. Boyce, The Development of a Reliable, Valid and Simple Office Lighting Survey, *Conference Proceedings—1995 IESNA Annual Conference* (New York: Illuminating Engineering Society of North America, 1995), 855–880.

[2] Exploratorium, Exhibit and Phenomena Cross–Reference: Sound–Audible (web page, 1995), http://www.exploratorium.edu/xref/phenomena/sound_-_audible.html. [Accessed November 4, 2000.]

[3] Rohles, F. H., Bennett, C. A. and Milliken, G. A. The effects of lighting, color and room decor on thermal comfort. ASHRAE Transactions, 1981.

Image ©digitalvision

Programming

4 John Flynn, "The Psychology of Light, Article 2, Orientation as a Visual Task," *Electrical Consultant*, January, 1973, 10–21.

5 D. H. Alman, "Errors of the standard photometric system when measuring the brightness of general illumination light sources," *Journal of the Illuminating Engineering Society*, 1977, no. 1: 61.

6 John Flynn, "The Psychology of Light, Article 5, Attitude Reinforcement through Lighting Design," *Electrical Consultant*, May, 1973, 42–45.

7 Dale Tiller, Lighting Quality, National Research Council of Canada, http://www.nrc.ca/irc/bsi/92-5_E.html [Accessed October 7, 2000.]

8 Belinda Collins, Evaluation of Subjective Response to Lighting Distributions: A Literature Review/NISTIR 5119 (Gaithersburg, MD: National Institute of Standards and Technology, 1993).

9 John E. Flynn, et. al., "Interim Study of Procedures for Investigating the Effect of Light on Impression and Behavior," *Journal of the Illuminating Engineering Society*, 1973, no. 3: 94.

10 Jennifer A. Vietch, ed. Full–Spectrum Lighting Effects on Performance, Mood, and Health, Institute for Research in Construction Internal Report No. 659, June, 1994, http://www.nrc.ca/irc/fulltext/ir659/contents.html [Accessed November 26, 2000.]

11 Lynne Lamberg, Medical News and Perspectives: Dawn's Early Light to Twilight's Last Gleaming…, *The Journal of the American Medical Association*, November 11, 1998, http://www.websciences.org/sltbr/jama.htm [Accessed November 26, 2000.]

12 Matthew Luckiesh and S. K. Guth, "Brightnesses in Visual Field at Borderline Between Comfort and Discomfort (BCD)," *Illuminating Engineering*, November 1949, vol. 44: 650–670.

13 Mark S. Rea, ed. *The IESNA Lighting Handbook: Reference and Application, Ninth Edition* (New York: Illuminating Engineering Society of North America, 2000), p. 11–3 and p. 19–4.

14 Illuminating Engineering Society, *IES Lighting Handbook, Second Edition* (New York: Illuminating Engineering Society, 1952), 10–58 and 10–69.

15 Gary Steffy, *Time–Saver Standards for Architectural Lighting* (New York: McGraw–Hill, 2000), p. 9–9.

16 Mark S. Rea, ed. *The IESNA Lighting Handbook: Reference and Application, Ninth Edition* (New York: Illuminating Engineering Society of North America, 2000), p. 1–22.

17 Mark S. Rea, ed. *The IESNA Lighting Handbook: Reference and Application, Ninth Edition* (New York: Illuminating Engineering Society of North America, 2000), chapter 10.

18 Mark S. Rea, ed. *The IESNA Lighting Handbook: Reference and Application, Eighth Edition* (New York: Illuminating Engineering Society of North America, 1993), p. 476.

19 Mark S. Rea, ed. *The IESNA Lighting Handbook: Reference and Application, Ninth Edition* (New York: Illuminating Engineering Society of North America, 2000), chapter 22.

20 Mark S. Rea, ed. *The IESNA Lighting Handbook: Reference and Application, Eighth Edition* (New York: Illuminating Engineering Society of North America, 1993), chapter 24.

21 Y. He, M. Rea, A. Bierman, and J. Bullough, Evaluating Light Source Efficacy Under Mesopic Conditions Using Reaction Times, *Journal of the Illuminating Engineering Society*, Winter 1997, (IESNA JIES, 1997), pp. 125–138.

22 A. L. Lewis, Equating Light Sources for Visual Performance at Low Luminances, *Journal of the Illuminating Engineering Society*, Winter 1998, (IESNA JIES, 1998), pp. 80–84.

23 Alan Lewis, Visual Performance as a Function of Spectral Power Distribution of Light Sources at Luminances Used for General Outdoor Lighting, *Journal of the Illuminating Engineering Society*, Winter 1999, (IESNA JIES, 1999), pp. 37–42.

4.10 General References

Agoston, G.A. 1987. *Color Theory and Its Application in Art and Design*. Berlin: Springer–Verlag.

Rea, Mark S., ed., and Thompson, Brian J., general ed. 1992. *Selected Papers on Architectural Lighting*. Bellingham, WA: SPIE Optical Engineering Press.

Rea, Mark S., ed. 2000. *The IESNA Lighting Handbook: Reference & Application, Ninth Edition*. New York: Illuminating Engineering Society of North America.

Rea, Mark S., ed. 1993. *The IESNA Lighting Handbook: Reference & Application, Eighth Edition*. New York: Illuminating Engineering Society of North America.

Schematic Design 5.1

Upon the completion of the programming phase, the designer is prepared to undertake schematic design: developing preliminary ideas or schemes for lighting of a particular project. Without much knowledge or experience in lighting techniques, light sources, and luminaires, the designer will find this schematic design phase to be a bit of a Catch–22. Much of what is written in later chapters will be instrumental in developing preliminary schemes. There are no conveniently packaged solutions or even rote techniques assigned for given programmed criteria. The designer is left to invent lighting solutions that address most, if not all, of the criteria established in the programming phase. Of course, this is a team effort. So inventions are welcome from the entire team, as are discussions and questions of schematic integrity.

5.1 Assessing architecture

While the lighting designer is programming lighting, the architects, landscape architects, and/or interior designers are likely programming their respective disciplines and may have begun some architectural, site, and/or interior design schemes. If interactive effort has not already gotten underway between team members, it is now necessary to do so. This may entail team meetings where exchanges of information occur. This may also involve design presentations by the architect. There may be design charrettes where all team members participate in a rapid succession of design concepts for the entire project. In any event, as design concept material becomes available, the lighting designer is then in a position to assess the landscape, the architectural, and the interiors schemes and begin to develop lighting schemes that fit with these concepts while also addressing the programming. At times, this can be an awkward situation. Frankly, no one wants to appear the fool— which may seem the case if "a bad design idea" is offered. This is not the case! First, in many situations, the worst ideas are NO ideas. Second, there have been instances where the oddest ideas have led the team to unique, successful installations. Finally, at such an early stage in the project, it is appropriate to stretch thought limitations with nontraditional ideas. Where programming seemingly cannot be accommodated with the proposed architectural, landscape, and/or interiors concepts, discussion with respective team members should occur. An effort should be made to find design concepts that all agree can help advance the programmed requirements.

Architectural, landscape, and/or interiors concepts may not be formalized at first. These may be quick sketches or, perhaps, tentative computer graphics that illustrate various explorations of design ideas. Many times, very rough sketches are accompanied by oral presentations. This is because during the early stages of schematic design, there may be very little in the way of formalized hard copy or computer graphics on architectural, site, and/or interiors schemes. This cannot and should not be used as an excuse to delay lighting schematics. Even when no information is forthcoming, the lighting designer can begin to offer tentative lighting schemes that address criteria established during programming. These schemes can then be presented to the design team and may actually help "start" the site, architectural, and/or interiors schematic design process.

Assessing the architectural design elements must go beyond simply absorbing whatever schematic information the architectural designers provide. This is an opportunity to interact with the architectural designers by

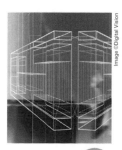

5.2

Schematic Design

Ethics are a value system. The system of values typically depends on a particular group or union to which an individual belongs or subscribes. The IALD has *Standards of Ethical Practice*. The NCQLP has a *Standard of Conduct*. In a perfect world, lighting design would be based on users' needs balanced with resource expenditures. See more on this topic in Section 12.1.

asking questions directly related to lighting programming. For example, if during the evaluation of existing conditions it becomes clear that users want "daylight" (and after some questioning it is apparent they want a view), yet the architectural designers have developed a subterranean structure, the lighting designer should pose the question about view—how can view be introduced for the users? Consider another example: During programming, the users made specific comments about feeling "confined" in office cubicles with very tall partitions and in a space with low ceilings. The lighting designer hopes to introduce indirect lighting and/or wall lighting in the new facility to help ease such perceptions, yet the architectural team proposes very low ceilings to minimize costs. The lighting designer should ask if there is any opportunity for additonal ceiling height in order to implement indirect lighting and to provide a better sense of open space. Further, the lighting designer should inquire about the open office furniture systems—are partitions likely to be tall? and if so, is there an opportunity to use sidelight and/or clerestory panels to offer the impression of a more open workstation arrangement and to permit more light to reach work surfaces.

This sort of interaction is crucial if there is hope of a successful environment for users. While egos have a tendency to be a burden during this step of the project, efforts should be made to explore (even if just for a few minutes of discussion) a variety of reasonable schemes that could address a host of programmed requirements. Patience, political skills, and humility are acquired and required attributes that will help the designer through this phase. Although the lighting designer's "client" on the project may be the architect, a moral obligation, if not an **ethical responsibility**, to the users of the area, space, or facility (with regard to comfort, quality, and quantity of the lighting) and to the public at large (with regard to energy use and sustainability) may necessitate some frank discussions.

5.2 Preliminary design

Lighting, while ultimately ubiquitous on every project, starts as bits and pieces of ideas considered for relatively small areas or spaces. The areas or spaces first addressed might be those considered most important or are those for which there is some architectural concept. In any event, the lighting concept will not simply and completely "come to mind" or "present itself." The process is typically quite fragmented. Simultaneously, however, a lighting design cannot simply be a menagerie of lighting ideas pieced together. In the end, lighting must be as cohesive as the site plan, the architecture, and the interiors. Further, it must be a maintainable system—hence, the umpteen lamps and luminaires that might result from a piecemeal approach simply are not appropriate.

A lighting scheme need not address all areas or spaces of a project. A scheme is a schematic. This is an overview or road map of how lighting might be used to meet the various program requirements while it also enhances and integrates with the architecture. Details are not yet at issue—and should not be addressed during schematic design. Completeness is undesirable—this makes it appear that the other design aspects are firmly resolved and that the lighting problem is solved with no remaining questions or further discussions necessary (a bit too final for most clients, users, and architectural designers at such an early phase of the project). General direction, though, is important.

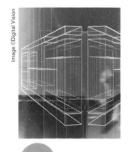

Schematic Design

For example, if the architect and/or liturgical consultant has developed a concept plan for a church renovation, discussion about lighting should revolve around how the space should look and where attention should be directed. Altar, chair, ambo, lectern, baptismal font, and the like are all focal elements. They should be identified as such in the schematic design phase, regardless how obvious this might seem. Now, however, it is a good time to consider what the background lighting should do for or with the observer. What is the architectural backdrop, and what is its significance to the task and/or experience? Drywall walls and ceilings may not deserve much attention via light. Depending on the size of the space, perhaps the focal elements alone will suffice as a balanced collection of visual components to make the space meaningful visually. Based on the illuminance requirements established in programming, how significant will the task lighting challenge be? For a moderate level in a relatively large room, the task lighting challenge is significant. How visible (or not) should lighting hardware be in such a space? Remember, downlights recessed in the cathedral ceiling may still be quite visible depending on their trim/cone finish, the depth of the lamp up into the luminaire, and the aperture size selected. Slope–adapted downlights create relatively large holes that are themselves relatively bright (and, therefore, quite visible—see Figure 5.1). This may be as or more objectionable than a bunch of hanging, cylindrical downlights. Perhaps some sort of uplighting? This would attract attention to the ceiling, however. A highlighted painted drywall surface probably won't set an appropriate meditation scene and may compete for visual attention with the focal elements. Perhaps a series of architectural slots can accommodate banks of adjustable lights that can be adjusted to uniformly light the congregation area. This may seem scattershot.

Another method is to think about lighting in layers (see Section 4.6.5)— ambient, task, and accent. The ambient or general lighting should relate to the architectural envelope—lighting up the architectural surfaces in a soft way. Ambient lighting might provide a third to a half of the total illuminance required for the task(s). Task lighting should relate more to the functional tasks and might provide two thirds to a half of the total illuminance required for the task(s). Accent lighting should relate to specific focal elements, architectural details, or features. The fewer layers of lighting, the less likelihood of a successful project.

It is crucial to look to the program established in Chapter 4. Of particular import are subjective impressions (See 4.5.3). These readily help direct lighting schemes. If spaciousness is an identified impression, then liberal wall luminance will be necessary. Wall lighting, preferably uniformly, is the concept. Now consider the schemes that can provide uniform wall lighting. For the uninitiated, a survey of manufacturers' literature can prime the idea pump. Of course, the surface coloration and reflectance value should be a part of this schematic thinking also. Indeed, perhaps the wall surfaces can be translucent and backlighted in order to provide the uniform wall luminances needed for the spaciousness impression. In–floor uplights can be used to uniformly light wall surfaces—a fresh change from the more usual ceiling–recessed lighting methods. If we're still considering the church, however, recognize that the upward light and shadow patterns may be percieved as a bit unnatural or even devilish.

In any event, schemes should not be lighting hardware driven. It is undesirable and certainly inexcusable to decide to use downlights in a project

Figure 5.1
Downlights in a sloped ceiling require slope–adapted cones/ trims. On relatively steep slopes, the apertures become rather large and quite luminous (the lamp is deeper in the housing, resulting in more spill light on the cone). This can be visually annoying. [Note: Gary Steffy Lighting Design Inc. did not provide any lighting consultation on this project.]

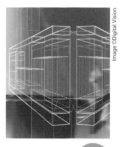

5.3 Schematic Design

The opening paragraph indicates the key programmatic theme—a more open, brighter setting. A succinct programming statement is best. When asked in oral presentations, this can be expanded and made more comprehensive. However, for most readers hard–pressed for time, simplicity is appropriate.

If sufficient solid information is unavailable, then presumptions must be made and should be so stated.

Sidebars should be used to help summarize for the reader the intent of the document. If photos are available (for renovation of existing facilities), consider including one or two images for reference.

Harking back to the program statement made in the first paragraph is important—to show the readers that the program is taken seriously and to illustrate the intentions of the designer to meet the program. Note the direct link—no longwinded, roundabout descriptions or flowery language is used.

Indicating here the kinds of light sources that will be considered helps gain immediate team feedback and also helps establish future work effort. Without some experience and/or preliminary design calculations, making such statements should not be made.

and then base spacing on illuminance requirements. This scheme does not holistically address all of the programming aspects discussed in Chapter 4. Inevitably, such thinking will result in lighting that doesn't address users' subjective impressions and their physiological requirements with regard to adaptation and comfort, and doesn't enhance the architectural elements and details the design team introduced.

Once schemes are pulled together for a reasonable portion of the project, a preliminary design can be documented. This is typically done in pencil on paper background plans provided by the architect or may be just a written brief—which is particularly acceptable on renovation projects where the architecture will substantially remain intact. Figure 5.2 illustrates a program/schematic brief for a sample church renovation project.

5.3 The budget

At about this time in the project schedule, if not before, the client and other team members will be quite anxious to determine if the project is likely to have a cost range consistent with preliminary estimates established by the client or others. In other words, is the project on track to be close to projected costs? Without making some progress toward a design scheme, this is difficult. Once some experience is gained, it is possible to pull together some

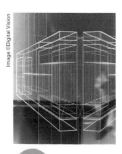

Image ©Digital Vision

Schematic Design

Schematic

Programming requirements have focused on the vestibule, nave, altar, apse, side aisles and balcony. Generally, the lighting scheme is intended to introduce a more open, brighter and more inviting worship setting. This suggests that much more attention should be given to lighting the architectural surfaces of the building.

Vestibule

Presumably the vestibule will remain a ceremonial space if not a fully functional vestibule. Refurbishing the existing pendents should be undertaken with a desire for restoration of the metal work and glass, and rewiring to higher output, longer–life halogen or fluorescent lamping. Uplighting should be implemented to highlight the ceiling and introduce a sense of brightness—this will better complement the brighter nave and offer better daytime transition. Control of these lights should be linked to church proper.

Nave

To enhance the decorative ceiling arches, and to introduce an improved sense of overall brightness, uplighting from the column capitals or transom onto the ceiling is recommended. To meet the task requirements of parishioners, downlights will be reconfigured and additional downlights introduced in the ceiling. This will necessitate top–relamped downlights for relamping from the attic which in turn requires architectural review of catwalk access. Given the great throw distance, the desire to achieve close to a maximum of 30 footcandles, and the apparent desire for setting of ceremonial settings that necessitates dimming, halogen or halogen infrared lamps will be necessary. Since these lamps are relatively short lived (e.g., rated life of 3,000 to 4,000 hours when not dimmed, and double this when dimmed), for day settings it is suggested that consideration be given to a second set of reduced quantity downlights and a few select accents using non–dim ceramic metal halide (with rated life of 9,000 to 12,500 hours depending on wattage and lamp type). Finally, the historic pendent lanterns could be reintroduced into the nave. This will help reduce the number of downlights in the ceiling and perhaps could even be used for the all–day setting (upon refurbishment, the lanterns could be lamped with longer life fluorescent lamps or, alternatively, could be lamped with two sets of lamps—incandescent for traditional service settings where dimming is required, and ceramic metal halide for all–day settings). The

Program

- Vestibule
- Nave
- Font
- Altar platform
- Apse
- Side aisles
- Balcony

Figure 5.2
An example of a schematic design and program brief (this figure continues on the following two pages). The brief was just three pages in length with an attachment related to cost magnitude. This project example is also shown later in Figures 11.4 and 11.5 as the project progressed into contract documents.

Lighting
The Project Name

1 ▲

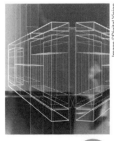

Image ©Digital Vision

5.3

Schematic Design

Lighting
The Project Name

The Project Name
Lighting Schematic Design Narrative

Schematic

historic lanterns are of sufficient scale to introduce a sense of intimacy to the nave. Various layouts of these pendent lanterns will be explored, including a pattern that emphasizes the altar location and a pattern that restores them to near their original layout.

Font

Accenting of the font should occur all around the font to provide not only a glow to the physical element, but to accentuate those being baptized. This permits greater focal attention to the event for all attendees. Depending on the final font location, this may necessitate lights mounted in two planes—the upper vaulted ceiling of the nave and the lower flat ceiling of the balcony. Again, depending on final font location, there is a likelihood that the front of the balcony will receive some spill light from the accents in the high ceiling. The lights should be controlled by a preset scene arrangement for maximum effect.

Altar

The planned location for the altar offers 360–degree viewing. As such, accent lighting should be planned around the altar in its entirety. This will necessitate groups of lights in the ceiling in a concentric pattern to the west and to the east as well as some downlights directly overhead. The presider's chair should be highlighted with perhaps four ceiling lights (two to the west and two to the east out in front of the chair)—although this will result in some accidental accenting of the paired columns in the background. Lights should be zoned to allow for several brightness intensities of the altar, the zone in front of the altar (for weddings, funerals, and the like), and the presider's chair, and to permit varying sequencing hierarchies between all three.

Apse

While the new organ is not intended to be of primary focus, its location here suggests that some soft lighting should be available to avoid the "dark hole" effect of an unlighted zone directly behind the altar (which by comparison will generally be lighted to high intensities). Significant accent lighting should be available for the cathedra and for the ambo. Finally, to accommodate the music center or stage presented by the apse, accent lighting should be made avail-

▼ 2

Schematic Design

Schematic

able to light choral or musical performers. At a minimum then, there should be four distinctive light groupings and each should be controlled by a preset system to ensure consistent results acceptable to most people. Note: no permanent theatrical or broadcast lighting is planned beyond the focal lighting and scene controls intended for liturgy and related musical performances. Consideration should be given to providing sufficient power locations for portable theatrical/broadcast lighting.

Side aisles
Stations of the cross are located in the side aisles. Lighting of these should be reexplored. Additionally, the original niches will be fully reintroduced. Lighting of these should offer a quiet backdrop. Finally, uplighting the side aisle ceilings will help carry the sense of brightness from the nave, and create a better sense of overall architectural connection to the nave. Each of the three lighting components just described should be separately controlled so that preset lighting arrangements can be established to enhance the program of the liturgy.

Balcony
As part of the nave, the balcony should be lighted in similar fashion as the nave. Hence, downlights will require reconfiguration as well as additional units introduced. As with the apse, to avoid a dark hole appearance, the organ pipes and/or the west wall should be lighted softly.

Lighting
The Project Name

3 ▲

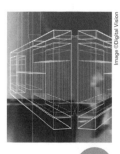

Image ©Digital Vision

5.3

Schematic Design

Appendix

Lighting Equipment Cost Magnitude

Area/Zone	Equipment	Quantity[1]	Unit Magnitude[2]	Subtotal	Rounded Total
Vestibule					US$26,000.
	Refurbished pendants	1	US$4,000.	US$10,000.	
	Uplights	6	US$400.	US$2,400.	
	Front entry sconces	2	US$3,500.	US$7,000.	
Nave pendants	Refurbish	12	US$10,000.	US$120,000.	US$120,000.
Nave[3]					US$75,000.
	Uplights	44	US$450.	US$19,800.	
	Downlights	70	US$375.	US$26,250.	
	Accents	70	US$375.	US$26,250.	
Apse					US$20,000.
	Downlights	20	US$375.	US$7,500.	
	Accents	36	US$375.	US$13,500.	
Side aisles					US$30,000.
	Uplights	22	US$450.	US$9,900.	
	Station accenting allowance	12 stations	US$1,000.	US$12,000.	
	Niche lighting allowance	10 niches	US$1,000.	US$10,000.	
House controls[4]	Allowance	Allowance	US$40,000.	US$40,000.	US$40,000.
Egress lighting[5]		na	na	na	na
Total Lighting Equipment Cost Magnitude (excluding installation)					US$320,000.

[1]Luminaire quantities are simply guesstimates to establish some magnitude costs. Final quantities likely to be different.
[2]Hardware magnitude is intended to cover the actual luminaires and lamps. These are guesstimates. As such, the bottom line should be considered an allowance. Deleting or reducing line item values may not result in complete savings of that value amount. No contingency is included and should be a part of the overall project cost magnitude.
[3]Includes balcony, font and altar.
[4]Controls magnitude covers house lighting, but does not include any studio/broadcast control board.
[5]Exit sign and egress lights magnitude need to be developed by registered professionals.

Lighting
The Project Name

7 ▲

Figure 5.3

An example of a schematic design cost magnitude. This may not be developed until much further study of the project (e.g., near the end of design development)—depending on the specific project scope and the designer's previous experiences (e.g., is there enough historic design information in the designer's files to permit such a guesstimate?).

historical references that can offer a cost magnitude per project type. For example, if over the course of three to five years, the designer has been involved in two or three church projects, the cost data and square footage data from these projects can be averaged to yield a "magnitude guess" on what these sorts of projects might cost. Be aware of several cautions. First, the projects averaged together must be of similar scope. A low–cost, "pole barn" church cannot be averaged together with a restoration of an early–20th century cathedral. Second, allow for inflationary and geographic differences. A project in Peoria, Illinois, is likely to be less costly than a project in Chicago. Third, make clear all assumptions and caveats. For example, references to "magnitude cost" or "cost magnitude" offer some latitude compared to simply "cost" or even "cost estimate." Further, unless the designer is comfortable developing such magnitudes, make clear that the lighting magnitude does not include installation costs—such is best left to installation professionals, the contractors. Figure 5.3 illustrates a sample cost magnitude.

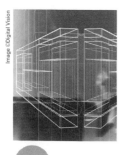
Image ©Digital Vision

Daylighting

Energy crises, renewable energy sources, sustainability, and health and wellbeing are renewing the interest in daylighting. Although these are, indeed, serious issues, it is much too easy to get caught in the whirlwind of political correctness. Daylighting as a strategy is akin to electric lighting as a strategy. Treating daylighting solely as a design element will likely wreak havoc on the occupants. Indeed, light needs to be treated with great care, regardless of its source.

Daylighting should be considered from the occupants' perspectives. While many, if not all, occupants want a view to the exterior, few, if any, can discern a daylight footcandle (or lux) from an electric light footcandle (or lux). Further, while no one wants to waste energy or earth resources, neither does anyone want to be debilitated. Unfettered daylight, or worse, daylight fettered incorrectly, can result in glare, task washout, veiling reflections, and adaptation effects that can seriously limit the occupants' levels of comfort and desire to remain in the space.

This means addressing daylight as a light source that requires reckoning! In the same way that bare lamps (regardless of type) hanging in front of an occupant are neither acceptable nor tolerated and, therefore, not designed, so, too, is the sun or bright clouds hanging outside unabated neither acceptable nor tolerated. Many books have been written on daylight—as a design and engineering media, as a health media, and as a sustainable media. The following text covers the primary issues and offers some direction toward avoiding serious blunders. This is presented on the basis that using an ostensibly sustainable source like daylight can lead to discomfort and human inefficiency and, ultimately, to wasting energy.

6.1 Defining daylighting

Any light that the sun produces and that strikes the earth directly, indirectly, or both is daylight. This includes sunlight (direct from the solar disc), skylight (whether clear or cloudy or somewhere in between), and sunlight and/or skylight reflected from other surfaces (e.g., the ground, other buildings, bodies of water, and the like, except the moon—which is considered moonlight). Daylight has been called natural light. Electric light has been called artificial light. However, light is light—visible radiation or visible wavelengths of the electromagnetic spectrum. These wavelengths are natural. There is no substantive, repeatable data proving that daylight illuminance is healthier than electric light at the intensities necessary or desirable for typical indoor human functions. Very high intensities of either daylight or electric light can be beneficial (see Health below). Certainly view is healthy. Some measure, albeit limited, of ultraviolet radiation is also beneficial (see Health below). In typical indoor environments, daylight can serve two functions: 1) offer a connection to the outside world; and 2) reduce the energy required to operate electric lights.

6.2 Assessing daylight

For the designer to assess daylight, programming should be done to better determine how and if daylighting is a part of users' expectations. As noted, daylighting means different things to different people. View, health, illuminance, luminance, and sustainability are criteria that are likely to drive why daylighting is introduced on a given project and how it is handled as a design and engineering element.

6.2   Daylighting

oculi (plural for oculus)

A circular or oval opening, such as a skylight. Latin for eye.

image-preserving media

Typically, a reference to window shades, glass, and acrylic, etc., that permits a clear view through. Image-obscuring media indicates that which does not permit a view through it, but typically allows some light to pass through it.

vision glass

Glass that allows a clear view. Synonymous with image-preserving media. Transmittances range from 5 up to 75%. The lower transmittances are achieved with tinted glass and/or with mirror coatings.

spectral power transmission

A measure of the power or intensity of electromagnetic energy transmitted through a material or medium. Identical to spectral power distribution, which is a term typically reserved for electric light sources. For glass used in windows, clerestories, and skylights, etc., spectral power transmission depends on the base glass itself (its iron content or lack thereof), any added tints, and/or any coatings, as well as the number of glass panels or panes used in the assemblies. For example, a dark bronze tint means that the blue and green light energy present in daylight will be absorbed or reflected, yielding transmitted light that is richer in orange and red.

Image ©EyeWire, Inc.

▶ *View:* View means that users are visually connected in real time (as opposed to some video arrangement) with the outdoors through windows or other architectural **oculi**. View offers a significant psychological benefit to users. The temporal qualities of the exterior environment offer important cues to users. Wanting to know weather conditions and the time of day is human nature. Seeing sun, shade, and/or intensity changes over time help us mark time and are part of the life experience. This cueing may play some role in our circadian rhythm physiology. These changes over time also may help users maintain an alert state necessary for motivation and continuing work and social interaction throughout the day.[1] View also acts as a distant focus for eye muscle relaxation from time to time during the day. If view is an important daylighting aspect, then the architecture will need to provide for an appropriate pattern of oculi through which people can see to the outdoors. Further, these oculi need to be filled with **image-preserving media**—typically **vision glass**. The critical questions, however, are how much and what kind of visible transmittance should this glass have? "How much" transmittance refers to the quantity of light that comes through the glass and influences how much sky and/or sun glare is present and, therefore, the method(s) for mitigating such glare (this may include manual, automated, or fixed architectural louvers, shades, blinds or drapes, or the greater challenge of developing windows that are sufficiently recessed, shaded, or oriented to avoid or at least minimize such glare issues). "What kind" of transmittance is more accurately termed **spectral power transmission**. So, a window may transmit 30 percent of the total light falling onto it and, with blue-green tinted glass panes for instance, may transmit mostly green and blue wavelengths and relatively fewer red and orange wavelengths. This would create a blue-rich view and would tend to yield bluer interior daylight quality—rendering nearby surfaces with a blue cast.

▶ *Health:* Daylight has significant health benefits. Unfortunately, daylight also carries serious health liabilities. Benefits include the physiological aspects of circadian rhythms (important to minimizing seasonal affective disorder [SAD]) and the production of vitamin D (important to calcium absorption in the body).[2] Unfettered daylight as experienced outdoors includes shorter wavelength ultraviolet radiation associated with skin cancer (also known as UV_B [315 to 280 nm]).[3] These wavelengths are also believed to cause yellowing of the eyes' lenses, resulting in cataracts.[3, 4] In any event, the health benefits of daylighting are a result of some reasonable combination of intensity and time exposure. For example, the circadian rhythm aspect appears to respond to a minimum of 250 fc (2500 lx) over a period of two hours or, alternatively, to a maximum of 1000 fc (10,000 lx) over a period of perhaps twenty minutes. Similarly, for vitamin D production, a daytime walk of perhaps thirty minutes is required. Since interior daylighting effects are achieved after daylight is transmitted through some sort of medium that typically limits UV transmission, then interior daylighting as a health benefit is limited to the circadian rhythm and to the psychological benefits associated with the temporal changes of daylight intensity and color. With respect to circadian rhythm, daylight intensities need to be between 250 fc (2500 lx) and 1000 fc (10,000 lx) for two hours and just twenty minutes respectively. Otherwise, these illuminance intensities are too high to support comfortable long term reading of paper tasks and computer screens. So, even as a health benefit, daylight for circadian rhythm

Daylighting

enhancement requires control mechanisms that the users can adjust to achieve the appropriate illuminances over the appropriate time range. Alternatively, circadian rhythm rooms might be advisable—where users can spend a period of time to experience appropriate daylight illuminance intensities.

▶ *Illuminance*: Daylight can provide much of the light needed to perform many of today's living and working tasks. Because daylight is highly variable, and because it has limited availability, designing the daylighting system in any building to meet illuminance targets requires an immense team effort and typically entails greater initial and maintenance costs. While this should certainly NOT prohibit daylight from consideration, it indicates the degree of care, finesse, integration, and user education that is necessary for a successful daylight–integrated installation. Illuminance from daylight, when correctly implemented, should result in reduced energy use.

▶ *Luminance*: Daylight can provide luminances necessary to meet some of the subjective impression requirements outlined earlier. Luminance balancing (from surface to surface) can also be achieved with daylight. As noted in the illuminance discussion above, however, the variability and intensities of daylight will create a serious challenge for the design team. Indeed, it must be said that daylight is not a free energy source. Initial capital expenditures higher than most clients or users may be expecting, ongoing maintenance requirement, sophisticated controls, and the teamwork necessary to achieve success—all equally experienced with successful, quality electric lighting systems—are elements of Implementing daylight.

▶ *Sustainability*: The very essence of sustainability is to attempt to achieve as much as possible with as little as possible—and particularly with natural, renewable resources. Daylight certainly offers such a means. At the risk of repetition, however, it is important to appreciate the enormity of the challenge to the team. Success of daylighting as a sustainable practice is very sensitive to the integration and interaction of the various building materials and systems (e.g., glazing systems on windows, skylights, clerestories, monitors, etc.; lighting systems, controls systems, HVAC systems, interiors, or furniture systems, etc.).

6.3 Daylight media

The sun (also called the solar disc) and the sky are the two most significant daylight sources readily available to designers. Reflected daylight from other surfaces is secondary. Any of these daylight sources can introduce luminances of such significance that one or several of the following may occur:

▶ Distraction
▶ Direct glare
▶ Reflected glare
▶ Veiling reflections
▶ Transient adaptation

Managing daylight to provide at the least a view, and at the most a view, illuminance, and luminance is the key to successful daylighting in today's architecture. Using such daylight media as monitors, clerestories, skylights, and windows with appropriate orientation, shading control, and room surface finishes along with proper electric lighting is necessary to achieve cost– and occupant–effective sustainable daylighting.

Image ©EyeWire, Inc.

6.3 Daylighting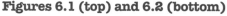

Image ©Photodisc, Inc.

Image ©RubberBall Productions

Figures 6.1 (top) and 6.2 (bottom)
Visual environment pleasantness: The daylighted composition of highly textured architectural dome of the Pantheon in Figure 6.1 is now considered quite pleasant and evocative by most people. The oculus and dome configuration permit a tracking of the time of day and yet also introduce a diffuse light into the lower space caused by the interreflection of light. The texture of the architecture is further strengthened by daylight, although this, too, changes with sky conditions and sun position. The ornate classical dome in Figure 6.2 also introduces diffused daylight into the lower space, but now via a clerestory at the base of the dome. In both situations, the volume and configuration of the space are an integral part of the success and charm of the daylighting. [Note: Gary Steffy Lighting Design Inc. did not provide any lighting consultation on these projects.]

Daylight as it relates to modern architecture is seldom offered the opportunity to reveal and interact with architecture and create a dynamic visual mystique for humans as it has in past practice. Further, today's humans' functions in buildings are much, much different than in the past. These are important distinctions. Many designers are awed by imagery of architectural masterpieces that are themselves rendered wonderfully in daylight. Most any attempt to recreate such splendor and awe solely with daylighting in modern buildings is a lost cause without the attention to architectural form, texture, and volume. Figures 6.1 and 6.2 illustrate historical references to daylight. Figure 6.3 illustrates a common modern reference to daylight in a work setting. Note the great disparity between historic references to daylighting and modern–day actuality. People's expectations today, certainly in work environments, call for a setting that is both comfortable and functional for purposes of their work directives. Full–strength daylight through building apertures will not satisfy most folks most of the time.

Where tasks are less demanding than the traditional office environment and where architectural form and volume, if not texture, lend themselves to interior daylight distribution, daylight can be a significant part of the experience of place and can also contribute to less electric light, at least during the daylight hours. Figures 6.4 to 6.8 offer examples of similarly functioning projects and an array of daylight resolutions.

Daylight media, their relevance in workspaces, and a variety of respective design goals are outlined in Table 6.1. Because many workspaces today involve reading and assessing electronic–based tasks along with hard copy tasks, daylight quality and quantity requirements are much different than those experienced in other kinds of spaces and in workspaces of the past (where many tasks were manually based and involved discrimination of fine

Image ©EyeWire, Inc.

Daylighting

Figure 6.3
Visual environment pleasantness: The simple introduction of daylight today evokes a sense of pleasantness, at least initially. Without baffles or louvers (here, wide–slat horizontal blinds act as baffles), this exposure would be uncomfortable for visual work (e.g., viewing television or working on a computer) on sunny conditions (as shown here). The geometry of space and, therefore, the lack of ability to introduce daylight high up into the space and out of primary field of view, do not lend themselves to soft, general distribution of daylight. [Note: Gary Steffy Lighting Design Inc. did not provide any lighting consultation on this project.]

detail and/or subtle color (e.g., sewing, woodworking, or painting with organic paints). In general, a daylight design should strive to provide for large areas of moderate–to–low uniform luminances and illuminances. This means not only controlling the daylight media with appropriate glass and shading, but also controlling room surface finishes and electric lighting with great care. With our continuing concern for energy conservation, daylight media are bound to become more important in new and renovation design work.

The orientation for daylight media depends on the geographic and topographic location of the project and its proximity to other structures. Generally, the more diffuse the daylight (e.g., northern exposure daylight in the northern hemisphere), the less cumbersome the control technique and the more uniform the luminance of the daylight media and other room surfaces. Nevertheless, diffuse north skylight luminances can exceed 3000 fL (10,200 cd/m²), which is more than ten times the luminance limit criteria for a work environment. Therefore, shade control techniques are advisable even for north–oriented daylight media. Control techniques range from simply using low– to moderate–transmission glass (10 to 30 percent transmittance), to overhangs, shelves, solar shades, or a combination of these. Low transmission glass, while allowing an unobstructed view of the outdoors, usually will alter the color of the view and of the incoming daylight. With gray–tinted glass, the exterior view appears grayed or dulled, imparting a "cloudy" or overcast look. The incoming daylight has a stark, cool appearance. Bronze tinted glass, while also skewing colors, seems more acceptable, as the exterior scene looks somewhat rosy and incoming light has a warmer cast. Low–emissivity (Low–E) glass tends to provide a spectrally neutral view of the exterior while incoming daylight is also spectrally neutral. These are desirable characteristics. Some of the moderate–transmission green glass selections offer a richer landscape and sky view. In any event, differences are significant, even from manufacturer to manufacturer. Samples and/or mockups should always be reviewed prior to final selection.

Frit pattern glass continues to increase in popularity. Frit is a ceramic coating that is an integral part of the glass and, thus, is permanent. The frit patterns can vary significantly, from dot patterns (round or square dots—Figure 6.7 shows such an example), to linear patterns reminiscent of Venetian blinds while still perserving the image beyond. The key to frit patterns is avoiding the lighter colored coatings (e.g., white, light gray, pale blue, or peach, etc.) and using primarily darker coatings (e.g., medium gray and dark

6.3 Daylighting

Table 6.1 Daylight Media Guidelines for Workspaces[a, b]

	Orientation[c]	Control Techniques	Surface Reflectance Guidelines Walls	Ceilings
Monitors	• North • East • West • South	• Moderate transmission glass (30 to 50%) • Architectural baffles or louvers (exterior) • Architectural setbacks • Overhangs • Light shelves (interior or exterior)	• Medium to light (30 to 50%)	• Very light (90%)
Clerestories	• North • East • West • South	• Moderate transmission glass (30 to 50%) • Architectural baffles or louvers (exterior) • Architectural setbacks • Overhangs • Light shelves (interior or exterior)	• Medium to light (30 to 50%)	• Very light (90%)
Skylights	[controllable only on sloped roofs] • North • East • West • South	• Very low transmission glass (2 to 10%) • Architectural baffles or louvers (exterior) • Deep skylight wells • Frit patterns • Solar shades[e] • Blinds	• Medium (30%)	• Very light (90%)
Windows	• North • East • West • South	• Low transmission glass (5 to 15%) • Significant overhangs • Architectural baffles or louvers (exterior) • Frit patterns • Solar shades[e] • Blinds	• Light (50%)	• Light to very light (80 to 90%)

[a] Suggestions intended for northern hemisphere climates.
[b] Guidelines can be relaxed in more casual, transient–type spaces where glare is not a significant concern to the function, and/or where the drama of the view or of the sky is paramount.
[c] Listed in order of preference from "most appropriate" to "least appropriate."
[d] All are with photocell/zoned controls to permit automated control of electric light as daylight is or is not available.
[e] Solar shades are intended to be photocell controlled to permit automated control as daylight is or is not available and as glare is or is not present.
[f] Use wallwashing liberally with direct lighting in order to balance window luminances with interior vertical surfaces.

gray) or using two layers of coatings (e.g., a dark gray or black layer toward the outside of the glass and a white or light gray layer toward the inside of the glass). On two layers, however, registration of the patterns is critical to the success. Further, this method is at least twice as costly as using single layers.

Other glass technologies that may ultimately offer a cost–effective means of daylight control are photochromic glass and electrochromic glass. Photochromic glass is composed of a special molecular substrate (or an inherent molecular structure) that fades from a transparent/high–transmission medium to a transparent/low–transmission or opaque medium when exposed to UV wavelengths found in daylight (reverting back to transparent/high transmission when the UV source is sufficiently small or not present). Electrochromic glass operates in a similar fashion, except that it is not activated by UV radiation, but by a control switch. This control switch can then be operated manually or automated with a photocell.

Solar shades also provide a reasonable way to reduce daylight transmission and yet preserve the view. These are many times known by the tradename MechoShade®. These shades and others are typically made of woven fiberglass that has a sufficiently open and consistent weave to permit view. The density of the weave establishes the degree of transmission, which ranges from about 3 percent to 15 percent or greater. Figures 6.9 and 6.10 illustrate the value of the solar shades. In larger installations, solar shades

Image ©EyeWire, Inc.

MechoShade® is a registered trademark of MechoShade Systems, Inc.

Daylighting

	More Appropriate Electric Lighting[c, d]	Application Notes
	• Indirect • Semi–indirect • Direct/indirect	• Avoid small, intermittent, punched openings • Assess time–of–day occupancy to establish best orientation(s)
	• Indirect • Semi–indirect • Direct/indirect	• Avoid small, intermittent, punched openings • Assess time–of–day occupancy to establish best orientation(s)
	• Indirect • Semi–indirect • Direct/indirect • Direct[f]	• Avoid large–area, shallow openings • Assess time–of–day occupancy to establish best orientation(s)
	• Indirect • Semi–indirect • Direct/indirect • Direct[f]	• Avoid small, intermittent, punched openings • Assess time–of–day occupancy to establish best orientation(s)

work best when automated using motorized rollers connected to photocell controllers. This automation helps offer consistent glare control and veiling reflection reduction throughout an environment.

Low–transmission glass, frit pattern glass, and photocell–controlled solar shades are very appropriate daylight control techniques for large areas that many people use. In these kinds of applications where many people are using the space(s), manually and independently controlled horizontal or vertical shades can be disastrous. A horizontal blind properly set for one person may cause glare or, alternatively, loss of view for another person. Vertical blinds are particularly problematic. Inevitably, if the vertical blinds are set appropriately for one side of the room, anyone on the other side of the room will likely have glare and/or veiling reflection issues. Drapes offer similar drawbacks. Once the drape is partially opened, glare and/or veiling reflections are the likely result for some of the space occupants. Hence, blinds and drapes should be reserved for single–occupancy spaces.

Where daylight media are used extensively in workspaces, finishes of wall and ceiling surfaces should be matte in order to prevent harsh, glary reflections from these surfaces. The walls should have a minimum reflectance of 30 percent, and the ceilings should have a minimum reflectance of 70 percent, with 90 percent preferable. These reflectances, when matte, allow the daylight to interreflect within the room, providing more efficient use of that light source. Also, these reflectances allow the designer to balance the room luminances by lighting those surfaces receiving little daylight to be electrically lighted efficiently. Luminance balancing yields better visual comfort and reduced veiling reflections.

Image ©EyeWire, Inc.

6.3 Daylighting

Figure 6.4

Airline terminals offer opportunities for both architectural diversity and daylight integration or daylight use. Here, visual tasks are not so demanding or of such duration that extreme glare control and veiling reflection control need to be taken. Nevertheless, the more pleasant the visual environment experience, the more pleasurable the waiting, if not flying, experience. At Chicago O'Hare International Airport, the United Terminal takes a less classical form while introducing daylight at multiple levels and various oculi configurations. Architectural surfaces need to remain light in tone to help with daylight interreflection and to minimize luminance ratios. To mitigate serious solar disc problems (direct glare), extensive use of fritted glass is used (note the softer shaded glass panels in the skylight noted as ❶ and in selected lower windows as shown in Figure 6.7). [Note: Gary Steffy Lighting Design Inc. did not provide any lighting consultation on this project.]

Figure 6.5

Here at the newest terminal at Ronald Reagan Washington National Airport, note the volume, form, and configuration of the architecture, as well as the texture. Daylighting is introduced at multiple levels and oculi to enhance overall luminances and illuminances while minimizing the glare hazard of smaller, less frequent daylight openings. Note the central oculi and upper clerestory references taken from historic examples. [Note: Gary Steffy Lighting Design Inc. did not provide any lighting consultation on this project.]

Figure 6.6

At Denver International Airport, the waiting concourses have a simple form with high ceilings and perimeter, continuous, tall windows. The high reflectance of the architectural surfaces in such flatter–ceiling, wide–box configurations is crucial to help with daylight interreflection and to minimize luminance ratios. All three spaces shown here in Figures 6.4, 6.5, and 6.6 offer daylighting. Recognize, however, one's perspective on the comfort and pleasantness of the space and how much the architectural form, volume, and texture contribute to such impressions. [Note: Gary Steffy Lighting Design Inc. did not provide any lighting consultation on this project.]

Balancing daylight luminances with other room surface luminances is best achieved by uniformly lighting the ceiling and walls. Hence, indirect or semi–indirect ambient electric lighting can be appropriate.

Overhangs, awnings, light shelves, and interior and exterior louvers and baffles are all architectural elements requiring modelling for various orientations, daytime and annual solar positions, and sky conditions. Alternatively, these architectural devices can be designed for worst case situations. For example, a study of **solar azimuth** and **altitude**s during the course of the year's shortest day, December 21st, can help the designer establish necessary overhang dimensions or baffle dimensions for a structure's south facing fenestration. Surface finishes of these devices should typically be light in color and matte in finish in order to minimize harsh

Daylighting

Figures 6.7 (above left) and 6.8 (above right)
Frit coatings on glass can help minimize the glare of the solar disc as found at Chicago O'Hare International Airport (note the nonfritted glass versus the fritted glass sections identified as ❶ in Figure 6.7). However, frit cannot sufficiently prevent veiling reflections from daylight luminances as shown with the notation ❷ in both Figure 6.7 (window wall facing east) and Figure 6.8 (bank of monitors facing east and "seeing" the effect of the window wall shown in Figure 6.7). Without operable, near–opaque window treatment, users will experience glare and/or veiling reflections for some duration of the day. [Note: Gary Steffy Lighting Design Inc. did not provide any lighting consultation on this project.]

contrast between sky and underside of architectural treatment and to limit glary reflections. Further, specular finishes of these elements, particularly light shelves, will result in harsh "flash" reflection bands or streaks on ceiling surfaces. These devices cannot act as "sun scoops" unless they are motorized and placed on a sun–tracking system in order to maintain the proper sun angle relationship necessary for optimum optical reflectance, or unless they are engineered as systems to take best advantage of available sun and daylight. These devices require a sufficient amount of design and analysis time to establish their validity and determine their best application on a given project. Several such systems and performance criteria have been outlined by others.[5]

more online @

```
http://www.mechoshade.com/m1.shtml
http://www.nrel.gov/buildings/windows/
http://www.advancedbuildings.org/main_t_building_spec_glazings.htm
http://www.lbl.gov/Science-Articles/Archive/cheap-photochromics.html
http://www.nahbrc.org/toolbase/pandt/tech/abstracts/elecwin.html
```

6.4 Daylight analysis

In analyzing daylight at a given location, there are three basic components to consider: direct sunlight, which impinges intermittently on the east, south, or west exposures of a building in the northern hemisphere; skylight, which impinges simultaneously and somewhat more consistently on all exposures of a building; and reflected light from the ground and nearby man–made structures. Each of these components will vary wildly with time of day, season, and prevalent atmospheric conditions.

Direct sunlight is an elusive, ever–changing source, both in its intensity and directionality. To assess its impact, designers must review illuminance data collected for the geographic locale of the given project site. Reference books offer tabular summaries of data, while online services also offer easily accessible and formatted data for a subscription fee.[6,7] Direct sunlight is best controlled by orientation and architectural devices, such as overhangs, awnings, light shelves, interior and exterior louvers and baffles, and solar shades. Depending on time of day, time of year, and geographic location,

6.5 Daylighting

solar azimuth

Viewing a site plan view of the building in question in the northern hemisphere, solar azimuth is the angle between due south and the horizontal position of the sun (if the sun is aligned with due south, the solar azimuth is 0°). See diagram below.

::::::::::::::::::

solar altitude

Viewing a section of the building in question, solar altitude is the angle between the ground plane and the vertical position of the sun. See diagram below.

::::::::::::::::::

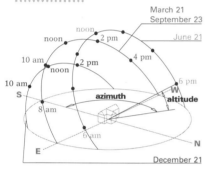

summer solstice

The date when the earth's North Pole is most steeply inclined toward the sun (for the northern hemisphere), resulting in the most intense sunlight exposure and the longest period of daylight in a day (typically occurs June 21).

::::::::::::::::::

winter solstice

The date when the earth's South Pole is most steeply inclined toward the sun (for the northern hemisphere), resulting in the least intense sunlight exposure and the shortest period of daylight in a day (typically occurs December 21).

::::::::::::::::::

Image ©EyeWire, Inc.

direct sunlight can generate 10,000 fc (100,000 lx) on horizontal surfaces (like skylights), and 3000 fc (50,000 lx) on vertical surfaces (like windows).

Skylight is more consistent than direct sunlight, although it, too, is variable to some extent in intensity and color. Skylight must be assessed in two situations—clear and cloudy. Skylight is essentially a large, diffuse, area source, offering a general distribution of daylight. Skylight is best controlled by glass transmission, frit pattern glass, and image–preserving shades. Depending on time of day, time of year, geographic location, and extent of cloud cover, skylight can generate 2000 fc (20,000 lx) on horizontal surfaces, and 1000 fc (10,000 lx) on vertical surfaces.

Reflected light is more consistent than direct sunlight and is less significant than direct sunlight or skylight. Unless specular reflecting surfaces are involved (e.g., large bodies of water or large expanses of neighboring glass buildings), reflected light is typically addressed in the same manner as skylight. Several hundred footcandles (perhaps 5000 lx) might reflect from the ground or nearby building surfaces.

Calculational methods abound for daylighting analyses (see the general references in Section 6.6). The designer must consider each elevation separately since orientation and sun position greatly affect daylight availability. Daylight data for at least three days of the year should be reviewed (the **summer** and the **winter soltice**s and the **vernal** or the **autumnal** equinox), and then for at least three times of each of the analyzed days (perhaps 9 am, noon, and 3 pm **solar time**), and each of these times for various sky conditions (typically clear, partly cloudy, and cloudy) in order to get a reasonable view of the likely highs and lows of daylight availability and their respective degrees of severity. This yields a minimum of 108 analyses— more if a review of various fenestration layouts and sizes and/or architectural elements (overhangs, louvers, etc.) are to be assessed. As such, these analyses are best done with the aid of a computer. Many of the commercially available lighting programs offer daylighting analyses. Here, the designer needs to input the lattitude and longitude of the building, as well as the design parameters of the building (e.g.,dimensions, geometry, fenestration, and surface reflectances).

more online @
http://www.glyphweb.com/esky/concepts/default.htm

6.5 Daylight and electric light integration

Daylighting is not an energy efficient nor a sustainable practice if electric lighting has not been scaled back (in terms of illuminances and luminances and, therefore, in terms of luminaires and lamps required, and/or automated controls have not been introduced. So the development of an electric lighting solution that works with the daylighting is paramount to an efficient and sustainable project. Automated controls are crucial to the success of daylight and electric light integration on a large project. Here, as daylight becomes available, electric light should be dimmed (preferably) or switched to lower levels, while luminance balances are maintained. This typically results in the use of a photocell or photocells, depending on the fenestration orientations, configuration(s) of interior space(s), and zoning of the electric lighting. Astronomical timeclocks may be desirable to offer time–of–day control beyond that offered by photocells, such as lunch hour or morning or after-noon breaks, or simply to offer a change in light quality and/or quantity over time. Dimming of lights seems least annoying to occupants, particularly if

Daylighting

©Robert Eovaldi

©Robert Eovaldi

Figure 6.9 (above left) and Figure 6.10 (above right)

Although the east facing exterior window wall is composed of low transmittance bronze glass (about 8% transmission, identified as ❶), morning sun and sky luminances create direct glare and undesirable silhouetting effects—the folks seated along the east side of the table are in silhouette as viewed by the folks seated along the west side of the table. Glare, silhouetting, and veiling reflections are mitigated with the introduction of a low transmittance (about 5% transmission) motorized MechoShade® system. The fabric of the MechoShade® is medium gray to limit the strong diffusion of lighter fabrics that would preclude a view to the exterior. Note the preservation of the exterior view and the reduction of veiling reflections on the table top.

electric lights are never fully extinguished, which itself can cause angst among users. Stepped switching of lights is more noticeable than dimming, but is also much less costly. The advent of addressable ballasts may offer some increased localized control advantages and some rearrangement advantages. In any event, all of this automation offers another layer of complexity to the system installation, commissioning, and maintenance.

6.6 Endnotes

[1] Heschong Mahone Group, *Daylighting in Schools: An Investigation into the Relationship Between Daylight and Human Performance* (San Francisco, CA: Pacific Gas and Electric Company, 1999).

[2] Dr. Damien Downing, The Daylight Robbery, http://www.ddowning.demon.co.uk/daylight/05.html [Accessed November 26, 2000.]

[3] World Health Organization/INTERSUN, Protection Against Exposure to Ultraviolet Radiation, http://www.who.int/peh-uv/publications/english/who-ehg-95-17.htm [Accessed November 26, 2000.]

[4] Steven A. Zilber, Review of Health Effects of Indoor Lighting, Architronic, http://architronic.saed.kent.edu/v2n3/v2n3.06.html [Accessed November 26, 2000.]

[5] M. Moeck, On Daylight Quality and Quantity and Its Application to Advanced Daylight Systems, *Journal of the Illuminating Engineering Society*, Winter 1998, (IESNA JIES, 1998), pp. 3–21.

[6] Claude L. Robbins, *Daylighting Design & Analysis* (New York: Van Nostrand Reinhold Company, 1986), pp. 332–681.

[7] Meteotest, Meteonorm, http://www.meteonorm.com/ [Accessed January 28, 2001.]

6.7 General References

Daylighting Committee. 1999. *Recommended Practice of Daylighting*. New York: Illuminating Engineering Society of North America.

Lam, William M. C. 1986. *Sunlighting as Formgiver for Architecture*. New York: Van Nostrand Reinhold Company.

Rea, Mark S., ed. 2000. *The IESNA Lighting Handbook: Reference & Application, Ninth Edition*. New York: Illuminating Engineering Society of North America.

Rea, Mark S., ed. 1993. *The IESNA Lighting Handbook: Reference & Application, Eighth Edition*. New York: Illuminating Engineering Society of North America.

Robbins, Claude L. 1986. *Daylighting Design & Analysis*. New York: Van Nostrand Reinhold Company.

vernal equinox

The date in the spring for the northern hemisphere when the earth's poles are at right angles to the sun, resulting in moderate sunlight exposure and in equal periods of daylight and nighttime in a day (typically occurs March 21). Equinox is Latin for equal night.

autumnal equinox

The date in the fall for the northern hemisphere when the earth's poles are at right angles to the sun, resulting in moderate sunlight exposure and in equal periods of daylight and nighttime in a day (typically occurs September 23).

solar time

Time that is defined based on the sun's position. Equal to standard time.

Image ©EyeWire, Inc.

Lamps

Defined as an industry standard to mean that point in time at which half of the lamps in a large group will have failed. Important note—rated life is not the point in time at which all lamps will have failed.

A long with daylighting, electric lighting equipment, whether standard or custom, is the crux of the design development stage. Lamps, luminaires, and light distribution devices are all included as equipment that comprises the lighting system. This chapter provides a review of many of the light sources that should be considered during design development. Lamps are the ultimate source of electric light. We might shade them, reflect them, refract them, louver them, dim them, or bare them, but these devices that produce visible electromagnetic radiation are called lamps. As a population, we have grown to prefer some lamps more than others. As technology moves forward, our common impressions of lamps become outdated. This chapter will discuss lamps as the technologies exist today. However, energy, sustainability, maintenance, and life–cycle issues, and a corporate desire to "hit a home run" with any product, including lamps, will continue to pressure lamp development. While many of the design principles and procedures outlined in this text are relatively unchanging, lamp and luminaire technologies evolve rather rapidly. Hence, what follows is a general review based on today's marketplace. Continuing education on lamps is a must.

7.1 Lamp families

There are five general families of electric lamps: incandescent, cold cathode, fluorescent, high intensity discharge (HID), and electrodeless. These lamp families provide the palette from which most lighting designers choose lamps. Incandescent and cold cathode lamps are used sparingly as decorative and accent sources for commercial and hospitality facilities. Incandescent lamps are used considerably in residential applications. Fluorescent lamps are making significant inroads in residential applications and remain a staple in commercial, hospitality, and healthcare facilities for both general lighting and decorative lighting. Until recently, HID lamps were used nearly exclusively in industrial and exterior applications. However, recent advances in the metal halide sector of HID lamps now means these sources have great potential in commercial, hospitality, and healthcare facilities. Electrodeless lamps are newcomers to architectural lighting. Electrodes are essentially filaments found in other lamp families used to strike an electric arc. These electrodes, however, wear out. Deleting them from lamps means much longer **rated life**. However, at the moment, the electrodeless lamp family covers the extremes in lighting—with very low output lamps and very high output lamps (and nothing in between). The high output electrodeless lamps are categorized as either versions of fluorescent or metal halide lamps. In this text, all electrodeless lamps will simply be categorized as electrodeless.

Certainly, as manufacturers continue lamp development and as designers become increasingly innovative in meeting a host of lighting criteria, we should see broader uses of all lamp types. Fluorescent lamps will continue to make inroads in residential and hospitality applications. HID lamps will gain in popularity in commercial and retail applications, both interior and exterior uses. Electrodeless lamps, as their development progresses, will likely see increased use in all applications. Without major advances in incandescent lamp technologies, applications of this family of sources should continue to shrink. Table 7.1 outlines the general lamp families and their relative respective operating characteristics. Discussions follow on each family.

The following discussions introduce some specific qualities about lamps. As such, there is a distinction that must be emphasized between efficacy (lumens per watt [LPW]) and candlepower (cp). As noted earlier in Chapter 4, Section 4.4.12, candlepower is a much better indication of a lamp's (and also a luminaire's)

7.2 Lamps

effectiveness in directing light to the area where light is desired. So, while LPW is a favorite metric of engineers and lamp manufacturers, it does not tell a complete story. The following example about a water hose might help. Suppose you have a spigot that can supply 30 gallons (114 liters [L]) of water per minute. If you hook a 1" (25 mm) diameter hose to the spigot, water flows out the end of the hose at 30 gallons (114 L) per minute. Now, put a nozzle on the end of the hose. While 30 gallons per minute of water will still flow through the hose, the nozzle concentrates or directs the water—a method more effective for washing objects. Think of "gallons per minute" as the equivalent of "lumens per watt," and think of the nozzle as the equivalent of a reflector and/or lens assembly on a lamp or luminaire. So, don't fall victim selecting lamps based solely on LPW ratings.

more online @

http://www.gelighting.com/na/specoem/index.html
http://www.sylvania.com/welcomej.htm
http://www.lighting.philips.com

7.2 Incandescent lamps

Incandescence is light emission from a heated object. In a traditional incandescent lamp, an electric current passes through a tungsten filament, heating the filament to the point of producing visible radiation. Incandescent lamps are, indeed, better heaters than illuminators. For architectural lighting, halogen and halogen infrared incandescent sources are most efficient. Even these lamps, however, pose a cooling load issue for HVAC systems, and use more energy to produce light than fluorescent or metal halide counterparts. Because most people prefer the color quality of incandescent lamps, all other lamp types are compared to incandescent. Hence, for fluorescent and metal halide lamps to have popular success, they must compare quite favorably with incandescent lamps.

Incandescent lamps remain the most popular lamps in America and in the rest of the world. There are simply too many sockets in place in existing construction (most of it residential) to effect a significant and fast switch to other lamp types. However, in response to energy consumption issues, manufacturers continue to explore and develop new technologies in order to improve incandescent lamps. The latest source development, commercialized by GE, is the halogen infrared technology.

Standard tungsten filaments boil away as the incandescent lamp ages. A typical household table light incandescent lamp is likely to have a blackened zone or area on the bulb envelope when it fails. This is where the evaporated tungsten has settled. During the several hundred hours of its life, a standard tungsten filament incandescent lamp loses light output—the filament boils away, leaving less filament to produce light and blackening the inside bulb wall, thereby reducing the overall transmittance of the lamp bulb. In the 1950s, it was discovered that halides or salts enclosed in a quartz capsule and heated to high temperatures would help capture the evaporating tungsten and redeposit it back onto the filament. Sort of a self–perpetuating filament! The halogen cycle permitted lamp manufacturers to offer lamps that are more efficient, are longer–lived, and have better **lumen maintenance** than standard tungsten counterparts. These early lamps were called quartz halogen—quartz being the only substance at the time that could withstand the very high temperatures. Many capsules today use ceramics.

In the 1980s, GE introduced a coating that could be applied to the halogen capsule that would take some of the heat (infrared radiation) generated by the tungsten filament and redirect this heat back onto the filament. More heat on the filament produces more light and permits a reduction in power (watts)

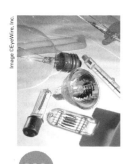

Image ©EyeWire, Inc.

Lamps

required. This, in turn, allows the use of fewer watts of power to achieve the same amount of light! At the moment, halogen infrared (HIR) incandescent lamps are about twice as efficient as standard tungsten filament incandescent lamps. As this HIR technology finds its way into the various lamp shapes, residential lighting and accent lighting in commercial applications will become more efficient.

Other technologies are allowing lamp manufacturers to squeeze more efficiency from halogen and HIR lamps. Osram Sylvania and Philips have pioneered special reflectors for accent lights that capture the light from the halogen and HIR capsules and redirect it more efficiently than has been possible or practical in the recent past. Table 7.2 outlines the more common halogen **mains voltage** lamps. Table 7.3 outlines the halogen infrared mains voltage lamps that are increasingly the lamps of choice for architectural applications where an incandescent quality is a necessity, but some measure of efficiency and better lamp life are also desired.

Finally, for most efficient accent lighting, smallest filaments are best. **Low voltage** (typically 12V) lamps permit filaments to be quite small—as close to a theoretical point source as is practical—and, therefore, allow for optically precise reflectors to be developed around them. Recent advances in low voltage halogen infrared lamps result in relatively long life (4000 and 5000 hours), very precisely controlled accent lights. Table 7.4 outlines the more common halogen low voltage lamps, and Table 7.5 outlines the halogen infrared low voltage lamps.

The halogen and HIR technologies are possible only because of extremely high operating temperatures near the filament. These lamps need to be used with great care. They should be used only in luminaires that are UL listed for operation of such a lamp; should be kept sufficient distances from flammable materials; should never be touched when in operation or soon after extinguishing; should never be in close proximity to human skin; should be enclosed in a protected outer bulb envelope or shielded with a tempered glass lens; and should not be used in portable lights that are easily tipped or are used without adult supervision.

Dimming of halogen and HIR lamps is very easy and costs little. Dimming has the advantage of increasing lamp life by as much as 400 percent. However, since the halogen cycle works only under high temperature conditions and since dimming reduces filament temperature, extensive dimming (to less than 90 percent of full output) for extended periods (more than 100 hours) will actually reduce lamp life. Therefore, periodically (perhaps once a month), halogen and HIR lamps that are consistently dimmed should be operated at full output for an hour or so. Dimming also affects light output (lumens) and wattage (power) consumption. Figure 7.1 offers several graphs showing the relationship of these various parameters as incandescent lamps are dimmed.

7.2.1 TB bulb shape/mains voltage

This is the modern–day equivalent to the A bulb shape (A stood for arbitrary shape—the soft curvilinear bulb profile shown below the TB shape in the upper left margin on page 116). As noted previously, halogen capsules require some sort of protective shielding in the off–chance the capsule should experience a nonpassive failure—in other words, explode. While not a common occurrence, if/ when a halogen capsule explodes (perhaps by coming in contact with moisture), the hot shards of glass and filament can cause a fire unless contained—hence, the protective shield, which is typically tempered glass. To develop a halogen

lumen maintenance

Referring to a lamp's ability to maintain light output over life. As all lamps age, they produce incrementally less light. Some lamps have better **lamp lumen depreciation (LLD)** than others.

lamp lumen depreciation (LLD)

A percentage value (less than 100%) indicating the total light output available from a given lamp at a certain time in its life. For example, a halogen lamp that has a rated life of 2000 hours will have 100% (1.00) of its rated light output at the start of its operation (or life). At 1400 hours of operation, enough filament will have burned away that the lamp produces 95% (0.95) of its initial rated output. At the end of rated life (2000 hours), the halogen lamp will produce 92% (0.92) of its initial rated output. In this text, LLD is reported at 70% of life.

mains voltage

Referring to the primary or main operating voltage of a typical electrical system. Typically, 120V or 277V in America, 230V in much of Europe, and 347V in Canada.

low voltage

Referring to the secondary operating voltage of some lamp types. Typically, 12V or 24V operation as opposed to the mains voltage of 120V or 277V in America, 230V in much of Europe, and 347V in Canada.

7.2.1 Lamps

Table 7.1 General Lamp Families and Respective Characteristics

	Incandescent[a]	Cold Cathode	Fluorescent[b]
Advantages	• Low initial cost • No auxiliary equipment • Withstand wide temperature range • Easily dimmed • Excellent optical control • Excellent color rendering • Preferred color temperature • Soft/diffuse to sharp/focused • Instant on to full output	• Fair efficiency • Small size • Custom formed to any shape • Many colors (saturated to pale) • Easily dimmed • Low glare potential • Very long life • Instant on to at least 50% output	• Good to excellent efficiency • Very long life • Low heat output • Good to excellent color rendering • Large area lighting • Soft/diffuse • Instant on to at least 50% output
Disadvantages	• Poor efficiency • Short life • High heat output • Easy failure due to physical shock • High operating costs • Frequent throwaways (landfill volume) • High glare potential • Transformers required for low volt lamps	• Large, noisy transformers required • Relatively high initial cost • Inconsistent quality (locally made) • High voltage cabling issues • Group relamping a necessity for color	• Ballasts required • Relatively high initial cost • Very temperature sensitive for full output • Expensive/problematic to dim • Confusing socket/ballast varieties • Inconsistent selection on low wattages
Color	• Highly preferred • Renders reds, yellows, and oranges well • 90 to 100 CRI • Warm tone (2500 to 3100°K)	• Variety of whites available • Variety of colors available • 0 to 100 CRI • Cool tone available (3500 to 5000°K) • Warm tone available (2500 to 3100°K) • Very cool tone available (6500 to 8500°K)	• Variety of whites available • Variety of colors available • 70 to 90 CRI • Cool tone available (3500 to 5000°K) • Warm tone available (2500 to 3100°K)
Applications	• Auditoriums • Ballrooms • Casino gaming • Church naves • Dance clubs • Galleries • Hair styling studios • Historical settings • Merchandising • Residential interior/exterior areas • Security lighting (motion sensed only) • Workbenches	• Atriums • Auditoriums • Ballrooms • Casino gaming • Dance clubs • Façades • Lobbies • Merchandising • Signage	• Art studios • Atriums • Auditoriums • Ballrooms • Basketball gyms • Casino gaming • Church naves • Concourses • Dance clubs • Façades • Filing rooms • Hair styling studios • Healthcare spaces • Historical settings • Industrial plants • Laboratories • Libraries • Machine rooms • Merchandising • Pedestrian paths/sidewalks • Residential areas • Videoconferencing • Workbenches

[a] Discussion based on halogen and halogen infrared incandescent lamps, and excluding standard tungsten filament incandescent lamps.
[b] Discussion based on triphosphor fluorescent lamps.

Lamps

	HID/Metal Halide[c]	HID/High Pressure Sodium	Electrodeless
Advantages	• Good to excellent efficiency • Moderate life • Good to excellent color rendering • Good to excellent optical control • Good to excellent color rendering • Sharp/focused	• Very long life • Good to excellent optical control • Sharp/focused	• Good to excellent efficiency • Extremely long life • Diffuse • Good to excellent color rendering • Low wattages very decorative/colorful
Disadvantages	• Ballasts required • High initial cost • Extremely expensive/problematic to dim • Inconsistent selection on low wattages	• Monochromatic (yellow) color of light • Relatively high initial cost • Useless for low–light applications • Useless where color perception desired • Disliked by people for most applications	• Transformers for low wattage lamps • Ballast/control gear for high wattage lamps • No moderate wattages • Limited application • No warm tone versions available
Color	• Variety of whites available • 70 to 90 CRI • Cool tone available (4100°K) • Warm tone available (3000°K)	• Yellow–orange • 20 CRI • 2100°K	**Low wattage lamps** Variety of white available Variety of saturated colors available **High wattage lamps** • 80 CRI • 3500°K
Applications	• Art studios • Atriums • Basketball gyms • Casino gaming[d] • Church naves[d] • Concourses • Façades • Galleries • Hair styling studios • Healthcare spaces • Historical settings[d] • Industrial plants • Laboratories • Libraries • Machine rooms • Merchandising • Parking lots • Pedestrian paths/sidewalks • Roadways • Videoconferencing[d] • Workbenches	• Storage facilities (low activity)	**Low wattage lamps (1 to 10 watts)** • Auditoriums (steplights) • Ballrooms (purely decorative) • Casino gaming (purely decorative) • Dance clubs (purely decorative) • Lounges (purely decorative) • Merchandising (purely decorative) • Residential areas (steplights) **High wattage lamps (80 to 150 watts)** • Atriums • Basketball gyms • Concourses • Façades • Industrial plants • Machine rooms • Parking lots • Pedestrian paths/sidewalks • Streets

[c] Discussion based on ceramic metal halide lamps.
[d] These lamps are not dimmable and not instant–on and, therefore, cannot be used in dimmable, quick on–off situations.

7.2.2 Lamps

A bulb, manufacturers had to come up with a thick glass bulb envelope. The first of these, by GE, was also covered in Teflon® hence, a Teflon® bulb, or TB lamp. Since the glass is cast (for tempering) and not blown, the bulb has a more angular shape than the traditional A bulb. These lamps are frosted or diffuse–coated to provide a general purpose lamp. Lamps are available in the "19" size (TB/H/19) only. As with any lamp designation, the numeric value immediately succeeding the bulb shape/type indicates the lamp's diameter in eighths of an inch (see Figure 7.2). This is very important when selecting luminaires. If a wall sconce cutsheet indicates that the sconce can accommodate an A15 lamp, then a TB/H/19 won't fit—the lamp will be ½" too big in diameter. For TB/H/19 lamps to provide any useful downlighting or soft wallwashing to a room, luminaire reflectors need to be specifically designed to accommodate them and best distribute their light optically. Even so, TB/H/19 lamps are best suited for low–level applications, such as residential transition spaces and some ceremonial commercial and hospitality spaces.

7.2.2 PAR bulb shape/mains voltage

PAR is an acronym for parabolic aluminized reflector, which describes the shape and type of the bulb. Made of cast glass and a precisely formed parabolic internal reflector, some varieties of PAR lamps can withstand direct contact with rain and snow, so they have been popular, albeit unsightly, as household security floodlights. Since this application contributes to light trespass and light pollution, such security floodlights should be used in conjunction with motion detectors to limit use. The large lens on a PAR lamp has a partially stippled, mostly stippled, to fully stippled pattern that, in conjunction with the PAR reflector, establishes the intensity and spread of light. PAR lamps are the most versatile of the incandescent lamps. Given their various beam spreads, wattages, and resulting candlepower, these lamps can be used as accents in low, moderate, or high ceiling applications, or can be used for general lighting.

Similar to the TB lamp designation, PAR lamps have a numerical suffix indicating the lamp diameter. However, other alphanumerics are used to distinguish the various versions of PAR lamps from one another. Figure 7.3 illustrates the extent of the lamp designation.[1]

PAR lamps can be used in bare sockets, in luminaires with little or no special reflectors, or in luminaires with reflectors specially designed to accommodate them. The higher wattage halogen infrared versions have efficacies of 21 LPW, and in the relatively large PAR38 reflector, excellent candlepower intensity is possible. For this reason, however, these lamps can be quite glary. Their best use is in deep downlights, deep adjustable accents, accents fitted with louvers, or spreadlens wallwashers.

7.2.3 T bulb shape/mains voltage

The quartz halogen tubular bulb, or T bulb, is so named because the bulb is a linear, cylinder shape. These are commonly known as halogen lamps to the consumer and have been responsible for a number of fires in recent years because of users' carelessness. As discussed previously, table lights or floor lights (many of which use these T lamps) must be fitted with tempered glass shield(s), must be kept from flammable materials, must be very stable in their construction and placement, and must be operated only under adult supervision.

Teflon® is a registered trademark of E. I. duPont de Nemours and Company.

Lamps

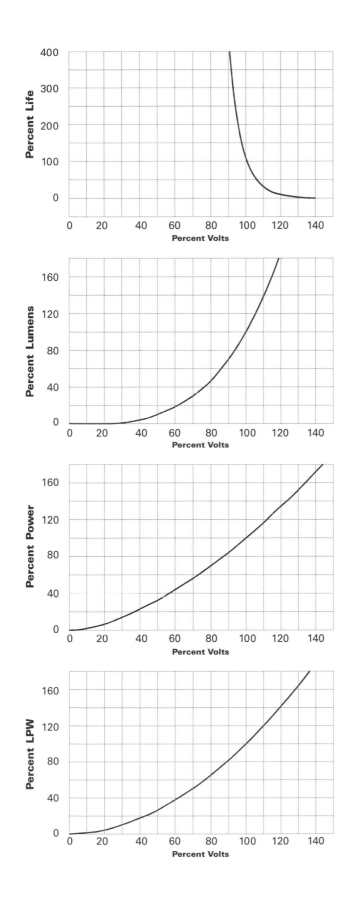

Figure 7.1
Dimming of an incandescent lamp significantly influences lamp life, light output (lumens), wattage (power) used, and efficacy (lumens per watt [LPW]).

Lamp Life Function
Dimming an incandescent lamp significantly increases lamp life. Halogen and HIR lamps, however, do require full run–up periodically in order to maintain the halogen cycle.

Lumen Output Function
Lumen output drops with dimming, but not in a linear fashion as shown here. When dimmed below 20%, little useful light is produced—although the effect can be much like candlelight.

Power Function
Lamp watts decline nearly linearly as volts are reduced.

Lumens per Watt Function
Lamp efficacy is seriously reduced as incandescent lamps are dimmed since light output falls faster than power used.

7.2.3 Lamps

Table 7.2 Common Halogen Mains Voltage Lamps for Architectural Lighting

Halogen Mains Voltage (120V)	Attributes	Luminaires
TB/H	• 14 LPW • Little candlepower punch • 2000 to 3500 hour life • 2800°K • 95% LLD • Medium screw base • Inexpensive • General service lamp	• Downlights • Wallwashers • Sconces • Table lights • Floor lights
PAR20/H	• 11 LPW • Fair candlepower punch • 2000 to 3500 hour life • 2800°K • 95% LLD • Medium screw base • Inexpensive • Accent lamp • NSP, WSP, NFL, and FL[a]	• Downlights • Adjustable accents • In–floor or in–grade uplights • Wallslots
PAR30S/H	• 12 LPW • Fair–to–moderate candlepower punch • 2000 to 3500 hour life • 2800°K • 95% LLD • Medium screw base • Inexpensive • Accent lamp • NSP, NFL, and FL[a]	• Downlights • Wallwashers • Adjustable accents • In–floor or in–grade uplights • Wallslots
PAR30L/H	• 13 LPW • Moderate candlepower punch • 2000 to 3500 hour life • 2800°K • 95% LLD • Medium screw base • Inexpensive • Accent lamp • NSP, SP, NFL, FL, and WFL[a]	• Existing R30/R40 downlights[b] • Existing R30/R40 wallwashers[b] • Existing R30/R40 adjustable accents[b] • Existing R30/R40 in–floor or in–grade uplights[b] • Existing R30/R40 wallslots[b]
PAR38/H	• 16 LPW • Moderate–to–high candlepower punch • 2000 to 4200 hour life • 2900°K • 95% LLD • Medium screw base • Moderately expensive • Accent lamp; pinspot lamp • NSP, SP, VWSP, NFL, FL, WFL, and VWFL[a]	• Downlights • Wallwashers • Adjustable accents • In–floor or in–grade uplights • Wallslots

Lamp art ©GE

[a] Beam spread designations as defined by Gary Steffy Lighting Design Inc. previously for convenient and consistent discussion reference.[1] Base your final specifications on actual lamp designation from respective manufacturers.
[b] R30 and R40 lamps are not sufficiently efficient to be used and essentially have been legislated out of existence. PAR30L (long neck) lamps are made to retrofit existing luminaires that originally used R30 and R40 lamps.

Lamps

Applications	Manufacturers	Illustrative Examples
• Low ceilings • Primary: residential • Secondary: hospitality • Soft general downlighting • Soft general wall lighting • Soft localized/conversational lighting	• GE • Osram Sylvania • Philips	Image ©C.M. Korab
• Low ceilings • Primary: residential, gallery, hospitality • Secondary: commercial, retail • General downlighting • Accent lighting • Specular wall lighting (grazing effect)	• GE • Osram Sylvania • Philips	Image ©Robert Eovaldi
• Low–to–moderate ceilings • Primary: residential, gallery, hospitality • Secondary: commercial, retail • General downlighting • Accent lighting • Feature lighting • Specular wall lighting (grazing effect)	• GE • Osram Sylvania • Philips	• HIR versions used for efficacy and longer life (see Table 7.3)
• Intended as retrofit for older inefficient R30 and R40 luminaires	• GE • Osram Sylvania • Philips	Image ©Balthazar Korab
• Moderate–to–high ceilings • Primary: gallery, hospitality • Secondary: commercial, retail • General downlighting • Accent lighting • Feature lighting • Pinspot lighting • Specular wall lighting (grazing effect)	• GE • Osram Sylvania • Philips	Image ©C.M. Korab

7.2.4 Lamps

Table 7.3 Common Halogen Infrared Mains Voltage Lamps for Architectural Lighting

HIR Mains Voltage (120V)	Attributes	Luminaires
PAR30S/HIR	• 18 LPW • High candlepower punch • 3000 hour life • 2800°K • 95% LLD • Medium screw base • Moderately expensive • Accent lamp; pinspot lamp • NSP, NFL, and FL[a]	• Downlights • Wallwashers • Adjustable accents • In–floor or in–grade uplights • Wallslots
PAR38/HIR	• 21 LPW • High candlepower punch • 3000 hour life • 2900°K • 95% LLD • Medium screw base • Moderately expensive • Accent lamp; pinspot lamp • NSP, SP, NFL, FL, and WFL[a]	• Downlights • Wallwashers • Adjustable accents • In–floor or in–grade uplights • Wallslots

Lamp art ©GE

[a] Beam spread designations as defined by Gary Steffy Lighting Design Inc. previously for convenient and consistent discussion reference.[1] Base your final specifications on actual lamp designation from respective manufacturers.

Lamp art ©GE

T 3 and T4 lamps are quite common and are available in clear or frost versions. The clear versions technically offer the best optics for many luminaires, but frosted versions soften striations and reduce glare. These lamps are particularly well–suited for wallwash and uplighting applications. The tiny, linear source allows for very efficient linear reflector designs to "shovel" the light toward walls or ceilings. Several base options are available—single–ended and double–ended. 120V Single–ended bases are typically either screwbase or direct–contact bayonet (DC bayonet). Figure 7.4 shows some typical T lamps. Accent lights in Figure C4 use T6 lamps.

T lamps are enjoying a rebirth with the infrared coating technology discussed previously. On higher wattage, double–ended lamps, the infrared coating allows about a 30 percent reduction in energy consumption. Efficacies approach 35 LPW. Figure C4 shows uplights using HIR T3 lamps.

7.2.4 Other bulb shapes/mains voltage

There are many other bulb types of mains voltage lamps. However, these are standard tungsten filament lamps, not halogen or halogen infrared lamps. Therefore, because of their great inefficiencies and short life, these lamps are relegated to niche status. Table 7.4 outlines these tungsten filament lamps and their limited applications. The designer is encouraged to consider these lamps only on very few projects and even then only in very limited applications. Several lamp types not listed here are now no longer worthy of the designer's consideration—including BR, ER, and R types. At one time, these lamps served good purpose, but with the advent of current technologies, these lamps are inefficient and short–lived by comparison. As such, existing installations with these kinds of tungsten filament lamps should be considered as retrofit candidates with the newer more efficient halogen and HIR lamps.

Image ©EyeWire, Inc.

Lamps

Applications	Manufacturers	Illustrative Examples
• Low–to–moderate ceilings • Primary: gallery, hospitality, retail • Secondary: commercial • General downlighting • Accent lighting • Feature lighting • Pinspot lighting • Specular wall lighting (grazing effect)	• GE • Osram Sylvania • Philips	Image ©GarySteffyLightingDesign Inc.
• Moderate–to–high ceilings • Primary: gallery, hospitality, retail • Secondary: commercial • General downlighting • Accent lighting • Feature lighting • Pinspot lighting • Specular wall lighting (grazing effect)	• GE • Osram Sylvania • Philips	Image ©C.M. Korab

7.2.5 T bulb shape/low voltage

Low voltage (12V or 24V) allows for a small filament in this tubular lamp, which is available in a bipin base configuration (shown in Figure 7.4). These small lamps allow for excellent optical control. Nevertheless, they are quite hot and require sufficient air circulation. The lower wattage versions are used in con tinuous light cove details (typically uplighting special residential ceilings), steplights, decorative downlights, and decorative pendents. Higher wattage versions are used in small–diameter monopoint, track, or recessed accents, and in recessed downlights and wallwashers.

7.2.6 MR bulb shape/low voltage

MR stands for multifaceted reflector—a highly polished, many–faceted mirror reflector surrounds a small halogen capsule to direct light quite precisely and efficiently. Traditionally, these lamps were used exclusively in slide projectors. As technologies and manufacturing quality control have advanced, these lamps now have sufficiently long lamp life and efficiencies to make them suitable for many architectural lighting applications.

Because of their tiny size yet high light output, these lamps are inherently glary. The best luminaires are relatively deep or offer an optional louver to control glare. Their tiny size, however, makes them very popular for architectural applications. MR11 and MR16 lamps fit into downlights and adjustable accents that are 4″ in diameter (the smallest aperture size permissible in most ceiling types in the United States). Appropriate applications include lighting objets d'art and artwork, as well as merchandise feature accenting, wallwashing, and downlighting.

An auxiliary, protective, tempered glass lens is required in front of the MR lamp. Some versions are available from lamp manufacturers with an integral cover glass.

To limit the amount of heat exiting the front of the lamp, a dichroic coating that selectively transmits infrared radiation (heat) and reflects visible radiation is applied to the reflector on many of the MR lamp types. This makes for a very

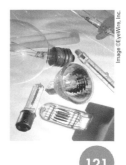

Image ©EyeWire, Inc.

7.2.7 Lamps

First numeric values identify lamp wattage

First letters identify bulb type

Second set of numeric values identify bulb diameter in eighths inches

Letter before first slash identifies neck length[a]

Letter(s) after first slash identifies halogen variety[b]

Letter after second slash identifies beam spread[c]

50PAR30S/H/SP

Figure 7.3

Anatomy of a PAR lamp designation. Check each lamp manufacturer's catalog for respective actual catalog designations and beam spreads.

[a] This letter appears on only PAR30 designations, with "S" indicating short neck and "L" indicating long neck.

[b] This letter(s) indicates halogen (H) or halogen infrared (HIR).

[c] In an effort to codify manufacturers' beam spread designations, it is proposed that:[1]

VNSP = Very Narrow SPot (7° or less beam spread)
NSP = Narrow SPot (8 to 10°)
SP = SPot (11 to 14°)
WSP = Wide SPot (15 to 18°)
VWSP = Very Wide SPot (19 to 23°)
NFL = Narrow FLood (24 to 32°)
FL = FLood (33 to 44°)
WFL = Wide FLood (45 to 55°)
VWFL = Very Wide FLood (56° or greater beam spread)

hot back of lamp and for a very crisp white light exiting the front of the lamp. As such, some residential applications are better served when a straw filter is used (if this is tempered, it can also serve as the required protective lens).

The infrared (IR) technology has also been married with the low voltage halogen technology in MR16/HIR lamps. Here, the IR coating on the halogen capsule is responsible for 25 percent improvement in efficiency—the same amount of light as standard MR16 counterparts at 25 percent fewer watts. With rated life of 4000 hours, these lamps offer a way of introducing some incandescent lighting in commercial and hospitality applications without breaking the power budget while also offering minimally acceptable maintenance cycles.

7.2.7 AR and PAR bulb shape/low voltage

Two other halogen low voltage lamps are worth discussion. AR (aluminum reflector) lamps and PAR (parabolic aluminized reflector) lamps operate much like the MR lamps—taking a small halogen capsule and putting a reflector around it. Here, however, the reflectors are sufficiently large, so that they can

Lamps

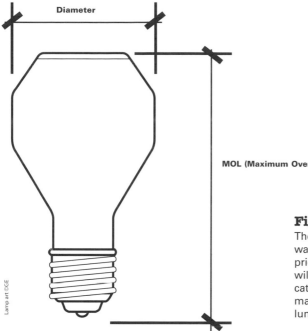

Diameter

MOL (Maximum Overall Length)

Lamp art ©GE

Figure 7.2
The common, critical dimensions of the lamp. Downlights, wallwashers, table lights, and floor lights all need to be checked prior to finalizing a specification to confirm that the desired lamp will fit properly within the luminaire. Each lamp manufacturer issues catalog data citing these common dimensions, and each luminaire manufacturer indicates on cutsheets which lamps fit within the luminaire.

Lamp art ©GE

achieve extremely tight (very narrow spot) pinspots. For high impact focal lighting in residential, retail, and hospitality spaces, where ceilings are relatively high and/or the objects to be highlighted are relatively small, these lamps are useful. One benefit of these lamps over MR lamps is the use of a filament cap. A cap placed over the filament, preventing its direct view, results in much less glare. AR and PAR lamps are so well controlled optically that there is no spill light, yielding very dramatic presentation unless ambient light is provided from other sources.

The AR version requires a tempered glass protective lens, whereas the PAR36 lamp does not. The AR lamp also seems to be a quieter lamp upon dimming. Dimming causes lamp filament hum or singing on many incandescent lamps. For many of the halogen and HIR lamps, however, the bulb envelope is sufficiently thick and the internal halogen capsule offers another acoustic isolation mechanism. For PAR36 lamps, however, likely because of their design originally as automotive lamps, filament hum is significant when dimmed.

7.2.8 Low voltage transformers

The low voltage lamps previously discussed require 5.5, 12, or 24 volts—each family has several varieties. To achieve this, transformers (which transform the mains or high voltage down to the required operating voltage) must be used at the lamp (integral to the luminaire) or remotely. Using a remote transformer eliminates hardware from each luminaire and typically allows the operation of more than one lamp from a single transformer. However, sizing the remote transformer and the wiring from the transformer become critical engineering assignments in order to maintain proper operating voltage at the lamp (remember, under voltage, or dimming, results in significantly longer life but less light, while over voltage results in significantly shorter life). Also, the location of the remote transformer(s) become a critical architectural and engineering issue. Transformers (which could be at least 8 by 8 by 12" (200 by 200 by 300 mm) must be easily accessible, well ventilated, and sound–isolated, and located in a code–compliant space.

Image ©EyeWire, Inc.

Lamps

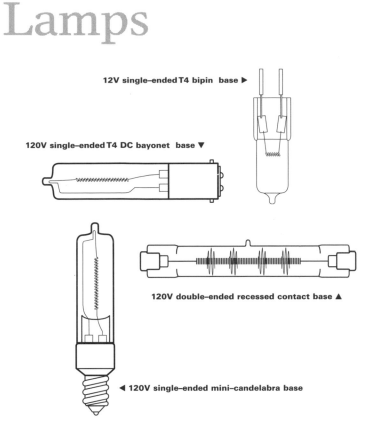

12V single–ended T4 bipin base ▶

120V single–ended T4 DC bayonet base ▼

120V double–ended recessed contact base ▲

◀ 120V single–ended mini–candelabra base

Figure 7.4

Tubular quartz halogen lamps are available in a variety of voltages, configurations, and base types, each serving a specific photometric and functional need. Because of their relatively short life (typically 2000 hours or less), these lamps have relatively limited application in architectural lighting. Many of these lamps have limited, specific orientations that must be followed to obtain rated lamp life and to minimize the hazard of fire. As with all lamps and luminaires, carefully read manufacturers' datasheets for application information.

Transformers that are used adjacent to lamps and are intended to operate just a single lamp usually are available in either an electromagnetic version (the old–style iron core with a continuous coil of wire wound around it) or an electronic version (solid state components). Each type has its benefits. The electromagnetic transformer is bulky and relatively heavy, but is also relatively quiet and easily dimmed. The electronic transformer is smaller and lightweight, but can be noisy when dimmed, and requires a special dimmer.

Low voltage transformers consume some energy just in the transforming process. Typically, this extra load is between 5 and 10 percent of the lamp wattage. This is a particularly important consideration when determining electrical loads for energy code compliance and for cooling loads.

7.3 Cold cathode lamps

Cold cathode lamps are so named because of the use of a filament–like device known as a cathode at each end of the lamp. These cathodes, installed in a tubular glass structure, strike an arc from one end of the tube to the other. Unlike typical fluorescent lamps that always retain a bit of heat at the cathodes (hence, "hot" cathodes) to help strike an instant light with ease, the cathodes in cold cathode lamps are not preheated (which would help start the arc through the tube), but rather are simply energized with very high voltages that drive an arc through the tube. This is an important distinction because cold cathode lamps, thus, require high–voltage transformers that have the potential to be noisy and hot, and require careful wiring/connecting

Lamps

Table 7.4 Niche Application Tungsten Filament Lamps

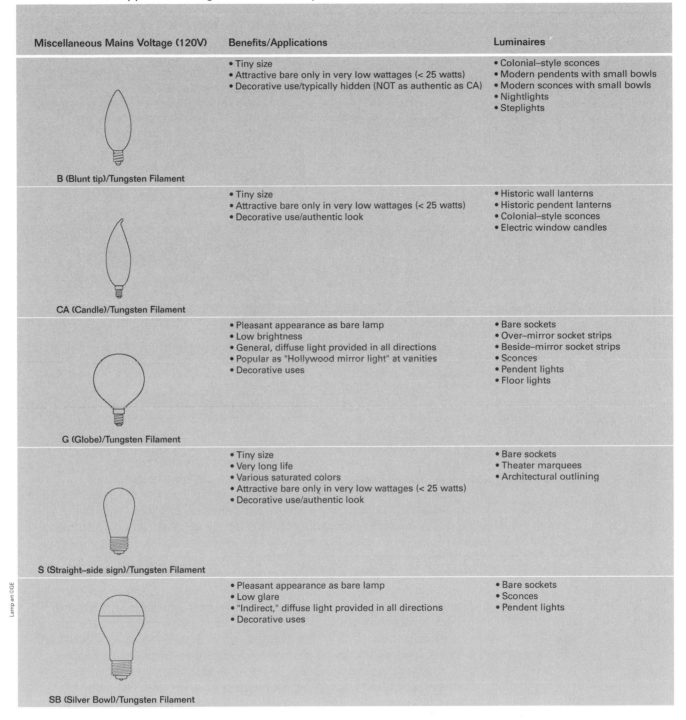

Miscellaneous Mains Voltage (120V)	Benefits/Applications	Luminaires
B (Blunt tip)/Tungsten Filament	• Tiny size • Attractive bare only in very low wattages (< 25 watts) • Decorative use/typically hidden (NOT as authentic as CA)	• Colonial–style sconces • Modern pendents with small bowls • Modern sconces with small bowls • Nightlights • Steplights
CA (Candle)/Tungsten Filament	• Tiny size • Attractive bare only in very low wattages (< 25 watts) • Decorative use/authentic look	• Historic wall lanterns • Historic pendent lanterns • Colonial–style sconces • Electric window candles
G (Globe)/Tungsten Filament	• Pleasant appearance as bare lamp • Low brightness • General, diffuse light provided in all directions • Popular as "Hollywood mirror light" at vanities • Decorative uses	• Bare sockets • Over–mirror socket strips • Beside–mirror socket strips • Sconces • Pendent lights • Floor lights
S (Straight–side sign)/Tungsten Filament	• Tiny size • Very long life • Various saturated colors • Attractive bare only in very low wattages (< 25 watts) • Decorative use/authentic look	• Bare sockets • Theater marquees • Architectural outlining
SB (Silver Bowl)/Tungsten Filament	• Pleasant appearance as bare lamp • Low glare • "Indirect," diffuse light provided in all directions • Decorative uses	• Bare sockets • Sconces • Pendent lights

Lamp art ©GE

by the installer. The reference "cold cathode" is at times used interchangeably with "neon." Technically, however, neon is a type of cold cathode lamp—one filled with neon gas and of small diameter (typically 15 mm). Red light results when the tube is filled with neon. Blue light results when the tube is filled with argon and some mercury. If the glass tube is coated with various phosphors, then other colors of visible light can be generated, including shades of white (from very pink or warm white, to very blue or daylight white).

7.3 Lamps

Figure 7.5
These three ceiling murals are painted on shallow coves that are uplighted by 15 mm cold cathode tubing. Since the diameter of each cove is relatively small, and to maintain a continuous lighted ring, the cold cathode lamp was selected. A high color rendering (85 CRI), 3000°K color temperature lamp was used. The 15 mm tubing allowed for a relatively small cove detail to be developed that is proportionally appropriate for the diameter of each cove. This provides most of the ambient light to the main floor elevator lobby in a hotel resort.

Cold cathode lighting, initially developed as signage lighting in the early 20th century, was a precursor to today's fluorescent lighting. Each installation is essentially custom. Tubing is purchased by a sign or local lamp manufacturer and is then shaped into the various configurations and lengths required for the given project. Tubes are cleaned, vacuum–pumped, and filled with the appropriate mixture of gas and elements for the color specified. Cold cathode lamps typically are three times as efficient as incandescent lamps with life ratings that can be as high as 25,000 hours. However, because these are custom lamps, when one lamp in a long run burns out, it may be necessary to replace all of the lamps. The new lamp will likely have a brighter appearance than and may even exhibit some color shift from the original lamps. If the lamps are exposed or backlighting signage, this brightness and color difference can be readily apparent and distracting. Even in cove lighting applications, this difference may be sufficiently bothersome. Group relamping is typically best. Finally, the custom nature of these lamps makes them somewhat expensive.

Cold cathode tubing diameters range from 12 to 25 mm. The smaller–diameter lamps can be neatly tucked into relatively small architectural coves, niches, and ledges as illustrated in Figures 7.5 and 7.6. Cold cathode was also used in a narrow wallslot detail in Figures 4.12 and 4.20, and in coves in the tiered oculus detail shown in Figure 4.21. Cold cathode lamps have the added benefit of being continuous "lines" of light that can be bent to almost any shape. Because these lamps are handmade to order from stock tubes that are usually 4' (1200 mm) in length, the tubes can be molded end to end to 8 to 12' (2.4 to 3.6 m) runs. Alternatively, special socket configurations called "bend backs" allow for a continuous lighted appearance with short lamp segments.

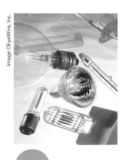

Lamps

©C.M. Korab

Figure 7.6

A cold cathode cove detail was developed using 15 mm copper neon tubing. Since this detail occurs at the intersection of two long corridors, and to help guests in the hotel readily identify such intersections from some distance, the copper color was selected. An added "surprise" as one approaches the intersection is the impact of the MR16 downlight accenting the carpet detail.

The National Electrical Code cites requirements regarding neon tubing. In residential applications, for example, the transformers must be specially sized and relatively low voltage. Check with the registered electrical engineer on the project and with the local building authorities for specific interpretation and guidance.

more online @

```
http://www.egl-neon.com/index.htm
http://www.eurocom-inc.com/color_chart.htm
http://www.nationalcathode.com
```

7.3.1 Cold cathode light output

The light output of cold cathode tubing depends on: the glass tube color, if any (many times the tube is clear); the glass tube phosphor, if any; the tube diameter; the electric current in milliamperes (ma); the gas fill in the tube; and the quality with which the tube is blown, vacuum pumped, filled, and sealed (in other words, the manufacturing quality control). Generally, mercury and argon filled 25 mm tubes with phosphor coating operating at the relatively high current of 120 ma will produce the greatest light output—as much as 500 lumens per linear foot for the various high–color–rendering whites.

Small–diameter tubes (12 to 15 mm) can be very bright—the smaller the tube, the brighter the appearance—to the point of being glary. However, it is the larger diameter tubes (20 and 25 mm) that produce the most light.

Light output is also dependent on the ambient temperature of the environment in which the cold cathode is to operate. Especially sensitive are tubes based on the mercury fill. At cold temperatures, below 50°F (11°C), the output of mercury–based cold cathode lamps is reduced. At freezing temperatures and lower, some mercury–based lamps may not start or may flicker dully. Neon–based lamps are best where temperatures are expected to be low for extended time periods.

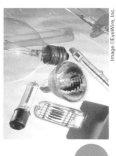

Image ©EyeWire, Inc.

7.3.2

Lamps

dedicated–socket

A reference to a socket and lamp combination that does not permit the interchange of various lamps. For example, a typical screwbase socket in a wall sconce or table light will permit the user to insert any number of lamp types and wattages—these simply screw into the screwbase socket. However, a dedicated socket wall sconce will permit, for instance, the use of only an F26Double/830/4P lamp. A 2–pin lamp won't fit and a different wattage or style (e.g., F26Triple/830/4P) 4–pin lamp won't fit. There are some exceptions, however. Some Triple lamps can operate on the same ballasts—F26Triple and F32Triple are typically interchangeable.

7.3.2 Cold cathode color of light

With the variables of glass tubing color, glass tubing phosphor coatings, and fill gases, cold cathode lamps can produce a rainbow selection of colored light. Saturated (ruby) red, orange, gold, emerald green, and cobalt blue are relatively standard. There are also variations of these saturated colors (intense neon red to bright cherry red, for example). Softer colors include peach, lavender, creamsicle, turquoise, orchid, and the like, are also available (visit http://www.eurocom-inc.com/color_chart.htm for a sample color chart). Variability in color and intensity can be achieved within the same tube. Here, the cold cathode lamp manufacturers can introduce various inert components (bits of glass and sand) and/or mix phosphors along the length of the tube to create randomly varying effects. Some refer to this as crackle neon or lightning neon.

more online @
http://www.signweb.com/neon/cont/crackle000505.html

7.3.3 Cold cathode transformers

Cold cathode lamps require transformers for starting and operation. Because these transformers are relatively high voltage, particularly on the secondary side (the electrical connection between the transformer box and the cold cathode lamps), they must be out of reach of the casual occupant. At the same time, these transformers need to be easily accessible for electrical connections, replacement, or repair.

These high–voltage transformers have a tendency to hum or buzz. For this reason, they should be located in a sound–isolated, code–compliant area. Operation at these high voltages also requires well–ventilated locations. Finally, to minimize magnetic interference, lamp/socket hum, and potential code compliance issues, transformers need to be located as close as practical to the cold cathode lamps.

7.4 Fluorescent lamps

Fluorescence is light emission from an ultraviolet (UV)–radiated material (the phosphor coating—a white, powdery substance—in lamps). When phosphors are radiated or bombarded by UV radiation, they react by emitting visible light. Typically, 20 to 35 percent of the radiation produced is visible, with the remainder being thermal. In a fluorescent lamp, the UV radiation is produced when gas in the tube is electrically charged and a minute amount of mercury is vaporized. Like cold cathode lamps, fluorescent lamps have cathodes that strike an electric arc from one end of the lamp to the other. With fluorescent lamps, these cathodes require preliminary heating to ease the electric arc through the lamp and, therefore, require less voltage "kick" from a transformer or ballast (an energy savings and a safer, more cost–effective method for mass production than the requirements for cold cathode lamps). Thus, fluorescent lamps are also known as hot cathode lamps. Two types of fluorescent lamps in common use today are preheat and rapid start. Lamp families commonly available and deemed most efficient for present–day and immediate–future use are linear and compact. In linear lamps, the most appropriate versions are: T8, T5 (standard and high output [HO]), and T2. In compact lamps, the most appropriate are the **dedicated socket** versions of single–tube, double–tube, and triple–tube. See Table 7.5 for application characteristics of these fluorescent lamps.

Lamps

Fluorescent lamps are much longer–lived than incandescent lamps. Typical rated life ranges from 10,000 to 24,000 hours. Most life ratings are based on 3–hours–per–start. That is, if the lamp is allowed to remain energized for three hours or more every time the switch is turned "on," then the lamps rated life should equal the ratings the manufacturers provide. This is an important aspect of lamps with cathodes. Recall that incandescent lamps produce light by heating a filament to the point of filament glow. In cathode lamps, like cold cathode or fluorescent lamps, the cathodes have to be heated sufficiently to actually cause an arc of electricity to travel the length of the lamp. This significant and sudden voltage surge obviously wreaks havoc on the cathodes, and eventually they fail. Since this voltage surge is only required when the lamp is energized, it is reasonable to presume then that the fewer times the lamp is energized (turned on), the less likely the cathodes are to fail. Indeed, most fluorescent lamp manufacturers admit (and in some instances advertise) that where lamps are used in situations where the on–cycle is 12–hours–per–start, life increases dramatically. Conversely, where lamps are switched off/on quite a bit (and, therefore, the "on" cycle might be limited to half an hour or an hour at a time), lamp life will be reduced significantly—apparently by 50 percent or even more). Another factor affecting lamp life is the ballast type used to start and operate a fluorescent lamp (more on this in 7.4.9 Ballasts).

Fluorescent lamps operate considerably cooler than incandescent lamps. However, the newer, smaller diameter and high wattage fluorescent lamps will exhibit quite a bit of heat at or near the ends (where cathodes are located). The lamps themselves are temperature sensitive. Larger diameter lamps appear to be most affected by ambient temperature. This means that luminaire design and ballast selection are important to the lamps' starting and operating abilities in cold settings. Manufacturers list the minimum starting temperature for each variety of fluorescent lamps. In cold–climate applications, fluorescent ballasts with starting temperatures of 0°F (–18°C) or even lower should be used.

Operating orientation for fluorescent lamps is universal—lamps can be oriented vertically, horizontally, or any position in between without significant adverse effect on color of light or lumen output. However, in the case of the smaller fluorescent lamps, the orientation of the lamp and/or the construction of the luminaire greatly influences how heat is retained or carried away from the lamp—and this factor can influence light output. Further, most fluorescent lamps have an optimum operating temperature (at which point the lamp produces its rated light output) that is different from typical room ambient temperature. So, when lamps are first energized, they are "cool" (at whatever ambient temperature is available in the room or the exterior environment). As the lamps warm, light output increases. If too much heat is retained in the luminaire over a period of time, then light output will, after having risen, actually fall to a point where equilibrium is reached with final operating temperature and final light output. What's this mean for the designer? First, recognize that such light output/temperature relationships exist and ask luminaire and lamp manufacturers about specific situations. A reduction factor may have to be applied to calculations or, alternatively, expect potential complaints if too little or too much light is provided in a given application. Second, recognize that most any fluorescent application will have a time lapse at the first "switch on" after perhaps a 30–minute off period

7.4.1 Lamps

until full light output is achieved. Hence, occupants may enter a space, switch on the lights, and over the first 10 to 20 minutes experience a "warm-up" period where lights transition from perhaps 30 percent output to 100 percent output. Although this is gradual, it may be annoying to users.

7.4.1 T8 fluorescent lamps

The introduction of T8 lamps in the early 1980s initiated a significant trend toward more compact, better color, and more efficient fluorescent lamps. T signifies a tubular lamp, and 8 indicates the lamp's diameter in eighths of an inch (just like incandescent lamp designations). Since these lamps are somewhat small in diameter, they lend themselves to improving luminaire efficiency. Any light source that approximates a line offers a better source around which reflectors can be designed to best distribute light.

Lamp efficacy is a direct result of the triphosphor (rare earth) coatings used inside the tubes. With these phosphors, T8 lamp efficacy is about 90 LPW (without ballast losses). T8 lamps are available in 2', 3', 4', and 5' (600 mm, 900 mm, 1200 mm, and 1500 mm) lengths (with respective wattages of 17, 25, 32, and 40).

There are two color rendering categories of T8 lamps—the 700 series and the 800 series. These designations indicate the color characteristics of triphosphor coatings. The 700–series lamps has a CRI of 75. The 800 series has a CRI of 85—considered deluxe triphosphor (XT) lamps. Lamp manufacturers have established a standard designation within each series that relates to the color temperature of the lamps. A "30" indicates a lamp with 3000°K color temperature. A "35" indicates 3500°K, and a "41" indicates 4100°K. The most efficient, longest–lived, and best color rendering T8 fluorescent lamps are the 800 series. Figure C3 shows use of an F25T8/830 lamp (exterior sconce).

Another important difference between the 700– and 800–series lamps is lamp lumen depreciation (LLD). The 700–series lamps' LLD is 0.87, while the 800 series have an LLD of 0.92. So, to maintain a certain light level over time, fewer 800–series lamps are needed—a more sustainable approach.

Luminaire aesthetics have improved with T8 lamps. The smaller lamp permits luminaire designers the latitude to develop smaller housings without sacrificing luminaire efficiencies. Alternatively, where large housings are acceptable, luminaire efficiencies exceed offerings available with previous fluorescent lamps technologies.

T8 lamps have revolutionized architectural lighting design over the past 18 years. Combined with the compact fluorescent lamps used in wall sconces, downlights, and wallwashers, T8 lamps have allowed designers and, hence, owners, clients, and users, to experience energy–efficient, cost–effective, comfortable, attractive, human–scale lighting approaches.

Continuing technological developments have enabled T8 lamps to dominate the fluorescent lamp market. Long–life versions offer 24,000 hour life. High–performance versions offer 97 LPW efficacies (without ballast losses). Low–mercury versions offer improved sustainability.

7.4.2 T5 standard output fluorescent lamps

These lamps, also known as high efficiency (HE—not to be confused with high output, or HO, versions), are the latest development in tubular, linear fluorescent lamps. At just over ½" (15 mm), these lamps are significantly smaller than their T8 counterparts. Indeed, the circumference of the tube is 40 percent less than that of a T8 tube, thereby significantly reducing the amount of glass, mercury, and rare earth phosphor necessary to make each lamp—more sustainably appropriate than the T8. Further, the T5 much more closely approximates a line source

Lamp art ©GE

Image ©EyeWire, Inc.

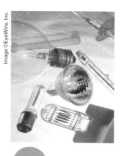

Lamps

Table 7.5 Fluorescent Lamp Types and Typical Applications and Characteristics

Applications	Characteristics[a]	T8[b]	T5[b]	HO[b]	T2[b]	FS[b]	FL/4P[b]	FD/4P[b]	FT/4P[b]
Steplighting	Very low level (<A)					■			
	Low level (A)						■	■	
	Moderate level (A)								■
Direct lighting (ceiling height <12′ (3.6 m))	Low level (A, B)						■	■	
	Moderate level (C, D)	■	■				■		■
	High level (D, E)	■	■	■					■
	Very high level (E, F)	■			■				
Indirect lighting	Low level (A, B)	■	■						
	Moderate level (C, D)	■	■	■			■		
	High level (D, E)	■	■	■			■		
Wallwashing/frontal	Moderate (commercial)	■	■		■		■		■
	High (retail)	■	■	■			■		
Wallwashing/grazing	Low (commercial)	■	■						
	High (commercial, retail)				■		■		
Sconces	Low level (A)					■		■	
	Moderate level (B)					■	■	■	
	High level (C)							■	■
Decorative/functional pendents	Low level (A)					■		■	
	Moderate level (B)						■	■	■
	High level (C, D)						■		■
Portable task lighting	Moderate level (C)					■			
	High level (D)						■	■	
Relative lamp/ballast cost	Lo/Mo/Hi/VHi	Lo	Hi	VHi	VHi	Lo	Mo	Mo	Mo
Relative lamp/ballast efficiency	Lo/Mo/Hi/VHi	Hi	VHi	Hi	Mo	Lo	Mo	Mo	Mo

[a] Letter categories associated with IESNA illuminance categories (see Section 4.6.5).
[b] See discussions of lamps in respective sections of Chapter 7.

than the T8 lamp, thereby improving luminaire efficiencies significantly—again, more sustainably appropriate.

The standard T5 lamp is the most efficacious white light source currently available on a large scale—104 LPW (without ballast losses). This is significant, and is not to be confused with the T5HO lamp that, while certainly producing lots of lumens, has an efficacy of 90 LPW (a result of its much higher wattage relative to the light output). T5 lamps are also the first metric

7.4.3 Lamps

T5 standard lamps...

- Most efficacious (104 LPW)
- Best color rendering (85 CRI)
- Excellent LLD (0.95)
- Small luminaires
- Most sustainable fluorescent
- 20,000 hour life

lamp introduced in the United States. The so–called 4' equivalent lamp, which requires 28 watts of power, is 46" (1163 mm) in overall length. Other lengths are 22", 34", and 58" (560 mm, 864 mm, and 1473 mm) (with respective wattages of 14, 21, and 35 watts).

Operating such small diameter tubing at such high levels of efficiency requires use of the higher quality triphosphors—so T5 lamps are available only in the 800 series. The quality of light, therefore, is excellent from T5 lamps. Its LLD is 0.95 at 70 percent life.

The small size of the T5 lamp has empowered luminaire manufacturers to introduce very small luminaires with excellent efficiencies. This has been particularly dramatic in indirect luminaires. Since the T5 lamp is nearly half the diameter of a T8 lamp—yet the T5 lamp produces nearly as much light as an equivalent length T8—the brightness of the T5 bulb is extremely high. Hence, these lamps work well in indirect applications.

T5 lamps will likely continue the evolution that began with T8 lamps. Indeed, the T5 lamps are nearly a paradigm shift in lighting. The optical characteristics of such a small, 20,000 hour lamp enable task lights under shelves or binder bins to use a single 22" (560 mm) lamp in a 2', 3', or 4' long housing to comfortably light a task area at just 14 watts when combined with low–to–moderate ambient lighting. Lamp and luminaire costs are relatively high, but should drop as use and replacement volume increases.

7.4.3 T5HO fluorescent lamps

T5HO lamps are the high output (HO) version of the T5 standard output lamps. Many times confused as the most efficacious lamps, these lamps offer the most lumens for a given lamp length. These lamps have many of the same characteristics as standard output counterparts, except lumen output and efficacy. HO lamps have efficacies of about 90 LPW and, therefore, are nearly 15 percent less efficacious than the standard output counterparts. Additionally, these high wattage lamps have lumen outputs that make them potentially significant glare sources. Where ceiling heights are sufficiently generous to permit acceptable luminance ratios, these lamps are successful in indirect luminaires. Otherwise, these lamps are not as helpful in meeting project energy goals as are the T5 standard output fluorescent lamps. Further, these lamps are even more costly than their standard T5 counterparts.

7.4.4 T2 fluorescent lamps

The smallest and newest fluorescent lamp commercially available today is this ¼" (6 mm) diameter lamp. Indeed, the ballast gear that powers the lamp is itself larger than the lamp. Available in wattages of 6, 8, 11, and 13 watts, and corresponding lengths of 8½" (218 mm), 12½" (320 mm), 16½" (422 mm), and 20½" (523 mm), these lamps appear well suited for task lighting and architectural detail lighting situations. Lamp life is rated at 10,000 hours, and lamps are available in the 830 color series. This lamp so closely approximates a virtual line source that excellent optical systems could be developed in relatively small luminaires to provide excellent light distributions and efficiencies. Cove luminaires and task luminaires come to mind as those where size and performance are significant positive attributes. Pitfalls include the potential heat of the lamp and the brightness of the lamp. Given the very

Lamps

small diameter tube, cathodes at each end of the lamp are in very close proximity to the glass bulb wall, and, therefore, surface temperatures of the glass bulb can get quite high. So the lamp is hot to the touch and requires sufficient space volume. Another fallout of the tiny bulb diameter is the brightness of the bulb wall. So much light exits from such a small source that a glare problem exists if direct view of the lamp is permitted. Finally, given their relatively new stature and low volume use, these lamps and their respective luminaires are expensive. As experience is gained with the lamp and applications increase, look for cost and availability to improve.

7.4.5 Fluorescent compact single–tube lamps (FSingle)

Lamp art ©GE

Compact fluorescent lamps were first introduced by Philips under the PL brand designation so many folks erroneously refer to the entire family of compact fluorescent lamps as PLs. A generic reference is CFL (compact fluorescent lamp). These original compact fluorescent lamps were so named for their relatively miniature size. Lamps are available in 5, 7, 9, and 13 watt versions (see Figure 7.7) in either electromagnetically ballasted or electronically ballasted versions (see more in 7.4.9). Each manufacturer has, unfortunately, elected to introduce its own "variation on a theme" for designating lamps. Hence, this text uses a generic designation system—review lamp manufacturers' literature for specific catalog designations for the various lamp types.

Similar to T5 lamps, in order to maintain the high efficacy and offer a stable, relatively long life lamp, manufacturers must use the XT or 800 series of phosphors. This has the added benefit of offering the best color rendering available. Depending on manufacturer, the FSingle lamps are available in 2700°K, 3000°K, 3500°K, and 4100°K. Unfortunately, not all colors are available in all wattages and socket types. This leads to a potential hodgepodge when specifying various luminaires or severely restricts the designer's luminaire options. In short, the 2700°K versions, originally thought to be appropriate for residential applications—where fluorescent lamps have yet to make an impact—are much too pinkish for most applications (including residential applications). The 4100°K versions are extremely cool white in appearance—the availability of this lamp is apparently driven by the old school of design where only cool white lamps were readily available and/or where the thinking was that in warm climates the cooler–toned lamps are somehow more appropriate. Of course, these lamps are perceived by most folks as too institutional in appearance, and wash out skin tones and warm tones. Hopefully, manufacturers will consolidate to 3000°K and 3500°K across all wattages and socket/ballast types.

Efficacy for these FSingle lamps ranges between 50 and 60 LPW ((without ballast losses), with higher wattages exhibiting the higher efficacies. However, the rated lamp life of 10,000 hours and the low–brightness, all–around glow available from these lamps make them excellent candidates for steplights, wall sconces, and task lights. These lamps are not useful in downlighting or wallwash lighting applications. Any exterior applications require the use of lamps with minimum starting temperatures of 0°F (–18°C). Further, with these low wattage lamps, consider limiting exterior use to well–protected luminaires very close to or integrated into building architecture.

As noted in Figure 7.7, there are two socket/ballast types for these lamps. The 2–pin base (2P—two metal pins exit the lamp base and make contact with the luminaire socket) operates only on electromagnetic ballasts,

Image ©EyeWire, Inc.

7.4.6 Lamps

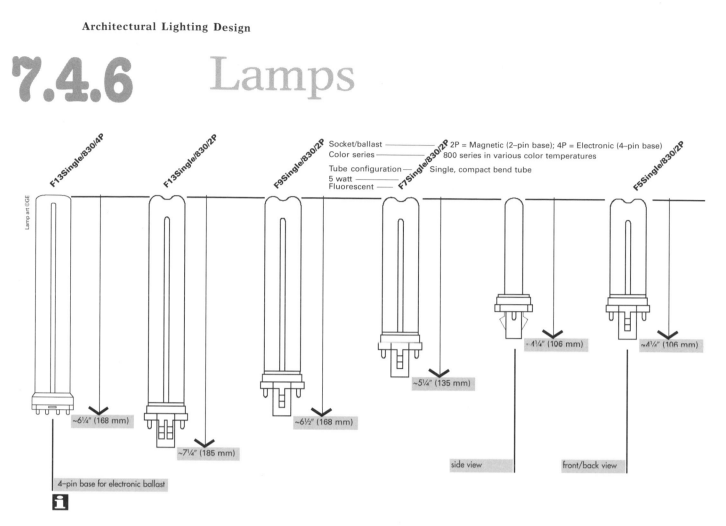

Figure 7.7
This represents the range of typical compact fluorescent single–tube lamps available. Sizes are relatively accurate. Recognize socket differences for electromagnetically ballasted lamps versus electronically ballasted lamps. The lamps are not interchangeable. Specification coordination by the designer with the lamp, luminaire, and ballast manufacturers is necessary to minimize incorrect lamp purchases.

ℹ You are encouraged to use electronic versions. These will likely become the standard shortly—offering better efficiency, no hum, no flicker, and typically better lamp life compared to electromagnetic versions.

resulting in lamp flicker and ballast hum. These effects are quite disturbing, particularly in task lights. The 4–pin base (4P—four metal pins exit the lamp base and make contact with the luminaire socket) operates only on electronic ballasts, resulting in more efficient operation with no flicker and no hum. Wherever possible, consider the 4P versions.

7.4.6 Fluorescent long compact, 4–pin lamps (FLong/4P)

These lamps offer excellent life and performance when the rapid–start, electronically ballasted versions are used. Wattages are 18 and 40 watts. The F18L–version is 10½" (267 mm) in overall length and the F40L is 22½" (572 mm) in length, and each has a rated life of 20,000 hours. These lamps are available in the 830, 835, and 841 color series. Figure 7.8 shows these two lamps. The F18L is typically used in sconces, small linear wallwashers, small square downlights (lamps oriented horizontally), small cove striplights or asymmetric luminaires, and freestanding tasklights. The F40L is typically used in indirect pendent luminaires (linear or large bowl type), and cove striplights or asymmetric luminaires. The F40L is typically too bright for direct lighting applications. These lamps are not suitable for exterior, cold–climate applications. An inherent problem with early compact fluorescent lamps was their tendency to have base meltdowns and/or cracked tubes near the base at the

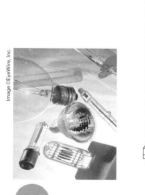

Lamps

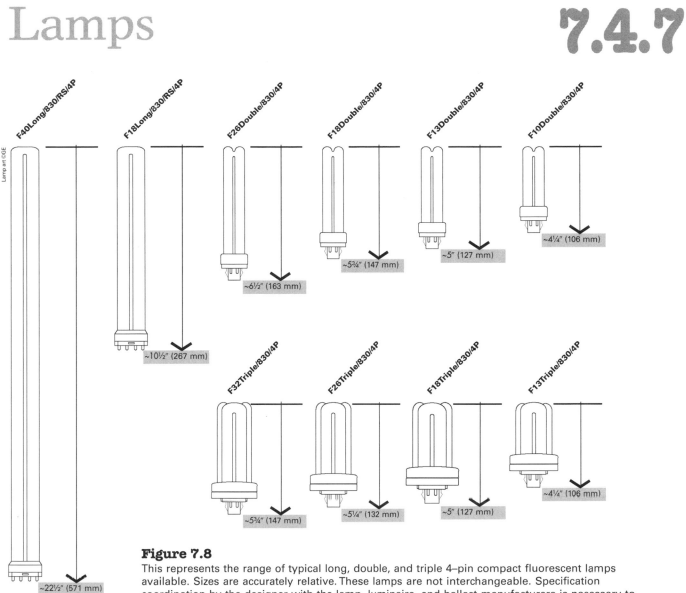

Lamp art ©GE

F40Long/830/RS/4P

~22½" (571 mm)

F18Long/830/RS/4P

~10½" (267 mm)

F26Double/830/4P

~6½" (163 mm)

F18Double/830/4P

~5¾" (147 mm)

F13Double/830/4P

~5" (127 mm)

F10Double/830/4P

~4¼" (106 mm)

F32Triple/830/4P

~5¾" (147 mm)

F26Triple/830/4P

~5¼" (132 mm)

F18Triple/830/4P

~5" (127 mm)

F13Triple/830/4P

~4¼" (106 mm)

Figure 7.8
This represents the range of typical long, double, and triple 4–pin compact fluorescent lamps available. Sizes are accurately relative. These lamps are not interchangeable. Specification coordination by the designer with the lamp, luminaire, and ballast manufacturers is necessary to minimize incorrect lamp purchases.

end of life. There are now two ways to avoid this messy and hazardous situation—by specifying lamps with end–of–life (EOL) detection or specifying ballasts with EOL.

7.4.7 Fluorescent compact double–tube, 4–pin lamps (FDouble/4P)

Manufacturers soon realized that the single–tube and long compact fluorescent lamps could be "folded" lengthwise in half to create a shorter lamp while maintaining the wattage and light output of the longer counterparts. While 2P and 4P versions are available, only the 4P versions offer high quality, flicker–free, no–hum, instant–on (no start-up flutter) light. Figure 7.8 illustrates the 4P series. Typical applications include wall sconces, downlights, wallwashers, and tasklights. However, the lower wattages (F10Double and F13Double) are best in the tasklight situations, otherwise the task area is overlighted and becomes too harsh. On the other hand, the F10Double and F13Double do not produce sufficient output for downlight and wallwash applications.

The double–tube lamps have efficacies of 60 to 65 LPW (without ballast losses) and exhibit the 800 series color characteristics. Rated lamp life is

Lamp art ©GE

Image ©EyeWire, Inc.

7.4.8 Lamps

10,000 hours. Some of these lamps are not suitable for exterior, cold–climate applications. Check each manufacturer's data for starting temperature requirements. As noted in 7.4.6, early compact fluorescent lamps tended to have base meltdowns and/or cracked tubes near the base at the end of life. There are now two ways to avoid this messy and potentially hazardous condition—by specifying lamps with EOL detection or specifying ballasts with EOL.

7.4.8 Fluorescent compact triple–tube, 4–pin lamps (FTriple/4P)

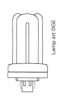

Soon after the double–tube lamps were introduced, manufacturers developed a triple–tube version in response to the need for even smaller, high–lumen light sources for downlight and wallwash applications. These lamps are only available in 4P versions for high quality, flicker–free, no–hum, instant–on (no start-up flutter) light. Figure 7.8 shows the range of wattages and sizes for the FTriple/4P lamps. Figure C1 illustrates an application (the pendent luminaires). Since these lamps are relatively new, applications currently include downlights and wallwashers, as well as in–grade uplights. However, these lamps could also have application in wall sconces and tasklights, although luminaire product development in these areas is required.

Triple–tube lamps have efficacies of 65 to 75 LPW (without ballast losses) and exhibit the 800 series color characteristics. Rated lamp life is 10,000 hours. Some manufacturers' versions are suitable for exterior, cold–climate applications. Check manufacturers' data for starting temperature requirements. Recognize that these lamps have a warm–up time to full on.

The triple–tube lamp marks the future of compact fluorescent lamps—smaller lamps with ever–greater light output while maintaining or reducing wattage requirements.

7.4.9 Fluorescent ballasts

Fluorescent lamps require a voltage surge to energize the lamp and then, once started, need a constant current flow to assure continuous, stable operation. The devices that serve these two functions are known as ballasts. As recently as the 1990s, most ballasts were relatively large, heavy black boxes. Heavy because they were filled with lots of windings of copper wire around an iron block or core. These kinds of ballasts are called electromagnetic and, besides being bulky and heavy, operate fluorescent lamps in such a way that the lamps flicker and the ballasts themselves hum. This is noticeable by some folks and can be quite annoying. More than twenty years ago, electronic ballasts were in initial development and production. The promise of electronics was to operate fluorescent lamps at high frequency (25,000 Hz or greater). Such operation increases lamp/ballast system efficiency by as much as 15 percent, and has the benefits of no audible hum (25,000 Hz is above human hearing) and no flicker. Up until 1995, however, these electronic ballasts were unreliable. Every three or four years from 1980 to 1995, a new electronic ballast model or manufacturer or both was introduced to the marketplace. By 1995, manufacturing processes and electronic technologies were sufficiently refined to permit production of good (not great or excellent) reliability. Since the mid–1990s, electronic ballasts have made significant progress in quality control and in the production chain for luminaire manufacturers. Today, electronic ballasts are commonplace and fairly reliable. When issues arise, the manufacturers typically respond quickly and decisively to correct the problem.

Lamps

Electronic ballasts are quite small today—this has been evolutionary as the electronic components have shrunk. Today, these small ballasts permit the design of smaller luminaire housings. The electronic components also allow ballast manufacturers to change ballast operating characteristics with relative ease or to assign functionality to chips.

Seven specific characteristics must be correctly specified to assure satisfactory operation of the lighting system: lamp starting sequence, end–of–life protection, electromagnetic interference protection, current crest factor, ballast factor, power factor, and total harmonic distortion. The lamp starting sequence is, perhaps, the single most important aspect with regard to maximizing lamp life. The three basic starting sequences are instant start, rapid start, and programmed start. Instant–start operation uses the least amount of energy, but is not well–suited where lamps are switched on/off more than four or five times each day. Rapid start uses a bit more energy than instant start, but is more suitable where lamps are switched on/off frequently throughout the day. Programmed start also uses a bit more energy than instant start, but is quite well suited for frequent on/off switching and is intended to offer the best lamp life.

EOL protection is desirable to avoid any physical meltdown and/or cracking of the fluorescent glass tube when the lamp fails. A ballast with EOL protection senses the lamp failure and disconnects electricity from the lamp until a new lamp is installed.

Electromagnetic interference (EMI) protection helps minimize ballast interference with other electrical devices, such as radios or televisions.

Current crest factor relates to the ratio of the peak electrical current and the operating current requirements of the lamp. The ballast should meet lamp manufacturers' current crest factor specifications. Typically this factor is 1.6 or so, and the ballast should not exceed 1.7.

Ballast factor (BF) expresses the percentage of rated light output to be expected from a lamp when operated on the given ballast. Based on an unfortunate and outdated industry standard, many ballasts operate lamps to only 88 percent output (a BF of 0.88)! Admittedly, lamp wattage is also reduce to 88 percent of full rating, but this certainly seems to deceive the public. Lamps are rated to produce a certain and expected amount of light. Many production ballasts, however, are purposely designed to operate lamps at 88 percent output. This means, of course, that to meet a specific light intensity, 14 percent more lamps, luminaires, and ballasts need to be used than would be required if the BF were 1.0 (100 percent). This is not sustainable practice. Hopefully all ballast manufacturers will expand the range of BFs available to include 1.0 across all ballast lines, voltages, and number of lamps operated.

It should be noted that BFs other than 1.0 are helpful in certain situations. For example, sometimes very low light levels are desired, but to maintain reasonably uniform intensity, luminaires must be spaced on a given pattern. While ballasts are available for many but not all lamp wattages that have BFs of 0.78, 0.88, 0.98, and 1.18, these vary from manufacturer to manufacturer and do not all offer the same starting sequences, EOL protection, and EMI characteristics. Most of the compact fluorescent lamp electronic ballasts are available with BFs of only 1.0.

Power factor relates to a building's wiring system and the electrical load that the ballast appears to place on that wiring. A power factor of 1.0 is best and is referred to as "high" power factor. As the power factor is reduced, a

Image ©EyeWire, Inc.

7.4.10 Lamps

building's wiring systems are increasingly burdened. A sufficient number of low power factor ballasts can actually create an electrical wiring system problem in a building. As such, power factors should be 0.95 to 1.0.

Total harmonic distortion (THD) and third harmonic distortion also relate to a building's electrical power distribution system. The lower a ballast THD, the better. The THD should not exceed 0.20, and third harmonic distortion should not exceed 0.10.

Electronic ballasts are available to dim fluorescent lamps. Dimming, however, remains a somewhat elusive feat. Cost, lamp life, lamp seasoning, and system reliability are unresolved issues. Further, dimming ballasts are not available for all of the more popular lamps and wattages. Finally, integration with dimming systems is not universal—some dimming ballasts require proprietary dimming controls, resulting in serious hardware aesthetic challenges with respect to the non–dim switches throughout a facility. When reviewing dimming ballasts, check low–end dimming ability (preferably down to 1 percent with no flicker), and check lamp/ballast warranty with the respective manufacturers. Dimming of fluorescent lamps will result in some shift in both color temperature and color rendering. When a series of fluorescent lamps must be dimmed, it is advisable that all of the lamps be identical in size, wattage, and color. Otherwise, noticeable and annoying color shifts will occur from lamp to lamp. For example, if a dimmable fluorescent cove is being designed for a conference room, and the cove is 15′ (4.6 m) long, then use five 3′ lamps rather than three 4′ lamps and one 3′ lamp.

Use only ballasts that are UL listed and labeled. Ballasts should be warranted for a minimum of two years and preferably for three or even five years. While the newer electronic ballasts have not been in operation long enough to tell, it is anticipated that ballasts will last twenty years.

Finally, electronic ballasts do offer excellent potential for precise, energy efficient operation of lamps. Computer chip circuitry now allows for addressable ballasts—that can actually be addressed via handheld wireless control devices. Look for continued development of electronic ballasts in the near future that will offer greater functionality (e.g., 2– and 3–level switching, and more reliable and lower cost dimming).

more online @

http://www.advancetransformer.com/products/electronic/electronic.asp
http://www.esavings.com
http://www.magnetek.com/ballast/
http://www.sylvania.com/ballast/prodinfo.htm

7.4.10 Other fluorescent lamps

The previously discussed fluorescent lamps have been in common use for fewer than fifteen years. There are many existing installations where T12 lamps are used. There are even some luminaires sold today that use T12 lamps and switch–start T8 and T5 lamps. These should be avoided. These are typically inefficient and operate on old–style ballasts that create annoying flicker and hum. Over the next ten years, many of these lamps and ballasts will be legislated out of existence given their poor efficiency.

Another group of lamps of passing interest is the retrofit, screwbase fluorescent lamps. These lamps are used in existing screwbase luminaires originally intended for incandescent lamps, but where the efficiency and life of fluorescent lamps are important. However, for optically active luminaires (those with reflectors or lenses), screwbase fluorescent lamps are useless. Very little light will be focused or directed given the relatively large size of the

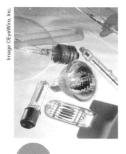
Image ©EyeWire, Inc.

Lamps

fluorescent lamp itself. Indeed, many of these retrofits result in wasting energy—not delivering nearly the light intensity in the right location for the wattage expended and the earth resources required for the glass, phosphor, and mercury components in the lamp. Further, screwbase lamps simply allow the user to exchange the fluorescent lamp for an incandescent alternative at any time, thereby negating the potential energy reduction. This is important when using screwbase fluorescent lamps in wall sconces, for example. In new or renovation construction, the wattage of screwbase fluorescent lamps cannot be counted in the power budgeting. Rather, the rated incandescent wattage of the sconce (or other luminaire in which a screwbase fluorescent lamp will be used) must be used in power budgeting. In other words, use the previously discussed dedicated–socket fluorescent lamps when specifying fluorescent lamps.

7.4.11 Fluorescent lamp/ballast sustainability issues

Fluorescent lamps, in order to operate efficiently, require the use of the heavy element mercury. Mercury is hazardous. Although the doses in fluorescent lamps are quite low, combining lots of these lamps (as might be expected to happen in landfills) is cause for concern. Most lamp manufacturers now offer extremely–low–mercury–content lamps. While recycling is always a preferred method of disposal, this lower dosage of mercury reduces the hazard of disposing great quantities of lamps.

Because sustainability is concerned with minimizing the number of earth resources used to make anything, including lamps and ballasts, then it is likely prudent to use the longest–life systems and the systems with the smallest (in physical size) components. T5 lamps, for instance, use nearly 40 percent less glass and less phosphor than T8 lamps, yet last as long. Programmed–start ballasts are the same size as other electronic ballasts, yet these ballasts promise longer lamp life. So, pulling together lighting systems that use as little in the way of hazardous components as practical but that also promise long life and energy efficient operations is a significant challenge for lighting designers.

7.5 High intensity discharge lamps

High intensity discharge (HID) lamps are so named for their ability to produce significant amounts of light by discharging electricity through a high–pressure vapor. There are three types of HID lamps: mercury vapor, metal halide, and high pressure sodium. These lamps are characterized by their warm–up time, restrike time, and color rendering (or lack thereof). Most HID lamps are not instant–on, requiring up to five minutes for full light output. If there is a power interruption while these lamps are on, they typically must cool down before they will restrike and warm back up to full light output. Therefore, where emergency lighting is required, auxiliary lighting systems are used to provide instant light during and immediately after power outages. This can be achieved with a quartz halogen restrike option—HID luminaires fitted with a quartz halogen lamp that switches on instantly in the event of a power outage, and remains on until the HID lamp is back to reasonable light output.

Like other lamp families, several bulb shapes are available for HID lamps. For most architectural lighting applications, bulb shapes include BD (bulbous dimpled), ED (ellipsoidal dimpled), PAR (identical to incandescent PAR shapes), and T (identical to incandescent T shapes). See Figure 7.9.

7.5.1 Lamps

In general lighting applications, HID lamps are not especially efficient compared to the newest deluxe triphosphor fluorescent lamps, but are more appropriate for most exterior lighting because they are less affected by temperature than fluorescent lamps. Further, HID lamps better approximate point sources and are, therefore, more easily controlled optically—resulting in more efficient luminaires and more carefully controlled nighttime lighting. For accent lighting applications, however, HID lamps in the PAR and T shapes are extremely efficient in providing concentrated lighting—making the newer ceramic metal halide lamps excellent candidates where efficient, long–life, near–incandescent color accent lighting is desired (e.g., retail, commercial accenting, façade accenting, etc.). Rated life for HID lamps ranges from 5000 to 40,000 hours. For lamps most appropriate for architectural applications where people are anticipated to use the areas or spaces, lamp life ranges from 5000 to 15,000 hours.

Like fluorescent lamps, HID lamps are enjoying the benefits of miniaturization and electronics. Luminaire sizes are smaller than ever, and electronic operation yields efficiency gains previously unanticipated. Further, electronic operation is quiet and flicker–free. Ballasts for HID lamps are traditionally huge and heavy, but the recently introduced electronic versions now offer smaller, lighter–weight options (currently only available for certain lamp types and wattages).

HID dimming has been attempted many times since 1990 with marginal success. While it can be done technically, it produces such lousy operating characteristics and has such limited range that the exorbitant costs simply are not worth it, except, perhaps, in sports arenas where dimming range is not critical, color quality during dimming is not an issue, and cost is not an issue. Dimmed HID lamps typically change drastically in color temperature and color rendering (both going "bad"). The range of dimming might be 30 to 100 percent. Cost might be as high as several hundred US dollars per lamp. Further, similar to fluorescent dimming, no comprehensive study has been undertaken to establish the effect of dimming on lamp life.

For architectural lighting applications where people are expected to use the areas or spaces and where any sort of color discrimination is important (even if to help identify vehicles responsible for moving violations or to help identify perpetrators' clothing color and skin tone), only metal halide lamps are recommended, and, therefore, only metal halide lamps are discussed here. Mercury lamps are too inefficient and potentially hazardous. High pressure sodium (HPS) lamps have such poor color rendering (with a CRI of 20) that they are useful only where color discrimination is not important. Further, as noted in 2.3, in exterior nightlighting situations, studies show that the monochromatic nature of HPS is inefficient relative to the fuller color nature of metal halide.

7.5.1 Metal halide lamps

Of the HID family of lamps, metal halide lamps provide the best color temperature and best color rendering. Since 1990, much research and development activity has centered around metal halide lamps. This has resulted in several major advancements: miniaturization, significant color rendering improvement, significant color temperature improvement, color consistency lamp–to–lamp and over life, efficacy improvement, and lamp life improvement. These advancements are the result of a new category of metal halide lamps—ceramic metal halide.

Image ©EyeWire, Inc.

Lamps

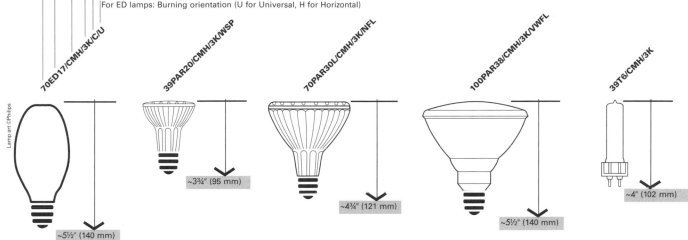

Wattage

Bulb shape (ED for Ellipsoidal Dimpled—there's a dimple on the top of the bulb) and bulb diameter (in eighths inches)

Ceramic Metal Halide

Color series (may be expressed in color temperature or as 800 series)

For ED lamps: Clear bulb for more focused light (blank) or coated bulb (C)
For PAR lamps: Beam spread (VNSP, NSP, SP, WSP, VWSP, NFL, FL, WFL, VWFL)

For ED lamps: Burning orientation (U for Universal, H for Horizontal)

70ED17/CMH/3K/C/U   39PAR20/CMH/3K/WSP   70PAR30L/CMH/3K/NFL   100PAR38/CMH/3K/VWFL   39T6/CMH/3K

Lamp art ©Philips

~5½" (140 mm)   ~3¾" (95 mm)   ~4¾" (121 mm)   ~5½" (140 mm)   ~4" (102 mm)

Figure 7.9

This represents the range of typical ceramic metal halide lamps available. Sizes are accurately relative. These lamps are not interchangeable. Specification coordination by the designer with the lamp, luminaire, and ballast manufacturers is necessary to minimize incorrect lamp purchases.

As Figure 7.9 illustrates, the PAR20, PAR30L, and T6 lamps are quite small. These make excellent choices where throws of light are relatively long, where efficiency is important, and where long lamp life is desired. The T6 lamps offer new opportunities for architectural lighting equipment manufacturers. Look for smaller, well–controlled (optically) downlights, accents, wallwashers, monopoints, and trackheads that take advantage of the T6 size, efficacy, and life.

Color rendering of ceramic metal halide rivals that of deluxe triphosphor fluorescent—ranging from 82 CRI to 93 CRI. Available color temperatures are 3000°K and 4100°K. The 3000°K lamps have a halogen color quality.

Color consistency has traditionally been a problem with metal halide lamps. Apparently, the doses of halide could not be sufficiently controlled to such minute degrees to minimize color shifting from lamp to lamp. Further, construction of the arc tubes could not be sufficiently controlled to prevent some eventual loss of halides during operational life, resulting in some color shift over time. Both problems have been addressed with ceramic metal halide.

Although ceramic metal halides are the promise of the present and future in HID lighting, some operational issues remain. These lamps, to date, are not available in instant–on versions. As with all metal halide lamps, there is potential for nonpassive failure (a kind reference to the lamp failing violently—exploding). Hence, some versions (some varieties of the ED lamps and all T6 lamps) of these lamps need to be used in enclosed luminaires (check with lamp and luminaire manufacturers before finalizing specifications on the lamp and luminaire combination). Another issue is that of LLD.

Image ©EyeWire, Inc.

7.6

Lamps

Historically, metal halide lamps have exhibited LLD as much as 50 percent over life. The ceramic metal halide lamps are better, exhibiting LLDs of about 35 percent over life. Nevertheless, this reduction needs to be accounted in the designer's calculations and might also suggest that group relamping is appropriate prior to end of rated life.

Efficacies range from 83 to 93 LPW (without ballast losses). This puts ceramic metal halide in the same category as some of the higher wattage compact fluorescent lamps and the T8 lamps.

Lamp life varies widely for ceramic metal halide lamps. First, the newer, smaller lamps have had little actual installation history. Hence, manufacturers must rate life based on what little experience exists in laboratory testing. Rated life ranges from 5000 to 15,000 hours depending on lamp type and wattage. Look for continued improvement in lamp life ratings over the next 10 year period.

Figures C1 and C3 illustrate use of ceramic metal halide PAR38 lamps. These lamps provide an incandescent quality of light to these building façades and details.

7.6 Electrodeless lamps

These lamps are the newest family in architectural lighting. Without electrodes or cathodes, there is no "weak link" to fail. These lamps typically have rated life in the range of 100,000 hours, which was heretofore unheard. For purposes of this text, there are two categories of electrodeless lamps—light emitting diode lamps (LEDs) and induction lamps.

LEDs are, at this publication date, very decorative in nature. Although they are long–life lamps, they are also typically very low in light output. This does mean, however, that they use very little power. LEDs are available in a cool white color, amber, green, red, and blue. These lamps are very tiny (perhaps $1/8$" across [3 mm]), and, therefore, each color of LED can be put into a larger bulb envelope to produce a wide range of colored light providing an electronic control device is added to the system (or by using dip switches located on the bulb envelope in some instances). Applications might include conversation pieces (something to encourage conversation, but not to provide sufficient light for conversation), decorative table lights, subtle wall accents (or dramatic accents if the wall is light in value and the surrounding environment is unlighted), steplights, and indicator or marker uplights in pavement or floors. Look for this technology to develop further and to have more significant architectural lighting influence.

Induction lamps operate on the principle of generating visible radiation by inducing high magnetic currents in order to generate atomic–level activity within the bulb. Philips and Osram Sylvania have production lamps available in relatively high wattages. Specific operating conditions are required for various wattage and lamp types. While the lighting equipment is relatively expensive, it does have rated life of 100,000 hours (about four times greater than the best T8 fluorescent lamp). Lamps are available in 3000°K, 3500°K, and 4100°K versions and offer a CRI of 80. This is an emerging technology. At the moment, Osram Sylvania classifies its induction lamp as fluorescent, while Philips classifies the lamp as HID. Experience with the induction process in various application settings will likely lead to improved guidance on system application recommendations. Frequently check with lamp manufacturers for updates.

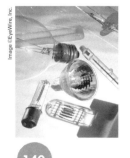

Lamps

7.8

more online @

http://www.colorkinetics.com/
http://www.lighting.philips.com/nam/prodinfo/hid/p5456.shtml
http://www.sylvania.com/prodinfo/business/fluorescent/icetron.htm

7.7 Mixing lamps on a project

On any given project, it is highly unlikely that a single lamp from one lamp family will meet all of the lighting criteria for all of the situations encountered. This has always meant that lamps must be mixed and matched on projects. Traditionally, this has been difficult. However, with the latest advances in deluxe triphosphor fluorescent lamps and in ceramic metal halide, these lamps can usually be mixed on projects with a good degree of success (see Figure C1). Further, these lamps can usually be mixed with halogen and HIR lamps. When mixing lamps on a project, it is preferable to maintain consistency with luminaire types at least in each space, if not across the entire project. Additionally, within the same space, mix lamps only if there are distinct functional differences between the various lights. Consider, for example, a building lobby. One wall is programmed to have many pieces of art on it, and it has been determined that wallwashing will permit most any size art to be positioned most anywhere (this also allows for future flexibility as the art changes). An opposite wall is to be fitted with the corporate logo that, based on its design, should be accented with pinspots. The wallwashing can be achieved with spreadlens wallwashers. Three varieties of wallwashers come to mind—halogen, compact fluorescent, and ceramic metal halide. Two varieties of adjustable spot accents come to mind—halogen and ceramic metal halide. To avoid the subtle but visible differences among these various sources, consider using the same lamp family for both the wallwashing and the logo accenting. Downlights, if used, could then be a different lamp type (e.g., compact fluorescent downlights). In any event, for a consistent appearance across the space in terms of color temperature and color rendering, it is suggested that all lamp color temperatures match (within 200°K) and that all lamp CRIs match (within 5 CRI points). Where distinct visual attention is required, a distinct change in color temperature may suffice.

Of course, to minimize maintenance lamp stocking requirements and to minimize confusion on relamping, it is desirable to minimize the variety of lamp types and wattages. Nevertheless, programming criteria established previously for the users of the space(s) should not be compromised just to make maintenance extremely simple. Maintenance staff should be NCQLP–certified (LC) in order to maintain an efficient yet program–compliant installation.

7.8 Lamp caveats

There are plenty of caveats on lamps, their limitations, intended uses, and operating characteristics. A specification cannot be written based solely on the material in this textbook. Determining the actual performance of any given manufacturer's product and establishing final specifications require review of manufacturers' literature on all products, including lamps. For lamps, some of the more common caveats include: base orientation or burning position; protection from moisture; temperature sensitivity; immediately replacing lamps with broken filaments, bulb walls, or bases; avoiding lamp shock while the lamp is operating; never changing lamps when the circuit is energized (all switches and circuit breakers controlling the lamp[s] being changed must be in the "off" position; high lamp operating tempera-

7.9 Lamps

tures and risk of burn or fire; using lamps only in luminaires with UL listings and labels indicating luminaire capacity to accommodate said lamps. Carefully read luminaire cutsheet data and lamp data, including any footnotes.

Beware of claims that sound too good or on which there is no bona fide scientific research. Long–life and super–long–life lamps, while no doubt lasting many thousands of hours, do so at the sacrifice of efficiency—and in a big way. These lamps are typically half as efficient as their "standard–life" counterparts. So, a maintenance person can be frugal on the labor budget (needed to change lamps), but can be contributing to increased energy consumption and the resulting pollution. Full–spectrum lamps typically are not. Yes, these may be "fuller" spectrum lamps than their common counterparts of ten or twenty years ago. However, given the latest lamp technologies, most high quality lamps offer a relatively full spectrum of radiation. Further, many so–called full–spectrum lamps have bluer cast to the light quality—actually making warm tones and skin tones look poor. As noted in Section 4.5.6, there is no benefit from full–spectrum lamps. As Section 2.8 indicates, light therapy is based on intensity rather than spectrum, and the intensity needs to be much greater than that experienced in most architectural lighting situations.

Finally, specify the lamps you believe are best for a given project. Do not fall victim to a lamp agenda espoused by an electrical distributor or a lighting rep. Furniture system manufacturers may wish to force a specific lamp on a project if they are supplying the task lights (which, of themselves, are typically overpriced and ergonomically inappropriate from lighting intensity, distribution, and control perspectives). Don't succumb to their tactics. The lighting design is intended to help people be comfortable and to be as productive as possible while maintaining reasonable energy use and maintenance strategies for many years.

7.9 Endnotes

[1] Gary Steffy Lighting Design Inc., *Time–Saver Standards for Architectural Lighting* (New York, New York: McGraw–Hill, 2000), p. 3–16.

7.10 General References

Energy Savings, Inc., 2000: *The Guide for Lighting Designers and Specifiers*. Schaumburg, IL, Energy Savings, Inc.
Gary Steffy Lighting Design Inc., 2000: *Time–Saver Standards for Architectural Lighting*. New York: McGraw–Hill.

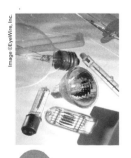
Image ©EyeWire, Inc.

Luminaires

8.1

Luminaires are the vehicles that deliver light. They house lamps, ballasts or transformers (if required), sockets and wiring components. Luminaires also typically house reflectors and/or lenses that are, in theory, designed to best distribute the light from the lamp to the functional area or zone intended. Luminaires should be built around lamps or, conversely, lamps should be built around luminaires. This chapter will discuss and give examples of some of the more important physical qualities and photometric aspects of luminaires, as well as the various families of luminaires available.

Luminaires are responsible for how light is distributed on room surfaces, work surfaces, tasks, plants, architectural elements and details, and people. Luminaires can be very noticeable—a significant part of the overall look of a setting may come from the actual hardware appearance of the luminaires (see Figure 4.16). Ironically, the lighting hardware may have more to do with the appearance of a setting when the luminaires themselves are unlit (see Figures 4.5, 4.6, 4.7, and the chapter icon in the lower corner below). On the other hand, luminaires can be very subtle, yet this too contributes to the overall look of a setting (see Figures 4.12 and 4.43). Many off–the–shelf or standard luminaires are available to meet many of today's lighting needs. The key is to start the design by establishing all of the appropriate lighting needs for a project (see Chapter 4) and then, based on these needs, to formulate schemes. Once the schemes are established, the designer is in a position to think about which lamps and luminaires can be used to achieve them.

Luminaires can be either off–the–shelf, modifications of standard equipment, or totally custom. Many times, a unique way of using off–the–shelf equipment will lead to a successful project. The arches in Figure 4.1 are uplighted with standard striplights in an architectural detail—a detail finalized by the architect to permit light leaks at the dentil work. Arriving at such a solution did not mean starting with the assumption that somehow, some way a striplight would be used on the project. The lighting program identified the need for spaciousness and daylight balancing in the lobby, while the architectural schematic presented a postmodern aesthetic. Lighting of the arches would introduce bright vertical and horizontal surfaces. The base detail at each arch was identified as a potential lighting element.

Understanding lighting hardware is critical to knowing if and how light can be introduced into a given space or architectural setting. Light reflection (Figures 4.38, 4.39, and 4.40) and light transmission (see Figures 4.41, 4.42, and 4.43) are both important concepts in developing lighting solutions. Understanding luminaire photometric qualities is also crucial to being able to resolve lighting design challenges.

more online @
http://www.lightsearch.com/

8.1 Lighting hardware

Clearly, lighting design is much more than just applying available equipment, more than tacking luminaires onto or into the architecture—hence, the importance of programming and schematic design. There comes a time, however, when hardware must be selected if the designer is to maintain control over the quality of the project, in terms of both aesthetics and performance. Lighting hardware is generally judged on quality of construction, quality of appearance, and quality of photometry (light distribution characteristics). The degree to which each of these factors contributes to luminaire selection depends on the use of the equipment. For example, the luminaires used to

8.1 Luminaires

baffles

A series of metal or plastic "blades" arranged in a consistently spaced pattern usually perpendicular to the lamp, and which shield (or cut off) the lamp(s) from view in at least two directions (view perpendicular to the width of the baffle blade). See Figure 11.3, "continuous fluorescent wallslot luminaire with baffle."

louvers

Two series of metal or plastic "blades" arranged in a consistently spaced pattern, and each series of baffles oriented perpendicular to the other series so as to create an eggcrate effect (hence, also termed "eggcrate louver"). Louvers shield the lamp(s) from view in at least the four cardinal viewing directions. See Figure 11.2, "2 x 2' (600 x 600 mm) parabolic luminaire." Louvers are typically less efficient (they block more light) than baffles. Louvers are necessary, however, whenever the likelihood is high that folks will view the luminaire from at least three if not four major viewing directions.

uplight the columns in Figure C1 need not be attractive. Given the scale of the application and the relative diminutive size of the luminaires, they simply need to be painted out to match the stonework—the quality of appearance is not so important if the units are relatively quite small and painted out to match the background. However, the quality of the luminaires' construction is critical to its success in this exterior application. Rugged and durable are keywords when exterior lighting is involved. The luminaires shown have cast and spun components of heavy gauge aluminum, along with tempered glass lensing, and are UL wet–labeled. Finally, luminaire photometry is critical in the application exemplified in Figure C1. Here, however, the choice of lamp—100PAR38/CMH/3K/WSP—offers the photometric distribution required to fully light the column sides bottom to top. The luminaire, a Sterner PD41270, need not provide any optical design except the clear domed glass lens (to allow for ready water runoff and to minimize debris buildup) in a light straw color (to ever–so–slightly warm the color of the light for best enhancement of the limestone).

Another example is the steplights shown in Figure 4.12. Given close proximity to people (readily seen and easy to touch), such luminaires should evoke quality over time—requiring a cast housing with no blemishes and a high quality paint job (so the quality of appearance is high). Additionally, the cast housing provides the durability needed to withstand an accidental foot kick or vacuum–cleaner hose hit (so quality of construction is high). Photometry needs to be sufficient to light the treads relatively uniformly without introducing glare. Clearly, then, whenever selecting a luminaire, the questions of construction quality, aesthetic quality, and photometric quality need to be asked—and the degree to which each, if any, of these is important needs to be established. Many off–the–shelf luminaires are available for many applications. Some offer quality construction, others offer quality aesthetics, still others offer quality photometry, and some offer some combination of these qualities.

Custom luminaires often are just unique assemblies of various off–the–shelf components. How these components are brought together makes a unique aesthetic and/or photometric character (see Figure 8.1). Here, it is critical to develop hardware that will be UL listed and labeled once completed. Further, to maintain integrity of luminaire construction and warranty, it is strongly suggested that the entire luminaire assembly and some significant portion of constructed components (e.g., 50 percent or so) be performed by the specified vendor. Sometimes custom luminaires are remakes, reworks, reconstructions, or restorations of existing (or previously existing) luminaires. For remakes, photographs or drawings of the missing luminaire are necessary for redevelopment. For reworks, reconstructions, and restorations, the existing luminaire is specified with new wiring, a new or refinished finish, new sockets, new lamps, new shades, and the like, all, which when completed, are UL listed and labeled as a complete lighting assembly. Any work on custom luminaires requires a bit of back and forth with luminaire manufacturers. The designer develops drawings as "cutsheets" to be used with the specification as part of the contract documents to convey an intent. The successful luminaire manufacturer should then develop a shop drawing for review by the design team. The team will likely mark up the shop drawing to clarify any issues not entirely understood in the process. For larger and more complicated custom luminaires, or for projects where time and team interest permit, the design team should then review samples of various components for quality and aesthetic. For luminaires that are intended to have a significant photometric function, portions of reflectors/lenses and lamp

Image ©GarySteffyLightingDesign Inc./luminaire by others

Luminaires

Figure 8.1

The lighting program for this hospitality space called for warm, more intimate, and human–scale lighting, both in terms of the lighting effects and in terms of the lighting hardware. Further, a cathedral–ceiling lounge (in the left background) required similar lighting treatment—hence, the scale of the lighting hardware was important. No off–the–shelf luminaires could simultaneously meet the challenge of the scale requirements and the aesthetic character of the architecture. Custom sconces were proposed, using a single sconce in the lower–ceiling corridor areas and using a triple sconce in the cathedral–ceiling lounge. Using heavy gauge copper and faux alabaster material from Sterling Products, Baldinger Custom Architectural Lighting made the sconces. Each sconce uses GE 90TB/H lamps to permit time–of–day dimming.

assemblies may need to be reviewed as sample mockups to assure photometric performance. This entire back–and–forth process may take from 12 to 24 weeks from the date that the manufacturer is awarded the project, to final shipment of finished luminaire(s). This timeframe depends on the complexity and scale of the project and the status of the economy.

Table 8.1 outlines the various components that may be involved in a luminaire's construction. This checklist can be used to assess luminaires for a given project and can be used to assist in the writing of the lighting specification for a given project.

8.2 Luminaire construction

Luminaires are likely to remain in a given installation for many years. Retail applications may be the least stable because these change with fashion, purchasing trends, economic conditions, and the like. Commercial and hospitality installations will likely remain intact for twenty or thirty years. Luminaires' abilities to withstand the environment, both indoor and out; their ability to withstand building system interaction (e.g., vibration due to mechanical equipment); and their ability to withstand, indeed encourage, proper maintenance are key construction qualities necessary for long life. Heavy gauge steel, extruded aluminum, and/or cast metal are good base construction methods for long–life luminaires. Connections are the most likely points of failure in any luminaire, and mechanical fasteners (e.g., screws or rivets) are more permanent than tab/slot construction or some of the newer "cost–creative" methods of double–sided tape and Velcro®.

Baffles and **louvers** should be of sufficient gauge and/or of such cell size to minimize torquing. Extruded aluminum baffles or double–sided (U–shaped) steel baffles lead to more sturdy, monolithic construction. Lenses should be virgin acrylic for best performance and for greatest resistance to discoloration over time. Where luminaires are in vandal–prone areas, consider UV–stabilized polycarbonate lenses for greater durability.

In order to judge luminaire construction, several techniques are available: review of manufacturers' literature; view and handle samples, preferably an operational sample; and view a mockup. These techniques should be used in a linear

Velcro® is a registered trademark of Velcro Industries B.V.

8.3 Luminaires

progression toward decision making. For example, if six different manufacturers' luminaires are under consideration, then carefully review the manufacturers' literature—including online resources that may include various installation examples. Of the six, perhaps three manufacturers indicate the use of heavier–gauge steel than the others. Order and review samples of these three remaining luminaires. After this review of the physical samples, perhaps two luminaires will surpass the third. Finally, consider a mockup to review the construction quality of the luminaires after installation by electrical contractors. The mockup also provides an excellent opportunity to review the quality of aesthetic appearance and of photometry.

8.3 Luminaire appearance

Selecting a luminaire for its appearance simply on the basis of reviewing some catalog or online photographs may produce surprising and disappointing results. For any luminaire, it is necessary to ascertain several factors firsthand: the consistency, sheen, and durability of the finish; methods of attachment to the architecture; methods of connecting various components to one another; baffle, louver, reflector, and/or refractor (lens) fit and finish; and for linear luminaires, long–run connector components. The lighting designer is not reviewing these sorts of details in an engineering nor installation role, but rather needs to determine if any of these details will result in a bad appearance of either the luminaire or the architecture. For example, a beautiful sconce, particularly if imported and retrofitted for the local market, may have a wall escutcheon or canopy that is bolted into the wall with exposed bolts! To review such details, an actual working sample or a visit to an installation using the luminaire in question is required. Reviewing an installation (a project or application) sometimes is preferable to obtaining a sample because the sample can be commandeered and perfected at the factory prior to presentation to the designer.

8.4 Luminaire photometry

The photometry or optical performance of a luminaire is quite critical to the success of the lighting design. Even decorative luminaires need to have some sort of particular optical performance if they are to serve their decorative function. Such photometry may rely solely on the lamp. For example, crystal wall sconces look good only if small, low–wattage, clear incandescent lamps (see Table 7.4, candle [CA] tungsten filament lamp) or actual candles are used. Only such point sources show off the crystal in a glittery fashion.

With the exception of the most decorative luminaires (such as crystal sconces), photometric information from manufacturers should be readily available (see Figures 8.2 and 8.3). This data is quite useful in the design development of a project in determining preliminary luminaire quantities (see the lumen method discussion in Chapter 10). During final design development and into the contract document phase, this photometric data should then be used to finalize lighting layouts.

Even here, however, reviewing actual working samples is recommended. Some aspects of light distribution are not reported in published photometric data (unintentionally—the photometers simply are not required to measure data at every possible angle [an infinite amount of data would be generated, requiring a never–ending process]). A classic example is with indirect

Image ©GarySteffyLightingDesign Inc./luminaire by others

148

Luminaires

fluorescent luminaires. Many, but not all, indirect luminaires that are fitted with specular reflectors will likely produce striations or streaks on the ceiling or upper wall. These striations are very annoying disturbances, particularly if they exhibit movement from air circulating across/around the indirect lights or from mechanical vibration. These striations, as obnoxious as they are, do not show up in photometric reports and can be experienced only firsthand. This is a good example of needing nothing more than a working sample, plugging it in and holding it near a light–colored, matte wall with the light oriented upward or toward the wall; and looking for striations on the ceiling or wall. Another example is with parabolic (direct) luminaires. No matter how the parabolic baffle or louver is formed and if specular or semi–specular aluminum material is used, if lamps are aiming light directly onto the baffle or louver assembly, then there will be some viewing angle when a flash or hot streak of light is observed. This is the angle–of–incidence/angle–of–reflection phenomena (see Figures 4.38 and 4.39) doing its magic (or horror, if this angle is near a typical viewing position). Photometric tests will, in all likelihood, show that the parabolic luminaires exhibit low, consistent luminance. Viewing a sample is important to discovering if such a photometric glitch exists and evaluating its significance, if any.

8.5 Manufacturers' literature

Many of the better luminaire manufacturers offer a wealth of catalog information in hard copy and online. Typically, this literature includes a photo or line drawing (or both) of the luminaire, along with product features, construction, finish, ordering information, and sometimes application ideas. Additionally, detailed photometric data are available from reputable manufacturers. This data might be presented in graphic and tabular hard copy or might be available on diskette or online for convenient use in lighting calculation and lighting simulation programs.

Many manufacturers have product literature available online, so only a few pieces of literature are illustrated here in Figures 8.2, 8.3, 8.6, and 8.7. Figure 11.6 also illustrates some literature. Listings of manufacturers and their respective luminaire capabilities appear annually in such magazines as *LD+A*, *Architectural Lighting*, *Interiors*, and *Lighting Dimensions*. Many of these resources have websites where additional listings are available, along with links to specific manufacturers' sites.

8.6 Specific luminaires

Getting to know specific luminaires will require hands–on work. Visiting local lighting representatives showrooms or offices can help, although the selection of hardware is likely to be limited since optional trims, finishes, and optical packages abound. Visiting luminaire manufacturers' studios, research and development facilities, or manufacturing facilities will likely lead to a greater breadth of equipment to see. Recognize the propriety or impropriety of such visits, however. If the luminaire manufacturers fund these junkets, then perhaps the designer will be more likely to specify those manufacturers' products over others that may better meet a given project's needs. Additionally, sessions that the designer funds may qualify toward CEU credits for, say, NCQLP recertification. Another method for viewing products is attending annual trade shows. In the United States, the premiere show is LightFair.

Image ©GarySteffyLightingDesign Inc./luminaire by others

8.6

Luminaires

Table 8.1 Luminaire Specification Issues

Status (✓)	Parameter	Issues
___	Luminaire dimensions	• length • width • height • diameter • projection • hidden dimensions (above ceiling/behind wall)

___	Intended mounting	• recessed (in wall or ceiling)
		• surface (on wall or ceiling)
		• suspended
		  • stem
		  • aircraft cable
		  • chain
		• furniture mount
		• freestanding (on floor or work surface)

___	Intended ceiling application	• lay–in tile
		  • standard T
		  • narrow T
		  • very narrow T
		  • concealed T
		• drywall/plaster
		• metal
		  • pan (concealed T)
		  • linear
		• other
		  • concrete
		  • wood

___	Thermal requirements	• insulation contact • insulation nearby • no insulation

___	Flange requirements	• overlap trim
		  • contiguous (no seam between cone and trim)
		    • same as cone/reflector finish
		    • painted white
		    • painted custom color
		  • white plastic ring (part of 2–piece flange)
		  • discontinuous (seam between cone and trim)
		    • same as cone/reflector finish
		    • painted white
		    • painted custom color
		• flangeless (requires precise installation)

___	Reflector requirements	• shape
		  • ellipsoidal
		  • parabolic
		  • combination
		• material
		  • plastic
		  • metal

Luminaires

Table 8.1 Luminaire Specification Issues *(continued)*

Status (✓)	Parameter	Issues

		• forming
		  • spun
		  • hydroformed
		  • bent/folded
		  • extruded
		• finish
		  • milligroove baffles
		    • plastic
		      • white
		      • black
		    • painted
		      • white
		      • black
		      • custom color
		  • specular, low iridescent processed aluminum
		  • semi–specular, low iridescent processed aluminum
		  • diffuse, low iridescent processed aluminum

▬	Lensing	• acrylic (specify virgin acrylic)
		  • pattern 12 prisms
		  • low brightness prisms
		    • small prisms
		    • medium prisms
		    • large prisms
		  • matte opal
		  • decorative faux stone
		• door style
		  • flush
		    • sheet steel
		    • extruded
		  • regressed/shallow
		    • sloped regress
		    • straight regress
		  • regressed/deep
		    • sloped regress
		    • straight regress
		  • reveal edge

▬	Orientation	• direct
		  • fixed downlight
		  • fixed wallwash
		  • adjustable accent
		    • degree of rotation
		    • degree of tilt
		    • locking mechanisms or friction adjustment
		• indirect or semi–indirect

▬	Distribution	• widespread • narrow • medium • asymmetric • symmetric • cutoff requirements

continued on next page

8.6

Luminaires

Table 8.1 Luminaire Specification Issues *(continued)*

Status (✓)	Parameter	Issues

―	Key photometric data	• maximum luminances
		• candlepower
		  • center beam
		  • maximum
		  • beam spread
		• wattage
		• efficiency

―	Lamping	• configuration
		  • linear
		  • compact
		  • envelope shape
		• number of lamps
		• orientation
		  • vertical
		  • horizontal
		• control
		  • all lamps on/off
		  • one lamp controlled separately from another
		• color temperature
		• color rendering
		• lumen output
		• life
		• base configuration
		  • screw base
		  • bi–pin

―	Ballasts	• voltage
		• sound requirements
		• number of lamps controlled
		• electromagnetic vs. electronic
		• dimming vs. nondimming
		• programmed start
		• end–of–life shutoff protection
		• addressable
		• size and fit within luminaire
		• location
		  • remote
		  • in–luminaire
		• high power factor
		• ballast factor
		  • 1.18
		  • 1.00
		  • 0.88
		  • 0.78
		• Class P thermal requirement

―	Safety glass	• contain violent lamp failures • withstand degree of abuse

Luminaires

Table 8.1 Luminaire Specification Issues *(continued)*

Status (✓)	Parameter	Issues
—	Vapor requirements	• UL damp listing and label • UL wet listing and label • UL explosion–proof listing and label

—	Louvering	• material
		  • acrylic
		  • metalized plastic
		  • metal
		    • specular, low iridescent processed aluminum
		    • semi–specular, low iridescent processed aluminum
		    • diffuse, low iridescent processed aluminum
		  • wood
		• configuration
		  • louver vs. baffle
		  • flat (smooth) straight blade
		  • ribbed straight blade
		  • parabolic blade
		  • hexcell blade
		• door style
		  • flush
		    • sheet steel
		    • extruded
		  • regressed/shallow
		    • sloped regress
		    • straight regress
		  • regressed/deep
		    • sloped regress
		    • straight regress
		  • reveal edge

—	HVAC function	• none (static) • return • supply
—	Architectural details	• cove • slot • valance
—	Underwriters Labs Inc.	• UL listing and label
—	International Brotherhood of Electrical Workers	• IBEW label

8.6 Luminaires

TRIPLES-V 26/6

recessed compact fluorescent downlight/wallwasher

FEATURES

Triples-V 26/6 is an efficient 6" aperture low brightness downlight designed for use with one 26-watt triple-tube compact fluorescent lamp of the 4-pin types made by GE, OSRAM/Sylvania or Philips. Triples-V 26/6 provides a shielding angle of 38°.

One housing allows interchangeable use of downlight and wallwash reflectors, permitting housings to be installed first and reflectors to be installed or changed at any time.

Triples-V 26/6 uses one 26-watt lamp providing 1800 lumens (more than a 100-watt incandescent), a 10,000-hour life, a color rendering index (CRI) of 82, and color temperatures as warm as 2700°K (nearly duplicating the color qualities of incandescent).

Reflectors are available in clear (natural aluminum), semi-specular etch clear or champagne gold Alzak® with Color-Chek® anodizing, virtually eliminating iridescence. Wallwash reflectors available are: wallwash (120°), corner wallwash (210°), and double wallwash (2x120°).

Triples-V 26/6 includes a pair of mounting bars (¾" x 27" C channel). Specialty bars for wood joist and T-bar installations are also available.

APPLICATIONS

Fixture is suitable for downlighting or wallwashing in nearly all architectural environments, especially those spaces where non-directional luminaires are preferred over rectangular troffers. These include offices, stores, lobbies, corridors, restrooms and public areas.

Fixture is ⓤⓛ listed for Damp Location (may not be suitable for some outdoor environments). Fixture is union made IBEW and in compliance with the component based efficiency standards of the 1995 New York State Energy Conservation Code. Fixture is prewired with high power factor Class P electronic ballast and approved for ten #12 wire 75°C branch circuit pull-through wiring. Removal of the reflector allows access to the ballast and junction box.

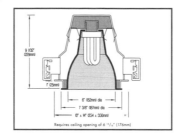

9 1/32" (229mm)

1" (25mm)

6" (152mm) dia
7 3/8" (187mm) dia
12" x 14" (254 x 300mm)

Requires ceiling opening of 6 15/16" (176mm)

PRODUCT CODE

For complete product code, list basic unit and select one item from each following box.

Basic Unit	TRP 26/6

Reflector Type		
Downlight .... no suffix	Corner Wallwash .... CWW
Wallwash .... WW	Double Wallwash .... DWW

Voltage		
120 volt service 120	277 volt service 277

Reflector and Flange Color	Overlap	Flush

Features of the luminaire are prominently outlined. A cross section is used to indicate aperture dimension and housing dimensions. General applications are cited, as are the various listing and labels that the luminaire exhibits. This particular luminaire is union made (and exhibits an International Brotherhood of Electrical Workers [IBEW] label). Product code information is then displayed, indicating the various standard options that are available on this particular luminaire (see Figure 8.3 also). If a desired option is not listed, the designer is encouraged to inquire about same with the local lighting representative. Many manufacturers have modified their respective products over the years and may be capable of providing an option not listed as a standard option. Obviously, options cost more money and may require longer leadtimes.

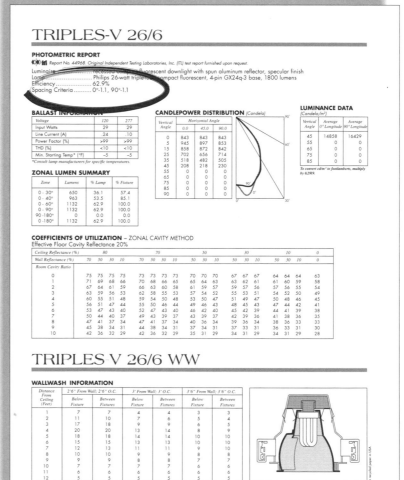

TRIPLES-V 26/6

PHOTOMETRIC REPORT

Report No. 44968. Original Independent Testing Laboratories, Inc. (ITL) test report furnished upon request.

Luminaire .... recessed compact fluorescent downlight with spun aluminum reflector, specular finish
Lamp .... Philips 26-watt triple-tube compact fluorescent, 4-pin GX24q-3 base, 1800 lumens
Efficiency 62.9%
Spacing Criteria .... 0°-1.1, 90°-1.1

BALLAST INFORMATION

Voltage	120	277
Input Watts	29	29
Line Current (A)	.24	.10
Power Factor (%)	>99	>99
THD (%)	<10	<10
Min. Starting Temp* (°F)	−5	−5

*Consult lamp manufacturers for specific temperatures.

ZONAL LUMEN SUMMARY

Zone	Lumens	% Lamp	% Fixture
0 - 30°	650	36.1	57.4
0 - 40°	963	53.5	85.1
0 - 60°	1132	62.9	100.0
0 - 90°	1132	62.9	100.0
90 -180°	0	0.0	0.0
0 -180°	1132	62.9	100.0

CANDLEPOWER DISTRIBUTION *(Candela)*

Vertical Angle	Horizontal Angle		
	0.0	45.0	90.0
0	843	843	843
5	945	897	853
15	858	872	842
25	702	656	714
35	518	482	505
45	208	218	230
55	0	0	0
65	0	0	0
75	0	0	0
85	0	0	0
90	0	0	0

LUMINANCE DATA

(Candela/m²)

Vertical Angle	Average 0° Longitude	Average 90° Longitude
45	14858	16429
55	0	0
65	0	0
75	0	0
85	0	0

To convert cd/m² to footlamberts, multiply by 6.2819.

COEFFICIENTS OF UTILIZATION – ZONAL CAVITY METHOD
Effective Floor Cavity Reflectance 20%

Ceiling Reflectance (%)	80				70				50				30				10			0
Wall Reflectance (%)	70	50	30	10	70	50	30	10	50	30	10	50	30	10	50	30	10	0
Room Cavity Ratio																		
0	75	75	75	75	73	73	73	73	70	70	70	67	67	67	64	64	64	63
1	71	69	68	66	70	68	66	65	65	64	63	63	62	61	61	60	59	58
2	67	64	61	59	66	63	60	58	61	59	57	59	57	56	57	56	55	54
3	63	59	56	53	62	58	55	53	57	54	52	55	53	51	54	52	50	49
4	60	55	51	48	59	54	50	48	53	50	47	51	49	47	50	48	46	45
5	56	51	47	44	55	50	46	44	49	46	43	48	45	43	47	44	42	41
6	53	47	43	40	52	47	43	40	46	42	40	45	42	39	44	41	39	38
7	50	44	40	37	49	43	39	37	43	39	37	42	39	36	41	38	36	35
8	47	41	37	34	47	41	37	34	40	36	34	39	36	34	38	36	33	32
9	45	38	34	31	44	38	34	31	37	34	31	37	33	31	36	33	31	30
10	42	36	32	29	42	36	32	29	35	31	29	34	31	29	34	31	29	28

TRIPLES V 26/6 WW

WALLWASH INFORMATION

Distance From Ceiling (Feet)	2'6" From Wall; 2'6" O.C.		3' From Wall; 3' O.C.		3'6" From Wall; 3'6" O.C.	
	Below Fixture	Between Fixtures	Below Fixture	Between Fixtures	Below Fixture	Between Fixtures
1	7	7	4	4	3	3
2	11	10	7	6	5	4
3	17	18	9	9	6	5
4	20	20	13	14	8	9
5	18	18	14	14	10	10
6	15	15	13	13	10	10
7	12	13	11	11	9	10
8	10	10	9	9	8	8
9	9	9	8	8	7	7
10	7	7	7	7	6	6
11	6	6	6	6	6	6
12	5	5	5	5	5	5

All vertical footcandles are initial values with no contribution from ceiling or floor reflectances. Computation performed with at least five wallwashers.

Cutsheet drawings courtesy of and ©Edison Price Lighting, Inc. Available online at http://www.epl.com

Luminaires

In this example (and that shown in Figure 8.2), photometric data is providing on the back of the cutsheet (aka, datasheet). Here are specific wattage data and luminaire efficiency data, as well as candlepower distribution and coefficients of utilization (more on these in Chapter 10). The luminaire in 8.2 has a 6" diameter aperture, and the one here has a 7" diameter aperture. Otherwise, the luminaires are identical—using the same lamps and available in the same finishes. One difficult decision the designer has to make, then, is whether to use a smaller diameter, more human–scale downlight (the 60 diameter unit), or use a slightly larger diameter downlight with nearly 10% greater efficiency (compare circled efficiency values). This phenomenon occurs across all luminaire and lamp types—larger luminaires are more efficient. This should be a decision of great care. Efficiency does not matter if folks don't like the space, or the increased glare potential.

TRIPLES-V 26/7

recessed compact fluorescent downlight/wallwasher

FEATURES

Triples-V 26/7 is a highly efficient 7" aperture low brightness downlight designed for use with one 26-watt triple-tube compact fluorescent lamp of the 4-pin types made by GE, Osram/Sylvania or Philips. Triples-V 26/7 provides a shielding angle of 40°.

One housing allows interchangeable use of downlight and wallwash reflectors, permitting housings to be installed first and reflectors to be installed or changed at any time.

Triples-V 26/7 uses one 26-watt lamp providing 1800 lumens (more than a 100-watt incandescent), a 10,000-hour life, a color rendering index (CRI) of 82, and color temperatures as warm as 2700°K (nearly duplicating the color qualities of incandescent).

Reflectors are available in clear (natural aluminum), semi-specular etch clear or champagne gold Alzak® with Color-Chek® anodizing, virtually eliminating iridescence. Wallwash reflectors available are: wallwash (120°), corner wallwash (210°), and double wallwash (2x120°).

Triples-V 26/7 includes a pair of mounting bars (¾" x 27" C channel). Specialty bars for wood joist and T-bar installations are also available.

APPLICATIONS

Fixture is suitable for downlighting or wallwashing in nearly all architectural environments, especially those spaces where non-

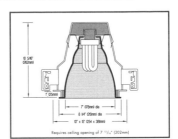

Requires ceiling opening of 7 ¹³/₁₆" (202mm)

PRODUCT CODE

For complete product code, list basic unit and select one item from each following box.

Basic Unit	TRP 26/7

Reflector Type			
Downlight	no suffix	Corner Wallwash	CWW
Wallwash	WW	Double Wallwash	DWW

Voltage			
120 volt service	120	277 volt service	277

Reflector and Flange Color	Overlap	Flush
Clear (Natural Aluminum)	COL	CFL
Champagne Gold	GOL	GFL
Semi-specular Etch Clear	ECOL	ECFL
Other reflector finishes are available on special order.		

Standard reflector flange continues reflector finish. White painted flanges and custom painted flanges are available on special order. Add WF (white flange) or CCF (custom color flange).

OPTIONS

Specify by adding to the basic unit.

Dimmable. Not for outdoor application .... – DM

Emergency battery pack operates lamp in event of power outage. Not for outdoor application .... – EM

Return Air Plenum. Modified for maximum performance in air return ceiling plenums .... – RA

⅛" (3mm) thick clear acrylic shield, spring-mounted within reflector .... – PS

▶ For combinations of the Options above, contact factory or Edison Price Lighting representative.

▶ An install-from-below version of this fixture, suitable for installation outside North America, is also available. Contact factory.

▶ Decorative reflector rings are available on special order. Contact factory.

EDISON PRICE LIGHTING

409 E 60 St, New York NY 10022, tel 212.521.6900 fax 212.888.7981 www.epl.com
®Copyright, Edison Price Lighting 2000

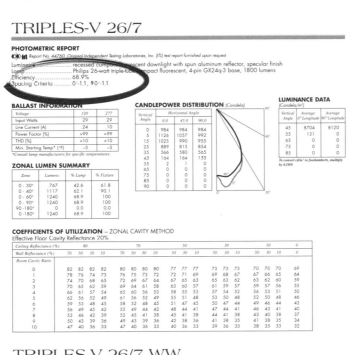

TRIPLES-V 26/7

PHOTOMETRIC REPORT

Report No. 44760. Original Independent Testing Laboratories, Inc. (ITL) test report furnished upon request.

Luminaire .... recessed compact fluorescent downlight with spun aluminum reflector, specular finish
Lamp .... Philips 26-watt triple-tube compact fluorescent, 4-pin GX24q-3 base, 1800 lumens
Efficiency 68.9%
Spacing Criteria .... 0°-1.1, 90°-1.1

BALLAST INFORMATION

Voltage	120	277
Input Watts	29	29
Line Current (A)	.24	.10
Power Factor (%)	>99	>99
THD (%)	<10	<10
Min. Starting Temp* (°F)	–5	–5

*Consult lamp manufacturers for specific temperatures.

ZONAL LUMEN SUMMARY

Zone	Lumens	% Lamp	% Fixture
0 - 30°	767	42.6	61.8
0 - 40°	1117	62.1	90.1
0 - 60°	1240	68.9	100
0 - 90°	1240	68.9	100
90 -180°	0	0.0	0.0
0 -180°	1240	68.9	100

CANDLEPOWER DISTRIBUTION *(Candela)*

Vertical Angle	Horizontal Angle		
	0.0	45.0	90.0
0	984	984	984
5	1126	1057	992
15	1025	990	955
25	889	815	854
35	566	580	565
43	164	164	133
55	2	1	0
65	0	0	0
75	0	0	0
85	0	0	0
90	0	0	0

LUMINANCE DATA
(Candela/m²)

Vertical Angle	Average 0° Longitude	Average 90° Longitude
45	8704	8120
55	131	0
65	0	0
75	0	0
85	0	0

To convert cd/m² to footlamberts, multiply by 0.2919.

COEFFICIENTS OF UTILIZATION – ZONAL CAVITY METHOD
Effective Floor Cavity Reflectance 20%

Ceiling Reflectance (%)	80			70				50			30			10			0
Wall Reflectance (%)	70	50	30	10	70	50	30	10	50	30	10	50	30	10	50	30	10	0
Room Cavity Ratio																		
0	82	82	82	82	80	80	80	80	77	77	77	73	73	73	70	70	70	69
1	78	76	74	73	76	75	73	72	72	71	69	69	68	67	67	66	65	64
2	74	70	68	65	72	69	67	64	67	65	63	65	63	62	63	62	60	59
3	70	65	62	59	69	64	61	58	63	60	57	61	59	57	59	57	56	55
4	66	61	57	54	65	60	56	53	58	55	53	57	54	52	56	53	51	50
5	62	56	52	49	61	56	52	49	55	51	48	53	50	48	52	50	48	46
6	59	53	48	45	58	52	48	45	51	47	45	50	47	44	49	46	44	43
7	56	49	45	42	55	49	44	42	48	44	41	47	44	41	46	43	41	40
8	53	46	42	39	52	45	41	38	45	41	38	44	41	38	43	40	38	37
9	50	43	39	36	49	43	39	36	42	38	36	41	38	35	41	38	35	34
10	47	40	36	33	47	40	36	33	40	36	33	39	36	33	38	35	33	32

TRIPLES-V 26/7 WW

WALLWASH INFORMATION

Distance From Ceiling (Feet)	3' From Wall: 3' O.C.		3'6" From Wall: 3'6" O.C.	
	Below Fixture	Between Fixtures	Below Fixture	Between Fixtures
1	7	6	5	4
2	8	8	6	6
3	11	9	7	6
4	14	14	9	9
5	14	15	11	11
6	14	14	11	11
7	12	12	10	10
8	10	11	9	9
9	9	9	8	8
10	8	8	7	7
11	7	7	6	6
12	6	6	5	5

All vertical footcandles are initial values with no contribution from ceiling or floor reflectances. Computation performed with at least five wallwashers.

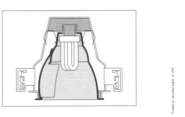

Printed on recycled paper in USA.

Image ©GarySteffy/LightingDesign Inc./luminaire by others

8.6.1 Luminaires

Other shows are cited in Section 1.8. Finally, requesting samples for review is also a good way to ascertain a luminaire's various qualities. However, these samples can be reviewed for only limited time before being returned to manufacturers.

Besides the downlights already discussed, a few other luminaire categories (which parallel application techniques) include wallwashing, ambient recessed, and ambient pendent. Each of these is represented in Figures 11.1, 11.2, and 11.3 in graphic plan–view form as they might be indicated on reflected ceiling plans.

8.6.1 Wallwash luminaires

Wallwash luminaires are available in two versions—those that graze a wall with light and those that flood a wall with light. The grazing light is typically used to accentuate architecture—the wall itself. The flooding wash is typically used to offer a flatter, frontal light for highlighting artwork. However, depending on the art and other criteria, such as cost and/or energy use, there are instances where grazing light works for art highlighting and where a flooding wash works for architectural highlighting. Grazing options are typically used where a more frontal flood would create harsh reflections from the wall surface into folks at seated positions nearby or where the wall has some translucency, in which case floods would direct some glare through the wall to users on the opposite side. Figures 8.4 and 8.5 illustrate the grazing wallwash or wallslot. These are continuous linear luminaires available in many trim, lamping, and baffling/louvering options. The construction of the slot luminaire is very important. Since these run for full lengths of walls, thin–gauge housings are undesirable since they result in snaking of the luminaire along the length of the wall, which is itself hopefully quite true/straight. Louver construction, as discussed in 8.2, is also important to the finished appearance. There are times, however, where wallslots occur on "dead end" walls—walls that are at the end of a corridor or perhaps at the end of a vestibule where users must make a path choice between left and right, but never can walk beneath or sight down the length of the slot. Here, inexpensive slots or slot details with striplights can be used to good advantage. Wall slots typically require some shielding. Further, if wall lengths are not on a module with lamps, some fiddling with end conditions is necessary. Further, corner conditions can be problematic. Many manufacturers do, however, have techniques to minimize these issues—from telescoping ends, to overlapping lamps, to indirect slot lighting techniques. In any event, some dark end conditions may result if care is not taken in selecting and specifying the wallslot. Overlapping lamps also helps to avoid socket shadows that are common in many, though not all, wallslots. However, the extent of the overlap may actually create a "brightened" or reverse socket shadow condition. Here, visual inspection of an installation or mockup is necessary to appreciate the degree of socket shadowing or end darkening, if any.

While the grazing wash is achieved with continuous wallslots, the flood wash has quite a few variants. The flood wash is typically achieved with open bottom downlight/wallwash combinations (see the lower right corners of the "second sheets" shown in Figures 8.2 and 8.3); spreadlens wallwashers; small, rectilinear halogen asymmetric lensed luminaires; or discrete fluorescent asymmetric slot luminaires. Each of these is intended to work best when placed several feet from the wall with center–to–center spacings of one to two times the distance from the wall (e.g., a wallwasher located 2′

Luminaires

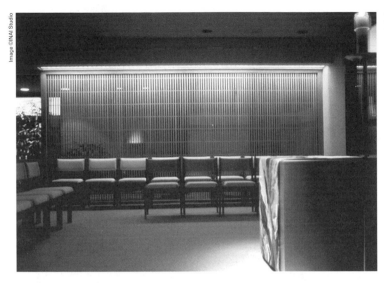

Figure 8.4
The lighting program for this hospital chapel called for a sense of privacy or intimacy. Further, the small meditation space in the background was developed so that one or a few people could have some very private time alone. To help provide the privacy, peripheral elements should be lighted with very low luminance in the field or zone of occupancy (see Section 4.5.3). To achieve this, the wood screen wall was grazed with a fluorescent wallslot (to prevent light and glare from interfering with those seated against this side of the screen wall and from those seated on the other side of the screen wall). A few accents (each lamped with GE 50PAR36/H/VNSP lamps) pinspot the tabernacle in the distance, but provide no other spill light—offering those meditating in this zone anonymity.

from the wall should be spaced on 2 to 4' centers if the wall is to be uniformly lighted). From experience, and by reviewing the photometric data—particularly the illuminance data included for wallwashers—downlight/wallwash combinations and spreadlens wallwashers provide a relatively soft light. These seem to have best impact when used relatively close to the wall (e.g., 1'–6" [450 mm] to 2'–0" [600 mm] where ceilings are 10' [3 m] in height or less) and spaced on a one–to–one ratio (spaced the same distance on center as they are spaced from the wall). With the advent of the ceramic metal halide lamp, there are now spreadlens wallwashers that offer significant visual impact to the wall while using less energy. Figure 8.6 shows a halogen spreadlens wallwash luminaire, while Figure 8.7 shows a ceramic metal halide wallwash luminaire.

Figure 8.8 illustrates use of the discrete fluorescent asymmetric slot luminaires. These range in length from 1' (300 mm), to as long as 4' (1200 mm). These kinds of units and their halogen/lensed counterparts can typically be spaced on center as much as 2 to 2.5 times their distance from the wall. This can yield some excellent efficiencies, in both energy and initial cost.

`some wallslot examples online @`
```
http://www.linearlighting.com/
http://www.litecontrol.com/
http://www.cooperlighting.com/brands/neo-ray/
```

8.6.2 Ambient recessed luminaires

Recessed luminaires are so named because the housing actually recesses above the ceiling plane. Several varieties are common for general lighting in many applications. These include lensed luminaires, parabolic luminaires, and shielded–lamp luminaires. All of these luminaires depend on a rigid housing. The thinner the gauge of metal used in the housing, the greater the likelihood that luminaires will not sit firmly into or be aligned with the ceiling grid or drywall flange. Further, most of these luminaires require some sort of mechanical door to access lamps for relamping. Again, thinner gauge metals and/or poor fitting lift–and–shift access doors will readily result in a poor look soon after the first relamping cycle.

Lensed luminaires are typically used in laboratories, healthcare facilities, and foodservice facilities where easy cleaning and/or the need to contain broken lamp fragments (by code in the case of foodservice facilities) are required. With proper gasketing, these luminaires are available in wet–rated versions. A wide range of lensing is available. However, the higher efficiency

8.6.2 Luminaires

Figure 8.5 (wallslot)

The lighting program for this open office called for soft, diffuse ambient light with dramatic accents in perimeter situations. This corridor portal offered just such a dramatic accent opportunity. The blue metal panel exhibits high gloss, yet the color deserves accenting to serve as an exciting visual element from the distance. A fluorescent wallslot was used to graze the wall. This slot, by Neoray, uses an indirect cove detail built into the luminaire so that the lamp can never be directly viewed—an important feature for such a glossy wall. Philips F32T8/830 lamps are used.

Figure 8.5 (ambient)

The ambient lighting hardware was selected for its very slim profile—considered important in a relatively low-ceiling space in order to maintain appropriate human–scale (large stuff looming overhead seems quite foreboding). With these small lines of light, by Peerless, straightness of run (particularly as viewed in the end–on condition) and rigidity (no sag or snake) are critical for observing a "perfect" installation. Philips F32T8/830 lamps are used.

©2001, Steelcase Inc. Reprinted with permission.

lenses typically are also the most glary and/or most unattractive. Typically, lenses with smaller prisms (e.g., the generic A20) have a better appearance and offer a softer distribution of light and less glare. Lens thickness will depend on the size of the luminaire, but is particularly important on luminaires with a footprint larger than 4 square feet (0.35 square meters). Thicker lenses exhibit less sag. Some luminaire manufacturers, including Legion, Lightolier, Neoray, and Prudential, offer deep regress lensed luminaires with opal lenses. The regress is achieved in most of these luminaires with an extruded edge, offering a clean, neat look. Regressing indicates that the lens itself sits at least an inch (25 mm) above the ceiling plane. If the lens is etched on the bottom surface, there are no glossy reflections—offering a richer look than the typically shiny plastic. Nice, but inefficient and better left to areas where appearance is a primary goal and direct fluorescent lighting is desirable.

Parabolic luminaires, introduced in the 1960s, have replaced lensed luminaires as the commodity light for most commercial applications. Four–lamp lensed 2 by 4' (600 by 1200 mm) were the popular, cheap way to achieve illuminances exceeding 100 fc (1000 lux). For the few employers who cared and the few architects who fought the battle, 4–lamp parabolic luminaires were a welcome reprieve from the glare of the lensed luminaires. By the mid–1980s, however, the energy crises had made their collective mark and 3–lamp parabolic luminaires became the standard. Engineers, in an attempt to maximize illuminance, minimize connected load, and minimize first costs, were laying out parabolic lighting systems that resulted in dark, cavelike spaces, and/or inflexible open plan offices, and/or severe VDT screen washout problems. A VDT screen positioned under a large, 2– or 3–lamp parabolic luminaire may exhibit washout. A user seated under such a luminaire may experience a form of glare, even if the luminaire is not in the overhead peripheral field of view. On the other hand, a user seated between luminaires may have a "dark hole" experience—the

Image ©GarySteffyLightingDesign Inc./luminaire by others

Luminaires

contrast between the relatively brighter surround and the immediate low brightness results in an impression of a very dark zone. The key is using low–lumen luminaires (e.g., a 2 by 2' (600 by 600 mm) parabolic using 3–F17T8/830 lamps, or a 1 by 4' (300 by 1200 mm) parabolic using 1–F32T8/830 lamp) on relatively close spacings (e.g., on staggered patterns of 4 by 4' [1.2 by 1.2 m] or on regular patterns of 6 by 6' [1.8 by 1.8 mm] for 8' [2.5 m] or 9' [2.75 m] ceiling heights). As computer tasks became prominent, parabolic luminaires were developed that maintained low luminances and illuminances. Figure 8.8 illustrates one such parabolic luminaire. One way to quickly assess a parabolic luminaire's glare control is to check the depth and cell size of the louver or baffle. The deeper the louver, in general, the better the glare control. Some louvers and baffles actually surround and almost engage the lamp for a very low glare situation (as is the case in the parabolic luminaire shown in Figure 8.8). Louvers or baffles that are less than 3" (75 mm) in depth should have blade spacings equal to the depth in order to maintain a 45 degree cutoff. Finally, the finish of the aluminum has a significant impact on the aesthetic quality of the luminaire and on the overall brightness impression. Three basic finishes are available, and all should be low iridescent (i.e., not exhibiting an oil-canning appearance that can occur with standard aluminum when lighted with the triphosphor fluorescent lamps—the three phosphor wavelength peaks are actually reflected at slightly different angles, thereby causing a rainbow effect on the aluminum. These three finishes are specular, semi–specular, and diffuse. Diffuse is the current favorite where some sense of brightness is desirable (which is most applications) and also hides fingerprinting—a very practical benefit with luminaire relamping.

A recent newcomer to recessed lighting is an approach whereby the lamps are actually hidden from direct view. The recessed luminaire acts as a miniature cove. Although the effect is somewhat like indirect lighting, the proximity of the lamps to the luminaire reflecting surface result in sufficient luminances that this luminaire is not appropriate for large open areas where VDT use is anticipated. These luminaires are best suited for small areas, such as private offices, conference rooms, copier centers, and the like, or circulation and transition spaces.

8.6.3 Ambient pendent luminaires

Where ceiling heights are greater than 9' (2.75 m) (preferably 10' [3 m] or more), pendent mounted lighting generally has promise. Indirect lighting can provide virtually glare–free conditions while giving the impression of brightness. Just as with parabolic luminaires, the success of this approach is driven by the lamping and spacing of the luminaires. Luminaire optics can vary significantly from manufacturer to manufacturer and from luminaire type to luminaire type. With the introduction of T5 fluorescent lamps, luminaire manufacturers are introducing very efficient luminaires with widespread distribution. However, standard T5 lamps tend to be more appropriate for most standard office applications. Single–lamp cross–section luminaires are best in order to meet energy code requirements.

Two key criteria for electronic office applications of indirect lighting are the ceiling luminance and the uniformity of this luminance. As reported in Table 4.9, office ceilings should not be any brighter than 250 fL (850 cd/m²), and as reported in Table 4.10, the luminance ratio on the ceiling surface should be 4:1 where computer use is intensive. The ambient lighting shown in Figure 8.5 meets these criteria—compliance depends on luminaire optics and lamping.

8.6.3 Luminaires

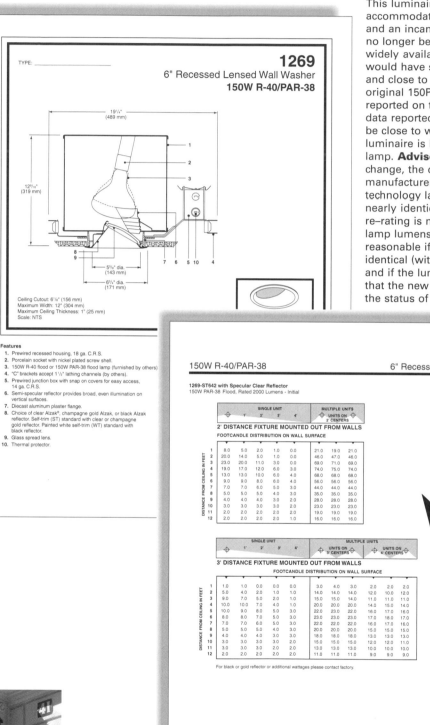

1269
6" Recessed Lensed Wall Washer
150W R-40/PAR-38

19¹/₄" (489 mm)
12⁹/₁₆" (319 mm)
5⁵/₈" dia. (143 mm)
6³/₄" dia. (171 mm)

Ceiling Cutout: 6¹/₈" (156 mm)
Maximum Width: 12" (304 mm)
Maximum Ceiling Thickness: 1" (25 mm)
Scale: NTS

Features

1. Prewired recessed housing, 18 ga. C.R.S.
2. Porcelain socket with nickel plated screw shell.
3. 150W R-40 flood or 150W PAR-38 flood lamp (furnished by others)
4. "C" brackets accept 1¹/₂" lathing channels (by others).
5. Prewired junction box with snap on covers for easy access, 14 ga. C.R.S.
6. Semi-specular reflector provides broad, even illumination on vertical surfaces.
7. Diecast aluminum plaster flange.
8. Choice of clear Alzak®, champagne gold Alzak, or black Alzak reflector. Self-trim (ST) standard with clear or champagne gold reflector. Painted white self-trim (WT) standard with black reflector.
9. Glass spread lens.
10. Thermal protector.

Figure 8.6

This luminaire was originally developed to accommodate both an incandescent R lamp and an incandescent PAR lamp. R lamps should no longer be used; however, PAR lamps are widely available. Today, a 100PAR38/HIR/FL would have similar light output (2070 lumens) and close to the same candlepower as the original 150PAR38/FL lamp for which data are reported on the second sheet (below). So, the data reported below can then be presumed to be close to what data will result when the luminaire is lamped with a 100PAR38/HIR/FL lamp. **Advisory**: As lighting technologies change, the designer must either re–rate manufacturers' published data for the new–technology lamps or attempt to find a lamp of nearly identical light output characteristics. If re–rating is necessary, use the ratio of new lamp lumens to old lamp lumens. This is only reasonable if lamp beam spreads are nearly identical (within a few degrees of one another), and if the luminaire manufacturer has indicated that the new technology lamp does not change the status of the luminaire's UL listing.

150W R-40/PAR-38 — 6" Recessed Lensed Wall Washer

1269-ST642 with Specular Clear Reflector
150W PAR-38 Flood, Rated 2000 Lumens - Initial

2' DISTANCE FIXTURE MOUNTED OUT FROM WALLS
FOOTCANDLE DISTRIBUTION ON WALL SURFACE

DISTANCE FROM CEILING IN FEET	SINGLE UNIT 1'	2'	3'	4'	MULTIPLE UNITS UNITS ON 2' CENTERS		
1	8.0	5.0	2.0	1.0	0.0	21.0	19.0	21.0
2	20.0	14.0	5.0	1.0	0.0	46.0	47.0	46.0
3	23.0	20.0	11.0	3.0	0.0	69.0	71.0	69.0
4	19.0	17.0	12.0	6.0	3.0	74.0	75.0	74.0
5	13.0	13.0	10.0	6.0	4.0	68.0	68.0	68.0
6	9.0	9.0	8.0	6.0	4.0	56.0	56.0	56.0
7	7.0	7.0	6.0	5.0	3.0	44.0	44.0	44.0
8	5.0	5.0	5.0	4.0	3.0	35.0	35.0	35.0
9	4.0	4.0	4.0	3.0	2.0	28.0	28.0	28.0
10	3.0	3.0	3.0	3.0	2.0	23.0	23.0	23.0
11	2.0	2.0	2.0	2.0	2.0	19.0	19.0	19.0
12	2.0	2.0	2.0	2.0	1.0	16.0	16.0	16.0

3' DISTANCE FIXTURE MOUNTED OUT FROM WALLS
FOOTCANDLE DISTRIBUTION ON WALL SURFACE

DISTANCE FROM CEILING IN FEET	SINGLE UNIT 1'	2'	3'	4'	MULTIPLE UNITS UNITS ON 3' CENTERS			UNITS ON 4' CENTERS		
1	1.0	1.0	0.0	0.0	0.0	3.0	4.0	3.0	2.0	2.0	2.0
2	5.0	4.0	2.0	1.0	1.0	14.0	14.0	14.0	12.0	10.0	12.0
3	9.0	7.0	5.0	2.0	1.0	15.0	15.0	14.0	11.0	11.0	11.0
4	10.0	10.0	7.0	4.0	1.0	20.0	20.0	20.0	14.0	15.0	14.0
5	10.0	9.0	8.0	5.0	3.0	22.0	23.0	22.0	16.0	17.0	16.0
6	8.0	8.0	7.0	5.0	3.0	23.0	23.0	23.0	17.0	18.0	17.0
7	7.0	7.0	6.0	5.0	3.0	22.0	22.0	22.0	16.0	17.0	16.0
8	5.0	5.0	5.0	4.0	3.0	20.0	20.0	20.0	15.0	15.0	15.0
9	4.0	4.0	4.0	3.0	3.0	18.0	18.0	18.0	13.0	13.0	13.0
10	3.0	3.0	3.0	3.0	2.0	15.0	15.0	15.0	12.0	12.0	11.0
11	3.0	3.0	3.0	2.0	2.0	13.0	13.0	13.0	10.0	10.0	10.0
12	2.0	2.0	2.0	2.0	2.0	11.0	11.0	11.0	9.0	9.0	9.0

For black or gold reflector or additional wattages please contact factory.

Presc•lite 1251 Doolittle Dr. • San Leandro, California 94577 U.S.A. • Phone (510) 562-3500
With representatives' offices in principal cities throughout North America.
Copyright© 1998 Prescolite, All Rights Reserved • Specifications subject to change without notice. • Printed in U.S.A. • RINC-042 • 3/98

Cutsheet drawings courtesy of and ©Prescolite, Inc. Available online at http://www.prescolite.com

Luminaires

Figure 8.7

Ceramic metal halide lamps offer great promise for efficient wallwashing using the spreadlens wallwash luminaire. Note below that the data is displayed for a 100PAR38/CMH/3K/NFL, presumably (if vague, this should be confirmed with the manufacturer). A multiplier of 0.60 is shown at the very bottom of the second sheet below for a 70PAR38/CMH/3K/NFL lamp. When the arrowed data is multiplied, the results are greater than what is anticipated from the arrowed data of the 100PAR38/HIR/FL lamp shown in Figure 8.6. This is likely a result of both the ceramic metal halide technology and the use of a slightly more focused PAR lamp here (the NFL here versus the FL lamp in Figure 8.6). Also, note that when the metal halide wallwash is moved to a distance greater than 3' (900 mm) from the wall, the upper portion of the wall goes dark. A wall is considered uniformly lighted if the maximum–to–minimum ratio is 10:1 top to bottom and left to right.

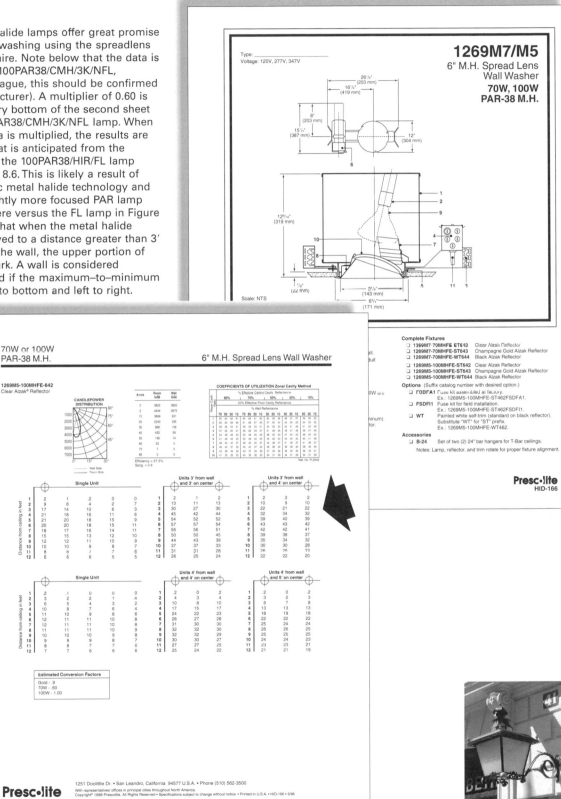

Image ©GarySteffy/LightingDesign Inc./luminaire by others

8.6.3 Luminaires

Image ©Robert Eovaldi

Figure 8.8

The very low ceiling condition combined with the desire for a "Class A" work environment of hushed conversation, and high–efficiency lighting (the client was driven to respect the earth's resources, so energy use and material resource use were to be kept to a minimum) resulted in the use of recessed parabolic luminaires for the direct ambient lighting. For best glare control, given the high use of VDTs, Lithonia Optimax luminaires were each lamped with one GE F32T8/830 lamp and spaced over workstations for best efficiency. To avoid a cave effect so common with parabolic luminaires (e.g., to enhance the sense of spaciousness—see Section 4.5.3), liberal wallwashing was used. Here, Columbia Parawash luminaires, each using one GE F18Long/830/RS/4P lamp, are spaced 2' (600 mm) from the wall and 4' (1200 mm) on center for a uniform wash. The interior architect carefully coordinated finishes to achieve the most lighting effect for the least wattage—hence, the light–colored walls.

Other pendent luminaires include the semi–indirect and direct/indirect versions. These tend to offer the most efficient lighting systems available today that also have the capability of providing the most comfortable environment. For any pendent lighting solution, including the indirect version, luminaires can be extruded aluminum or formed steel. They can be modular or essentially built to suit (usually in 1' [300 mm] increments). They can be suspended by aircraft cable (as in Figure 8.5), which is essentially invisible or via tubular stems. These suspension components need to be on some consistent spacing that the manufacturer recommends for the given luminaire to assure a level, plumb run. Power feeds need to occur ever so often and are available in straight or coiled white or black cords. The coiled cords, while initially looking firm and neat, eventually sag so that the coils are all bunched toward the bottom of the cord. With aircraft cable, luminaires can be attached to some grid systems, depending on the local code requirements. Otherwise, cable attachment points are typically located in the center of ceiling tiles, at least laterally (with the luminaire width).

The luminaires discussed here are widely available for review online. Cutsheets and photometry are easily accessed at various manufacturers' websites. There is no need to guess about lighting equipment or optics. There is no reason to use generic luminaires from outdated texts and references. The designer should treat every project as fresh and new, and should research programming, schematics, and solutions accordingly.

Image ©GarySteffyLightingDesign Inc./luminaire by others

Luminaires

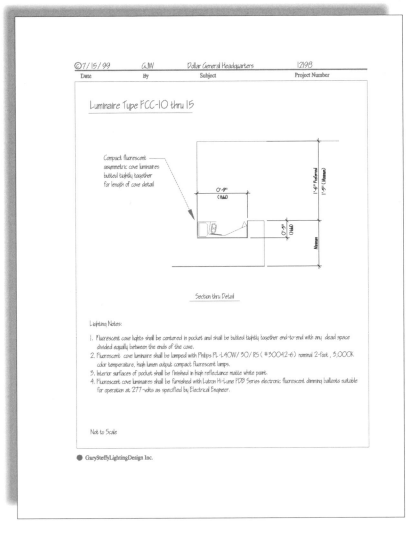

Figure 8.9

This fluorescent cove detail expresses the important dimensions for purposes of getting the luminaire into the detail and getting light out of the detail. This particular cove was detailed around the Peerless ECX–style cove luminaire with an F40Long/830/RS/4P lamp. This detail would accompany the lighting specification, which itself would reiterate the size of the Peerless luminaire, outline the lamping and ballast requirements, and cite the specific Peerless catalog number. A plan view used for the lighting layer of a reflected ceiling plan is shown in Figure 11.2 ("architectural cove with asymmetric luminaires"). This detail is similar to that used along the top of the tall wall in Figure 4.43.

8.7 Lighting details

Some luminaires are intended for use in architectural details. Here, the designer must develop concept sketches indicating the relevant detail dimensions around which the architect and/or engineer will then develop structural and architectural finish details to support and hide the luminaire. Perhaps the most significant issue for any detail is its intended function—decorative, functional, or both. The more functional details will have to be developed around the photometric qualities of the luminaire. Fluorescent asymmetric distribution cove lights, for example, are intended to spread light across a ceiling above the cove detail. Calculations show the height of the cove opening is critical to optimal performance of the asymmetric cove luminaire. Figure 8.9 illustrates such a detail concept.

8.8 General References

Gary Steffy Lighting Design Inc. 2000. *Time–Saver Standards for Architectural Lighting Design.* New York: McGraw–Hill.

Image ©GarySteffyLightingDesign Inc./luminaire by others

Controls

Controls for lighting can be simple electromechanical devices that literally connect a light to electricity or disconnect a light from electricity—depending on the position of the switch that a given user has manually configured (typical toggle switch has an up position for "on" and a down position for "off"). However, with the great developments and size and cost reductions in electronics, controls for lighting are increasingly capable of many functions. Because of their direct interface with the electrical distribution system, controls are devices that ultimately are the responsibility of the registered engineer on the project. The designer needs to indicate how lights are grouped and where switches are to be located. The designer should also provide a suggestion on the kind of control involved—hence, the following discussion.

9.1 Switches (on/off operation)

Traditional on/off switches need to be addressed in terms of type (e.g., toggle, slide, electronic push-button, or rocker), location, and quantity. Typical locations for switches include wall, door jamb, or remote control by phone or handheld infrared or radio frequency device. For wall–mounted switches, the height above finished floor (AFF) and the lateral location from nearby walls or door jamb must be established by the architect or interior designer. It should be noted that consistent lateral dimension from door jambs and mounting height from floor are desired for the best look as well as for a consistent "find" for users. To be ADA–compliant, switches need to be at or less than 4' (1.2 m) AFF.

For any user, the number of switches increases the complexity of space use. Typically, more than three switches introduces significant confusion. Further, more than three switches will consume a significant amount of wall space. This introduces at least two problems. First, the wall area may be sufficiently full that artwork or other wall–mounted niceties are prohibited. Second, this looks awful. If more than three wall switches are a necessity, then consideration should be given to networked or preset switching systems.

Table 9.1 outlines some controls designations that might be considered when indicating controls on drawings. With regard to the last two designations (S_L and $S_{Room\ No.}$), there are certainly variations on the theme. In any event, reference to these designations is then required in the Controls' Specification (see Section 11.5) so that the contractor can purchase appropriate devices. For spaces where preset scene controls are specified or where switches are the networked or preset type, it is suggested that the control designation be $S_{Room\ No.}$ in order to attract specific attention to its special nature (see discussions below).

Switches should be selected based on intended function and users' needs. Toggle switches are extremely easy to comprehend (up is "on" and down is "off") and easy to use. Other switch types are available, including push-button and rocker. These are typically considered more decorative than the toggle switch; however, a review of switch type with the building owner and/or users may be advised to confirm that these styles are acceptable. Also, screwless plates are considered more aesthetically pleasing in most situations, and switches are now available in many styles. Typically, the screws are hidden beneath a snap–over switchplate. Where security is an

Image ©EyeWire, Inc.

9.2  Controls

astronomical timeclock

A timeclock that has built–in software to keep track of the solar calendar and, if so programmed, track daylight savings time and standard time changes. Such a timeclock, then, knows, for example, sunrise and sunset times and can program lights on or off accordingly. Astronomical timeclocks can perform complete operation of lights, providing there is no concern about darkness due to impending storms (which only a photocell could detect).

issue, switches can be the keyed type, where insertion of a key into the switch is necessary for its function. However, the registered professional(s) on the project needs to ascertain the code requirements for switching types and locations.

more online @

```
http://www.cooperwiringdevices.com/iemain.html
http://www.geindustrial.com/industrialsystems/panelboards/catalog/lc-main/
    index.htm
http://www.hubbell-bryant.com/
http://www.leviton.com/sections/prodinfo/newprod/npleadin.htm
http://www.passandseymour.com/
```

9.2 Switches (on/dimming/off operation)

Where incandescent lighting is prevalent and/or where lighting intensity is intended to change based on space use, dimming switches are appropriate. Dimming for incandescent lamps has the added benefit of extending lamp life. As Figure 7.1 illustrates, dimming incandescent lamps just 5 percent can yield a 200 percent increase in lamp life.

Dimming of low voltage and fluorescent lamps requires special dimmers. When selecting and specifying dimmers, then it is necessary to determine if the desired dimmer can safely and satisfactorily dim the lighting that is intended to be dimmed. Manufacturers' literature is clear in this regard. However, where questions arise, contact respective switch and luminaire manufacturers.

As with on/off switches, dimmers should be selected based on anticipated use. If users are elderly, then the ease of the on/off function and the ease of the dimming function (and the clarity of how these are done) will be crucial. If users are likely to set the dimmer setting once in a while (rather than always changing the setting), then dimmers that have a small, nearly hidden slider immediately adjacent to the toggle, push-button, or rocker might be appropriate (the slider is so small that it is not convenient for intermittent dimming control throughout the day). Rotary dimmers are considered old–fashioned by many people and may be difficult to operate for the elderly. Slider dimmers may be easier to use, but have an inherent flaw with the "off" mode. "Off" is when the slider is pushed down and "clicked" off. Since the lights dim to what appears to be "off" at the downward push just prior to clicking off, most folks fail to realize that the final "click to off" is necessary. Hence, the lights continue to draw a bit of power, but not sufficiently to glow.

more online @

```
http://www.cooperwiringdevices.com/iemain.html
http://www.geindustrial.com/industrialsystems/panelboards/catalog/lc-main/
    index.htm
http://www.hubbell-bryant.com/
http://www.leviton.com/sections/prodinfo/newprod/npleadin.htm
http://www.litetouch.com/main.html
http://www.lithonia.com/controls/synergy/default.htm
http://www.lolcontrols.com/products/default.asp
http://www.lutron.com/
http://www.passandseymour.com/
```

9.3 Networked switching

Depending on the size of the project and the number of switches and/or dimmers ultimately used on the project, it may be desirable to network all or many of the switches for centralized control. There are two basic systems—one for residential and some smaller hospitality and commercial applica-

Image ©EyeWire, Inc.

Controls

Table 9.1 Control Device Designations

Designation	Lighting Intent	Issues
S	Single on/off switch (may be ganged with others)	• Convenient/obvious upon entering room • Permits turning off lights immediately prior to exiting room without walking through darkened room • Convenient to operate (simple to understand) • Controls all architectural lights in room or combined with other switches for complete control
S_d	Single dimmer switch (may be ganged with others)	• Convenient/obvious upon entering room • Permits turning off lights immediately prior to exiting room without walking through darkened room • Convenient to operate (simple to understand) • Controls all architectural lights in room or combined with other switches for complete control
S_3	3–way switch (control lights from two locations)	• At least one switch is convenient/obvious upon entering room • At least one switch permits turning off lights immediately prior to exiting room without walking through darkened room • Convenient to operate (simple to understand) • Controls all architectural lights in room or combined with other switches for complete control
S_4	4–way switch (control lights from three locations)	• At least one switch is convenient/obvious upon entering room • At least one switch permits turning off lights immediately prior to exiting room without walking through darkened room • Convenient to operate (simple to understand) • Controls all architectural lights in room or combined with other switches for complete control
S_L	Single on/off switch with indicator light	• Typically mounted outside of room (e.g., walk–in refrigerator, closet, etc.). • Can be turned off by others external to lighted room
S_M	Single on/off switch with integral motion sensor	• Various sensing technologies and combinations available • Appearance of switch device • Location/orientation of switch critical to successful operation and depends on range and area of coverage available from switch device
$S_{Room No.}$	Special control devices ($S_{Room No.-A, B, C, etc}$ for multiple special controls in each room)	• At least one switch is convenient/obvious upon entering room • At least one switch permits turning off lights immediately prior to exiting room without walking through darkened room • Convenient to operate (simple to understand) • Controls all architectural lights in room or combined with other switches for complete control

tions, and one for large–scale commercial applications. Here, the desire for centralized control from specific locations is important. For example, in a large residence, it becomes tedious at bedtime for the owner to check all rooms to make certain lights are off. Further, it is desirable, perhaps, to have centralized function of exterior security lights. There may be a desire to have quick access to all or many house lights in the event of an emergency or an intrusion. Finally, it may be desirable to interconnect some or all lights with the security alarm system. All of these desires can be achieved if lighting controls are networked together and then are made centrally programmable. These systems typically have such available features as photocell control (to automatically switch some or all landscape lights on at dusk or when a storm passes, for example) and **astronomical timeclock** control. Some systems

Image ©EyeWire, Inc.

9.4 Controls

also have special features, such as vacation mode and "lighted path home." Here, the system tracks and memorizes weekly lighting rituals (which lights are turned on/off and at what times by users of these spaces) and then can play back the previous week's lighting when occupants go on vacation—giving the residence the "someone's home" appearance due to oddly timed on/off and varied room lighting schedules. The "lighted path home" feature allows users to call ahead on cell phone to activate certain lighting scenes (such as site lighting or security lighting). A similar feature interfaces the garage door opener with lighting scenes—when the garage door opener is activated, certain lights can also be switched on.

These networked systems are quite popular in large residences or where the occupant is looking for convenience. However, they are also appropriate in smaller hospitality and commercial applications. Country clubs, conference centers, conference suites, executive office suites, multi–roomed dining facilities, and the like are potential applications. Networked systems can range in cost from just US$1500 or so for a series of rooms, to several hundred thousand dollars for an entire commercial building.

more online @

```
http://www.geindustrial.com/industrialsystems/panelboards/catalog/lc-main/
    index.htm
http://www.leviton.com/sections/prodinfo/newprod/npleadin.htm
http://www.litetouch.com/main.html
http://www.lithonia.com/
http://www.lolcontrols.com/products/default.asp
http://www.lutron.com/
```

9.4 Preset switching

For some facilities or spaces, the time comes when a bunch of dimmer switches on the walls to each room or area offers occupants and/or passersby too many opportunities to dim the lighting to the wrong intensity or to an inappropriate effect or mood. Examples include auditoriums, restaurants, conference facilities, building lobbies and atriums, ceremonial reception and/or office areas, and home dining rooms, family rooms, living rooms, and even kitchens. Because of the various functions that might occur over various times of the day and night, it is desirable to "set the scene" for each specific function and/or time of day. With a wall full of switches and dimmers, this means some sort of marking code for the dimmers along with a legend on when each marked code is to be used and when switches are to be "on" or "off." Obviously, this is tedious for the users and soon is dismissed as an annoyance. Preset controls are based on a dimming system that actually keeps track of all the lights and switches and/or dimmers in a room or suite of rooms (or for exterior lights and related switches and/or dimmers) and allows the specification of usually one, two, four, six, eight, twelve, sixteen, etc., preset scenes.

A preset scene is established when the lights in a room or area have been grouped and dimmed to provide a specific light intensity and/or aesthetic look. For example, in a restaurant with wall sconces, pendents over banquettes, recessed art accents, a special highlight accent for the maitre d' station, and special display case lighting, there is a desire to set each of these groups of lights to specific intensities for lunch, to different specific intensities for dinner, and to yet other different intensities for clean up. So, the three scenes are lunch, dinner, and clean up. A three–button preset control station (or wall switchplate) is not a standard item, but a four–button control station is readily available. The fourth button would be kept as a spare or perhaps simply assigned a desirable, but unnecessary function—such as "closing" (which

Image ©EyeWire, Inc.

Controls

9.5

Table 9.2 Control Zone and Preset Scene Example

Zone	Lunch (Scene 1)[a]	Dinner (Scene 2)[a]	Closing (Scene 3)[a]	Clean up (Scene 4)[a]
(1) Sconces	0.80	0.35	0.90	1.00
(2) Pendents	0.65	0.25	0.75	1.00
(3) Art accents	0.80	0.45	0.80	0.00
(4) Maitre d'	0.95	0.60	0.00	0.85
(5) Display case	0.95	0.45	0.00	0.00

[a] Value cited is based on 1.00 as full on (100% light output) and 0.00 as full off (0% light output).

might be a scene of lighting that is brighter and less aesthetic than the "dinner" scene, but not as harsh as the "clean up" scene) that could be used fifteen minutes prior to closing to indicate to patrons that time is running out. There are five zones of lights—sconces, pendents, art accents, maitre d' station accent, and display case. Table 9.2 outlines the various scenes and the settings of each zone proposed for each scene. Most preset systems are easily reprogrammed, so that after several days or weeks of operation, changes can be made. However, any staff member can readily set lights properly for each scene with a simply push of a button. Of course, scene buttons need to be properly labeled. The smallest preset scene system (for a small room or group of rooms) is likely to cost US$2000 installed.

more online @

    http://www.geindustrial.com/industrialsystems/panelboards/catalog/lc-main/
        index.htm
    http://www.litetouch.com/main.html
    http://www.lithonia.com/
    http://www.lolcontrols.com/products/default.asp
    http://www.lutron.com/

control zone

A specific light or group of lights identified to be separately controlled from all other light and/or groups of lights in a space or area. See Figure 11.5 for a control zone loop diagram.

9.5 Timeclocks

Timeclocks can be used to automatically sequence lighting at predetermined times. These devices range from the very simply electromechanical types to electronic devices with many functions. Timeclock selection is based on the extent of the required function and the number and types of lighting equipment being controlled. For example, a few exterior lights at a residence could be timed "on" and "off" with a simple electromechanical timeclock. However, if the front lawn is to be controlled separately from the back lawn, and if some interior security lights are also to be controlled at yet another time, then either three simple timeclocks are required or an electronic timeclock that can handle the multiple functions should be specified. As noted earlier, astronomical timeclocks are convenient since they also keep track of the solar time (actual sunrise and sunset times throughout the year, as well as tracking daylight savings and standard times). Timeclocks can also be specified with battery backup in case of power failure. Generally, the most convenient timeclock and the one consistently yielding the best tailored energy use and sustainability timeclock arrangement is an electronic, astronomical timeclock with battery backup; however, these are also the most expensive timeclocks.

more online @

    http://www.lutron.com/
    http://www.passandseymour.com/
    http://www.tork.com/

9.6 Controls

9.6 Motion sensors

Motion sensors can be integrated into switches or can be independently mounted devices—typically mounted on the ceiling. Motion sensors offer the promise of, and usually deliver energy savings by, switching lights off when lighted areas are unoccupied for a predetermined period. Placement of motion sensors is important to their successful function. If sensors are located out of the line of sight of occupants, then it is likely the sensors won't sense occupants and may inadvertently switch lights off. Additionally, sensor technology influences how well it detects occupants. Some sensors use infrared technology, others use ultrasonic technology, and still others use a combination. The dual technology appears to offer the best coverage for a variety of occupancy situations. Motion sensors aren't appropriate if spaces are always or likely to be occupied.

Where motion sensors control fluorescent lights, it is important to determine the likely frequency of on/off switching. Fluorescent lamps have a shortened life if they are switched off and on frequently. Programmed start ballasts offer the softest and smoothest lamp start and are intended to improve lamp life even if frequent on and off switching occurs. If it is suspected that the motion sensor(s) will only activate fluorescent lights up to four times each day, then instant start and rapid start ballasting would be reasonable. If more frequent activation is expected, programmed ballasts should be used. Even though the lamps may not last their full rated life because they are expected to be off much of the day, their actual time in service (in place until relamping is required) is likely to be quite long.

more online @

    http://www.hubbell-bryant.com/
    http://www.leviton.com/sections/prodinfo/newprod/npleadin.htm
    http://www.lithonia.com/
    http://www.lolcontrols.com/products/default.asp
    http://www.lutron.com/
    http://www.passandseymour.com/
    http://www.tork.com/
    http://www.wattstopper.com/webc/home.htm!

9.7 Photocells

Where daylighting is available, consideration should be given to dimming or switching off electric lights when the daylight intensities are sufficient to accommodate the task(s). This is only practical when automated and activated by a photocell. Photocells are available for indoor use and for exterior use. Location of photocells should relate quite directly to their intent (e.g., if lighting along a north window wall is to be photocell controlled, the photocell should not be located on the south wall). Typically, in large applications, more than one photocell is necessary to relate directly to the locale and architectural conditions of each area to be controlled. Photocells must be kept cleaned and should be kept away from the influence of electric light.

more online @

    http://www.leviton.com/sections/prodinfo/newprod/npleadin.htm
    http://www.lithonia.com/
    http://www.lolcontrols.com/products/default.asp
    http://www.lutron.com/
    http://www.passandseymour.com/
    http://www.tork.com/
    http://www.wattstopper.com/webc/home.htm!

Image ©EyeWire, Inc.

Controls

9.8 Switching strategies

Where rooms are small and/or lighting layouts are simple, then individual switches to each light or group of lights is a reasonable approach to switching. Always plan for a switch at the entry to a space or area so that people can light a path immediately upon entering and extinguishing the lighted path immediately upon exiting.

Where lighting layouts are more complicated and/or include distinct light groupings intended to operate independently, consideration might be given to preset switching. Where such complicated lighting persists in other rooms or areas of a facility, then networked switching and/or networking of the preset switches is desirable so that lighting can be centrally controlled. Alternatively, where an area or group of areas simply have lots of luminaires, centralized control offered by networked switching is desirable. These centralized systems are automated and can be easily orchestrated by computer.

Combine photocell and astronomical timeclock functions with computer–controlled networked switching for the most efficient and, therefore, the most sustainable lighting approach. With each upgrade in switching technique and technology, initial costs increase. Further, maintenance requirements become more sophisticated. Finally, few complete systems can be easily specified and integrated with all technologies combined. This puts greater burden on the designer, the registered professionals, and the installation contractor.

9.9 Device styles, arrangements, and function

For any control devices, recognize there will be decisions and/or issues regarding color, finish, mechanical attachment, ganging, button type consistency, and backlighting, if any. Most control devices are plastic, although some metal devices are available. Colors are typically limited to white (a certainty), ivory (a near certainty), brown (a possibility), and black (a possibility). If mixing one vendor's devices with another's, count on the colors not matching. Additionally, the finish itself is likely to be glossy, satin, or matte. Again, this is likely to be inconsistent from vendor to vendor.

Many control devices screw to switchboxes in the wall. Two screws are ever–present on the faceplate. However, several manufacturers have developed screwless (at least in appearance) options. These faceplates have a clean, architectural appearance and are considered aesthetically appropriate in many residential and commercial applications.

Ganging of controls is desired if two or more devices are in or near one location. This becomes increasingly difficult when the devices are from different manufacturers and will be difficult if each device has significantly different functions (e.g., a preset switch with four buttons is difficult to gang with a single on/off switch since the buttons and switch do not have similar appearances).

Some switches are available with an internal, soft light source. This is more easily identifiable in the dark upon entering a space or when wakening in the middle of the night. Some switches are available in an engraved, backlighted configuration that makes it easy to identify preset switch functions in the dark. Finally, some switch devices are themselves internally illuminated computer screens that can have a nightlight presence or activate upon the touch of the screen.

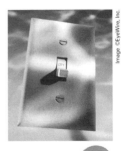

Image ©EyeWire, Inc.

9.9 Controls

To assist in any of these selection criteria and to ease integration of various switch functions, it is best to standardize on a family of vendor–specific control products most appropriate for each project. Further, control operations should be carefully reviewed with the client and/or users. Where infrared (IR) or radio frequency (RF) are to be used as remote control devices, users must be comfortable with such issues as keeping remotes consistently available (they may easily be lost or inadvertently left in other spaces or areas); the use of such devices around other IR or RF devices in the same room, area, or building; and, for IR devices, maintaining a line of sight between the remote device and the IR receiver (the advantage of RF over IR is its ability to work "around corners" and in "blind" setups where the receiver is not visible from the point where the remote control is actually being used); and if more than one IR or RF device is in use, the potential for cross–talk and cancellation between the devices (e.g., if Joe is using the remote to change lights in his office or workstation, can he inadvertently change the lights in Sue's office?).

Design Tools

The design development phase of a project cannot be considered complete until it is known that the proposed solution(s) will work. To know this, however, requires considerable experience and/or quantifiable documentation. Because considerable experience can be gained only over a significant period of time, this text deals with the quantifiable documentation aspects. There comes a time on a project when the designer, other team members, and the client want some degree of confidence that the proposed lighting solution will, indeed, meet most or all of the needs most or all of the time. The most definitive way to determine a proposed solution's success is to build it. This is, however, an extremely costly method of testing a solution. Many design tools are available that will help build a level of confidence with the proposed solution(s)—or will not, in which case the solution(s) needs to be reevaluated and revised accordingly.

Most design tools are part of an iterative process. A design is established, however tentative, and some "test" of that design is made. As the design is finessed, so, too, are the tests. Indeed, the tests will likely help finesse the design. Design, then test, then redesign based on test results, then test again, and so on. Design tools can be classified into qualitative tools and quantitative tools. Qualitative tools allow the designer to assess the lighting quality aspects of the design. For example, will a particular design really result in an impression of spaciousness when compared against other possible designs? On the other hand, quantitative tools allow the designer to assess the lighting quantities—luminances, luminance ratios, and illuminances to name a few.

10.1 Qualitative design tools

Before getting bogged down in all sorts of technical data and calculations, it is desirable to know if the lighting design will be successful in meeting the softer, more subjective, or psychological criteria. After all, it is relatively easy to achieve certain luminances and illuminances—this is done by revising final luminaire selections, spacings, and lamping after lighting techniques have been established. However, establishing lighting techniques is much more difficult. This depends on how the space is to look and feel, which areas and surfaces are to be relatively light, which are to be relatively dark, and which are to be somewhere in between. Two– or 3–dimensional visualizing provides the most appropriate qualitative design tools. This includes mood shots, field trips, lighting renderings, models, and mock-ups.

10.1.1 Mood shots

Sometimes clients and/or users are clearly most comfortable after having seen examples of installations that are similar to the design work being proposed for their specific project. Photos and magazine images can serve this purpose, but this technique must be used with great care. Often professional photos include photographer's fill light, which makes the scene especially attractive as photo art. Indeed, a fine exercise in art is to take the latest architectural and interior design magazines and attempt to determine where fill light was applied (few of these shots are done without fill light). Look for odd shadows (e.g., chair leg shadows raked across the floor for more than a foot or two mean that fill light is likely located off to one side [the side away from which the shadows are directed] at a few feet above the floor). Look for vivid detail (e.g., if floor covering, seating upholstery, wall coverings, and the

10.1.2 Design Tools

like are dark in tone, but subtle patterning is visible, then fill light is likely used to overlight the pattern). Look for odd luminance patterns (e.g., odd wall scallops [although these may be from poorly aimed architectural lighting], or odd floor scallops or ceiling scallops [a dead giveaway that fill was used]). Look for image washout (if the entire photo appears to be effusively lighted to the point of looking as if the installation would be glary or uncomfortable, then banks and banks of fill light were likely used). So, if a client is shown a mood shot that has been filled by the photographer and this isn't appreciated or explained by the lighting designer, it is likely the client will be disappointed with the end result (because it won't look like the picture looked!). To avoid such disappointment, use photos that are believed to present a reasonable facsimile of the actual installed lighting effects; use photos of similar space, style, taste, and budget as the project under consideration; and/or clearly state that the image is being shown for the lighting effects (as opposed to the furnishing's/finishes' styles and character).

Some photographers have taken the time and patience to learn and apply techniques that avoid harsh and unrealistic fill light, yielding photography that is itself and art, while portraying space and light realistically. Many images throughout this text were so taken and prepared. Finally, remember that there is no substitute for seeing an installation firsthand to appreciate actual light characteristics.

10.1.2 Field trips

Viewing the actual lighting installation is best. Field trips to the actual installations are preferable to photo imagery. On larger projects, it is very reasonable to take a one or two day trip to a distant locale to view projects of similar lighting scale and scope. Even though several thousands of dollars may be expended, this is no more costly than the time/fee involved in developing models or computer analyses. Of course, this technique is appropriate only when the project being viewed has quite close character and lighting solutions as the proposed project. Field trips also allow the client to review in situ conditions with workers in place and the comings and goings of visitors, and to experience the importance of maintenance (or lack thereof).

10.1.3 Light renderings by hand

Expressing a sense of light and dark, and shade and shadow to a client will be necessary if the client is uninitiated in lighting or if new techniques or modified applications are to be used on a project. Although some expression can be conveyed in written form, being "there" (through virtual reality or mock-ups) or seeing a picture or light rendering of "there" will be the most expeditious means of convincing a client of your intentions. Lighting renderings are also excellent learning tools—helping the designer better visualize the space or area and allow for exploration of more appropriate solutions.

Light renderings can take many forms. Relatively simple pencil sketches can address spatial form, shade, shadow, and highlighting. Figure 10.1 shows such a sketch. The architect established the perspective wireform and the lighting designer shaded the wireform to illustrate the anticipated effect of a particular lighting concept. Here, the structural ceiling coffer is proposed to be uplighted to accentuate the height of the space, maintain an "open" or "airy" feeling, and to articulate the coffer structure. Luminaires were proposed along the interior–side upper bulkhead running the length of the atrium circulation space. The luminaires were proposed to be asymmetric

Design Tools

10.1.3

Image courtesy of ard ©GE

Figure 10.1

This pencil sketch was based on a wire perspective diagram supplied by the architect. After a lighting concept was discussed with team members, the sketch was then made by developing shade, shadow, and brightness patterns that were both desired for the environment and anticipated from the lighting. Recognize that this is an interactive process. The sketch attempts to illustrate the desired light patterns, and then the lighting equipment and exact placement are established.

Figure 10.2

The sketch shown to the left in Figure 10.1 was used to convince the team, including the client, that the proposed lighting approach would be an appropriate method of lighting the linear atrium. The actual installation, shown here, has a remarkable resemblance to the pencil sketch. This photo was taken from a second floor bridge over the linear atrium space, hence the different perspective and the view of the second floor interior wall. Of course, extensive lighting calculations were done to convince the team that appropriate luminances and illuminances could be achieved. Calculations also helped finalize surface finishes.

throw—to throw light out across the ceiling toward the window wall. The sketch convinced the design team and the client that the aesthetic was appropriate. Quantitative calculations were performed to ascertain the luminance and illuminance components. Figure 10.2 shows the finished lighted effect.

Pencil and charcoal sketches can be quick and effective. The key, of course, is understanding what light will do—how it will shade, shadow, highlight, sparkle, wash, streak, and so on. This can be learned only through observation. A journal (sketchbook) of observations is a convenient if not necessary reference for such work. Pencil and charcoal are limited to monochromatic renderings, but can be used quite effectively to illustrate the effect of lighting. Learn to establish which kinds of lights are in a given space and then attribute various lighting effects to them. Airbrushing with marker is another technique that can be used to show not only shade, shadow, and highlight, but can also show the subtle gradations between these and can illustrate the effect of color. Figure 10.3 shows an airbrush rendering, and Figure 10.4 shows the finished project. As presentations are made to upper management on the larger projects, and as the criticality of the decision tends to increase, it may be necessary to develop more refined presentation renderings.

If a professional renderer is retained as a consultant to the design team, then careful explanation of both the lighting hardware and its likely effects will need to be made to the renderer. Otherwise, lighting patterns are likely to

Image ©GarySteffyLightingDesign Inc.

10.1.3 Design Tools

Figure 10.3
During the conceptual design phase for the exterior lighting of the Michigan State Capitol, an airbrushed elevation was developed to convey the key components of the structure for which lighting was proposed. This helped convince the design team that an overall façade wash was unnecessary. Indeed, it was agreed that even the flatness expressed on the rendering was undesirable and that additional enhancement of the architectural character of the structure was desired.

Figure 10.4
The finished result shows more dramatic lighting than initially proposed in the airbrushed rendering. The architectural lintels and details are dramatized by shadows they create on upper façade areas, yet some accenting of the upper pediments is used to help define the overall structure. The dome, while completely lighted, exhibits a strong flood from the lower colonnade, with soft, fading light grazing the dome, and then strong accenting of the cupola.

be wrong (as the renderer may simply render in a "high contrast" mode for dramatic effect of the image) or even nonexistent (as the renderer may simply render in "100 percent" daylight).

Light renderings can be convenient, requiring a relatively small investment of time and money to illustrate lighting concepts for the design team's edification and the client's comprehension. A variety of techniques are available that lend themselves to black/white/gray value studies or to color renderings. Although light renderings can be a good way to capture the look of a space, a good sense of how a space may feel and function cannot be acquired through renderings.

10.1.4 Light renderings by computer
Computer software has improved since 1990 to the point that fairly quick, yet rough, visualizations can be made. The Illuminating Engineering Society has an annual listing of available lighting software and its proclaimed capabilities. While there is little doubt that these software are accurate in their ability to calculate illuminance and luminance data, many are fraught with quirks of input style and recitation, presentation format, and output style and capabilities.

Design Tools

10.1.5

Image ©GarySteffyLightingDesign Inc.

Figure 10.5
Some lighting software performs relatively simple light renderings to help the designer visualize the lighting effects. Here, Lumen Micro (from Lighting Technologies, Inc.) generated an image of an elevator lobby lighting scheme. This scheme was later used in more rigorous rendering software (see Figure 10.6.2) to show the client various lighting schemes. Recognize, however, that computer time is drastically different between that required for this image (perhaps ten minutes) versus that required for Figure 10.6.2 (perhaps six hours).

Unfortunately, these programs are essentially the product of computer programmers, not lighting designers or even lighting savvy computer programmers. The programs include such oddities as no input mirror on the output, pagination errors, wasted paper, import/export dyslexia, and goofy presentation scales and tables. But if all you need is an answer, and an accurate one, then this software will be fine. If additional time is put into reworking formatting and output details, the resulting printouts can be quite useful for review with other team members and possibly even clients. Perhaps the most ubiquitous of these is Lumen Micro from Lighting Technologies, Inc. Anyone interested in lighting should have a minimum capability of performing Lumen Micro imagery, an example of which is shown in Figure 10.5. For those with great patience and computer aptitude, such programs as Lightscape™ and Radiance can provide excellent imagery. Examples of Radiance renderings are shown in Figure 10.6. These are extraordinarily time–consuming, even for the computer literate and software–able; however, the gain is usually worth the pain. Results are stunning—and typically sufficient to help convince a client of a particular solution. If educational facilities and talent are available for tutorial on Lightscape and/or Radiance, take advantage of this—this skill for lighting design work is quite valuable.

more online @
http://www3.autodesk.com/adsk/section/0,,152898-123112,00.html
http://www.lighting-technologies.com/
http://radsite.lbl.gov/mirror/radiance/book/

10.1.5 Models

Models have long been used to establish architectural layout, cadence, and form. With some innovation, models can be used to illustrate daylighting and electric lighting effects. Models are particularly effective in conveying a total spatial look (including colors and/or finishes), providing additional insight into the subjective aspects of the entire architectural design. Photographs, and especially slides or video, of models can be very effective communication devices for the client. Shoebox–sized models do not require much time or money and yet can be helpful in establishing team consensus on an approach.

Models can be used to show both interior and exterior lighting concepts. Further, one model can be used to explain various lighting scenes proposed for the project or can be used to experiment with various lighting concepts. Figure 10.7 illustrates the use of a single model in order to develop various

Image ©GarySteffyLightingDesign Inc.

Lightscape™ is a registered trademark of Autodesk, Inc.

10.1.5 Design Tools

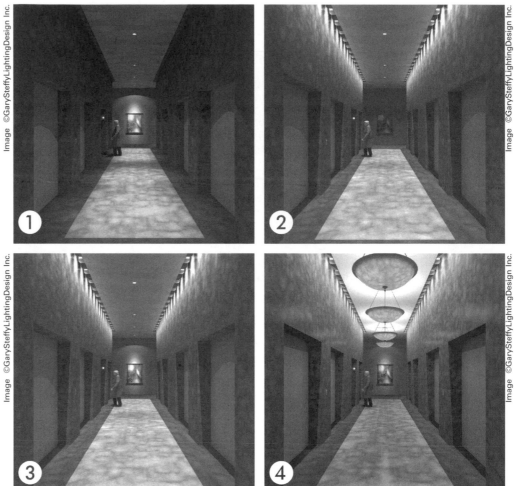

Figure 10.6

These renderings were generated with Radiance/Unix. A relatively narrow elevator lobby is planned on the first floor, and the developer is uncertain if more than downlighting is required. Finishes are honed marble in light and dark varieties, with a plaster ceiling of a relatively light–toned paint. Option 1 is the original preference of the developer–downlights with an art accent. The imagery evokes a confining, cavelike space. For a more spacious appearance, wallwashing is suggested. However, given the slightly glossy nature of the stone, the wallwash must be grazing to avoid harsh glare reflections. Option 2 illustrates this effect. Option 3 includes the art accent, seen as critical to the overall formal effect desired and to the prevention of the dark hole effect experienced as one exits the elevator. Decorative pendents were thought to be one method of also enhancing a sense of spaciousness, so this was illustrated in Option 4.

lighting scenes based on space function. Of particular interest are images 10.7.1 versus 10.7.2, and then 10.7.3 versus 10.7.4. While the architecture remains unchanged, lighting effects vary. In 10.7.2, the artwork that was accented in 10.7.1 is now unlighted. Note how the space has a drab, more institutional, and overall less interesting appearance. In 10.7.4, end wall emphasis is achieved, while in 10.7.3, side wall emphasis is achieved. Note how the corridor seems to continue forever in 10.7.3, while the corridor is visually shortened by comparison in 10.7.4. Alternatively, note how the corridor actually seems wider in the near zone in 10.7.3 than in 10.7.4. A final resolution should then combine these two scenes into one. While the model in this particular example is complicated and aggressive in its effects, working with apertures and light helps offer an understanding of how light can work with and react to architectural form and desired subjective impressions.

Design Tools

10.1.6 Mock-ups

Mock-ups are very effective qualitative techniques that can, in some instances, also be used for quantitative purposes. Mock-ups need not be full–scale or highly refined or detailed, and they sometimes can be done with just a few hundred dollars' worth of materials. Indeed, mock-ups can be made of Fome–Cor® and sheets (these materials are then painted or dyed for reasonably close hue and value).

Many mock-ups are done for aesthetic reasons, but sometimes mock-ups are necessary for quantitative reasons. Providing the mock-up is sufficiently large (so that edge effects can be ignored) or is sufficiently accurate (with daylight apertures and architectural surface colors and finishes as planned), lighting measurements can be made to confirm the proposed lighting resolutions will meet criteria or to permit further design changes in order to meet criteria.

Although full–scale mock-ups may sound expensive and time–consuming, in the context of a building worth tens of millions or hundreds of millions of dollars, a US$100,000 mock-up may be very well worth the price. Additionally, as the building is constructed, there are plenty of opportunities to "test" schemes. This requires close work with the electrical contractor in order to be kept apprised of the windows of opportunity for such mock-ups.

Finally, mock-ups need not be grand, full–scale efforts. It is quite reasonable to request a few sample luminaires and then to mock-up these few lights in your studio space to ascertain quantity and quality of light and effect from the subject luminaire(s). This also permits assessment of the manufacturer's quality control on the assembly and quality of the base luminaire materials.

10.2 Quantitative design tools

There comes a time when the designer and the client need to know how, and then if, the proposed design will meet the luminance and illuminance criteria. Specifically, it is necessary to assess average, maximum, and minimum luminances; luminance ratios; maximum, minimum, and average vertical illuminances; and maximum, minimum, and average horizontal illuminances. The designer need not be a calculus or computer whiz, but does need to know which criteria are important for a given project and which specific target values should be achieved. Final in–depth calculations can be performed by engineering consultants or by manufacturers if need be.

Some basic calculations can assist designers in early budgeting phases and help start layouts. These include templates, the zonal cavity (or lumen) method, the inverse square method, and computer simulations. Initial attempts at any one of these will be somewhat dubious. The designer needs to try any or all of these techniques several times and test actual results against predicted results in order to establish the method(s) that are both convenient and reasonably reliable.

10.2.1 Templates

Templates can be useful in establishing a preliminary equipment layout. Primarily used for site lighting or path lighting, templates are commonly available for postlights and steplights. These templates consist of isocontour plots or lines of lux/footcandle values printed on white paper.

Fome–Cor® is a registered trademark of International Paper.

10.2.1 Design Tools

Figure 10.7

The scale model is initially planned based on lighting criteria (including the architectural form that is given) and anticipated lighting effects from various cutouts (which themselves are "treated" with either colored acetate or diffusing media of varying transmittances depending on the intensity, diffusion, and color desired). With electric light applied near the cutouts, effects can be tested and ultimately photographed for the client's and/or team's consideration. The model allows for easy reconfiguration when effects are not as potent as desired or are deemed too strong. This particular example illustrates a corridor leading into a corporate presentation room. Figure 10.7.1 shows the corridor with sidewall displays accented. Figure 10.7.2 shows no sidewall display accenting, but maintains a focus on the corporate logo on the back wall of the conference room. Figure 10.7.3 shows a general circulation scheme that accentuates architectural elements. Figure 10.7.4 emphasizes the conference room itself. Figure 10.7.5 shows one lighting scheme in the conference room. Figure 10.7.6 shows the relative scale of the model and the lighting rigging used. Example courtesy of the University of Kansas ARCE 690 Fall 2000 Class (David Brown, Hyun Young Cho, Matthew Hendel, Sunwong Jung, and Avraham Mor) taught by Dr. Martin Moeck. **Advisory**: Extreme care must be taken in the lighting of such models. Lamp heat and proximity can be a hazard and must be monitored at all times.

Design Tools

10.2.2

Through the overlaying of tracing paper or vellum onto the white–paper template, the designer can begin to lay out luminaire spacings. This is based on horizontal illuminance only, however. The illuminance values provided with the contours should be considered as **initial values** without any **interreflection**. Although templates are a quick technique, they are not sufficiently accurate to qualify as a final design. Figure 10.8 shows a luminaire cutsheet that includes both the luminaire dimensional specifics and some illuminance isocontour plots. Figure 10.9 discusses the isocontour plots and specifically assesses one contour.

10.2.2 Lumen method

The lumen method, or zonal cavity method, of calculation is no doubt the simplest method of establishing a uniform luminaire layout based on horizontal illuminance criteria (typically at floor height for corridors and circulation spaces or desk height for workspaces). Although lots of factors, coefficients, lamp lumen data, and other values must be sought from a variety of references, the calculation itself entails nothing more than simple addition, multiplication, and division. Because this technique does require some research time to collect the appropriate data, and because the calculation formula has a cumbersome appearance (giving it an appearance of scientific accuracy), many designers believe it is the extent of lighting design. Considering the lumen method to be the be all and end all to lighting design is an incorrect assumption. *The lumen method is only a single–criterion compliance technique and only for uniform luminaire layouts.* Figure 10.10 illustrates the layout uniformity concept necessary for the success of the lumen method. The lumen method is essentially an illuminance–only design tool. Table 10.1 outlines the characteristics of the lumen method calculation technique, along with those of some of the other calculation techniques available to the designer.

The single greatest benefit of the lumen method is its general ease of use in establishing preliminary lighting layouts for initial budget projections and initial layout development and preliminary architectural design integration. With some calculational and room geometry tricks, the lumen method can serve as a fairly accurate design layout tool, even for somewhat nonuniform lighting. However, this does require a good understanding of the lumen method technique.[1] Generally, more accurate, final calculations by one of the computer methods using flux transfer or ray tracing techniques are suggested to better meet illuminance, luminance, and energy criteria.

The lumen method is so named for the axiom that illuminance on a large surface is equal to the total lumens falling onto that surface divided by the area of the surface. In its simplest form, then, the lumen method is simply the total number of lumens available in a room divided by the area of the room. The lumen method can be used in a number of ways, to find: the initial average illuminance on a horizontal surface to be expected from a proposed layout; the maintained average illuminance (average illuminance to be expected over time, compensating for dirt buildup and depreciation factors) to be expected from a proposed layout; the quantity of lamps required in a given space in order to achieve a specific average maintained illuminance on a horizontal surface with a specific luminaire; or the quantity of luminaires required in a given space in order to achieve a specific average maintained illuminance on a horizontal surface. These four lumen method variations are formulated in Table 10.2. Table 10.3 outlines the various factors needed to

initial values

All lighting literally loses its luster over time. As lamps burn, electrodes, filaments, gases, phosphors, and the like decompose. As luminaires age, they get dirty and their metal finish deteriorates. Further, architectural surfaces also deteriorate and reflect slightly less light. These factors yield maintained levels of light over time. Hence, at system start-up, initial levels or values of light are available that are higher than will be available after some time of operation—typically a year or so.

interreflection

Except in totally black rooms or in outer space, light strikes surfaces and reflects to other surfaces and so on, until the light finally hits the surface (task area) of interest. All of these reflections are known as interreflection. Depending on the surface reflectance values in a given setting, interreflections can account for a significant amount of light. Hence, to design the most efficient lighting layout, interreflection must be considered. This is typically achieved with the aid of the computer—which can either account directly for all of these interreflections by ray diagramming (very time intensive, even for a computer) or perform difficult mathematical analyses to mimic the effect of interreflections (complicated for humans, but more expedient for the computer than ray diagramming).

Image ©GarySteffyLightingDesign Inc.

10.2.2 Design Tools

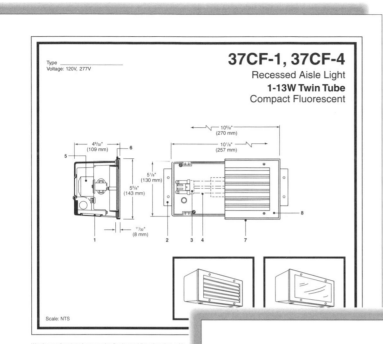

Type _____
Voltage: 120V, 277V

37CF-1, 37CF-4
Recessed Aisle Light
1-13W Twin Tube
Compact Fluorescent

10⅝"
(270 mm)

10⅛"
(257 mm)

4²³⁄₃₂"
(109 mm)

5¹⁄₈"
(130 mm)

5⅝"
(143 mm)

¹¹⁄₃₂"
(8 mm)

Scale: NTS

Weatherproof, gasketed, recessed wall units providing a low glare, wide spread light pattern. For outdoor or indoor use. Separate trim allows flush installation in wet surfaces or overlaps dry surfaces.
Do not install in brick structures with high calcium mortar.

Features
1. Diecast aluminum housing. White baked enamel finish.
2. Galvanized steel mounting brackets.
3. Injection molded Valox® lamp holder.
4. One (1) 13W compact fluorescent twin tube lamp (not included).
5. One (1) 13W encased and potted NPF ballast. 120V or 277V, specify.
6. Neoprene weatherproof gasket.
7. Diecast aluminum trim allows flush installation in wet surfaces or overlap in dry surfaces (optional). Brushed aluminum finish.
8. Diecast aluminum louvered faceplate with clear glass (37CF-1) or clear prismatic glass lens with diecast frame (37CF-4). Textured grey finish.

Labels
UL, CSA listed.
Suitable for wet locations.
Suitable for concrete pour.
Non-type I.C.

Figure 10.8
This luminaire uses the F13Single compact fluorescent lamp and is intended to be used as a steplight. The cutsheet offers two different isocontour plots for illuminance. One plot is for the glass lens steplight, while the other plot is for the louvered steplight. **Advisory**: Note that the steplight comes standard with an "NPF" ballast. This designates a normal power factor ballast. For best efficiency and best operating parameters, specify "HPF" or high power factor ballasts whenever available. Also, note that this is a "Non–type I.C." luminaire. If this luminaire is to be mounted in any open wall construction, then all insulation must be kept at least 3" (75 mm) away from the luminaire housing (this requires special construction by the contractor) to avoid overheating.

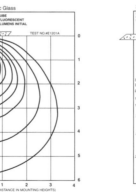

1-13W TT Compact Fluorescent   Recessed Aisle Light

37CF-4 with Prismatic Glass

INITIAL HORIZONTAL FOOTCANDLES
Mounting Heights

13W TWIN TUBE COMPACT FLUORESCENT
RATED 900 LUMENS INITIAL

TEST NO.#E1201A

3.9 2.5 1.7 1.3
3.1 2   1.4 1.0
2.3 1.5 1.0 .77
1.6 1   .69 .51
1.2 .75 .52 .38
.78 .50 .35 .26
.39 .25 .17 .13
.20 .13 .09 .07

(DISTANCE IN MOUNTING HEIGHTS)

37CF-1 with Louvered Faceplate

INITIAL HORIZONTAL FOOTCANDLES
Mounting Heights

13W TWIN TUBE COMPACT FLUORESCENT
RATED 900 LUMENS INITIAL

TEST NO. E1196A

3.9 2.5 1.7 1.3
3.1 2   1.4 1.0
2.3 1.5 1.0 .77
1.6 1   .69 .51
1.2 .75 .52 .38
.78 .50 .35 .26
.39 .25 .17 .13
.20 .13 .09 .07

(DISTANCE IN MOUNTING HEIGHTS)

Presc•lite   1251 Doolittle Dr. • San Leandro, California 94577 U.S.A. • Phone (510) 562-3500
With representatives' offices in principal cities throughout North America.
Copyright® 1996 Prescolite. All Rights Reserved • Specifications subject to change without notice. • Printed in U.S.A. • AL-1 • 6/96

Cutsheet drawings courtesy of and ©Prescolite, Inc. Available online at http://www.prescolite.com

Design Tools

10.2.2

Figure 10.9 and cutsheet content

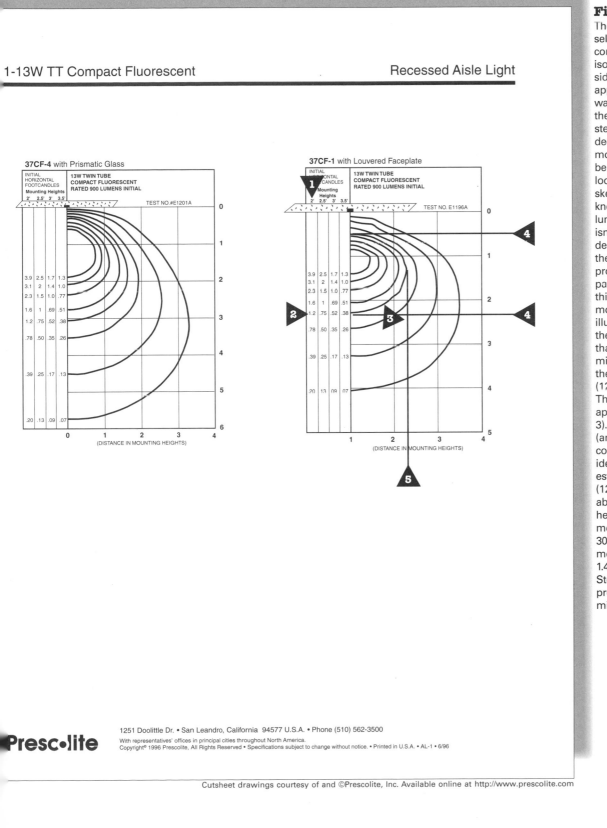

1-13W TT Compact Fluorescent   **Recessed Aisle Light**

37CF-4 with Prismatic Glass

INITIAL
HORIZONTAL
FOOTCANDLES
Mounting Heights
2' 2.5' 3' 3.5'

13W TWIN TUBE
COMPACT FLUORESCENT
RATED 900 LUMENS INITIAL

TEST NO.#E1201A

2'	2.5'	3'	3.5'
3.9	2.5	1.7	1.3
3.1	2	1.4	1.0
2.3	1.5	1.0	.77
1.6	1	.69	.51
1.2	.75	.52	.38
.78	.50	.35	.26
.39	.25	.17	.13
.20	.13	.09	.07

(DISTANCE IN MOUNTING HEIGHTS)

37CF-1 with Louvered Faceplate

INITIAL
HORIZONTAL
CANDLES
Mounting
Heights
2' 2.5' 3' 3.5'

13W TWIN TUBE
COMPACT FLUORESCENT
RATED 900 LUMENS INITIAL

TEST NO. E1196A

2'	2.5'	3'	3.5'
3.9	2.5	1.7	1.3
3.1	2	1.4	1.0
2.3	1.5	1.0	.77
1.6	1	.69	.51
1.2	.75	.52	.38
.78	.50	.35	.26
.39	.25	.17	.13
.20	.13	.09	.07

(DISTANCE IN MOUNTING HEIGHTS)

Figure 10.9
The louvered steplight is selected for better glare control. Hence, the isocontour on the right side of the cutsheet applies. There are several ways to use or "work" the contour plot. Here, as step 1, the designer decides that the mounting height should be 2' (600 mm) (this looks best in an elevation sketch and/or the kneewall into which the luminaire will be placed isn't very high). Now the designer is looking for the spacing necessary to provide 1 fc (10 lx) on a path that is 3' wide. Since this contour plot (like most) is based on INITIAL illuminance, and since the designer anticipates that light losses over time might be close to 20%, then a contour of 1.2 fc (12 lx) is targeted (step 2). This identifies the appropriate contour (step 3). Contours are additive (and so a trace overlay could be made). Step 4 identifies the boundary established by the 1.2 fc (12 lx) requirement. From about ½ the mounting height (half of the mounting height is 1' or 300 mm) to about 2⅓ the mounting height (4'–8" or 1.4 m) from the steplight. Step 5 indicates that a preliminary spacing might be 4'–8" (1.4 m).

1251 Doolittle Dr. • San Leandro, California 94577 U.S.A. • Phone (510) 562-3500

With representatives' offices in principal cities throughout North America.
Copyright© 1996 Prescolite, All Rights Reserved • Specifications subject to change without notice. • Printed in U.S.A. • AL-1 • 6/96

Presc•lite

Cutsheet drawings courtesy of and ©Prescolite, Inc. Available online at http://www.prescolite.com

10.2.2 Design Tools

undertake a lumen method calculation: maintained illuminance criterion; area of the space; initial lamp lumens; recoverable light loss factors; nonrecoverable light loss factors; and the luminaire's coefficient of utilization (CU).

The maintained illuminance criterion was established in programming. See Section 4.6.5 as well as the latest IESNA Handbook, or for the experienced designer, consider past experiences. This criterion is intended to be a target value maintained over time. Note the distinction. Unless otherwise cited in IESNA literature, illuminance criteria are not to be considered initial, nor maximums nor minimums, but rather the target maintained over time toward which a designer should aim. It is well understood that lighting is dependent on so many variables, and that precise prediction is impractical. Nevertheless, the designer is to do his/her best.

The area of the space is simply the entire free area from wall to wall. This is where the lumen method can be undesirable. If an office has a single occupant and is 300 ft² (27 m²) and the horizontal illuminance criterion on the desk is 50 fc (500 lx), then using the lumen method as a design tool will result in 50 fc (500 lx) average over the entire room area. This will probably be a waste of energy if the desk and return work surfaces compose only 30 ft² (2.7 m²). Indeed, it may be more appropriate to establish an ambient or general illuminance of perhaps 20 or 30 fc (200 or 300 lx) throughout the room, and then research a desk light that can provide the remaining 20 to 30 fc (200 to 300 lx) on the work surface proper to achieve the 50 fc (500 lx) desired.

Initial lamp lumens are reported in lamp manufacturers' literature. Depending on the lamp type, manufacturers might list mean lumens and centerbeam candlepower also. Make certain to use initial lamp lumens for all lumen method calculations.

Recoverable light loss factors (RLLF—see Table 10.3) include all of the light loss factors (LLFs) that can be "recovered" over the course of an installation's lifetime. As discussed in Chapter 7, lamps lose some light output over time. This is barely perceptible with halogen lamps and deluxe triphosphor fluorescent lamps, but is noticeable with ceramic metal halide lamps. This particular recoverable light loss is known as lamp lumen depreciation (LLD). By group relamping at 70 to 80 percent of rated lamp life, LLD can be recovered on a regular, ongoing basis. This is typically more cost–effective and may be more sustainable than purchasing and installing more luminaires and lamps initially. Further, this reduces ongoing maintenance costs since group relamping is less expensive per lamp than spot relamping (which requires retrieval of the ladder every time a lamp burns out). A second RLLF is luminaire dirt depreciation (LDD). As a building is operated over time, dust collects on luminaire reflectors, lenses, louvers, and lamps. These losses might amount to a few percent decrease in light output over time in buildings with newer HVAC systems. Higher losses have been reported and may be experienced; however, this suggests more frequent cleaning cycles for lamps/luminaires (which might typically be every few years). Otherwise, more lamps/luminaires are required during initial installation—which is not considered an efficient nor sustainable approach.

Finally, room surface dirt depreciation (RSDD) is also a recoverable factor. As room surfaces age, they collect dirt; and although this is certainly a secondary factor compared to LLD or LDD, it can have some impact on reducing reflected light. Through the repainting and/or refinishing of walls, floors, and ceilings from time to time, this factor is minimized. These surface losses might amount to a few percent decrease in light output over time.

©Glen Calvin Moon

©Glen Calvin Moon

©Glen Calvin Moon

Figure C1

This historic bank façade (Detroit's First National Bank Building) lacked night identity without façade lighting. Rather than flooding the entire façade in flat light (and exacerbating light pollution and energy use), architectural features were selected for discrete accenting. Indeed, the program was "To establish the nighttime presence of the historic façade in a way that enhances the architectural structure and 3–dimensional character of the details." 100PAR38/CMH/3K/WSP ceramic metal halide lamps are used in an uplight on either side of each column (detail close up shown in upper left). Historic lantern wall brackets were introduced along the ground floor. Each of these is lamped with a long life incandescent lamp for a soft, authentically historic appearance. The entry lobby (see detail shown in lower left) also adds significant visual presence to the façade lighting. This is done not by overlighting the lobby, but by lighting its architectural surfaces. Ceilings are washed with cold cathode coves (lamped with 15 mm tubing operated at 60 ma and of 3000°K color temperature in triphosphor version for best color rendering and best color matching with fluorescent lighting in the lobby), and historically sympathetic pendents are lamped with F32Triple/830/4P fluorescent lamps. Notice how the ceramic metal halide column accents offer a color quality identical to the incandescent wall brackets and the lobby lighting. [Note: on the night of the photo shoot, the streetlight in front of the building happened to be out. Although this makes the photo more dramatic, even when the streetlight is functioning, the façade has a similar, dramatic, and highly visible appearance.]

Figure C2

This 1930s skyscraper's (Detroit's Penobscot Building) upper setbacks are lighted with a mix of floodlights and spotlights using the same lamp (but in luminaires with different reflector/lens assemblies)—a 150E17/3K/U standard metal halide warm–tone lamp (this was just before ceramic metal halide lamps became available in this wattage; otherwise, ceramic metal halide would have been used for richer color rendering and better consistency in color match from lamp to lamp). The lighted façade elements are lit to an average between 15 and 20 fc (150 to 200 lx). More light would result in a more significant focal in the night skyline, but would also exacerbate light pollution and energy use. Less light would result in a sufficiently weak focus whereby energy would be arguably wasted since the feature would not be readily identifiable against the night skyline. The façade is limestone—a relatively light finish. Darker stone would require more light for an equivalent luminance or brightness.

©Glen Calvin Moon

Figure C3

The street–level presence of the tower shown in Figure C2 is achieved with select feature accenting. Programming was identical to that cited in Figure C1—light was to enhance the historic character of the architecture, using these unique features (which today would cost a small fortune to detail/build) to benefit in establishing a nighttime presence. The main entry arch is uplighted with six 100PAR38/CMH/3K/WSP ceramic metal halide lamps (three lamps at each base of the arch). The sculptural element above the arch is lighted with two 100PAR38/CMH/3K/WSP ceramic metal halide lamps (one on the end of each flagpole—see detail shown in bottom image). Wall sconces are used at the ground floor level to introduce a more human scale element. However, to maintain an appropriate proportion to the scale of the building, each sconce is 2' (600 mm) in width by 4' (1200 mm) in height. Sconces are lamped with F25T8/830 fluorescent lamp and ballasted with low temperature ballasts.

©Glen Calvin Moon

C3

Figure C4 (above images)
This early 20th century cathedral (Grand Rapids' St. Andrew) was restored in 2000. Lighting intensities in such facilities are trending toward 20 to 30 fc (200 to 300 lx) at lap height to accommodate older parishioners. To achieve such intensities (most historic churches typically were lighted to between 3 and 7 fc (30 and 70 lx)), strong downlighting is necessary. Given the nature of liturgical ceremonies, these lights typically must be dimmable to allow for change in focus and spatial impression during the service. Here, 250PAR38/H/NSP quartz halogen downlights offer much of the functional lap light. Uplights lamped with 350T3/C/HIR lamps flood the vaulted ceiling with light—accentuating the grandeur of the space's height and also contributing some functional lap light. More importantly, the uplights serve to mitigate the harshness and glare common with just downlights, filling shadows that are common with downlights. The Mary icon to the right is lighted with 100PAR38/HIR/SP lamps. The reredos is accented with theatrical spotlights lamped with 575T6/H lamps. Pipe rails were used for mounting theatrical spot– and floodlights (see detail photo—one of the pipe rails and sets of theatrical accents for the reredos).

Figure C5 (right image)
The beautifully detailed Victorian architecture of the Michigan State Capitol offered many opportunities for developing layers of lighting that ultimately offer the entire splendor of visual experience and collectively contribute to the safe and functional lighting needed for circulation throughout the facility. Triphosphor fluorescent lamps are used in the flag cases (filled with reproduction flags to avoid the issues associated with conservation of such historic textiles) and in the picture lights (just visible) on the second floor rotunda balcony to light governors' portraits. Long life incandescent traffic signal lamps are used inthe flag case decorative globes and in the small pendent globes attached to the ornate structural cantilevers on the upper floors. The oculus in the dome is uplighted with blue–filtered metal halide (100ED17/3K/U lamps) to accentuate the deep blue painted sky and further enhancing the height (regression) of that element. The dome is uplighted with a combination of 250PAR38/H/NSP lamps (to accentuate the gold leaf) and metal halide floodlights (lamped with 100ED17/3K/U lamps to flood the blue–toned field of the dome). 250PAR38/H/NSP accent lights (hidden on an upper, inaccessible–to–the–public balcony) highlight artwork on the lower dome.

©Balthazar Korab, Ltd.

Figure C6

Just like its interior, the ornate architecture of the Michigan State Capitol offered great opportunities for developing layers of lighting that ultimately sets the entire splendor of visual experience and collectively contribute to the safe and functional lighting needed for circulation around the exterior facility. To minimize maintenance stocks of lamps and to permit better cost control on lamps, many lamps used in the interior of the facility were also used on the exterior. Long life incandescent traffic signal lamps are used in the historic postlights flanking the entry and spaced sparingly along walkways. The lower façade is lighted with a series of spotlights and floodlights lamped with metal halide (100ED17/3K/U lamps) to accentuate the lower zone of the building. Pinspot luminaires also using the 100ED17/3K/U lamps were placed in underground pits in the front lawn to accent the upper pediments. These same extraordinary spotlights were used to highlight the upper dome and the cupola (spotlights by ARC Sales/Mini and standard BMF models). Standard floodlights also using the 100ED17/3K/U metal halide lamps were strategically placed on upper balconies at the central entry and around the based of the dome colonnade.

©Dietrich Floeter Photography

©Dietrich Floeter Photography

Figures C7 (upper left) and C8 (lower left)

This 1920s theater (Muskegon's Frauenthal Theater) was restored in 1998. For purposes of finite dimming, most all sources used here are incandescent. Wall brackets, wall sconces, surface mounted lights (below each balcony ceiling), and pendents are the obvious decorative luminaires that also contribute to functional lighting for circulation and conversation before the show (and during intermission). Decorative niches above the exit doors are backlighted for dramatic effect to minimize dark voids that can be common in such large volume spaces. Large ceiling coves serve to hide key theatrical stage lighting positions and also offer an opportunity for functional/ decorative lighting of the cove itself. This also serves to minimize a large dark volume by lighting significant areas of the ceiling. Many of these techniques have been lost over the years essentially due to "budget." Architecture plays such a significant role in our lives and in our psyche that saving what amounts to just a few bucks on lighting is detrimental to the human experience we call life. [Note: to accentuate the dark finishes of the floor and seating for the purposes of the photo, extensive fill light was used— hence the brightness patterns in the seating layout.] [Note: Gary Steffy Lighting Design Inc. provided the architectural lighting design, but did not provide any theatrical lighting consultation on this project.]

©Dietrich Floeter Photography

Figure C9
This closeup view of the stage offers some idea of the scale and, therefore, the area of coverage achieved with the ceiling cove. [Note: Gary Steffy Lighting Design Inc. provided the architectural lighting design, but did not provide any theatrical lighting consultation on this project.]

Design Tools

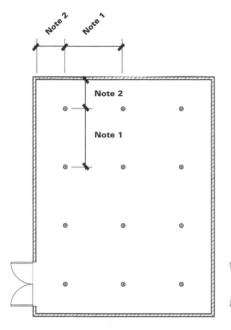

Figure 10.10.1
Lumen method spacing guidelines for downlights.
Note 1
Spacing distance S (should not exceed spacing to mounting height ratio [S/MH] offered by luminaire manufacturer). See Figure 8.2 for example spacing criteria.
Note 2
Preferably between 0.5S and 0.3S (typically not less than 1' [300 mm] nor more than 3' [900 mm] unless other perimeter lighting techniques are used). Other perimeter lighting techniques are desirable to avoid a bland or drab setting.

Figure 10.10.2
Lumen method spacing guidelines for parabolic luminaires.
Note 1
Spacing distance S (should not exceed spacing to mounting height ratio [S/MH] offered by luminaire manufacturer). See Figure 8.2 for example spacing criteria.
Note 2
Preferably between 0.5S and 0.3S (typically not less than 1' [300 mm] nor more than 3' [900 mm] unless other perimeter lighting techniques are used). Other perimeter lighting techniques are desirable to avoid a bland or drab setting.

Figure 10.10.3
Lumen method spacing guidelines for pendent luminaires (indirect, semi–indirect, or direct/indirect).
Note 1
Spacing distance S will depend on ceiling heights and ceiling luminance criteria. See Section 4.6.2.
Note 2
Preferably between 0.5S and 0.3S (typically not less than 1' [300 mm] nor more than 4' [1200 mm] unless other perimeter lighting techniques are used). Some perimeter accenting is desired.
Note 3
Preferably about 0.3S (typically not less than 1' [300 mm] nor more than 4' [1200 mm] unless other perimeter lighting techniques are used). Some perimeter accenting is desirable.

Higher losses have been reported and may be experienced, but just as with LDD, this suggests more frequent cleaning or refinishing of room surfaces rather than the more costly and less sustainable approach of installing more lamps and luminaires to account for a greater RSDD loss.

Nonrecoverable light loss factors (NRLLF–see Table 10.3) include all those factors that negatively affect the lighting system and are permanent. These are factors that account for real–world conditions and that are laboratory constants when testing lamps and luminaires. During photometric tests, for example, very exacting voltage and temperature conditions are established in the laboratory. Reference transformers or ballasts are used so that all lamps and luminaires are operated under similar situations, and, therefore, their ratings and data are all relative. This allows the designer to compare one manufacturer's lamp or luminaire performance against another's and know that any performance differences are due to lamp or luminaire design and engineering rather than to odd testing situations.

Voltage factor is an NRLLF and is a result of the nominal voltage to the lamp, ballast, or transformer not being maintained. Voltage drop because of long wiring runs and/or incorrect wire sizes, voltage surges, and primary voltages above or below nominal conditions from the utility can reduce light output.

Another NRLLF is ballast factor (BF). BF accounts for the differences experienced when operating a fluorescent lamp on a ballast having characteristics that vary from the test reference ballast used in measuring lamp performance in the test lab. BF can result in significant under performance of a lighting system. Unfortunately, this situation continues to

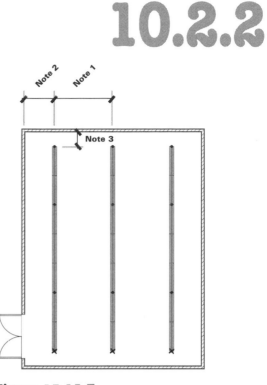

10.2.2 Design Tools

Table 10.1 Quantitative Design Tools

	Templates	Lumen Method	Point Method
Technique	• Hand (pencil, paper, and brain) • Hand (calculator)	• Hand (calculator) • Computer	• Hand (calculator) • Computer
Luminances	No	Yes	Yes
Horizontal Illuminances	Yes	Yes	Yes
Vertical Illuminances	No	No	Yes
Accuracy	• Poor for interior • Fair for exterior	• Fair to good	• Good
Advantages	• Quick	• Quick	• More accurate
Disadvantages	• Single criterion compliance • Questionable accuracy • Initial values (must apply correction factors) • No interreflection • Assumes empty room/area (no objects)	• Single criterion compliance • Average value basis (no min or max) • Assumes empty room/area (no objects)	• Time–consuming • No interreflection • Assumes point source • Large sources must be discretized
Uses	• Exterior applications • Interior applications • Uniform applications • Nonuniform applications • Establish preliminary layout • Budget estimating	• Interior applications • Uniform applications • Establish preliminary layout • Budget estimating • Final layout for noncritical spaces • Fair for indirect • Good for direct	• Exterior applications • Interior applications • Uniform applications • Nonuniform applications • Establish exact layouts for accenting • Establish exact layouts for general lighting • Establish exact layouts for task lighting

[a] With any calculation that is performed by a computer, it is easy to get caught up in the "accuracy" of such answers. However, in most cases it is impossible to ever measure within 10% or so of predicted (calculated) values.
[b] So much output is possible in such short timeframe that it is easy to print out reams of paper with data.

Design Tools

	Flux Transfer	Ray Tracing
	• Hand (calculator) • Computer	• Computer
	Yes	Yes
	Yes	Yes
	Yes	Yes
	• Good to excellent	• Good to excellent
	• More accurate	• Excellent visualization imagery
	• Results only as good as data input • False sense of accuracy[a] • Potential tree killer[b]	• Limited by data input • Limited by available time • False sense of security[a] • Potential tree killer[b]
	• Exterior applications • Interior applications • Uniform applications • Nonuniform applications • Establish exact layouts for accenting • Establish exact layouts for general lighting • Establish exact layouts for task lighting	• Exterior applications • Interior applications • Uniform applications • Nonuniform applications • Establish exact layouts for accenting • Establish exact layouts for general lighting • Establish exact layouts for task lighting

10.2.2 Design Tools

Table 10.2 Lumen Method Variables and Formulations

Variable	Description
E_i	Initial average illuminance predicted
E_m	Maintained average illuminance criteria
CU	Coefficient of utilization
RLLF	Recoverable light loss factor • lamp lumen depreciation (LLD) • luminaire dirt depreciation (LDD) • room surface dirt depreciation (RSDD)
NRLLF	Nonrecoverable light loss factor • voltage factor • ballast factor • thermal factor • partition factor

To determine initial average illuminance (E_i) from a given layout

$$E_i = \frac{\text{Lumens per lamp * Number of lamps per luminaire * Number of luminaires * CU * NRLLF}}{\text{Work area}}$$

To determine maintained average illuminance (E_m) from a given layout

$$E_m = \frac{\text{Lumens per lamp * Number of lamps per luminaire * Number of luminaires * CU * RLFF * NRLLF}}{\text{Work area}}$$

To determine the quantity of lamps required for a given luminaire in a given room and for a given illuminance target

$$\text{Number of lamps} = \frac{E_m * \text{Work area}}{\text{Lumens per lamp * CU * RLFF * NRLLF}}$$

To determine the quantity of luminaires required for a given room and a given illuminance target

$$\text{Number of luminaires} = \frac{E_m * \text{Work area}}{\text{Lumens per lamp * Lamps per luminaire * CU * RLFF * NRLLF}}$$

be exacerbated by ballast manufacturers with nearly all "standard electronic" ballasts for T8 fluorescent lamps having BFs of 0.88. To achieve a lamp manufacturers' rated light output, a BF of 1.0 is required. Thus, designers may find themselves accidentally short of the illuminance target by 12 percent, or conversely may find that their clients need to purchase 13 percent more lamps and luminaires for the initial installation. This is not very energy– or sustainably–appropriate.

Ballast factors can help the designer finely "tune" a design. Think of BFs as permanent dimmers. There may be a need to maintain a certain luminaire spacing for uniformity, yet the lowest wattage lamp is already in place but the illuminance value is predicted to be too high. Using ballasts with a BF of 0.88 or 0.78 could help in this situation. Other times, however, it is more sustainably appropriate to stick with a specific layout, and rather than add luminaires and lamps, look for a ballast with a BF of 0.98 or 1.18 to achieve

Design Tools

Table 10.3 Lumen Method Variable References and Estimates

Variable		Reference Source	Rough Estimate
E_m		• Table 4.13 • IESNA Handbook • Client criteria • Experience • Codes and/or ordinances	• See Table 4.13
Work area		• Floor plan (new and renovation) • Measurements (renovation)	[not applicable]
Initial lamp lumens		• Lamp manufacturers' data	• 50TB/H = 710 lumens[2] • 90TB/H = 1580 lumens[2] • 35PAR20/H = 385 lumens[2] • 50PAR30S/HIR = 750 lumens[2] • F13Triple/830/4P = 900 lumens[2] • F32Triple/830/4P = 2350 lumens[2] • F28T5/830 = 2900 lumens[2] • F32T8/830 = 2950 lumens[2] • 70ED17/CMH/3K = 5250 lumens[2]
RLLFs	• Lamp lumen depreciation (LLD)	• Lamp manufacturers' data	• Halogen = 0.95 • Triphosphor fluorescent = 0.95 • Ceramic metal halide = 0.85 to 0.75
	• Luminaire dirt depreciation (LDD)	• IESNA Handbook • Experience	• 0.97
	• Room surface dirt depreciation (RSDD)	• IESNA Handbook • Experience	• 0.97
NRLLFs	• Voltage factor	• Electrical engineer • IESNA Handbook	• 1.0
	• Ballast factor	• Ballast manufacturers' data	• 0.78 • 0.88 (most common for F/T8) • 0.98 (most common for F/T5 and F/T5HO) • 1.18
	• Thermal factor	• Luminaire manufacturer • Lamp manufacturer	• 0.95
	• Partition factor	• Not readily available	• See Table 10–4
CUs		• Manufacturers' data	[not applicable]

the illuminance target. This BF range of 0.78 to 1.18 seems to define the limits within which the lamp manufacturers would prefer lamps to operate in order to achieve rated life.

Another NRLLF is the thermal factor. This accounts for the difference in luminaire ambient temperature between that experienced in the lamp/ luminaire testing lab and the real environment. A reasonable thermal loss is perhaps 5 percent, although this does vary from lamp type to lamp type. For example, the newer T5 triphosphor fluorescent lamps are designed to operate optimally in a higher ambient temperature—more appropriate for the smaller, more confining luminaires anticipated with T5 lamps.

Perhaps the most problematic and frequently overlooked NRLLF is the partition factor. A partition factor is considered in those spaces where partial height partitions are used to subdivide space into office cubicles or workstations. Generally, the lower the ceiling and the higher or taller the partition, the worse the partition factor. Partition factors are usually worse for direct, well–controlled luminaires (e.g., parabolic luminaires) and usually better for indirect, widespread distribution luminaires. Table 10.4 outlines

10.2.2 Design Tools

some approximate partition factors for various ceiling heights and partition heights. Accommodating this effect typically results in the use of smaller luminaires, each with fewer lamps, but uses more total luminaires (since they need to be spaced closer together to overcome the losses attributable to the partitions). Here, clerestories and sidelights in partition systems help significantly. For example, if a partition is 80″ (2032 mm) in height, but the top 18″ (457 mm) is a clerestory, then for lighting purposes the partition will act similar to a 72″ (1828 mm) high partition in the way light is blocked, absorbed, or redirected.

It is conceivable to have total LLFs (adding the RLLFs and NRLLFs) approaching 0.70 for some commercial lighting applications. For typical office settings, however, total LLFs should range from a low of 0.80, to 0.90.

Coefficients of utilization (CUs) are an expression of the lighting system's efficiency in producing lumens on the work surface in the given room geometry, reported in decimal form. Some light output (lumens) from the lamps is absorbed by the luminaire, walls, and ceiling. The CU depends on: efficiency of the luminaire; distribution of light from the luminaire (narrow, medium, or widespread); room surface reflectances; and geometry (size and proportions) of the room. CU values are found in manufacturers' data. Reported in tabular form, CUs are determined by the designer, on the basis of given room proportions and room surface reflectances. Figures 8.2 and 8.3 offer exemplary CU tables.

Room proportions for CU data are identified by a single number, known as the room cavity ratio (RCR). Figure 10.11 illustrates the variables that affect the RCR. This ratio, the formula for which may look complicated, is actually quite simply determined. The only information required to establish the RCR is: the mathematical constant of 2.5; the room perimeter (for rectangular spaces this is simply the length and the width); and the height of the cavity from the workplane or floor to the bottom of the luminaires. See Figure 10.11 for the formula that is used.

After the RCR is established, the room surface reflectances must be estimated. For purposes of using the lumen method as an early estimator, and because the floor reflectance has little impact on the illuminance level on the workplane or floor, the floor reflectance can be presumed to be 20 percent. Again, for purposes of this lumen method estimator tool, wall and ceiling reflectance values need not be finalized, but rather can be categorized as light, medium, or dark. Tables 4.10 and 4.11 offer reflectance estimates.

Now the CU can be determined from the manufacturer's data. Find the CU table, and locate the appropriate ceiling reflectance zone, and then the appropriate wall reflectance column. Then locate the RCR column (generally the left–most column), and read down to the RCR for the room in question. Read across from the appropriate RCR and down the appropriate ceiling/wall reflectance to find the CU. The CU must be in decimal form to be used in the lumen method formula.

Refinements can be made for more accurate calculations based on specific wall, floor, and ceiling reflectances, and based on floor cavities (a floor cavity is the cavity between the workplane and the floor plane if they are not one in the same) and ceiling cavities (a ceiling cavity is the cavity between the plane defined by the bottom of the luminaires and the ceiling if they are not one in the same). Typically, however, these are tedious and cumbersome calculations that result in mathematically insignificant changes—and time that would be better spent using computer simulations to determine more precisely lighting layouts and light intensities and patterns.

Design Tools

Table 10.4 Partition Factor Estimates

Ceiling Height	Partition Height	Approximate Partition Factor
Between 8' 6" and 9' 0" (2.6 m and 2.75 m)	• Less than 42" (1067 mm)	• 1.0
	• 43 to 54" (1092 to 1372 mm)	• 0.95
	• 55 to 65" (1397 to 1651 mm)	• 0.85
	• 66 to 80" (1676 to 2032 mm)	• 0.75
Between 9' 0" and 9' 6" (2.75 m and 2.9 m)	• Less than 42" (1067 mm)	• 1.0
	• 43 to 54" (1092 to 1372 mm)	• 0.97
	• 55 to 65" (1397 to 1651 mm)	• 0.90
	• 66 to 80" (1676 to 2032 mm)	• 0.80
Between 9' 6" and 10' 0" (2.9 m and 3.0 m)	• Less than 42" (1067 mm)	• 1.0
	• 43 to 54" (1092 to 1372 mm)	• 0.97
	• 55 to 65" (1397 to 1651 mm)	• 0.95
	• 66 to 80" (1676 to 2032 mm)	• 0.85

10.2.3 Point method

The point method, or inverse square method, is used to check illuminance at a specific point or series of points that are intended to be lighted by more directional point sources (e.g., halogen or HIR PAR and MR lamps); or to get an idea of the appropriateness of a downlight prior to developing a layout using the lumen method (which, remember, is intended to provide a uniform layout of lighting equipment in order to achieve an average illuminance throughout an entire space). Figure 10.12 illustrates two variations on the point method. One variation is used to determine maintained illuminance at a point on a vertical surface (wall or art), while the other variation is used to determine maintained illuminance at a point on a horizontal surface (workplane or floor).

Interreflection is not taken into account in the point method as it is in the lumen method. Since even the light aimed onto artwork will ultimately reflect from the artwork and eventually hit the floor, counting on interreflection can significantly reduce initial hardware purchases and, thus, reduce lamp replacement and energy use over time. So, the point method should be used to get an idea of a lamp/luminaire's likelihood of meeting criteria, but final layouts should be based on computer software that includes the effects of interreflection.

The point method is particularly accurate for exterior lighting and for interiors with black walls and ceilings.

10.2.4 Computer calculations

As noted previously in 10.1.4, quite a few software programs are available for the calculation of design problems. These programs not only offer the visualization tools discussed in 10.1.4, but also include methods for calculating quantitative values. Some manufacturers offer programs at cost or even free of charge. Quick calculation programs are available online at several manu-

10.2.5 Design Tools

facturers' websites to help the designer establish preliminary layouts and quantities. Confirm that the programs distributed for use on your computer are using sophisticated flux transfer or ray tracing techniques (which are more accurate and do require a fair amount of computer running time) and not just computerized lumen method or point method techniques (which are less accurate). These programs should allow the designer to develop nonuniform, task– or area–specific lighting solutions that are more energy efficient and sustainable than uniform lighting systems stretching from room corner to room corner.

Because the computer spews forth reams of printed input and output data, computer calculations can easily eat trees. Attempt to be judicious in determining the calculations that should be printed out for review. Further, these reams of information give the false impression of flawless finality and degree of accuracy. First and foremost, the accuracy of computer calculations is limited by the accuracy of the input data—the luminaire photometry, the lamp lumen data, all of the RLLFs and NRLLFs, room surface reflectances, room geometry, partition factors, and the like need to be as accurate as is known at the time of the assessment. Second, as mentioned previously, the computer software may not be much more than simple hand calculation techniques put on a machine—this doesn't make the answer any more accurate. Third, the accuracy of any calculation technique is difficult to ascertain because measured light levels usually are, at best, only within 10 to 20 percent of calculated values. This is a result of light meter inaccuracies, voltage fluctuations on the lighting system, room surface reflectance variations, and so on.

Whenever computer calculations are made, the RLLF and NRLLF values discussed previously are applicable and need to be used. This is especially important when a third party (manufacturer or engineer, for example) runs computer calculations for the designer. Such third parties may use LLFs different from those reported in Table 10.3, may elect to use no LLFs or may only use selected LLFs. Room surface reflectance assumptions can significantly alter calculations. Many manufacturers and engineers have standardized on 80 percent ceiling reflectance, 50 percent wall reflectance, and 20 percent floor reflectance. Clearly, these may not relate to actual design conditions and, therefore, calculations may be off by as much as 30 percent.

Computer calculations permit more detailed analyses of various lighting layouts which can result in more efficient lighting applications. Lighting layouts need not be in a regular array of consistent spacing for computer analysis. Lighting can then be oriented according to task locations, according to subjective aspect requirements, or both.

10.2.5 Spreadsheets

Quantitative data extend beyond illuminance and luminances. Power budgets are another criterion that must be assessed. Some of the lighting software programs will also attempt to address power budgeting; however, these may not correctly track lamp wattage and BF (and, therefore, ballast wattage). As such, the designer must pull together a spreadsheet either by hand or by computer (e.g., Excel, Quattro Pro, Lotus 1•2•3, etc.) outlining luminaire type, lamp, lamp wattage, transformer (for low voltage luminaires) wattage or ballast (for fluorescent and metal halide) wattage, number of lamps/ballasts

Image ©GarySteffyLightingDesign Inc.

Design Tools

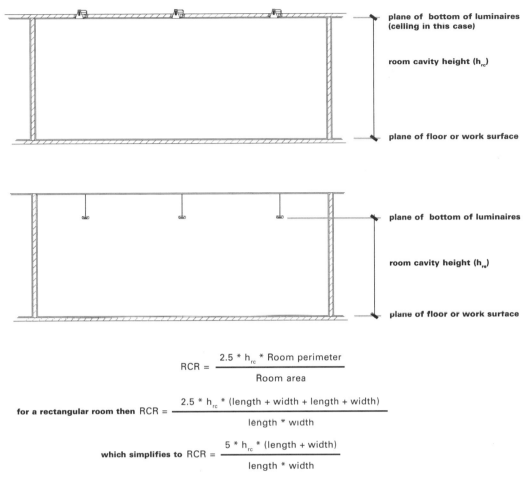

plane of bottom of luminaires (celling in this case)

room cavity height (h_{rc})

plane of floor or work surface

plane of bottom of luminaires

room cavity height (h_{rc})

plane of floor or work surface

$$RCR = \frac{2.5 * h_{rc} * \text{Room perimeter}}{\text{Room area}}$$

for a rectangular room then $RCR = \dfrac{2.5 * h_{rc} * (\text{length} + \text{width} + \text{length} + \text{width})}{\text{length} * \text{width}}$

which simplifies to $RCR = \dfrac{5 * h_{rc} * (\text{length} + \text{width})}{\text{length} * \text{width}}$

Figure 10.11
These room sections illustrate the dimensions that must be known in order to determine a room cavity ratio (RCR).

per luminaire, and luminaire count in order to eventually tally total lighting wattage on a per room basis. Further, tracking the net square footage of each room is necessary in order to establish the power load (watts per square foot [per square meter]) that the design imposes on the building. This is then used to determine if the power budget criterion has been met. When the designed lighting load is equal to or less than the power budget criterion, then compliance is achieved. When the lighting load is greater than the power budget criterion, the design must be reworked to reach compliance.

10.3 Endnotes

[1] Mark S. Rea, ed., *The IESNA Lighting Handbook: Reference and Application, Ninth Edition* (New York: Illuminating Engineering Society of North America, 2000), pp. 9–28 to 9–46.
[2] Gary Steffy, *Time–Saver Standards for Architectural Lighting* (New York: McGraw–Hill, 2000), pp. 3–9, 3–28, 5–22, 7–6, 8–12, 8–18, 8–49, 8–53.

Image ©GarySteffyLightingDesign Inc.

10.3 Design Tools

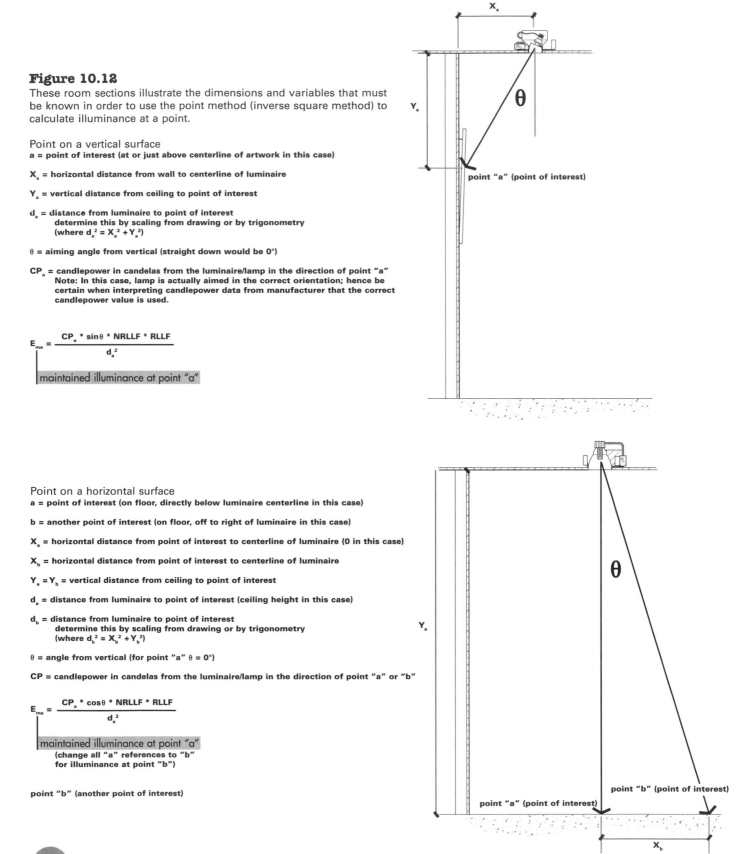

Figure 10.12

These room sections illustrate the dimensions and variables that must be known in order to use the point method (inverse square method) to calculate illuminance at a point.

Point on a vertical surface

a = point of interest (at or just above centerline of artwork in this case)

X_a = horizontal distance from wall to centerline of luminaire

Y_a = vertical distance from ceiling to point of interest

d_a = distance from luminaire to point of interest
    determine this by scaling from drawing or by trigonometry
    (where $d_a^2 = X_a^2 + Y_a^2$)

θ = aiming angle from vertical (straight down would be 0°)

CP_a = candlepower in candelas from the luminaire/lamp in the direction of point "a"
    Note: In this case, lamp is actually aimed in the correct orientation; hence be certain when interpreting candlepower data from manufacturer that the correct candlepower value is used.

$$E_{ma} = \frac{CP_a * \sin\theta * NRLLF * RLLF}{d_a^2}$$

maintained illuminance at point "a"

Point on a horizontal surface

a = point of interest (on floor, directly below luminaire centerline in this case)

b = another point of interest (on floor, off to right of luminaire in this case)

X_a = horizontal distance from point of interest to centerline of luminaire (0 in this case)

X_b = horizontal distance from point of interest to centerline of luminaire

$Y_a = Y_b$ = vertical distance from ceiling to point of interest

d_a = distance from luminaire to point of interest (ceiling height in this case)

d_b = distance from luminaire to point of interest
    determine this by scaling from drawing or by trigonometry
    (where $d_b^2 = X_b^2 + Y_b^2$)

θ = angle from vertical (for point "a" $\theta = 0°$)

CP = candlepower in candelas from the luminaire/lamp in the direction of point "a" or "b"

$$E_{ma} = \frac{CP_a * \cos\theta * NRLLF * RLLF}{d_a^2}$$

maintained illuminance at point "a"
(change all "a" references to "b"
for illuminance at point "b")

point "b" (another point of interest)

Contract Documents

11.1

CAD

CAD, or computer aided design, refers to the method of recording a design in plan, elevation, and, perhaps, 3–D electronic files. These electronic files can then be transmitted easily to other team members and/or can be plotted to paper for distribution.

First and foremost, the contract documents on a project are provided by registered professionals to the client/owner for release to contractors for bidding. The lighting designer can assist the registered professionals by developing documentation for their review and recommended disposition. The contract documents typically contain the detailed, dimensioned, and accurate architectural reflected ceiling plans, elevations, sections, details, specifications, and cutsheets needed to convey design information to a contractor(s). Throughout the construction process, contract documents will also include shop drawings. Any particular project is only as good as its contract documents. Typically, the reflected ceiling plans contain information indicating the luminaire type or designation, the luminaire location and/or spacing, and, if necessary, the luminaire orientation or direction of light throw.

Elevations and sections are shown for lighting purposes when luminaires are floor– or wall–mounted or have a unique profile or inner optical characteristic that must be illustrated. These elevations and sections can be particularly useful in conveying ADA–compliance aspects.

Details are used to convey the exact architectural dimensions and construction parameters necessary for a particular luminaire or lighting effect.

Specifications are, perhaps, the most critical aspect of any lighting design because they outline some of the expected duties of the contractor; indicate specific lamp, ballast, transformer, and luminaire requirements; and cite applicable industry standards and code references.

11.1 Reflected ceiling plans

Reflected ceiling plans are so named because they are a mirror–image (reflected) view of the ceiling. Imagine that you are looking down onto a mirror inserted as a plane about 4 feet above the floor, and the luminaires and various ceiling elements are all visible in this mirror. This view constitutes a reflected ceiling plan.

To develop reflected ceiling plans, the designer needs to know equipment locations, spacings, and focus or aiming directions (if applicable). Symbols are needed to provide a cohesive indication of specific luminaires throughout a project.

The ANSI standards for lighting symbols are quite limited—appearing more appropriate for the designer short on time and with a very limited palette of lighting options. To make drawings more meaningful at initial glance to both designers and contractors, a more diverse and realistic representation of luminaires is appropriate. Figures 11.1, 11.2, and 11.3 illustrate various possible luminaire symbols. Such symbols are appropriate for the architectural and electrical reflected ceiling plans that typically are used to show lighting, and/or can be used on separate lighting plans that are referenced by the architectural and electrical reflected ceiling plans. These symbols are entered in **CAD** databases as templates and then drawn to scale on reflected ceiling plans.

Figure 11.4 shows a reflected ceiling plan for a particular project. Note that luminaires are tagged or typed for easy cross reference to the specfication. This tag or type designation is usually located adjacent to each luminaire or series of luminaires (whichever is clearest). Where luminaires are intended to

11.2 Contract Documents

be centered in ceiling tile, it is not necesssary to give luminaire dimensions, although notational references periodically throughout the plan may help avoid any misunderstanding since grid backgrounds (particularly in CAD) might move during final design documentation. For drywall ceilings, dimensions to all luminaires are necessary. Where luminaire dimensions from walls and/or other luminaires are quite repetitive, such can be noted without showing all dimensions repetitively. In any event, the contractor should be directed not to scale dimensions from drawings since drawing reproduction may have actually shrunk or expanded the actual inked plan somewhat. The lighting designer should be given an opportunity to review the final reflected ceiling plans that the registered professionals developed to confirm that the lighting intent remains intact.

11.2 Design details

The concept details developed during design development (discussed in Chapter 8) now must be finalized. The lighting designer needs to confirm exact detail dimensions. The registered professionals need to identify appropriate supports, connections, integration details, and finishes. The lighting designer should be given an opportunity to review the final details that the registered professionals developed to confirm that the lighting intent remains intact given the construction detail requirements.

11.3 Specifications

Lighting specifications are the backbone of any successful lighting project. Specifications should be just that—specific, detailed descriptions of the work to be done and citation of a specific manufacturer's or several specific manufacturers' hardware that the lighting designer/specifier has deemed capable of meeting the project lighting criteria. The designer has an implicit, if not explicit, understanding with the client to assimilate the client's criteria, prioritize that criteria (since it is very unlikely that all criteria can always be met), analyze solutions to best meet that criteria, and lay out and specify those solutions. As such, the specification, along with drawings, becomes a legal document. Therefore, it must be drafted carefully, reviewed with the project team, presented to the registered professionals (if the lighting designer is not also the architect or electrical engineer on the project), released to the contractors, and used as a resource during bidding, shop drawing review, and construction.

The seed for a good specification is not how well one writes or how many details are outlined in lamp and luminaire descriptions. The integrity of the lighting design solution sets the stage for the integrity of the specification. Extensive review of hardware alternatives, and review of interior and/or exterior architectural and task requirements, energy and other building code requirements, lighting calculations and analyses of various solutions, and integration of the lighting with other building systems constitute the lighting design—a task demanding the entire design team's attention. If any one or

Format and content.........................

- Depend on consultant's status (registered or not)
- Should be reviewed periodically by legal counsel

Image ©EyeWire, Inc.

Contract Documents

◎ pinhole downlight

○ small downlight (4″ diameter)

◯ typical downlight (6″ diameter)

◈ wallwash luminaire (6″ diameter)

◀◯ adjustable accent luminaire (6″ diameter)

□ small square or rectlinear downlight

▢ typical square or rectlinear downlight

◧ typical square or rectllnear wallwash luminaire

◀▭ typical square adjustable accent luminaire

▨ typical rectilinear compact fluorescent wallwash luminaire

typical monopoint accent luminaire

typical recessed–slot, 4–head accent luminaire

Figure 11.1
These are some plan–view graphic representations for a variety of ceiling recessed, small aperture luminaires. A wall (in plan) is represented to the far left for reference orientation on wallwash luminaires and adjustable accents.

several of these aspects are not addressed or are only briefly considered, then the lighting specification will represent a weak design—one that can be called to question with little or no rebuttal and enabling contractors, distributors, lighting reps, and even the client to make substitutions with no substantiation of their own and, more importantly, with little or no refutation by the lighting designer. After all, if little design preparation went into the lighting layout and specification, then little rationale will exist for that layout and specification. As such, little defense can be made when others challenge that layout and specification.

Before writing a specification then, a solid design must be developed. During a robust design process, sufficient information becomes available regarding the lamp, ballast, and luminaire requirements necessary to meet project criteria. This information should be documented clearly and in detail in the specification so that others may understand what equipment needs to be purchased and installed in order to achieve the anticipated results. Table 8.1 (in Chapter 8) outlines a checklist of issues or elements that should be considered for inclusion in the specification of luminaires.

11.3   Contract Documents

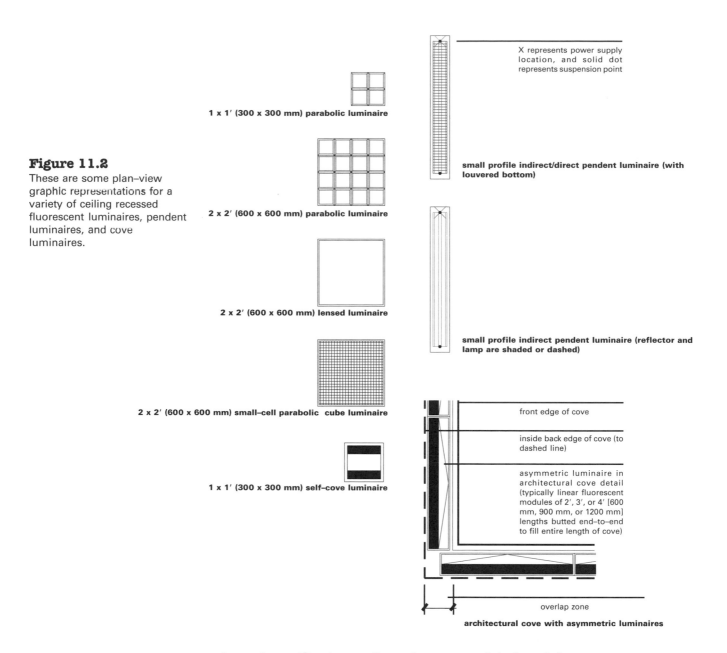

X represents power supply location, and solid dot represents suspension point

1 x 1' (300 x 300 mm) parabolic luminaire

2 x 2' (600 x 600 mm) parabolic luminaire

2 x 2' (600 x 600 mm) lensed luminaire

2 x 2' (600 x 600 mm) small–cell parabolic cube luminaire

1 x 1' (300 x 300 mm) self–cove luminaire

small profile indirect/direct pendent luminaire (with louvered bottom)

small profile indirect pendent luminaire (reflector and lamp are shaded or dashed)

front edge of cove

inside back edge of cove (to dashed line)

asymmetric luminaire in architectural cove detail (typically linear fluorescent modules of 2', 3', or 4' [600 mm, 900 mm, or 1200 mm] lengths butted end–to–end to fill entire length of cove)

overlap zone

architectural cove with asymmetric luminaires

Figure 11.2
These are some plan–view graphic representations for a variety of ceiling recessed fluorescent luminaires, pendent luminaires, and cove luminaires.

A good specification outlines the expected duties of the contractor above and beyond the general standard of care and practice expected from a licensed electrician. Further, a good specification outlines all of the lighting equipment required for a complete project that is expected to meet lighting criteria developed and agreed upon by the design team and met by its solutions. A good specification never cedes equipment selection to contractors or distributors unless it has been determined that any selection will meet criteria. This is an important point and a key distinction between specifications and design guidelines. In final specifications, using such terms as "or equal" or simply listing five, ten, or fifteen manufacturers with no catalog numbers for various luminaire designations is simply shirking design responsibility. No client should accept such work as that of professionals—indeed, such work should be

Contract Documents

typical half–bowl wall sconce

small linear (vertically) or cylindrical wall sconce

typical triangular sconce

wall bracket luminaire

continuous PAR–lamp wallslot luminaire with baffles between each lamp

continuous fluorescent wallslot luminaire with baffle

Figure 11.3
These are some plan–view graphic representations for a variety of wall sconce and wallslot luminaires. A wall (in plan) is represented to the far left for reference orientation.

viewed skeptically since it will be unclear if the designer did any design work to substantiate layouts and hardware selections.

The following pages illustrate a sample specification used on a project. The specification roughly follows formatting the Construction Specifications Institute (CSI) established—lighting is categorized as section 16500. Key components of the specification include the preface, contents, general, products (including a schedule of specific luminaire types and respective manufacturers' catalog ordering codes), and execution. Annotations on the pages following Figure 11.5 outline the rationale for various sections of the specification. Specifications should include only those requirements with which the designer is comfortable, familiar, and willing to uphold, and may be as long or as short as desired and/or necessary to convey the designer's requirements. Ultimately, however, a project's success depends on the integrity of the design and of the specification of that design.

more online @

http://www.csinet.org/technic/techhome.htm
http://www.lightforum.com/design/ALM0503.html
http://www.lightforum.com/design/ALM093.html

11.3

Contract Documents

Figure 11.4

A sample reflected ceiling plan layer as generated by the lighting designer for review and recommended disposition by the registered professionals. Many times, the lighting reflected ceiling plans are combined with architectural and engineering plans, in which case a good bit of other information is also shown on the drawing, including walls and window and door locations. Figure 11.5 shows the same plan with control loops. Note: for clarity on this sample "layer" drawing, dimension lines have been removed—these are shown in relationship to wall locations and/or ceiling plane changes.

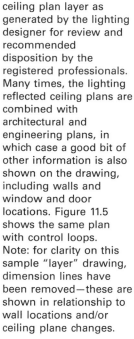

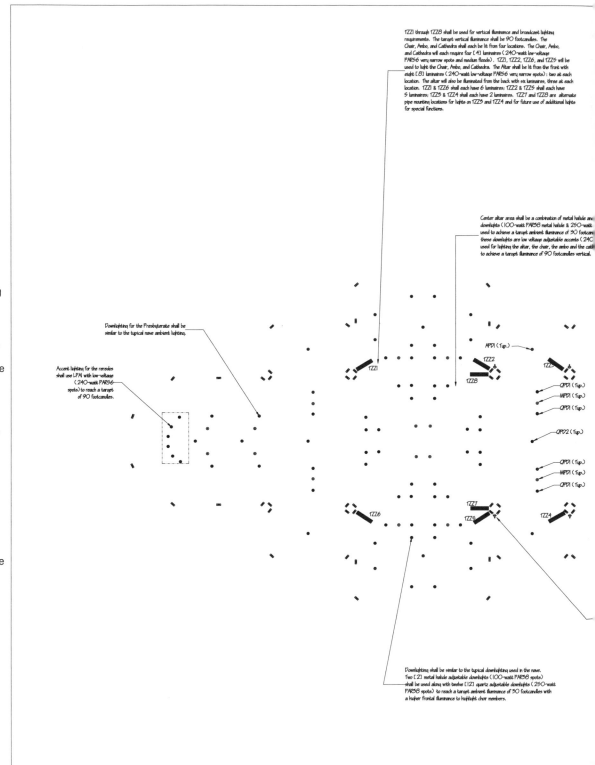

Contract Documents

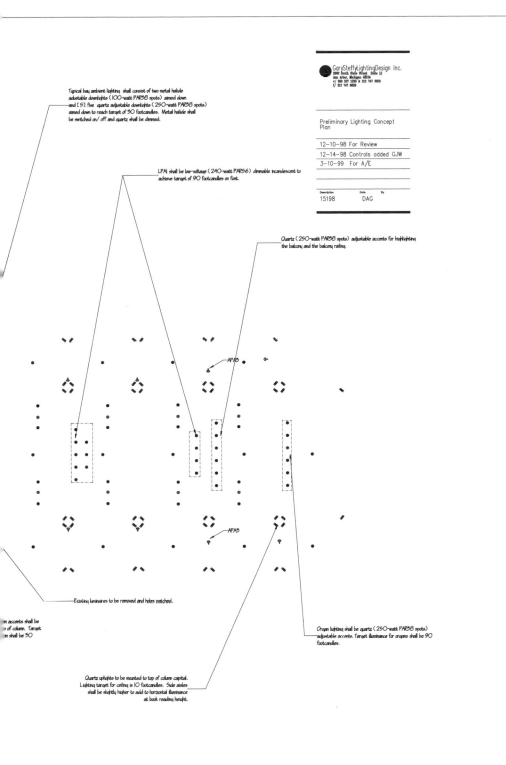

Typical bay ambient lighting shall consist of two metal halide adjustable downlights (100-watt PAR38 spots) aimed down and [5] five quartz adjustable downlights (250-watt PAR38 spots) aimed down to reach target of 50 footcandles. Metal halide shall be switched on/off and quartz shall be dimmed.

LPAI shall be low-voltage (240-watt PAR56) dimmable incandescent to achieve target of 90 footcandles on font.

Quartz (250-watt PAR38 spots) adjustable accents for highlighting the balcony and the balcony railing.

Existing luminaires to be removed and holes patched.

...m accents shall be ...s of column. Target ...n shall be 50

Organ lighting shall be quartz (250-watt PAR38 spots) adjustable accents. Target illuminance for organs shall be 90 footcandles.

Quartz uplights to be mounted to top of column capital. Lighting target for ceiling is 10 footcandles. Side aisles shall be slightly higher to add to horizontal illuminance at book reading height.

GarySteffyLightingDesign Inc.
2900 South State Street, Suite 12
Ann Arbor, Michigan 48104
v/ 800 537 1230 & 313 747 6630
f/ 313 747 6629

Preliminary Lighting Concept Plan

12-10-98 For Review
12-14-98 Controls added GJW
3-10-99 For A/E

Description	Date	By
15198	DAG	

11.3 Contract Documents

Figure 11.5
A sample lighting controls plan layer showing the lighting layer (from Figure 11.4) with the control loops indicating how lights are intended to be controlled.

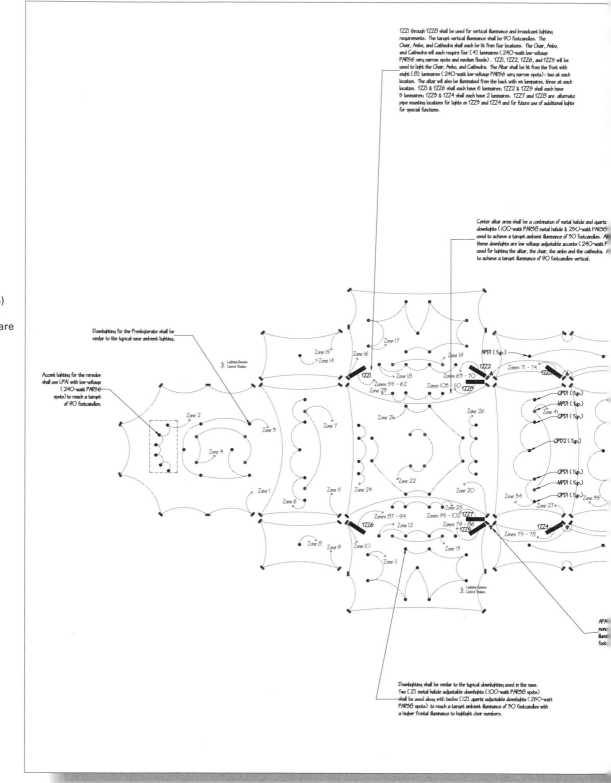

Contract Documents

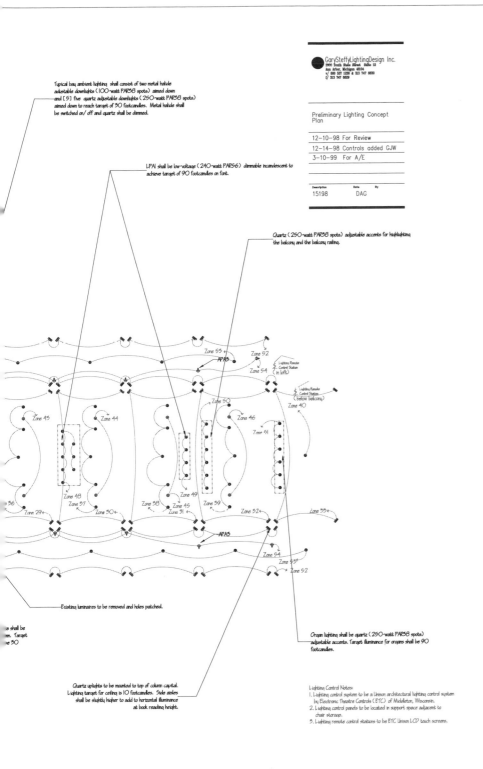

Typical bay ambient lighting shall consist of two metal halide adjustable downlights (100-watt PAR38 spots) aimed down and [5] five quartz adjustable downlights (250-watt PAR38 spots) aimed down to reach target of 50 footcandles. Metal halide shall be switched on/off and quartz shall be dimmed.

GarySteffyLightingDesign Inc.
3900 South Shula Street Suite 10
Ann Arbor, Michigan 48104
v/ 800 537 1230 & 313 747 6630
t/ 313 747 6629

Preliminary Lighting Concept
Plan

12-10-98 For Review

12-14-98 Controls added GJW

3-10-99 For A/E

Description	Date	By
15198	DAG	

LPA1 shall be low-voltage (240-watt PAR56) dimmable incandescent to achieve target of 90 footcandles on font.

Quartz (250-watt PAR38 spots) adjustable accents for highlighting the balcony and the balcony railing.

Zone 53+   Zone 52
APA5   Zone 54

Lighting Remote
Control Station
(in loft)

Lighting Remote
Control Station
(below balcony)
Zone 40

Zone 45   Zone 44   Zone 46   Zone 51

Zone 48   Zone 49
Zone 57   Zone 58   Zone 45   Zone 59
Zone 50+   Zone 51+   Zone 52+   Zone 55+
Zone 29+   APA3
                                  Zone 54
                                  Zone 53+
                                  Zone 52

Existing luminaires to be removed and holes patched.

...s shall be
...n. Target
...e 30

Organ lighting shall be quartz (250-watt PAR38 spots) adjustable accents. Target illuminance for organs shall be 90 footcandles.

Quartz uplights to be mounted to top of column capital. Lighting target for ceiling is 10 footcandles. Side aisles shall be slightly higher to add to horizontal illuminance at book reading height.

Lighting Control Notes:
1. Lighting control system to be a Unison architectural lighting control system by Electronic Theatre Controls (ETC) of Middleton, Wisconsin.
2. Lighting control panels to be located in support space adjacent to chair storage.
3. Lighting remote control stations to be ETC Unison LCD touch screens.

11.3 Contract Documents

Lighting Specification

The Project Name /S1679901   ©May 24, 2000 /16500–1

1 May 24, 2000

3 # Project Name
Project City, State

5

Preface — Registered Professionals
7 The following specification is intended to express lighting design
concepts and will need the input, review and approval or revision by
9 registered professionals on, but not limited to these issues prior to
being used as part of any contract document:
11 ▶Voltage.
▶HVAC integration/requirements.
13 ▶Mechanical fit with ceiling, walls, furniture, paving, earth,
foundations.
15 ▶Required architectural openings, footers and/or foundations.
▶Structural requirements.
17 ▶Color/finish.
▶All cutsheet copyrights, trademarks, and/or luminaire patents are
19 protected by the respective manufacturers and may not be
copied for the purpose of assessing substitutions or seeking
21 other manufacturers' so–called equals.
▶This specification is a copyrighted document and may not be
23 altered in any substantive way without the express written
permission of Gary Steffy Lighting Design Inc.
25

Preface — Contractor
27 Contractor shall follow the enclosed specification, except when directed
otherwise by the architect or engineer. In addition to practicing
29 industry–accepted care in construction and to following the
specification, the contractor shall address the following issues:
31 ▶All cutsheet copyrights, trademarks, and/or luminaire patents are
protected by the respective manufacturers and may not be

GarySteffyLightingDesign Inc.
2900 South State Street Suite 12
Ann Arbor, Michigan 48104
v/ 800 537 1230 & 734 747 6630
f/ 734 747 6629

Image ©EyeWire, Inc.

204

Contract Documents

The header should include the name of the project for which the specification is being written, the date, and the page number. It is also most convenient to include the electronic filename for future reference. If the specification is to be included as part of the typical architectural specification package, then the section number "16500" will help to categorize the lighting specification and its location within the larger overall specification. This is based on the Construction Specifications Institute (CSI) format.

more online @
http://www.csinet.org

Prominently display the date of issue for this specific specification version.

State the title of the project for which the specification is being provided.

State the location of the project.

A preface to the (other) registered professionals should outline any issues that need others' attention. Typically, registered professionals need to review, confirm, and/or revise the specification to meet specific architectural and/or engineering requirements. If the specification is being submitted by a registered professional (an electrical engineer, for example), then it may need the review of other team registered professionals (such as the architect, and other team engineers, such as the mechanical and/or structural engineer).

Including line numbering may be beneficial for specific review and reference. This is most helpful when quite a few bidders are anticipated and/or quite a few manufacturers are included in the specification—both situations increasing the likelihood of questions throughout the document and a need for precise, convenient referencing guides.

Some key issues may be conveyed in a preface to the contractor. Like the preface to the registered professionals, this may be seen as a "belts and suspenders" approach—identifying some highlights that are considered industry standard practice and/or included throughout the body of the specification.

The footer should contain some identification of the authoring body/firm of the specification. This should include voice and fax phone numbers to allow convenient reference by other team members, including the contractor and owner, during the project's construction.

Extra space on the outside margin allows for notations and for lots of page use without wearing text off the page (which would occur with small outside margin).

11.3 Contract Documents

Repetition of items that may be considered standard practice or standard of care anticipated from others for whom this document is intended helps clarify specifier's and client's expectations. This is particularly useful when very low bidders may later claim the price did not include such common practices as pulling permits and warranty followup.

Reiterate the electronic file name within the text in case the headers and footers are cut off by copying practices or by registered professionals incorporating the text into their respective documents.

Image ©EyeWire, Inc.

Contract Documents

Lighting Specification

The Project Name /S1679901   ©May 24, 2000 /16500–2

1   copied for the purpose of assessing substitutions or seeking
     other manufacturers' so–called equals.

3   ▶This specification is a copyrighted document and may not be
     altered in any substantive way without the express written

5   permission of Gary Steffy Lighting Design Inc.
     ▶Secure all necessary permits if/when/as required.

7   ▶As applicable and necessary, construct appropriate enclosures
     around non–insulation–contact–rated lighting equipment to

9   provide at least 3–Inches of air space on all sides of the
     luminaire.

11   ▶Maintain an appropriately professional relationship with the
     electrical inspector, coordinating appropriate inspection

13   sequencing, reviewing detail and hardware items for compliance
     with the inspector's requirements, and installing hardware and

15   details necessary to meet the inspector's requirements for code
     compliance.

17   ▶Strictly follow manufacturers' installation instructions on all
     luminaires, controls and necessary auxiliary equipment.

19   ▶Address all warranty issues as/if they arise with the respective
     manufacturers—this is not the responsibility of any entity other

21   than the contractor except for all lighting equipment
     direct–purchased by the Owner (which then is the sole

23   responsibility of the Owner).

25   File S1679901

GarySteffyLightingDesign Inc.
2900 South State Street   Suite 12
Ann Arbor, Michigan 48104
v/ 800 537 1230 & 734 747 6630
f/ 734 747 6629

11.3   Contract Documents

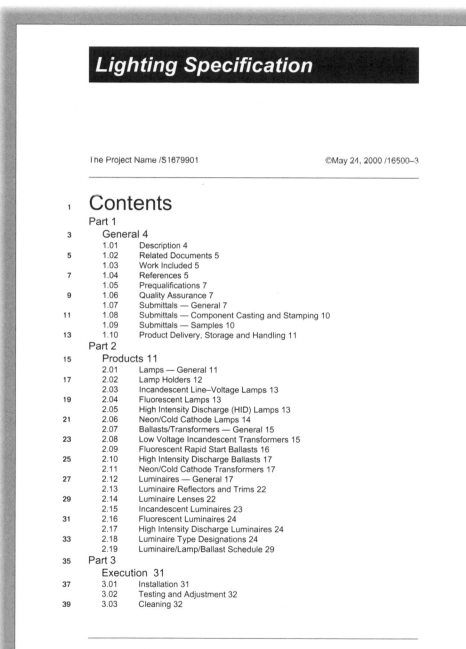

Lighting Specification

The Project Name /S1679901   ©May 24, 2000 /16500–3

GarySteffyLightingDesign Inc.
2900 South State Street Suite 12
Ann Arbor, Michigan 48104
v/ 800 537 1230 & 734 747 6630
f/ 734 747 6629

Contract Documents

A table of contents within the lighting specification is very convenient for reference during the construction documentation phase and during bidding and construction. At a minimum, section headings and subheadings should be included. A complete lighting specification will consist of thirty or forty pages or more, depending on the project size and the number of different luminaire types required. It may not be necessary to reissue all of the sections of the lighting specification when making revisions. This will depend on the number of contractors on the project, the amount of time that has passed since the last issuing of the specification, and the quality of the contractor's work evidenced by the specifier.

11.3   Contract Documents

A "General" section is essentially an introduction to the specification. This introduction should include the specific project for which the specification is intended and a few key remarks outlining the intent of the specification, how revisions are handled, and any special caveats of paramount importance.

It is crucial to alert all readers that the specification is intended to assure lighting design criteria compliance and is not intended to cover other disciplines' related aspects (unless, of course, it is written by a firm with capabilities in all of these disciplines, in which case the specification may indeed address other disciplines' issues).

Some clear, consistent methodology must be established and outlined regarding the handling of revisions. One possibility is to underline all changes or additions to a revised release of the specification and strike out all deletions from a revised release of the specification. The example illustrated in this chapter is one of a first release of the specification (hence, the file name in the upper left of the header of "S1679901" where "S" represents a specification document, "16799" represents a project number (number 167 in the year 1999), and "01" represents the version or release number). The point: keep track of changes.

more online @
http://www.ul.com

Underwriters Laboratories Inc. is a not–for–profit product safety testing and certification organization. Lighting products intended for permanent installation should be UL listed and labeled. Codes demand such for commercial applications and many residential applications. It is prudent to require that even portable lighting products be UL listed and labeled. Some manufacturers, particularly importers, will claim to use UL listed components. This is not equivalent to a complete UL listed assembly. In other than United States venues, other product safety testing, listing, and labeling services may be required. Always confirm this with local building authorities and/or code officials.

Substitutions and "knock offs" of specified products are a danger to the client and the design team. Such products are likely to NOT offer identical performance characteristics (e.g., photometric properties, efficiencies, on/off/dimming, and so on), aesthetics, and size as the originally specified products or the required UL listings and labels. Further, the illicit use of copyrighted, trademarked, and/or patented materials and products to seek substitutions may result in serious liability for the construction team and, if not explicitly forbidden by the design team and client, this liability may extend to the design team and client.

Image ©EyeWire, Inc.

Contract Documents

11.3

Lighting Specification

The Project Name /S1679901   ©May 24, 2000 /16500—4

1 # Part 1
   # General

3 ## 1.01 Description:

   A. Lighting Systems Specification for Luminaires, Lamps, Ballasts and
5   Transformers for The Project Name, Project City, State.
   B. This specification is generated to assure lighting design
7   compliance with lighting criteria. This is not Intended nor does it
       presume to cover Mechanical, Electrical, Civil or Structural
9   Engineering nor any Architectural or Landscape Architectural
       issues. These areas shall be addressed by the respective
11   disciplines and coordinated by Contractor to assure safe, aesthetic
       and operationally complete lighting installations.
13 C. <u>Revisions to this specification are indicated by underlining the
       area(s) which have been revised, as shown here.</u>
15 D. ~~Deletions to this specification are indicated by strikeout of the
       area(s) which have been deleted, as shown here.~~
17 E. All equipment and parts specified herein shall bear the "U.L.
       Approved" label. All luminaires shall be U.L. listed and labeled for
19   installation in fireproof or non–fireproof construction, dry, damp, or
       wet locations as required. Alternatively, respective labels may be
21   attributed to testing agencies other than U.L. providing the tests
       required for the labeling are according to U.L. standards and
23   procedures and providing the testing organization is recognized by
       Building Officials and Code Administrators International (BOCAI);
25   the International Conference of Building Officials (ICBO); or other
       relevant code authority recognized by the jurisdiction within which
27   the project is being constructed.
   F. Products identified herein and cutsheets which may be attached or
29   referenced represent copyrighted and/or patented and/or
       trademarked material and may not be freely copied nor distributed
31   for any purposes other than the purchase of the specified products.

GarySteffyLightingDesign Inc.
2900 South State Street Suite 12
Ann Arbor, Michigan 48104
v/ 800 537 1230 & 734 747 6630
f/ 734 747 6629

more online @
http://www.bocai.org
http://www.icbo.org

11.3

Contract Documents

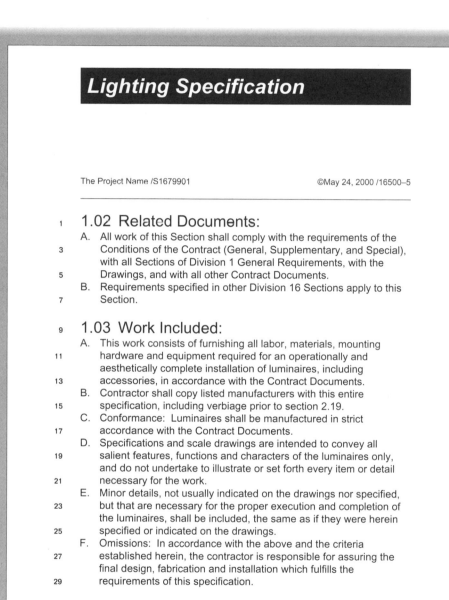

Lighting Specification

The Project Name /S1679901   ©May 24, 2000 /16500–5

1   ## 1.02 Related Documents:
    A. All work of this Section shall comply with the requirements of the
3   Conditions of the Contract (General, Supplementary, and Special),
        with all Sections of Division 1 General Requirements, with the
5   Drawings, and with all other Contract Documents.
    B. Requirements specified in other Division 16 Sections apply to this
7   Section.

9   ## 1.03 Work Included:
    A. This work consists of furnishing all labor, materials, mounting
11   hardware and equipment required for an operationally and
        aesthetically complete installation of luminaires, including
13   accessories, in accordance with the Contract Documents.
    B. Contractor shall copy listed manufacturers with this entire
15   specification, including verbiage prior to section 2.19.
    C. Conformance: Luminaires shall be manufactured in strict
17   accordance with the Contract Documents.
    D. Specifications and scale drawings are intended to convey all
19   salient features, functions and characters of the luminaires only,
        and do not undertake to illustrate or set forth every item or detail
21   necessary for the work.
    E. Minor details, not usually indicated on the drawings nor specified,
23   but that are necessary for the proper execution and completion of
        the luminaires, shall be included, the same as if they were herein
25   specified or indicated on the drawings.
    F. Omissions: In accordance with the above and the criteria
27   established herein, the contractor is responsible for assuring the
        final design, fabrication and installation which fulfills the
29   requirements of this specification.

31 ## 1.04 References:
    A. National Fire Protection Association (NFPA):
33   1. NFPA 70, "National Electrical Code", (NEC).

GarySteffyLightingDesign Inc.
2900 South State Street   Suite 12
Ann Arbor, Michigan 48104
v/ 800 53/ 1230 & /34 /47 6630
f/ 734 747 6629

more online @
http://www.nfpa.org

Contract Documents

The specification should cite other relevant documents that are critical to the implementation of a reliable and successful lighting system. Many of these documents may have related construction details, may outline additional electrical and/or architectural requirements, and may have additional location/dimensional information important for the successful construction and installation of the lighting system.

A paragraph outlining the work that is expected to be included and undertaken by the contractor should be succinct—citing key requirements and setting the tone for the quality of work and the compliance parameters. This does not presume to supersede the complete specification, but early in the reading does advise the contractor of the design team's intentions for a complete and operational installation meeting at a minimum the standard care and practice common to the industry.

All reputable manufacturers of UL listed and labeled lamps, luminaires, ballasts, and/or transformers should also subscribe to recognized industry standards, practices, recommendations and, of course, applicable codes. This section in the specification should cite many of the respective reference documents and agencies. This helps assure that hardware provided on the project does comply with appropriate quality and safety standards and practices.

11.3 Contract Documents

Documents referenced from the Illuminating Engineering Society of North America (IESNA) address photometric measurement and testing methods.

American National Standards Institute (ANSI) documents are referenced that address physical and operational characteristics of lighting–related electrical components.

National Electrical Manufacturers Association (NEMA) documents address complete luminaire and system requirements.

Lighting Specification

The Project Name /S1679901   ©May 24, 2000 /16500–6

---

1   B.   Illuminating Engineering Society of North America (IESNA):
1.   IES Approved Method for Life Performance Testing of General
3   Lighting Incandescent Filament Lamps, LM-49.
2.   IES Approved Method for Electrical and Photometric
5   Measurements of General Service Incandescent Filament
Lamps, LM-45.
7   3.   IES Approved Method for Life Performance Testing of
Fluorescent Lamps, LM-40.
9   4.   IES Approved Method for the Electrical and Photometric
Measurements of Fluorescent Lamps, LM-9.
11 5.   IES Approved Method for Life Testing of High Intensity
Discharge Lamps, LM-47.
13 6.   IES Approved Method for Photometric Measurements of High
Intensity Discharge Lamps, LM-51.
15 7.   IES Approved Method for Photometric Testing of Indoor
Fluorescent Luminaires, LM-41.
17 8.   IES Approved Method for Photometric Testing of Indoor
Luminaires Using High Intensity Discharge Lamps, LM-46.
19 C.   American National Standards Institute (ANSI):
1.   ANSI C78.1, "Dimensional and Electrical Characteristics of
21   Fluorescent Lamps - Rapid Start Types".
2.   ANSI C82.1, "Specifications for Fluorescent Lamp Ballasts".
23 3.   ANSI C82.4, "Specifications for High Intensity Discharge Lamp
Ballasts (Multiple Supply Type)".
25 4.   ANSI N540, "Classification of Radioactive Self- Luminous Light
Sources".
27 5.   ANSI C78 Series, Physical and Electrical Characteristics of
High-Intensity Discharge Lamps.
29 6.   ANSI C81 Series, Electric Lamp Bases and Holders.
D.   National Electric Manufacturer's Association (NEMA):
31 1.   NEMA LE1, "Fluorescent Luminaires".
2.   NEMA LE2, "HID Lighting System Noise Criterion (LS-NC)
33   Ratings".
3.   NEMA FA1, "Outdoor Flood Lighting Equipment".

GarySteffyLightingDesign Inc.
2900 South State Street   Suite 12
Ann Arbor, Michigan 48104
v/ 800 537 1230 & 734 747 6630
f/ 734 747 6629

more online @
http://www.iesna.org

more online @
http://www.ansi.org

more online @
http://www.nema.org
http://www.nema.org/
products/div2/

11.3

Contract Documents

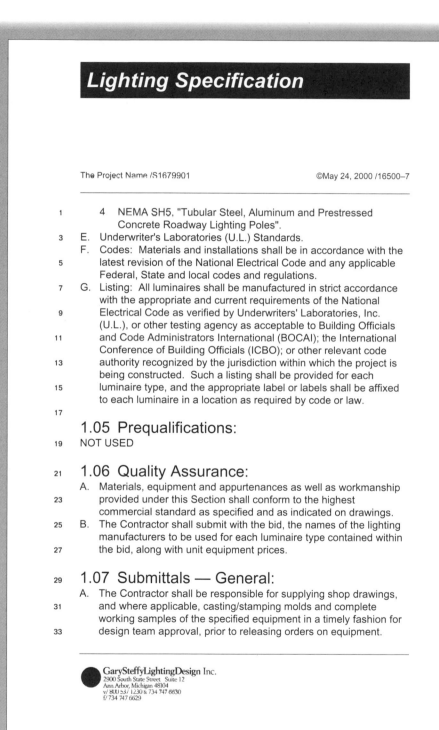

Lighting Specification

The Project Name /S1679901   ©May 24, 2000 /16500–7

1   4   NEMA SH5, "Tubular Steel, Aluminum and Prestressed
       Concrete Roadway Lighting Poles".

3   E.   Underwriter's Laboratories (U.L.) Standards.

    F.   Codes: Materials and installations shall be in accordance with the

5   latest revision of the National Electrical Code and any applicable
       Federal, State and local codes and regulations.

7   G.   Listing: All luminaires shall be manufactured in strict accordance
       with the appropriate and current requirements of the National

9   Electrical Code as verified by Underwriters' Laboratories, Inc.
       (U.L.), or other testing agency as acceptable to Building Officials

11   and Code Administrators International (BOCAI); the International
       Conference of Building Officials (ICBO); or other relevant code

13   authority recognized by the jurisdiction within which the project is
       being constructed. Such a listing shall be provided for each

15   luminaire type, and the appropriate label or labels shall be affixed
       to each luminaire in a location as required by code or law.

17

1.05 Prequalifications:

19   NOT USED

21   1.06 Quality Assurance:

    A.   Materials, equipment and appurtenances as well as workmanship

23   provided under this Section shall conform to the highest
       commercial standard as specified and as indicated on drawings.

25   B.   The Contractor shall submit with the bid, the names of the lighting
       manufacturers to be used for each luminaire type contained within

27   the bid, along with unit equipment prices.

29   1.07 Submittals — General:

    A.   The Contractor shall be responsible for supplying shop drawings,

31   and where applicable, casting/stamping molds and complete
       working samples of the specified equipment in a timely fashion for

33   design team approval, prior to releasing orders on equipment.

GarySteffyLightingDesign Inc.
2900 South State Street Suite 12
Ann Arbor, Michigan 48104
v/ 800 537 1230 & 734 747 6630
f/ 734 747 6629

Contract Documents

11.3

Underwriters Laboratories (UL) Inc. standards and testing practices are referenced for all lighting components and complete luminaires.

When custom luminaires, historic luminaires, or luminaire restorations are part of the design and if a strong desire exists to include as many manufacturers as possible for these custom luminaires, a section outlining qualifications will be appropriate. For public construction, this section may be a necessity. This section should outline the kinds of requirements expected of each manufacturer in order to minimize misunderstandings about the design of the luminaires: the level of detail required on shop drawing submittal, the attention to mockups required, the quality of manufacture, appropriate shipping requirements, and installation instructions and support service. **Note:** Where only one or several manufacturers are, in the estimation of the designer, most capable of meeting all of the design requirements, the designer may elect to list only the one or several manufacturers. In this case, no Prequalification Section is necessary.

Quality assurance must include some statement regarding the expected level of quality. Here, the contractor is told that the workmanship shall conform to the highest commercial standard. While this is an open-ended statement (and could, therefore, be argued both ways), it does alert the contractor that the designers and/or the client may, during inspections, cite work that needs redoing or at least needs revision if it is not up to what may typically be expected of good workmanship. Another quality assurance item relates to the lighting hardware that will be provided by the contractor. Here, 1.06.B informs the contractor that the names of the lighting manufacturers from which the contractor will purchase the project's luminaires must accompany the bid, as must line item unit prices. This provides the client with the option of sharing such information with the design team and seeking opinions about likely compliance with the specification and whether or not pricing is reasonable.

The contractor should be informed which kinds of submittals, if any, are anticipated. 1.07.A indicates that shop drawings are required along with casting and stamping molds and complete working samples if/as specified in the Luminaire/Lamp/Ballast Schedule (Section 2.19). The contractor is also forewarned that some luminaires may require long leadtimes and that the contractor is responsible for orchestrating shop drawing submittals and/or sample submittals in sufficient advance time so that the ultimate delivery date is not compromised. Sometimes contractors may seek to pull a "bait and switch" during the project by claiming that the leadtimes will result in the project not being completed on time. This section puts the burden on the contractor to maintain the schedule and also to maintain the originally specified equipment.

11.3 Contract Documents

This portion of Section 1.07 identifies for the contractor the extent of calculational and design detail from which the lighting specification progressed. To continue to thwart the "bait and switch" and put the burden of proving other alternatives as suitable, the contractor is alerted to some of the lighting criteria used (ASHRAE/IESNA 90.1 and California Title 24) and warned that in all likelihood substitutions will not meet all of the project's requirements and priorities. The contractor is also advised that his/her obligation to the project cost and schedule must be based on the originally specified equipment and not on substitutions. Of course, if the client changes priorities during construction (e.g., quality be damned, let's look for fast and cheap), then other solutions may have greater validity.

Lighting calculations, no matter who performs them, are only as accurate as the data on which they are based. Here, the contractor is alerted that if substitutions are permitted by the team and if they are then to be seriously considered, the substitutions must be accompanied by sufficiently accurate technical data (as outlined).

The contractor is advised that he/she is responsible for negotiating with the team prior to any substitution submittal to assure that fees are available to even assess substitution(s). Essentially, this requires that the contractor pay for the redesign effort required to determine if and then how the substituted products can meet the lighting criteria. Finally, the contractor is told that all substitutions, if any, must be identified at the time of bid (this prevents surprises later since the client could simply reject the bid due to substitutions). Further, the contractor must negotiate with the design team prior to the bidding in order to assure that fees are available to review the proposed substitutions.

Contract Documents

11.3

Lighting Specification

The Project Name /S1679901   ©May 24, 2000 /16500–8

1   Some luminaires may require at least 12 to 16 weeks of lead time -
the Contractor is responsible for allowing sufficient time for the
3   review process. Substitutions will not be accepted on the basis of
the contractor's obligation to make any deadlines, contractual or
5   otherwise, agreed by the contractor toward the completion of this
project. Lamp submittals are as important and necessary as
7   luminaire submittals and must be supplied by the Contractor to
assure correct lamp wattage, color and efficacy.
9   B.   The lighting equipment specified herein has been carefully chosen
for its ability to meet the luminous environment requirements of this
11   project. Calculations (LUMEN-Point and LUMEN-Micro) are
generally performed to determine luminances, luminance ratios,
13   and horizontal and vertical illuminances. In some instances, virtual
reality "images" have been generated (with RADIANCE or
15   Lightscape) to assist the Lighting Designer, the Architect and/or the
Owner in assessing the lighting quality of the space(s). Equipment
17   and/or manufacturers which have been shown to comply with
established criteria, including ASHRAE/IES 90.1/1999 (or
19   California Title 24 where applicable), is specified herein.
Substitutions in all likelihood will be unable to meet all of the same
21   criteria as the specified equipment.
C.   Where permitted, substitution submittals shall consist of a physical
23   description, dimensioned drawing and complete photometric and
electric data of the proposed lamp and luminaire. Working
25   samples of lamp and luminaire substitutions must also be supplied
for visual check of finish, operating and photometric characteristics
27   and aesthetic design. Photometric reports must list the actual
candela values of the luminaire's distribution with specified or
29   similar lamp in at least five horizontal planes with elevation angles
in increments not greater than 5° from nadir to zenith. Candela
31   curves, footcandle and lumen tables and iso-footcandle contours
are not acceptable. The Contractor shall be responsible for
33   negotiation with the Client, Lighting Designer and Electrical
Engineer prior to substitution submittal to assure fees are available

GarySteffyLightingDesign Inc.
2900 South State Street Suite 12
Ann Arbor, Michigan 48104
v/ 800 537 1230 & 734 747 6630
f/ 734 747 6629

more online @
[LUMEN-Micro]
http://www.lighting-
technologies.com

more online @
[RADIANCE]
http://
www.radsite.lbl.gov/
radiance/refer/
long.html

more online @
[Lightscape]
http://
www3.autodesk.com/
adsk/section/
0,,152898,00.html

more online @
http://
www.ashrae.org

11.3 Contract Documents

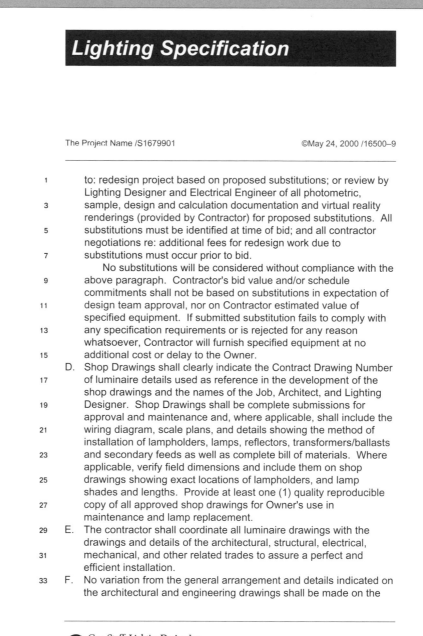

Lighting Specification

The Project Name /S1679901   ©May 24, 2000 /16500–9

1   to: redesign project based on proposed substitutions; or review by
  Lighting Designer and Electrical Engineer of all photometric,
3   sample, design and calculation documentation and virtual reality
  renderings (provided by Contractor) for proposed substitutions. All
5   substitutions must be identified at time of bid; and all contractor
  negotiations re: additional fees for redesign work due to
7   substitutions must occur prior to bid.
    No substitutions will be considered without compliance with the
9   above paragraph. Contractor's bid value and/or schedule
  commitments shall not be based on substitutions in expectation of
11   design team approval, nor on Contractor estimated value of
  specified equipment. If submitted substitution fails to comply with
13   any specification requirements or is rejected for any reason
  whatsoever, Contractor will furnish specified equipment at no
15   additional cost or delay to the Owner.

  D.   Shop Drawings shall clearly indicate the Contract Drawing Number
17   of luminaire details used as reference in the development of the
   shop drawings and the names of the Job, Architect, and Lighting
19   Designer. Shop Drawings shall be complete submissions for
   approval and maintenance and, where applicable, shall include the
21   wiring diagram, scale plans, and details showing the method of
   installation of lampholders, lamps, reflectors, transformers/ballasts
23   and secondary feeds as well as complete bill of materials. Where
   applicable, verify field dimensions and include them on shop
25   drawings showing exact locations of lampholders, and lamp
   shades and lengths. Provide at least one (1) quality reproducible
27   copy of all approved shop drawings for Owner's use in
   maintenance and lamp replacement.

29   E.   The contractor shall coordinate all luminaire drawings with the
   drawings and details of the architectural, structural, electrical,
31   mechanical, and other related trades to assure a perfect and
   efficient installation.

33   F.   No variation from the general arrangement and details indicated on
   the architectural and engineering drawings shall be made on the

GarySteffyLightingDesign Inc.
2900 South State Street Suite 12
Ann Arbor, Michigan 48104
v/ 800 337 1230 & 734 747 6630
f/ 734 747 6629

Contract Documents

The contractor is told quite clearly that no substitutions will even be considered without compliance with the previous paragraph. The contractor is also alerted that the bid value may not be based on an expectation that substitutions can later be introduced and their acceptance forced in order to hold the bid or in order to seek additional funds for simply providing the originally specified lighting equipment. Finally, the contractor is warned that even if substitutions are considered but fail acceptance by the team, then the contractor must provide the originally specified equipment at no additional cost to the client.

Shop drawing submittal is a critical step in the success of a project. Here, the contractor is told the level of detail and markings anticipated on shop drawings. It is incumbent on the contractor to forward this information to the luminaire manufacturers, so that the manufacturers know the extent of the information they need to provide for the project team's review.

It is necessary for the contractor to coordinate shop drawings with the respective design plans and details to assure that the installation can be made in an efficient manner that will be considered as perfect for the particular project application. It is the contractor's responsibility to alert team members of any discrepancies and/or of any conflicts with other systems and trades. Essentially, the contractor is being advised that the integrity of the lighting equipment performance, installation, and warranty may not be waived.

To avoid changes in lighting layouts and/or details, the contractor is advised not to deviate from the drawings unless written permission is granted by the architect and then any permitted variations shall be noted on shop drawings submitted for approval.

11.3   Contract Documents

Sometimes, to save time, manufacturers, manufacturers' reps, distributors, and/or contractors will submit "beauty shots" of lighting equipment. This material, while perhaps illustrating the type of luminaire specified, may not show all relevant information like some or all of the following: size (in three dimensions), reflector and/or trim finishes, ceiling integration capability, lamping, ballasting, voltage, lensing and/or louvering, and so forth. If such a shop drawing is "approved" by the team and the unit arrives in the wrong finish, voltage, size, etc., then the team may be held responsible for correcting the issue(s). So, only detailed cutsheets should be accepted as shop drawings.

The contractor is being alerted to the fact that the team's review of shop drawings does not waive any of the contractor's contract requirements.

Maintenance is difficult enough on many modern lighting devices. Every attempt should be made to provide the owner with complete operating manuals that should outline tools required to maintain the luminaire; types of cleaners that should be used and how they should be applied; and replacement parts list and warranty. Further, the manual should include a reproducible copy of the final as–built shop drawing.

When custom luminaires, historic luminaires, or luminaire restorations are part of the design and if these luminaires will have special stampings and/or castings, a section outlining sample submittal requirements should be used. This typically requires that the contractor submit casting and stamping molds for review by the design team or alternatively provide transportation (and subsistence as necessary) to the manufacturer(s) factory(ies) to review the molds.

If so required in any such luminaire descriptions outlined later in Section 2.19, then the contractor must furnish one complete luminaire sample and specified lamp for design team review.

To minimize incorrect submittals, the shop drawings must first be reviewed and "approved" or "approved as noted" prior to sample submittal.

To offer the best reviewing situation, it is advised that the luminaire be mounted and electrified as directed by the architect (on the actual project site if the project is sufficiently complete to allow such a mockup) and allowed to remain in place for at least one week so that the entire team may review the luminaire(s) and assess any time–invoked issues (e.g., sagging of bracket arms after a few days indicates castings of insufficient strength).

Some reasonable turnaround time must be agreed by the design team, so that the contractor can accommodate this in his/her schedule.

Lighting Specification

The Project Name /S1679901   ©May 24, 2000 /16500–10

1 shop drawings unless required to suit the actual conditions on the
   premises, and then only with written acceptance of the Architect.
3 All variations must be clearly marked as such on drawings
   submitted for approval.
5 G. Catalog cuts lacking sufficient detail to indicate compliance with
       contract documents will not be acceptable.
7 H. Review of shop drawings or samples does not waive contract
       requirements.
9 I. The Contractor shall be responsible for obtaining from his
       supplying lighting manufacturers, for each luminaire, a
11   recommended maintenance manual including:
       1. Tools required
13   2. Types of cleaners to be used
       3. Replacement parts identification lists
15   4. Final, as built shop drawings (quality, reproducible copies)
       5. Warranty
17

1.08 Submittals — Component Casting and
19 Stamping:
   NOT USED
21

1.09 Submittals — Samples:
23 A. The Contractor shall furnish one complete luminaire, including
        specified lamp, for each type so designated as requiring "review
25   sample" submittal.
    B. This shall occur after the shop drawing review process is complete
27   and approved for designated luminaires and prior to their
        fabrication.
29 C. Review sample luminaires shall be mounted and electrified
        according to Architect's directions to allow for a one–week review
31   period by the design team.

GarySteffyLightingDesign Inc.
2900 South State Street Suite 12
Ann Arbor, Michigan 48104
v/ 800 537 1230 & 734 747 6630
f/ 734 747 6629

11.3 Contract Documents

Lighting Specification

The Project Name /S1679901 ©May 24, 2000 /16500–11

1   D. Within two weeks of sample installation, the Architect shall notify the Contractor in writing of approval/rejection/comments necessary
3   for manufacturing or resubmittal.
     E. All review samples shall become the property of the Owner, but
5   may be used as a prototype by the manufacturer during the fabrication process. Approved review samples may be counted as
7   project quantities.
     F. Review samples must be made from parts to be used on project
9   luminaires and according to shop drawings and specifications. For example, stamped metal components are unacceptable if final
11   parts are to be cast.

13   ## 1.10 Product Delivery, Storage and Handling:
     A. The Contractor shall provide, receive, unload, uncrate, store,
15   protect and install lamps, luminaires and auxiliary equipment as specified herein. Lamps for miscellaneous equipment shall be
17   provided and installed by the Contractor according to equipment manufacturers' guidelines.
19

Part 2

21   ## Products
     ### 2.01 Lamps — General:
23   A. For color consistency, lamp maintenance consistency and for light output consistency, do not mix lamps from different manufacturers,
25   and do not mix so-called similar "Energy Saver" lamps with "Standard" lamps (this has the same effect as mixed die lots on
27   fabrics -- when placed side-by-side, they may not have the same appearance). Use one brand and type for each of the different
29   lamps specified.
     B. Lamps which fail within 90 days after acceptance shall be replaced
31   at no cost to the Owner.

GarySteffyLightingDesign Inc.
2900 South State Street Suite 12
Ann Arbor, Michigan 48104
v/ 800 537 1230 & 734 747 6630
f/ 734 747 6629

Contract Documents

Depending on project conditions, particularly including schedule, this paragraph may not be appropriate as illustrated here. The intent as written is to assure the client that the sample is an actual as–built model and that it shall serve as the quality and aesthetic guide or template (providing it is approved) for all other identical luminaires on the project.

Sometimes in the rush to order and deliver lamps to a job site, particularly on larger projects, the contractor may choose to have several sources or suppliers of lamps. It is essential that all lamps are as specified. Changing brand names or changing from "standard output" to "high output" or "energy saver" versions will likely result in a visibly noticeable change in color temperature and/or color rendering (SPD) and/or in light output.

To assist the client during initial relamping phases, it is advisable to have some "attic stock" or spare lamps purchased by the contractor that are the originally specified types. Some clients have their own rule of thumb on attic stock quantities required by the contractor.

11.3 Contract Documents

Some basic requirements of lamps should be cited. This may help assure that lamps are the most efficacious, highest quality available. Listing GE, Osram Sylvania, and Philips as the acceptable lamp vendors helps minimize off–brand lamps, long–life lamps, and so–called full–spectrum lamps from use on the project.

Requiring the contractor to provide lamps for all luminaires that are identified in the specification as part of the electrical contractor's work. This prevents any potential confusion if/when luminaires are shipped without lamps.

Since most incandescent lamps have a relatively short life, the contractor is advised not to use such lamps for purposes other than initial testing of the lighting.

Image ©EyeWire, Inc.

Contract Documents

11.3

Lighting Specification

The Project Name /S1679901   ©May 24, 2000 /16500–12

1   C. Contractor shall supply a quantity of lamps equal to 5% of each
        lamp type required for each luminaire, but no fewer than 12 of each
3   lamp type and no more than 60 lamps of each type unless
        otherwise indicated in the Luminaire Schedule (Section 2.19).
5   These lamps shall constitute the Owners initial replacement stock
        and are not to be used as warranty replacements in compliance
7   with section 2.01.B.

    D. Lamps shall conform to ANSI C78 Series Dimensional and
9   Electrical Characteristics of Lamps.

    E. Lamp performance (initial lumen output, life, color and lumen
11   maintenance) shall be as specified in the Luminaire Schedule.

    F. Initial lumen output shall be as measured after 100 hours of
13   operation.

    G. Lamp color for light sources shall be as specified in either color
15   temperature (degrees Kelvin) or CIE chromaticity coordinates
        measured by means of spectroradiometry.

17   H. Lamp performance shall be in accordance with the manufacturer's
        latest published data for the lamp types and respective
19   manufacturers specified.

    I. Manufacturer: Lamps shall be manufactured by General Electric,
21   Osram Sylvania or Philips unless otherwise specified. All lamps of
        a given type shall be supplied by the same manufacturer.

23   J. If a specific manufacturer is noted in the Luminaire Schedule, only
        that manufacturer shall be acceptable.

25   K. Provide lamps for all luminaires (furnished as part of the electrical
        work).

27   L. Incandescent and tungsten halogen lamps shall not be operated,
        other than for initial testing, prior to final inspection.

29   M. Replace defective and burned out lamps at the date of substantial
        completion as determined by the Architect.
31

2.02 Lamp Holders:

33   A. Unless otherwise specified, all line–voltage incandescent
        luminaires using screw–base lamps shall be equipped with U.L.

GarySteffyLightingDesign Inc.
2900 South State Street Suite 12
Ann Arbor, Michigan 48104
v/ 800 537 1230 & 734 747 6630
f/ 734 747 6629

more online @
[General Electric]
http://
   www.gelighting.com/
   na/specoem/
   index.html

more online @
[Osram Sylvania]
http://
   www.sylvania.com/
   welcomej.htm

more online @
[Philips]
http://
   www.lighting.philips.com

Image ©EyeWire, Inc.

11.3 Contract Documents

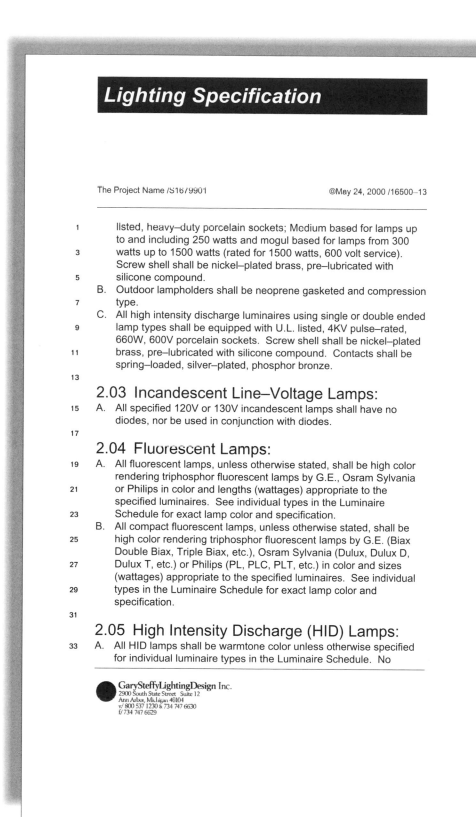

Lighting Specification

The Project Name /S16/9901   ©May 24, 2000 /16500–13

1   listed, heavy–duty porcelain sockets; Medium based for lamps up
     to and including 250 watts and mogul based for lamps from 300
3   watts up to 1500 watts (rated for 1500 watts, 600 volt service).
     Screw shell shall be nickel–plated brass, pre–lubricated with
5   silicone compound.
     B. Outdoor lampholders shall be neoprene gasketed and compression
7   type.
     C. All high intensity discharge luminaires using single or double ended
9   lamp types shall be equipped with U.L. listed, 4KV pulse–rated,
         660W, 600V porcelain sockets. Screw shell shall be nickel–plated
11   brass, pre–lubricated with silicone compound. Contacts shall be
         spring–loaded, silver–plated, phosphor bronze.
13

2.03 Incandescent Line–Voltage Lamps:

15   A. All specified 120V or 130V incandescent lamps shall have no
         diodes, nor be used in conjunction with diodes.
17

2.04 Fluorescent Lamps:

19   A. All fluorescent lamps, unless otherwise stated, shall be high color
         rendering triphosphor fluorescent lamps by G.E., Osram Sylvania
21   or Philips in color and lengths (wattages) appropriate to the
         specified luminaires. See individual types in the Luminaire
23   Schedule for exact lamp color and specification.
     B. All compact fluorescent lamps, unless otherwise stated, shall be
25   high color rendering triphosphor fluorescent lamps by G.E. (Biax
         Double Biax, Triple Biax, etc.), Osram Sylvania (Dulux, Dulux D,
27   Dulux T, etc.) or Philips (PL, PLC, PLT, etc.) in color and sizes
         (wattages) appropriate to the specified luminaires. See individual
29   types in the Luminaire Schedule for exact lamp color and
         specification.
31

2.05 High Intensity Discharge (HID) Lamps:

33   A. All HID lamps shall be warmtone color unless otherwise specified
         for individual luminaire types in the Luminaire Schedule. No

GarySteffyLightingDesign Inc.
2900 South State Street Suite 12
Ann Arbor, Michigan 48104
v/ 800 537 1230 & 734 747 6630
f/ 734 747 6629

Contract Documents

For a time during the late 1980s and early 1990s, in order to save energy and increase life, some incandescent lamps were fitted with diodes (devices that actually switched the filament "on" and "off" so fast it was technically imperceptible. Unfortunately, some folks could see this as a faint flicker, particularly in peripheral vision. This flicker was very annoying. Off brand lamps may still employ this technique. Another method of lengthening lamp life is to operate an incandescent lamp at less than its rated voltage—which is essentially permanently dimming the lamp. While this increases lamp life by perhaps 200 percent, it also reduces lumen output by about 30 percent, thereby resulting in a less efficacious lamp. This is not advisable unless the design and calculations are based on these reductions.

Reiteration and confirmation that the fluorescent lamps need to be high color rendering versions, which are the most efficacious lamps and offer the best light for chromatic contrasts and skin tones.

An alert that cool–tone HID lamps are not acceptable. Further, because HID lamps are difficult to manufacture, and, therefore, each manufacturer's lamps are likely to have either significantly different life, light output, and/or color characteristics, it is noted that no substitutes will be approved.

11.3 Contract Documents

Cold cathode lamps, including neon, are made to order. As such, if careful measurements of field conditions are not made, lamps may not fit or may not properly fit—leaving unsightly gaps (shadows) or overlaps (hotspots). Further, if the lamps are not consistently fit into details or along ceiling or wall surfaces, odd scallop patterns can occur. Finally, because these are made–to–order lamps, it is possible that one series of tube "blanks" may come from a batch or lot that is different from another series; this can result in color inconsistencies from lamp to lamp. Any of these issues result in an unacceptable appearance.

Cold cathode lamps are hand–bent and assembled. Without proper cleaning and filling, lamps will not provide the hoped–for light output and/or color.

Cold cathode lamps are hand–bent and assembled. Without proper cleaning and filling, lamps will not provide the hoped–for light output and/or color.

Some warranty should be established.

It is important to alert the electrical contractor that any neon/cold cathode vendor needs to be approved by the owner and the architect. This minimizes the possibility of having an unqualified vendor working out of a "back garage" and providing the neon/cold cathode for the project.

Image ©EyeWire, Inc.

Contract Documents

11.3

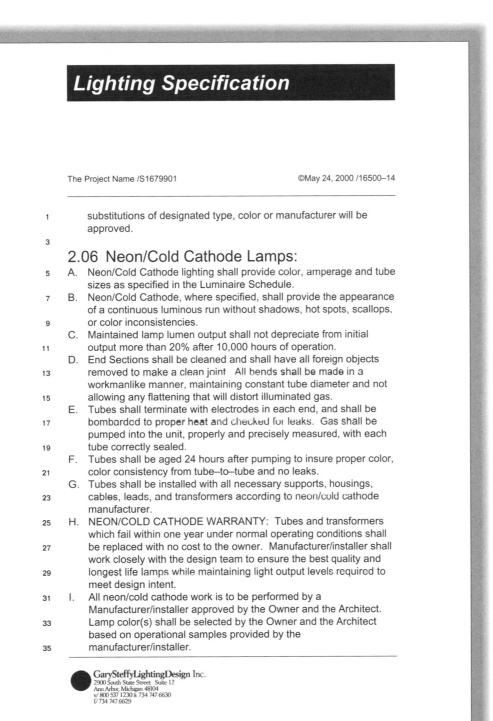

Lighting Specification

The Project Name /S1679901   ©May 24, 2000 /16500–14

1   substitutions of designated type, color or manufacturer will be
     approved.
3

2.06 Neon/Cold Cathode Lamps:

5   A.   Neon/Cold Cathode lighting shall provide color, amperage and tube
     sizes as specified in the Luminaire Schedule.

7   B.   Neon/Cold Cathode, where specified, shall provide the appearance
     of a continuous luminous run without shadows, hot spots, scallops,
9   or color inconsistencies.

   C.   Maintained lamp lumen output shall not depreciate from initial
11   output more than 20% after 10,000 hours of operation.

   D.   End Sections shall be cleaned and shall have all foreign objects
13   removed to make a clean joint All bends shall be made in a
     workmanlike manner, maintaining constant tube diameter and not
15   allowing any flattening that will distort illuminated gas.

   E.   Tubes shall terminate with electrodes in each end, and shall be
17   bombarded to proper heat and checked for leaks. Gas shall be
     pumped into the unit, properly and precisely measured, with each
19   tube correctly sealed.

   F.   Tubes shall be aged 24 hours after pumping to insure proper color,
21   color consistency from tube–to–tube and no leaks.

   G.   Tubes shall be installed with all necessary supports, housings,
23   cables, leads, and transformers according to neon/cold cathode
     manufacturer.

25   H.   NEON/COLD CATHODE WARRANTY: Tubes and transformers
     which fail within one year under normal operating conditions shall
27   be replaced with no cost to the owner. Manufacturer/installer shall
     work closely with the design team to ensure the best quality and
29   longest life lamps while maintaining light output levels required to
     meet design intent.

31   I.   All neon/cold cathode work is to be performed by a
     Manufacturer/installer approved by the Owner and the Architect.
33   Lamp color(s) shall be selected by the Owner and the Architect
     based on operational samples provided by the
35   manufacturer/installer.

GarySteffyLightingDesign Inc.
2900 South State Street Suite 12
Ann Arbor, Michigan 48104
v/ 800 537 1230 & 734 747 6630
f/ 734 747 6629

11.3   Contract Documents

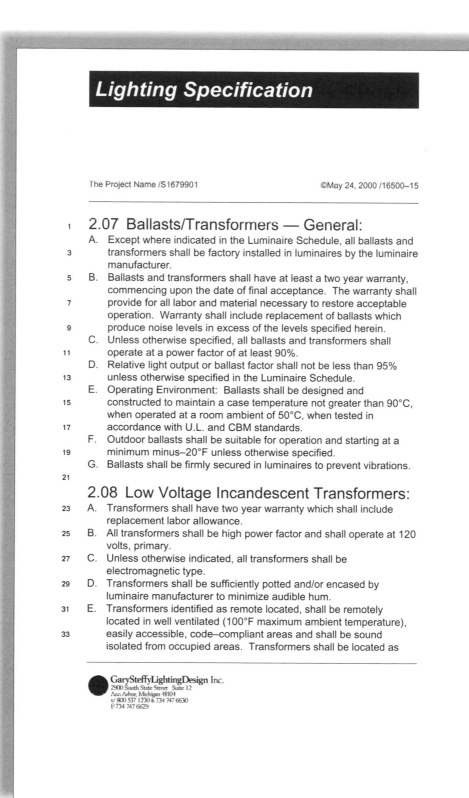

Lighting Specification

The Project Name /S1679901   ©May 24, 2000 /16500–15

2.07 Ballasts/Transformers — General:

A. Except where indicated in the Luminaire Schedule, all ballasts and transformers shall be factory installed in luminaires by the luminaire manufacturer.

B. Ballasts and transformers shall have at least a two year warranty, commencing upon the date of final acceptance. The warranty shall provide for all labor and material necessary to restore acceptable operation. Warranty shall include replacement of ballasts which produce noise levels in excess of the levels specified herein.

C. Unless otherwise specified, all ballasts and transformers shall operate at a power factor of at least 90%.

D. Relative light output or ballast factor shall not be less than 95% unless otherwise specified in the Luminaire Schedule.

E. Operating Environment: Ballasts shall be designed and constructed to maintain a case temperature not greater than 90°C, when operated at a room ambient of 50°C, when tested in accordance with U.L. and CBM standards.

F. Outdoor ballasts shall be suitable for operation and starting at a minimum minus–20°F unless otherwise specified.

G. Ballasts shall be firmly secured in luminaires to prevent vibrations.

2.08 Low Voltage Incandescent Transformers:

A. Transformers shall have two year warranty which shall include replacement labor allowance.

B. All transformers shall be high power factor and shall operate at 120 volts, primary.

C. Unless otherwise indicated, all transformers shall be electromagnetic type.

D. Transformers shall be sufficiently potted and/or encased by luminaire manufacturer to minimize audible hum.

E. Transformers identified as remote located, shall be remotely located in well ventilated (100°F maximum ambient temperature), easily accessible, code–compliant areas and shall be sound isolated from occupied areas. Transformers shall be located as

GarySteffyLightingDesign Inc.
2900 South State Street Suite 12
Ann Arbor, Michigan 48104
v/ 800 537 1230 & 734 747 6630
f/ 734 747 6629

Contract Documents

11.3

potted
Having encased electromagnetic ballast components in a compound that acts like an acoustic insulator, an electrical insulator, and a thermal insulator.

To maintain factory warranties and UL listings, ballasts and transformers that are intended to be a part of the luminaire should be installed in the luminaire at the factory.

Cheap and even some good ballasts have ballast factors (BFs) significantly less than 1.0. If lighting calculations for the design are based on BFs of 1.0, then reduced output ballasts will lead to lower light intensities on the project.

For ballasts used in outdoor applications in colder climates, it is essential that the ballasts have starting capabilities at or below 0°F.

Transformers for most low voltage incandescent lights can be either electronic or electromagnetic. In the recent past, electromagnetic transformers have proved more reliable, particularly when dimming. Review this on a project–by–project basis, because the electronic technologies change rapidly. Note: electromagnetic transformers can cause an audible hum (which is annoying) unless properly **potted** and installed at the factory.

11.3   Contract Documents

Include a clause regarding ballast warranties. Review warranties periodically, and update this clause accordingly. Some warranties are valid from the date the ballast is purchased from the ballast manufacturer rather than the date of installation in the project.

Certified Ballast Manufacturers (CBMs) have had a ballast standard in place for years on electromagnetic ballasts. To date, no ballast standard exists for electronic ballasts—hopefully, one will soon be available so that lamp and electrical operating characteristics are common among all electronic ballast manufacturers' products.

Polychlorinated biphenyls (PCBs) were produced in America from 1929 to 1977 and used as insulating material in electrical transformers and ballasts (as potting compound), among other things. PCBs are highly toxic and, hence, no longer used in America.[1]

For preset scene dimming control applications, fluorescent dimming is complicated and problematic. Lutron has an approach that appears most reliable, although periodically problems arise—and Lutron is quick to address these problems. A newcomer, ESI, may prove to have a reliable fluorescent dimming system as well; however, there remain issues regarding interface with total building control systems such as that provided by Lutron.

A very recent development is in programmed rapid start ballasts—which have the promise of improved lamp and ballast life (although this is yet to be proved—the system is too new to have in situ applications of 20,000–plus hours of operation). Also, lamp and ballast manufacturers have finally realized that end–of–life (EOL) situations in the recent past caused lamp base meltdowns and premature ballast burnout. Now, ballasts offer EOL sensors—when the ballast senses the lamp is about to fail or has failed, the ballast switches off power to the lamp and will not restart until a new lamp has been installed. Hence, electronic ballasts should be specified with these features.

Lighting Specification

The Project Name /S1679901   ©May 24, 2000 /16500–16

1   symmetrically as possible in relation to the wiring runs and shall be
      enclosed in code–compliant housings with secondary and primary
3   connectors with a service switch for every transformer.

5   ### 2.09 Fluorescent Rapid Start Ballasts:
      A.   Electronic and electromagnetic ballasts shall have at least a two
7   year warranty which shall include replacement labor allowance.
      B.   All ballasts shall conform to U.L.935 Fluorescent Lamp Ballasts
9   Standard, and shall be U.L. listed with class P thermal protection.
      C.   All ballasts shall be CBM certified.
11   D.   All ballasts shall conform to ANSI C82 Series Specification for
           Ballasts.
13   E.   All ballasts shall contain no PCB.
      F.   All ballasts shall have a minimum sound rating of 'A'.
15   G.   All electromagnetic fluorescent ballasts shall be premium
           energy-saving type suitable for operating lamps as specified and
17   shall be by Advance or Magnetek for maximum energy efficiency,
           minimum flicker and minimum noise. All luminaires shall be fused
19   on the primary side of the ballast.
      H.   All fluorescent dimming ballasts intended for preset scene
21   operation shall be Lutron Hi-Lume FDB–type, capable of dimming
           all lamps simultaneously from full output to 1% for T8 and T12
23   lamps and from full output to 5% for T5 lamps, without audible
           noise or visible flicker. All lamps to be dimmed by Lutron ballasts
25   shall be supplied by Lutron and shall match contractor's choice of
           those lamps specified herein.
27   I.   All non–dim electronic fluorescent ballasts shall exhibit
           programmed rapid start and end–of–life protection, unless
29   otherwise specified, and shall be manufactured by Advance, FSI,
           Magnetek/Triad, Osram Sylvania and shall operate lamps at full
31   rated light output, unless otherwise specified, and without noise or
           flicker.

33

GarySteffyLightingDesign Inc.
2900 South State Street   Suite 12
Ann Arbor, Michigan 48104
v/ 800 537 1230 & 734 747 6630
f/ 734 747 6629

more online @
[Advance]
http://
    www.advancetransformer.com/
    products/

more online @
[Magnetek]
http://
    www.magnetek.com/
    ballast/

more online @
[Lutron]
http://
    www.lutron.com/

Image ©EyeWire, Inc.

11.3   Contract Documents

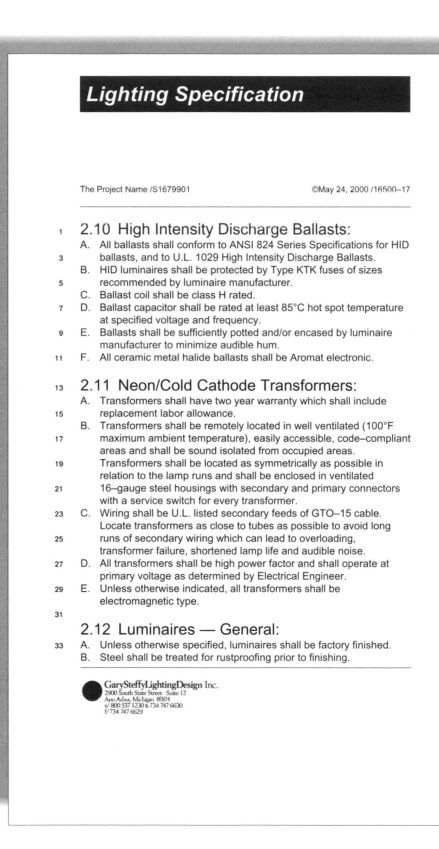

Lighting Specification

The Project Name /S1679901   ©May 24, 2000 /16500–17

2.10 High Intensity Discharge Ballasts:
A. All ballasts shall conform to ANSI 824 Series Specifications for HID ballasts, and to U.L. 1029 High Intensity Discharge Ballasts.
B. HID luminaires shall be protected by Type KTK fuses of sizes recommended by luminaire manufacturer.
C. Ballast coil shall be class H rated.
D. Ballast capacitor shall be rated at least 85°C hot spot temperature at specified voltage and frequency.
E. Ballasts shall be sufficiently potted and/or encased by luminaire manufacturer to minimize audible hum.
F. All ceramic metal halide ballasts shall be Aromat electronic.

2.11 Neon/Cold Cathode Transformers:
A. Transformers shall have two year warranty which shall include replacement labor allowance.
B. Transformers shall be remotely located in well ventilated (100°F maximum ambient temperature), easily accessible, code–compliant areas and shall be sound isolated from occupied areas.
   Transformers shall be located as symmetrically as possible in relation to the lamp runs and shall be enclosed in ventilated 16–gauge steel housings with secondary and primary connectors with a service switch for every transformer.
C. Wiring shall be U.L. listed secondary feeds of GTO–15 cable. Locate transformers as close to tubes as possible to avoid long runs of secondary wiring which can lead to overloading, transformer failure, shortened lamp life and audible noise.
D. All transformers shall be high power factor and shall operate at primary voltage as determined by Electrical Engineer.
E. Unless otherwise indicated, all transformers shall be electromagnetic type.

2.12 Luminaires — General:
A. Unless otherwise specified, luminaires shall be factory finished.
B. Steel shall be treated for rustproofing prior to finishing.

GarySteffyLightingDesign Inc.
2900 South State Street Suite 12
Ann Arbor, Michigan 48104
v/ 800 537 1230 & 734 747 6630
f/ 734 747 6629

Contract Documents

Where high wattage, standard metal halide, or high pressure sodium lamps are used, ballasts should conform to items 2.10.A to 2.10.E.

Where low wattage, ceramic metal halide lamps are used, ballasts should be electronic. These lamps and, therefore, these ballasts are relatively new to the market. Aromat appears to have a reliable product that meets the lamp manufacturers' operating requirements.

Neon/cold cathode transformers are big and bulky. There is no luminaire housing in which these transformers fit (as is the case with fluorescent ballasts, for example). Because of the voltages involved, these transformers must be housed in code–compliant areas that are relatively close to the neon/cold cathode tubing that they energize.

Expectations of the luminaire manufacturers should be outlined in the specification. This further establishes requirements of any vendors that attempt to substitute products.

11.3 Contract Documents

Finish not only establishes the manufacturer's level of quality, but consistency of finish requirements help eliminate the possibility of receiving batches of lights made months or years apart that can result in difference in color and/or texture of finish. This can happen if the manufacturer ships lights from different production batches or if the contractor shops around to several distributors, each with lots or batches of product from different dates of manufacture.

Complete factory wiring helps assure UL compliance and minimizes field errors. This also minimizes the likelihood that a vendor vends out all manufacturing capabilities—shipping cartons of parts to the job site for the contractor to assemble. Such vending can lead to significant quality control issues and to UL compliance issues.

For those projects where detailed luminaire castings have been developed and approved or where catalogued cast luminaires have been selected, it is important to note that the final castings need to match the approved patterns. Otherwise, for schedule and/or cost sake, casting patterns may be streamlined or even standardized from one luminaire type and size to another.

The contractor should be informed specifically if he/she is to also provide any necessary mounting hardware for a complete installation of lights. The architect should approve any auxiliary mounting hardware, so that the entire installation has a cohesive look, as well as structural integrity—something only a registered professional can judge (even if the architect does not wish to do this, it is his/her responsibility to retain a structural engineer or other registered professional to make such a judgment).

The need for plumb, level, and neat–appearing luminaires, connections, and mountings cannot be overstated.

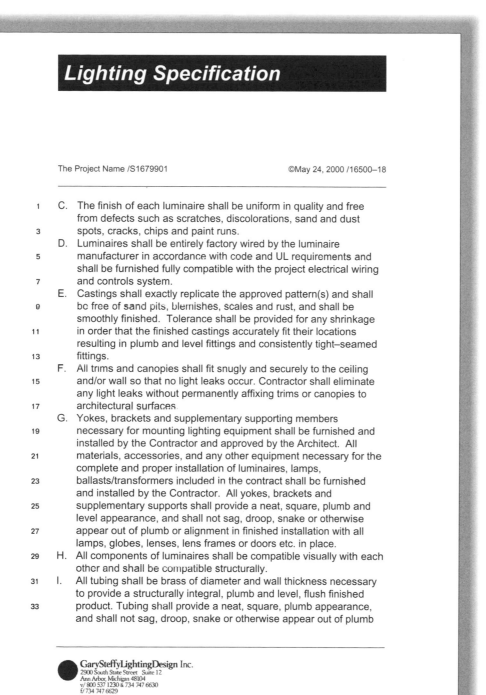

Lighting Specification

The Project Name /S1679901   ©May 24, 2000 /16500–18

1   C. The finish of each luminaire shall be uniform in quality and free
        from defects such as scratches, discolorations, sand and dust
3   spots, cracks, chips and paint runs.
    D. Luminaires shall be entirely factory wired by the luminaire
5   manufacturer in accordance with code and UL requirements and
        shall be furnished fully compatible with the project electrical wiring
7   and controls system.
    E. Castings shall exactly replicate the approved pattern(s) and shall
9   be free of sand pits, blemishes, scales and rust, and shall be
        smoothly finished. Tolerance shall be provided for any shrinkage
11   in order that the finished castings accurately fit their locations
        resulting in plumb and level fittings and consistently tight–seamed
13   fittings.
    F. All trims and canopies shall fit snugly and securely to the ceiling
15   and/or wall so that no light leaks occur. Contractor shall eliminate
        any light leaks without permanently affixing trims or canopies to
17   architectural surfaces.
    G. Yokes, brackets and supplementary supporting members
19   necessary for mounting lighting equipment shall be furnished and
        installed by the Contractor and approved by the Architect. All
21   materials, accessories, and any other equipment necessary for the
        complete and proper installation of luminaires, lamps,
23   ballasts/transformers included in the contract shall be furnished
        and installed by the Contractor. All yokes, brackets and
25   supplementary supports shall provide a neat, square, plumb and
        level appearance, and shall not sag, droop, snake or otherwise
27   appear out of plumb or alignment in finished installation with all
        lamps, globes, lenses, lens frames or doors etc. in place.
29 H. All components of luminaires shall be compatible visually with each
        other and shall be compatible structurally.
31 I. All tubing shall be brass of diameter and wall thickness necessary
        to provide a structurally integral, plumb and level, flush finished
33   product. Tubing shall provide a neat, square, plumb appearance,
        and shall not sag, droop, snake or otherwise appear out of plumb

GarySteffyLightingDesign Inc.
2900 South State Street Suite 12
Ann Arbor, Michigan 48104
v/ 800 537 1230 & 734 747 6630
f/ 734 747 6629

11.3

Contract Documents

Regardless of new or historic luminaires, methods of connection are important from both an appearance and a structural integrity perspective. In efforts to cut both cost and manufacturing time, some manufacturers may attempt to limit connections in number or quality. Indeed, manufacturers have been known to make connections with double-sided tape!

Lighting Specification

The Project Name /S1679901   ©May 24, 2000 /16500–19

1   or alignment in finished installation with all lamps, globes, lenses, lens frames or doors, etc. in place.

3   J.   Castings for historic luminaires shall be bronze or brass with at least 80% copper component. Aluminum shall be unacceptable
5   unless otherwise specified. All castings shall provide a neat, square, plumb and level appearance, and shall not sag, droop,
7   snake or otherwise appear out of plumb or alignment in finished installation with all lamps, globes, lenses, lens frames or doors etc.
9   in place.

  K.   Stampings for custom historic replicas shall be brass with at least
11   80% copper component. All stampings shall provide a neat, square, plumb and level appearance, and shall not sag, droop,
13   snake or otherwise appear out of plumb or alignment in finished installation with all lamps, globes, etc. in place.

15   L.   All connections shall be fixed rigid by screws, rivets and/or soldering. Screws and rivets shall not be visible. Soldering shall be
17   ground smooth to a clean, contiguous surface. All connections shall provide a neat, square, plumb and level appearance, and
19   shall not sag, droop, snake or otherwise appear out of plumb or alignment in finished installation with lamps, globes, lenses, lens
21   frames or doors etc. in place. No double–sided tape or Velcro shall be an acceptable means of connection of any luminaire
23   component.

  M.   All materials, accessories, and other related luminaire parts shall
25   be new and free from any defects and shall be effectively protected from any damage from time of fabrication until final acceptance of
27   the work by the Architect.

  N.   Luminaire enclosures shall be manufactured with a minimum of
29   #20 gauge (0.0359 inch thick) cold rolled sheet steel. Enclosures may be constructed of other metals, provided they are equivalent in
31   mechanical strength and acceptable for the purpose. Luminaires which are to be finished in vitreous porcelain enamel shall be
33   manufactured from a minimum of #20 gauge enameling steel.

  O.   All sheet metal work shall be free from tool marks and dents. All
35   bends shall exhibit sharp, accurate corner angles as practical with

GarySteffyLightingDesign Inc.
2900 South State Street Suite 12
Ann Arbor, Michigan 48104
v/ 800 537 1230 & 734 747 6630
f/ 734 747 6629

Contract Documents

11.3

Some luminaires have variable socket settings to permit the use of various lamp wattages and sizes in the same housing. Sockets should be factory set based on the specified lamping, or alternatively shall be set in the field by the contractor (sometimes contractors fail to notice this important aspect—hence, this note in the specification). Lamp sockets not properly set for the specified lamping can result in poor optical performance, inefficiency, and overheating.

Lighting Specification

The Project Name /S1679901   ©May 24, 2000 /16500–20

1   the gauges of the metal. All intersections and joints shall be
    formed true and of adequate strength and structural rigidity to
3   prevent any distortion after assembly.
    P. All electrical components shall be easily accessible and
5   replaceable without removing luminaires from their mountings or
    disassembling of adjacent construction.
7   Q. All lamp sockets shall be suitable for the indicated lamps and shall
    be preset at the factory or set during installation by the contractor
9   so that lamps are positioned in the optically correct relation to all
    luminaire components for the specified lamp.
11 R. As ceiling system(s) requires, each recessed and semi–recessed
    luminaire shall be furnished with a mounting frame or ring that is
13 compatible with the ceiling in which luminaires are to be installed.
    The frames and rings shall be one piece or constructed with
15 electrically–welded butt joints, and of sufficient size and strength to
    sustain the weight of the luminaire.
17 S. Contractor shall be responsible for coordination with Manufacturor,
    Architect, Structural Engineer and related trades to ensure that
19 proper and adequate structural reinforcement is provided within
    ceilings and building structure to support pendent mounted lighting
21 equipment for a secure, neat, square, plumb and level appearance.
    Pendents shall not sag, droop, snake or otherwise appear out of
23 plumb or alignment in finished installation with all lamps, globes,
    lenses, lens frames or doors etc. in place.
25 T. Contractor shall be responsible for coordination with Manufacturer,
    Architect, Structural Engineer and related trades to ensure that
27 proper and adequate structural reinforcement is provided within
    walls and building structure to support wall mounted lighting
29 equipment for a secure, neat, square, plumb and level appearance.
    Wall brackets shall not sag, droop, snake or otherwise appear out
31 of plumb or alignment in finished installation with all lamps, globes,
    lenses, lens frames or doors etc. in place.
33 U. Luminaires designated for outdoor use or for use in damp locations shall
    be suitably gasketed and/or sealed to prevent the entrance of moisture.

GarySteffyLightingDesign Inc.
2900 South State Street Suite 12
Ann Arbor, Michigan 48104
v/ 800 537 1230 & 734 747 6630
f/ 734 747 6629

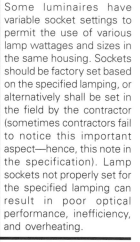

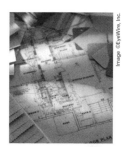

11.3 Contract Documents

Locking mechanisms greatly assist the maintenance folks during relamping. Without locking mechanisms set in place by the contractor, the first time a lamp requires changing, it is likely that the maintenance personnel will bump the lamp out of aiming alignment—and have no reliable method for aiming it back to its intended position. Locking mechanisms, when implemented correctly by the manufacturer and when set on final installation by the contractor, eliminate this problem.

Many of these citations may seem obvious. However, a robust specification will help minimize the possibility of unqualified shops from supplying lighting equipment for the specific project, or will assist the owner/client in getting warranty assistance from the contractor.

Lighting Specification

The Project Name /S1679901   ©May 24, 2000 /16500–21

1   All dissimilar metal materials shall be separated by non–conductive materials to prevent galvanic action.

3   V.   For steel and aluminum luminaires, screws, bolts, nuts and other fastening and latching hardware shall be a cadmium plated or
5   equivalent. For stainless steel luminaires, hardware shall be stainless steel. For bronze luminaires, hardware shall be stainless
7   steel or bronze.

W. All luminaires and their associated ballasts shall be capable of
9   operating within the temperature limits of their design and as specified by Underwriters Laboratories Inc. (U.L.), in the
11   applications and mounting conditions specified herein.

X.   Each luminaire which has a beam angle adjustment shall have
13   durable, easy–to–operate and access angle– and rotation–locking devices.

15   Y.   Each luminaire which has a lamp with an oval or rectangular shape beam pattern shall contain lamp orientation locking devices to
17   ensure that beam orientation is not disturbed during luminaire lamp replacement or cleaning.

19   Z.   Each luminaire which has a spreadlens shall contain lens orientation devices to ensure that lens orientation is not disturbed
21   during luminaire lamp replacement or cleaning.

AA. All materials, accessories, and any other equipment necessary for
23   the complete and proper installation, wiring and controls of all luminaires included in these construction documents shall be
25   furnished by the Contractor.

BB. Welding shall be in accordance with recommendations of the
27   American Welding Society. Welds exposed to view shall be ground flush and dressed smooth

29   CC. Extruded aluminum frames and trims shall be rigid and manufactured from high quality aluminum without blemishes in the
31   installed product. Miter cuts shall be accurate, joints shall be flush and without burrs. All seam alignments shall be maintained with the
33   luminaire located in its final position.

DD. Warranty: The Contractor shall warrant the luminaire, its finishes,
35   and all of its component parts, except ballasts, to be free from

GarySteffyLightingDesign Inc.
2900 South State Street Suite 12
Ann Arbor, Michigan 48104
v/ 800 537 1230 & 734 747 6630
f/ 734 747 6629

Contract Documents

11.3

Lighting Specification

The Project Name /S1679901   ©May 24, 2000 /16500–22

1   defects for a period of at least one year from date of acceptance by
     the Owner if operated within rated voltage range. Replacement of
3   faulty materials and the cost of labor to make the replacement shall
     be the responsibility of the Contractor.
5 EE. All luminaires for recessing in suspended ceilings shall be supplied
     with prewired junction boxes.
7

2.13 Luminaire Reflectors and Trims:

9   A. Alzak cones, reflectors, baffles and louvers shall be warranted
        against discoloration for at least ten [10] years. In the event of
11   premature discoloration or finish degradation, they shall be
        replaced by the manufacturer, including the cost of both materials
13   and labor. Alzak shall be low–iridescent type.
    B. Aluminum cones, reflectors, baffles and louvers shall be finished
15   specular, semi–specular or diffuse as specified and shall meet or
        exceed Alzak specifications. All material shall be low–iridescent
17   type.
    C. All cones, reflectors, baffles and louvers shall be removable for
19   lamp access and luminaire cleaning, however, they must otherwise
        be positively and securely held in–place.
21 D. There shall be no light leaks around the interface between
        cone/reflector/shade trim flanges and the ceiling or wall.
23 E. All cone/reflector trim flanges shall fit plumb and flush with the
        ceiling surface.
25 F. All cones, reflectors, baffles and louvers and visible trim of all
        luminaires shall be turned over to the Owner clean and free of
27   scratches, smudges and fingerprints. All cleaning shall be in
        accordance with respective manufacturers' instructions (securing of
29   which is the responsibility of the Contractor.

2.14 Luminaire Lenses:

31 A. Unless otherwise specified, plastic used for lenses and diffusers
33   shall be formed of colorless 100% virgin acrylic. The quality of the
        raw material must meet ASTM standards as tested by an

GarySteffyLightingDesign Inc.
2900 South State Street   Suite 12
Ann Arbor, Michigan 48104
v/ 800 537 1230 & 734 747 6630
f/ 734 747 6629

Trims and canopies should not be held in place by caulk or other sealant. This precludes easy access to lamps and/or ballasts and transformers. Further, when these sealants are "broken" to access components in the luminaire, a serious mess is made of the ceiling, with likely damage to the trim or canopy.

Light leaks around ceiling or wall junctures with luminaire canopies or trims are common problems. The contractor should be responsible for eliminating light leaks as much as practical. For example, some luminaire manufacturers supply gasket rings to mount between canopies or trims and architectural surfaces. Further, the contractor's ability to install junction boxes, back boxes, and housings in a plumb and level fashion greatly influences light leaks or the lack thereof.

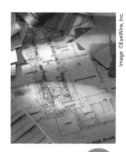

11.3 Contract Documents

Lighting Specification

The Project Name /S1679901   ©May 24, 2000 /16500–23

Similar remarks as made in other sections regarding the need to use quality materials in the manufacture of the lenses, the need to easily access lamps and ballasts, and the need for cleanliness.

1   independent test laboratory. Acrylic plastic lenses and diffusers shall be properly cast, molded or extruded as necessary to meet
3   the intent of the specified optics, and shall remain free of any dimensional instability, discoloration, embrittlement, or loss of light
5   transmittance for at least 15 years after installation.

B. Glass lenses and diffusers shall be tempered for high impact and
7   heat resistance with a transmittance of not less than 88%. For exterior luminaires glass lenses and refractors shall be borosilicate,
9   Corning #7740 or equal.

C. Optical lenses shall be free from spherical and chromatic
11   aberrations and other imperfections which may hinder the optic performance.

13 D. All lenses or other light diffusing elements shall be removable for lamp access and luminaire cleaning, however, they must otherwise
15   be positively and securely held in–place.

E. There shall be no light leaks between the lens and the lens frame.
17 F. There shall be no light leaks around the interface between lens door trim flanges and the ceiling or wall.
19 G. All lens door trim flanges shall fit plumb and flush with the ceiling or wall surface.
21 H. Lenses shall be installed and turned over to the Owner clean and free of dust, bugs, scratches, smudges and fingerprints. All
23   cleaning shall be in accordance with respective manufacturers' instructions (securing of which is the responsibility of the
25   Contractor.

27 ## 2.15 Incandescent Luminaires:

A. Luminaires using tungsten halogen sources shall be designed and
29   constructed so that lamp seal temperatures do not exceed lamp manufacturers' specifications when tested in accordance to the
31   relevant UL standard.
B. Lead wires for luminaires using tungsten halogen sources shall be
33   rated for 250°C operation.

GarySteffyLightingDesign Inc.
2900 South State Street Suite 12
Ann Arbor, Michigan 48104
v/ 800 537 1230 & 734 747 GG30
f/ 734 747 6629

Contract Documents

11.3

Lighting Specification

The Project Name /S1679901   ©May 24, 2000 /16500–24

1   **2.16 Fluorescent Luminaires:**
   A.   Luminaires with integral ballast(s) shall be constructed so that
3   ballast(s) can be serviced or replaced without removal of housing.
   B.   Rapid–start and programmed start lamps shall be mounted within
5   one inch of a grounded metal component, minimum one inch wide
   and as long as the lamp.
7

   2.17 High Intensity Discharge Luminaires:
9   A.   Open bottom luminaires shall be equipped with tempered clear
   glass lamp shield below lamp unless specified with explosion–proof
11   lamps suitable for use in open–bottom luminaires.

13 **2.18 Luminaire Type Designations:**
   A.   Luminaires (including lamps and ballasts/transformers) have been
15   assigned type designations consisting of three letters followed by a
   number in order to facilitate communication between the Design
17   Team, the Construction Team and the Owner. The first three letters
   indicate the source type, lamp (bulb/envelope) type and general
19   photometric distribution, respectively; The number distinguishes
   luminaires of the same type that have only minor differences,
21   explained in the specific description for each luminaire.
   B.   This specification and these luminaire designations have been
23   forwarded to respective manufacturers and to other team members
   and may not be changed without the written permission of the
25   Lighting Designer or the Architect. If permission is granted to
   change designations, the party changing the designations shall be
27   responsible for developing a cross–reference chart to the
   designations cited herein; and shall be responsible for notifying all
29   manufacturers and other team members of such changes.

31

GarySteffyLightingDesign Inc.
2900 South State Street   Suite 12
Ann Arbor, Michigan 48104
v/ 800 537 1230 & 734 747 6630
f/ 734 747 6629

Although newer lamp technologies may not require this condition, many linear fluorescent lamps require some grounded metal strip to be near the lamp and running the length of the lamp in order to help start the electric arc inside the lamp.

To keep track of the various luminaires and their respective lamps on any given project, the designer must assign a designation or "type" for each version of a luminaire/lamp on the project. This allows easy referencing by all team members. Since the lighting designer's effort is intended to be a part of the architect's or engineer's work, it is possible that either of those individuals or entities will want to change luminaire type designations to their respective "standards." This is not a problem as long as the party changing the designations develops a cross–reference table, so that as questions arise, folks have some convenient means of keeping track of various luminaire types. Since the specification has likely been circulated to lighting reps and other team members, it is inadvisable to change luminaire type designations.

Image ©EyeWire, Inc.

11.3 Contract Documents

Here, a standard type designation has been devised based on basic source type (e.g., incandescent, fluorescent, and metal halide, etc.), specific lamp type (e.g., A lamp, compact fluorescent, and PAR lamp, etc.), luminaire functional type (e.g., adjustable accent, downlight, and pendent, etc.), and on the number of versions of the specific luminaire that exist on the project (e.g., one version might be mounted in a lay-in ceiling, while another version is mounted in a drywall ceiling). This standard, then, serves as the basis for establishing luminaire type designations on every project. This consistency helps reps identify more readily the kind of lights being proposed and permits more confident communication among the design team over the course of a project.

Lighting Specification

The Project Name /S1679901   ©May 24, 2000 /16500–25

---

1 Example: AAA1
      ┌─ Source Type (e.g., Std. Incandescent)
3   ┌─ Lamp Type (e.g., A–Lamp)
           ┌─ Distribution Type (e.g., Adj. Accent)
5   ┌─ Similar Type Number

7   A A A 1

1. First Letter Designations — Source Type

9   A = Standard Voltage Incandescent or Halogen
      C = Cold Cathode
11   F = Fluorescent
      H = Mercury
13   L = Low Voltage Incandescent
      M = Metal Halide
15   N = Neon
      Q = Quartz
17   S = Sodium (High or Low Pressure)
      T = Track/Theatrical Hardware
19   Z = Assignable (Blank)

2. Second Letter Designations — Lamp Type and
21   Characteristics
      A = A–Lamp Envelope
23   B = B–Lamp Envelope
      C = Compact Fluorescent
25   E = E–Lamp Envelope
      G = G–Lamp Envelope
27   M = Multi–Reflector (e.g., MR16)
      P = PAR Lamp Envelope (2 piece reflector)
29   R = R–Lamp Envelope (1 piece reflector)
      S = S–Lamp Envelope
31   T = Tubular
      U = Tube/Strip Lights (e.g., Tivoli)
33   Z = Assignable (Blank)

GarySteffyLightingDesign Inc.
2900 South State Street Suite 12
Ann Arbor, Michigan 48104
v/ 800 537 1230 & 734 747 6630
f/ 734 747 6629

Contract Documents

11.3

Since each lamp family has what amount to proprietary lamp shapes, then each lamp family is likely to have varying functional qualities. In other words, photometric qualities are inconsistent from one lamp family (e.g., incandescent) to another (e.g., fluorescent). So, in this example of standardized designations, the third letter has different meanings for different lamps (which are then detailed on this page and the following two pages).

Lighting Specification

The Project Name /S1679901   ©May 24, 2000 /16500–26

---

1   3.   Third Letter Designations — Photometric Distribution

3   ▶*Incandescent Sources:*
         A = Adjustable Accent
5   B = Bollard
         C = Cove - Architectural (Indirect)
7   D = Open Downlight
         E = Exposed (Bare Lamp)
9   F = Flood
         G = Globe
11   H = Holiday "strings"
         I = [UNUSED]
13   J = "Junk"
         K = Steplight
15   L = Lensed Downlight
         M = Mirror Detail
17   N = Area Posttop (Globe)
         O = Spot
19   P = Pendant
         Q = Sconce
21   R = Reading/Task Light ("Table Lamp")
         S = Slot
23   T = Track Head/Theatrical
         U = Uplight
25   V = Valance
         W = Wallwash
27   X = Exit/Emergency
         Y = Torchiere
29   Z = Assignable (Blank)

GarySteffyLightingDesign Inc.
2900 South State Street   Suite 12
Ann Arbor, Michigan 48104
v/ 800 537 1230 & 734 747 6630
f/ 734 747 6629

11.3

Contract Documents

Lighting Specification

The Project Name /S1679901 ©May 24, 2000 /16500–27

1   3. Third Letter Designations — Photometric Distribution

3   ▶*Fluorescent Sources:*
     A = Asymmetric Indirect
5   B = Bollard
     C = Cove—Architectural (Indirect)
7   D = Downlight
     E = Exposed (Bare Lamp)
9   F = Furniture–integrated (Indirect)
     G = General Direct
11   H = General Direct/Indirect
     I = Industrial
13   J = "Junk"
     K = Steplight
15   L = Luminous Element
     M = Mirror Detail
17   N = Area Posttop (Globe)
     O = [UNUSED]
19   P = Pendant (General Indirect)
     Q = Sconce
21   R = Wraparound lens
     S = Slot—Architectural (Direct)
23   T = Task (Freestanding or Panel–hung)
     U = Furniture–integrated Task
25   V = Valance
     W = Wallwash
27   X = Exit/Emergency
     Y = Torchiere (Freestanding)
29   Z = Assignable (Blank)

31

GarySteffyLightingDesign Inc.
2900 South State Street Suite 12
Ann Arbor, Michigan 48104
v/ 800 337 1230 & 734 747 6630
f/ 734 747 6629

Contract Documents

11.3

Lighting Specification

The Project Name /S1679901   ©May 24, 2000 /16500–28

1   3. Third Letter Designations — Photometric Distribution

3   ▶*High Intensity Discharge Sources:*
          A = Area
5   B = Bollard
          C = Furniture-integrated Indirect
7   D = Open Downlight
          E = [UNUSED]
9   F = Floodlight
          G = General Direct
11   H = General Direct/Indirect
          I = Industrial
13   J = "Junk"
          K = Steplight
15   L = Lensed Downlight
          M = Hi–mast
17   N = Area Posttop (Globe)
          O – [UNUSED]
19   P = Pendant
          Q = Sconce
21   R = Decorative Low–level
          S = Spotlight
23   T = [UNUSED]
          U = Uplight
25   V = [UNUSED]
          W = Wallwash
27   X = [UNUSED]
          Y = Torchiere
29   Z = Assignable (Blank)

 GarySteffyLightingDesign Inc.
2900 South State Street   Suite 12
Ann Arbor, Michigan 48104
v/ 800 537 1230 & 734 747 6630
f/ 734 747 6629

11.3

Contract Documents

Lighting Specification

The Project Name /S1679901   ©May 24, 2000 /16500–29

---

1   **2.19 Luminaire/Lamp/Ballast Schedule:**

Contractor and/or supplier shall provide line item unit cost to owner and
3   lead time for luminaire. Proprietary luminaires are copyrighted designs by
the respective luminaire manufacturer and reproductions that are
5   unauthorized by said manufacturer are not permitted. All cutsheets
attached, if any, are copyrighted by respective manufacturers and may not
7   be reproduced without written permission of the respective manufacturer(s).

Type	What	Brief Description	Watts
FCD1	**Ambient Lighting** ▶Typical downlighting in servery	Recessed (lay–in) ceiling compact fluorescent downlight shall exhibit an aperture of about 0–feet/7–inches in diameter with an overall housing height of about 0–feet/9¾–inches. Luminaire shall consist of a formed steel housing, about 0–feet/10½–inches in width by 1–foot/1¼–inches in length, recessed above the ceiling and spun aluminum reflector with matching overlap flange trim. Luminaire reflector shall exhibit a low iridescent, semi–diffuse, clear Alzak finish. Luminaire shall be fitted with a clear acrylic shield for application above food service areas. Luminaire shall be furnished with an electronic programmed start, high power factor, THD <10%, ballast factor of 1.0, and shall exhibit end–of–llife cutoff suitable for operation at voltage as specified by the Electrical Engineer. Luminaire shall be lamped with one [1] Philips PL–T32W/30/4P/ALTO (#26832–6) 32–watt, 3000K, GX24q-3, 4–pin base, compact fluorescent lamp. ▶Lightolier 8020SSP/6132EVolts ▶Edison Price TRP32/7–Volts–ECOL–PS ▶Kurt Versen P926–SC–Volts ▶Zumtobel/Staff S5D6308H S2 6313HR MC	35

GarySteffyLightingDesign Inc.
2900 South State Street   Suite 12
Ann Arbor, Michigan 48104
v/ 800 537 1230 & 734 747 6030
f/ 734 747 6629

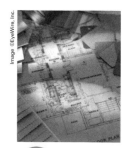

Contract Documents

To help avoid the scams associated with packaging lighting into one big dollar value (e.g., the lighting costs US$129,459), a demand that line item pricing be provided for each and every luminaire type on the project is included. This also assists the designer in assessing the fairness of pricing by judging the luminaire costs quoted by the contractor against the distributor net (DN) values obtained from the local lighting representatives. If one luminaire type is marked up 23 percent while another type is marked up 74 percent, this is cause for concern on the number of parties involved in the purchasing chain and/or whether the client is receiving the fairest prices.

The left–most column identifies the luminaire type designation. The second column indicates what the luminaire is intended to do and where it is intended to be used on the project. The third column is a brief description—brief, but not devoid of information. Such issues as luminaire aperture size, housing size, ballasting (for fluorescent and metal halide luminaires), finish(es), special features, and lamping should be addressed here. Acceptable manufacturers are listed, along with catalog numbers (see note below). The last column indicates the approximate total wattage (including any losses for ballasts or transformers) for each luminaire.

Only those manufacturers with products that the designer believes will meet the needs of the project should be listed here. Luminaires never before seen by the designer or for which no photometric data exists, or for which no calculations have been performed should not be listed.

Image ©EyeWire, Inc.

11.3 Contract Documents

The contractor's responsibility includes installing luminaires according to the industry standard of care and according to code. Additionally, the contractor is responsible for installing products according to the manufacturers' instructions (which the contractor is responsible for obtaining from the respective manufacturers).

Wherever any conflicts exist, the contractor must review the situation with the architect and obtain a resolution the architect approves. While the lighting designer may be asked for an opinion as it relates to the finished effect (lighting quality) or quantity of light, the architect, as the registered professional, must address such issues and direct the contractor.

Image ©EyeWire, Inc.

Contract Documents

Lighting Specification

The Project Name /S1679901   ©May 24, 2000 /16500–30

---

1 # Part 3
   # Execution

3 ## 3.01 Installation:

A. All equipment, wiring and installation shall be in accordance with
5   the National Electrical Code, applicable local codes, and accepted
       industry standard of care and practice, and shall be thermally
7   protected where necessary and shall not void any UL listings or
       labels. This shall include the integration of lighting equipment and
9   controls.

B. Install lighting equipment, including but not limited to luminaires,
11   controls, auxiliary devices and the integration of same in strict
       conformance with all manufacturers' recommendations and
13   instructions the securing of which shall be the responsibility of the
       Contractor.

15 C. Luminaires shall be integrated with controls in accordance with
       respective luminaire manufacturers' and controls manufacturers'
17   recommendations and instructions and to provide a complete,
       troublefree operation without compromising safety, code and/or UL
19   requirements.

D. Contractor shall be responsible for sealing all outdoor luminaires
21   for wet locations (ie. all knock-outs, all pipe and wire entrances,
       etc.) as is standard industry practice to prevent water from entering
23   luminaires.

E. The Contractor shall coordinate the lighting system installation with
25   the relevant trades so as to eliminate interferences with hangers,
       mechanical ducts, sprinklers, pipes, steel, etc.

27 F. For installation in suspended ceilings, ensure that the luminaires
       are supported such that there is no resultant bowing or deflection
29   of the ceiling system greater than 1/360 of the length of the total
       span of the ceiling member.

31 G. Mounting heights and configuration of the luminaires shall be as
       specified in the Luminaire Schedule and/or indicated on the
33   drawings, and where conflicts exist, as approved by the Architect.

GarySteffyLightingDesign Inc.
2900 South State Street Suite 12
Ann Arbor, Michigan 48104
v/ 800 537 1230 & 734 747 6630
f/ 734 747 6629

11.3 Contract Documents

For luminaires requiring aiming adjustments (e.g., adjustable accents), the contractor should be made responsible for making the adjustments under the observation of the lighting designer and architect. This means the contractor needs to provide the appropriate tools (ladders, scaffolds, and lifts, etc.) to reach and adjust the lights and to provide the manpower to adjust the lights. Finally, it is important to advise the contractor that depending on daylight conditions, it may be necessary to make aiming adjustments at night. If these kinds of statements are in the contract documents against which the contractor bid on the project, then there can be no argument that aiming was not a part of the project's cost, or that night aiming can't be done without additional money to cover the contractor's night hours' overtime rates.

Lighting Specification

The Project Name /S1679901   ©May 24, 2000 /16500–31

1   H   Suspended luminaires shall be installed plumb and level and at a
        height from finished floor as specified on the drawings, details and
3   Luminaire Schedule. In cases where this is impractical, refer to the
        Architect for a decision.
5   I. Luminaire finishes which are disturbed in any way during
        construction shall be touched up or refinished in a manner
7   satisfactory to the Architect.
    J. Reflector cones, louvers, baffles, lenses, trims and other decorative
9   elements shall be installed after completion of ceiling tile
        installation, plastering, painting and general cleanup.
11 K. Whenever a luminaire or its hanger canopy is installed directly to a
        surface mounted junction box, a finishing ring painted to match the
13   ceiling, shall be used to conceal the junction box.

15 ### 3.02 Testing and Adjustment:
    A. As required, all adjustable luminaires shall be aimed, focused,
17   locked, etc., by the Contractor under the observation of the
        Architect. As aiming and adjusting is completed, locking setscrews
19   and bolts and nuts shall be tightened securely by the Contractor.
    B. The Architect shall indicate the number of two member crews
21   required for aiming and adjusting. All aiming and adjusting shall be
        performed after the entire installation is complete. The Contractor
23   shall be responsible for notifying the Architect of appropriate time
        for final luminaire adjustment.
25 C. All ladders, scaffolds, lifts, etc. required for aiming and adjusting
        luminaires shall be furnished by the Contractor.
27 D. The Contractor shall be responsible for notifying the Architect of
        appropriate time for staking any outdoor luminaire locations which
29   are called out as "to be field located" on drawings and Luminaire
        Schedule, and shall supply equipment and personnel for staking at
31   the direction of the Architect.
    E. Where possible, units shall be focused during the normal working
33   day. However, where daylight interferes with seeing lighting
        effects, aiming shall be accomplished at night.
35

GarySteffyLightingDesign Inc.
2900 South State Street   Suite 12
Ann Arbor, Michigan 48104
v/ 800 537 1230 & 734 747 6630
f/ 734 747 6629

Image ©EyeWire, Inc.

254

Contract Documents

Lighting Specification

The Project Name /S1679901   ©May 24, 2000 /16500–32

1   ## 3.03 Cleaning:
    A. All luminaires and accessories shall be thoroughly cleaned after
3   being installed. All fingerprints, dirt, tar, smudges, drywall mud and
        dust, etc. shall be removed by the Contractor from the luminaire
5   bodies and lens/louver material prior to final acceptance. All
        reflectors shall be free of paint other than factory–applied, if any.
7   All optical reflectors, cones and lenses shall be cleaned only
        according to manufacturers' instructions.

The contractor must clean all luminaires and accessories according to manufacturers' instructions.

GarySteffyLightingDesign Inc.
2900 South State Street   Suite 12
Ann Arbor, Michigan 48104
v/ 800 537 1230 & 734 747 6630
f/ 734 747 6629

Image ©EyeWire, Inc.

11.4 Contract Documents

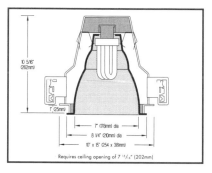

Figure 11.6

An example of a luminaire cutsheet accompanying a specification. Note the type designation label in the lower left corner. The label should not block other graphics/text on the cutsheet, should be readily obvious (e.g., placed in one of the four corners), and should be consistently located if possible (always in the same corner from cutsheet to cutsheet for ready identification by the reader). Arrows are affixed that indicate specific items of interest for this particular luminaire type. For example, this cutsheet represents Type FCD1, which is a downlight with a semi–specular reflector. Since this downlight will be used in a food serving area in a cafeteria, a clear acrylic shield is also required (by code to prevent lamp fragments from falling onto food).

TRIPLES-V 32/7

recessed compact fluorescent downlight/wallwasher

COMPACT FLUORESCENT 1-18

FEATURES

Triples-V 32/7 is a highly efficient 7" aperture low brightness downlight designed for use with one 32-watt triple-tube compact fluorescent lamp of the 4-pin types made by GE, Osram/Sylvania or Philips. Triples-V 32/7 provides a shielding angle of 40°.

One housing allows interchangeable use of downlight and wallwash reflectors, permitting housings to be installed first and reflectors to be installed or changed at any time.

Triples-V 32/7 uses one 32-watt lamp providing 2400 lumens (nearly that of a 150-watt incandescent), a 10,000-hour life, a color rendering index (CRI) of 82, and color temperatures as warm as 2700°K (nearly duplicating the color qualities of incandescent).

Reflectors are available in clear (natural aluminum), semi-specular etch clear or champagne gold Alzak® with Color-Chek® anodizing, virtually eliminating iridescence. Wallwash reflectors available are: wallwash (120°), corner wallwash (210°), and double wallwash (2x120°).

Triples-V 32/7 includes a pair of mounting bars (¾" x 27" C channel). Specialty bars for wood joist and T-bar installations are also available.

APPLICATIONS

Fixture is suitable for downlighting or wallwashing in nearly all architectural environments, especially those spaces where non-directional luminaires are preferred over rectangular troffers. These include offices, stores, airports, schools, hotels, lobbies and public spaces.

Fixture is cULus listed for Damp Location (may not be suitable for some outdoor environments). Fixture is union made IBEW and in compliance with the component based efficiency standards of the 1995 New York State Energy Conservation Code. Fixture is prewired with high power factor Class P electronic ballast and approved for ten #12 wire 75°C branch circuit pull-through wiring. Removal of the reflector allows access to the ballast and junction box.

Type FCD1
(This cutsheet and design are copyrighted and shown for construction team reference—reproduction is not permitted.)
● GarySteffyLightingDesign Inc.

10 5/16" (262mm)
1" (25mm)
7" (178mm) dia
8 1/4" (210mm) dia
10" x 15" (254 x 38mm)
Requires ceiling opening of 7 15/16" (202mm)

PRODUCT CODE

For complete product code, list basic unit and select one item from each following box.

Basic Unit .... TRP 32/7

Reflector Type			
Downlight .... no suffix	Corner Wallwash .... CWW
Wallwash .... WW	Double Wallwash .... DWW

Voltage	
120 volt service 120	277 volt service 277

Reflector and Flange Color	Overlap	Flush
Clear (Natural Aluminum) .... COL	CFL
Champagne Gold .... GOL	GFL
Semi-specular Etch Clear .... ECOL	ECFL
Other reflector finishes are available on special order.		

Standard reflector flange continues reflector finish. White painted flanges and custom painted flanges are available on special order. Add WF (white flange) or CCF (custom color flange).

OPTIONS

Specify by adding to the basic unit.

Dimmable. Not for outdoor application .... – DM

Emergency battery pack operates lamp in event of power outage. Not for outdoor application .... – EM

Return Air Plenum. Modified for maximum performance in air return ceiling plenums .... – RA

⅛" (3mm) thick **clear acrylic shield,** spring-mounted within reflector .... – PS

► For combinations of the Options above, contact factory or Edison Price Lighting representative.

► An install-from-below version of this fixture, suitable for installation outside North America, is also available. Contact factory.

► Decorative reflector rings are available on special order. Contact factory.

EDISON PRICE LIGHTING
409 E 60 St, New York NY 10022, tel 212.521.6900 fax 212.888.7981 www.epl.com
©Copyright, Edison Price Lighting 2000
1-18

Cutsheet drawing courtesy of and ©Edison Price Lighting, Inc. Available online at http://www.epl.com

11.4 Luminaire cutsheets

The lighting specification should also include cutsheets of the various luminaires specified. This allows the other team members to have a better idea of the appearance and size characteristics of the luminaires. Cutsheets also help the contractor better understand the lighting equipment that will need to be purchased and installed. This is an effort to limit misunderstanding or confusion on the luminaires and their attributes.

Cutsheets are copyrighted documents. Reproduction is restricted. Most manufacturers have come to realize that in order for other team members, contractors, lighting reps, and distributors to clearly understand what is

Contract Documents 11.6

being specified on any given project, cutsheets need to accompany the specification. Nevertheless, the specification, as well as tags on the cutsheets, should clearly indicate this material is for purposes of understanding and quoting the specified product—it is not to be copied or circulated for purposes of seeking substitutions or knockoffs. Figure 11.6 illustrates a cutsheet for luminaire type FCD1 on a particular project. From the cutsheet, the catalog information that needs to be entered into the specification is: Edison Price TRP32/7–Volts–ECOL–PS. Figure 11.7 illustrates a sample luminaire type tag for use on cutsheets.

11.5 Control specifications

Controls might be as simple as individual wall switches to turn respective individual or groups of lights on and off. Increasingly, however, controls' schemes are more complicated either for functional reasons (presentation rooms) or for energy–savings reasons (daylight activated dimming). The lighting designer must convey to the team how each luminaire is to be controlled. This is done on reflected ceiling plans and in specifications. Figure 11.5 illustrates a looping diagram overlayed on a lighting layer plan. This conveys which lights are to be on which control loops. Switching locations are identified in a rough sense. The architect is then responsible for establishing exact mounting heights and distances from jambs and/or wall interesection corners to locate the control or switch box, and for coordinating switch locations with other wall device locations (e.g., thermostats, music controls, and intercoms, etc.). The engineer is responsible for sizing wiring, distribution panels, energy management control systems, preset scene control systems, and the like.

Table 9.1 outlines some controls designations that might be considered when indicating controls on drawings. With regard to the last two designations (S_L and $S_{Room No.}$), there are certainly variations on the theme. In any event, reference to these designations is then required in the Control Specification, so that the contractor can purchase appropriate devices. For spaces where preset scene controls are specified or where switches must have special functions, it is suggested that the control designation be $S_{Room No.}$ to attract attention to its special nature.

Many projects do not involve sophisticated control schemes. Here, standard switches (one, two, or three) are used in each room to control groups of lights. While the lighting designer should indicate how the groups of lights are controlled (e.g., downlights are controlled separately from accent lights), the actual switching specification might be generated by the electrical engineer. In this situation, the lighting designer provides a control loops diagram, but perhaps does not forward a specification for the engineer's consideration. These formalities need to be determined on a case–by–case basis and mutually agreed on by the team members.

A control specification can be developed to parallel the lighting specification. The next several pages illustrate excerpts from a control specification.

11.6 Endnotes

[1] Rensselaer Polytechnic Institute, Chemical Origin (web page, undated), http://www.rensselaer.edu/~spilln/chemo.html. [Accessed December 29, 2000.]

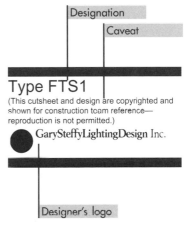

Figure 11.7
An example of a luminaire type designation tag for use on cutsheets. This is considered a minimum of information. Other information that can be useful include the designer's address and/or phone number (for quick reference should a question arise on a given cutsheet) and a date.

11.6 Contract Documents

A control specification should parallel the lighting specification, with a "General" section outlining what is expected of the contractor; a "Products" section outlining the kinds of products and components that are expected, including a specific description(s) and catalog number(s) of the controls being specified; and an "Execution" section outlining the contractor's anticipated handling of installation and setup.

Control Specification

The Project Name/C1679901   ©May 24, 2000/16500-3

1   # Contents

GarySteffyLightingDesign Inc.
2900 South State Street Suite 12
Ann Arbor, Michigan 48104
v/ 800 537 1230 & 734 747 6630
f/ 734 747 6629

Image ©EyeWire, Inc.

The lefthand most column in the table (called column #1) identifies the "Control Channel." In other words, and this occurs in no particular order, a group of lights has been identified with the requirement that all lights within the group be controlled together all the time. The next column, column #2, indicates the (hopefully) convenient label that should be used to identify the respective control channel. In this case, for this church project, the reredos was sufficently large and detailed, so that uplights could be placed behind it (hence, "Reredos Up" as the name for Control Channel 1). Column #3 offers a brief description of the lights involved. This is added for clarity. Column #4 outlines the luminaire types assigned to the designated control channel. Column #5 indicates if the lights are to be dimmed (Y for yes) or simply switched (in which case the N for no dimming). The last column (far right), Column #6, indicates the estimated wattage load. If fluorescent lights are covered or if low voltage lights are covered, then ballast and transformer losses must be included in the wattage load estimate. This information is necessary for the engineer and for the dimming equipment supplier.

Control Specification

The Project Name/C1679901   ©May 24, 2000/16500-12

6. Control station color shall match color samples supplied by, and/or reviewed and approved by the Architect and Lighting Designer.

2.05 Quality Control:
A. All devices shall be fully tested from proper operation prior to shipment from the factory.

2.06 Preset Control Zone Schedule:
The attached control zone schedule(s) indicates the controls design intent of the lighting designer only. The schedule(s) does not presume to cover Electrical Engineering issues and final documentation on loads must be prepared by the Electrical Engineer.

Control Channel	Label	Description	Luminaire Types	Dim Y/N	Approx. Total Load (watts)
1	Reredos Up	Reredos Ceiling Uplights	QTU1	Y	2800
2	Reredos Dn	Reredos/ Presbyterate downlight	QPD1&2	Y	1500
3	Reredos	Reredos Accents	LPA1&2	Y	4000
4	West MH	Metal Halide Front	MPD1	N	1800
5	Pres. Up	Presbyterate Uplights	QTU1	Y	4200
6	Altar Up	Altar, Choir, Seating Uplights	QTU1	Y	5600
7	Altar Dn	Altar Downlights	QPD1&2	Y	800
8	Altar	Altar Focus Downlights	QPD1&2	Y	400
9	Choir Dn	Choir Downlights	QPD1&2	Y	800

GarySteffyLightingDesign Inc.
2900 South State Street Suite 12
Ann Arbor, Michigan 48104
v/ 800 537 1230 & 734 747 6630
f/ 734 747 6629

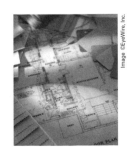

11.6

Contract Documents

This table is used to identify the number of control stations (wall switch locations), identify a label for each control station, describe briefly the control station function, and include any manufacturer–specific control catalog numbers (the column labeled "Control Types"). In this example, in the nave (near door 125D), a remote control station is specified. Remote means that only a limited number of functions can be performed at this control station. In this case, the control station has seven buttons (one for each of four scenes, one for brightening [raising] all lights, one for lowering [dimming] all lights, and one for switching all lights off. A "scene" is used to identify how a particular room setting/function is enhanced by lighting. For example, during the sermon, it is appropriate to consider dimming all focals except the lectern and dimming house lights. This could be called the "sermon" scene. Where full control of all lights is desired in this example, a liquid crystal display (LCD) station is specified. This is essentially a flat computer touchscreen through which all lighting channels can be accessed and dimmed separately and through which all scenes can be accessed. A laptop PC connection port permits for the easy programming and downloading of various scenes and the respective intensities of lights in those scenes.

Control Specification

The Project Name/C1679901   ©May 24, 2000/16500-15

Lighting Control Remote Station Design Intent			
Control Location	Label	Description	Control Types
Nave (Mechanical shaft wall adjacent to Door 125D)	Sanctuary Remote #1	7 Button Stations with 4 Scenes, Raise/Lower and Off	U10007
Choir (Exterior wall adjacent to Door 101B)	Sanctuary Master #1	LCD Station and PC Connector Station	ULCD and U2RSP
Corridor (Wall inside Corridor 109)	Sanctuary Remote #2	LCD Station	ULCD
Choir Loft (North mechanical shaft wall)	Sanctuary Master #2	LCD Station and PC Connector Station	ULCD and U2RSP

Part 3

Execution

3.01 Installation:

A. The lighting control system and wall box controls shall be installed in accordance with these specifications, the contract drawings, and the manufacturer's recommendations.

B. The Electrical Contractor shall run separate neutrals for all branch circuit loads.

C. Upon completion of installation and prior to removal of the dimmer bypass jumpers, the contractor shall verify all line, load and control wiring for accuracy of connections. Jumpers shall remain in place until all loads have been checked for short circuits or other wiring defects.

GarySteffyLightingDesign Inc.
2900 South State Street   Suite 12
Ann Arbor, Michigan 48104
v/ 800 537 1230 & 734 747 6630
f/ 734 747 6629

Image ©EyeWire, Inc.

Construction

After the contract documents have been passed along to the registered professionals for their review, correction, updating, and use (if they so choose), they will issue a complete set of construction documents to the owner and the rest of team for a final review, or issue the documents to contractors for bidding. Once a contractor is awarded the bid, the construction gets underway. Throughout this process of the registered professionals issuing construction documents, a contractor being awarded the bid, and construction, there are several ways the lighting designer may be called upon for assistance. For purposes of this text, these activities make up the Construction Administration Phase, or simply Construction.

12.1 Contract document review

The lighting designer may be asked to review the architect's and/or electrical engineer's lighting plans to confirm that lights were not erroneously moved around, deleted, or types changed. Sometimes components, such as structure, sprinklers, HVAC ducts, and the like, require lights to be rearranged. The designer should confirm that these rearrangements do not significantly alter the lighting intent.

12.2 Bidding and cost magnitudes

During the bidding process, questions may arise from contractors and/or electrical distributors about lighting hardware, lamping, and potential substitutions. At or near the end of bidding, the lighting designer may be asked to review the lighting bids or may be asked to defend the cost of the lighting bids. This is when the process can get dicey. Knowledge and/or expectations are important here. To understand the steps involved in pricing, a review of team member responsibilities and some backtracking to how lighting design gets done are necessary.

12.2.1 Client responsibilities

The client has the ultimate authority on how any project is specified. Indeed, the client quite likely will direct the team to specify certain products, develop certain details, and/or provide certain layouts based on the client's own experiences or desires. However, design aspects affecting life safety or compliance with codes or ordinances are the responsibility of the registered professionals on the team and/or of the building authorities that have jurisdiction in the municipality of the project. The client has a responsibility to know and understand the lighting purchasing chain, an example of which is shown in Figure 12.1. The client also has the ultimate authority on decisions regarding bid awards, substitutions, and what ultimately gets done on a project.

12.2.2 Conflicts of interest

Some designers are also buyers and sellers of lighting equipment. Manufacturers' representatives may have design support. Electrical distributors may have design departments. Luminaire manufacturers may have design or application groups. Construction managers and contractors may have in-house design consultants. Value engineers like to portray themselves as an independent, qualified design or engineering group. In each case and for most projects, these potential construction team members may, therefore, bring conflicts of interest to the party. While not all of these potential team

Image ©EyeWire, Inc.

12.2.3 Construction

members indulge in questionable conflict–of–interest activities, there remains such a preponderance of this activity that the client would be well advised to clear the air in advance of executing any project contract with any individual or entity. Divulging conflicts of interest or what may appear to be conflicts of interest to the client is only fair before proceeding with any contract. At times, the client either overlooks these conflicts for the promise of saving money on the project or is simply unaware of the behind–the–curtain arrangements that may exist. In many of these situations, the potential exists for some money savings to the client, but with, perhaps, an equal or greater proportion of these savings being diverted to the very construction team members making the recommendations "that save money." Client skepticism could run high.

Any team member, regardless of affiliation or independence, can offer the client some degree of integrity by subscribing to the NCQLP *Standard of Conduct.* The *Standard* outlines standards of performance, education, confidentiality, disclosure, courtesy, and professional representation aspects that encourage professional conduct and continuing education. NCQLP–certified individuals are expected to conduct themselves according to these standards. Clients would be well advised to use Lighting Certified (LC) individuals. Students are encouraged to pursue this certification—one that identifies an individual's level of lighting knowledge. Note the distinction. LC relates to one's knowledge level, not to one's practice level or to one's design capabilities. Since so many people are involved in the chain of lighting specification, purchasing, distribution, and installation, and since lighting so significantly influences energy use and users' comfort and productivity, the lighting community established the NCQLP and the LC certification to set a required level of knowledge for all involved in lighting. Hence, the public's better interests are served by lighting designers, representatives, distributors, installers, and maintainers who are certified to this common level of lighting knowledge, and who therefore are more likely to operate in unison to deliver and maintain efficient, comfortable lighting installations to the public.

more online @
http://www.ncqlp.org/

12.2.3 Standards of conduct

Any individual and/or corporation involved in any business should have or subscribe to a code or standard of conduct, a code of ethical practice, or a code of ethics. For lighting designers independent of any financial ties other than practicing lighting design, the IALD has a *Standards of Ethical Practice* as well as by–laws that indicate expected conduct of members. The idea is to establish a standard of professional conduct expected of all IALD members, thereby offering the public some degree of confidence and consistency in an IALD member's conduct.

The IALD *Standards of Ethical Practice* outlines obligations to the public as well as to the client and to the profession. Obligations to the public include endeavoring to improve the human environment, and acting in a manner that brings dignity and honor to the lighting design profession. Obligations to the client (or employer) include serving the best interests of the client—which means having no financial ties or other interests that might influence the designer's judgment (e.g., a financial interest in an electrical distributorship might influence or even have the appearance of influencing the selection of lighting hardware and/or how much of that hardware is

Construction

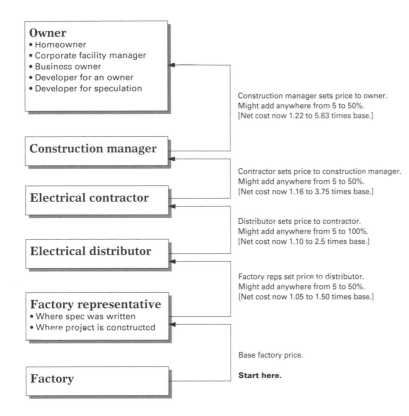

Owner
• Homeowner
• Corporate facility manager
• Business owner
• Developer for an owner
• Developer for speculation

Construction manager sets price to owner.
Might add anywhere from 5 to 50%.
[Net cost now 1.22 to 5.63 times base.]

Construction manager

Contractor sets price to construction manager.
Might add anywhere from 5 to 50%.
[Net cost now 1.16 to 3.75 times base.]

Electrical contractor

Distributor sets price to contractor.
Might add anywhere from 5 to 100%.
[Net cost now 1.10 to 2.5 times base.]

Electrical distributor

Factory reps set price to distributor.
Might add anywhere from 5 to 50%.
[Net cost now 1.05 to 1.50 times base.]

Factory representative
• Where spec was written
• Where project is constructed

Base factory price.

Start here.

Factory

Figure 12.1
A flow chart illustrating the possible, and for most projects the likely, purchasing chain for lighting equipment. Start at the "Factory" (bottom). Each link in the chain results in a cost markup on the original base price. Clients should endeavor to select a construction team that agrees to a reasonable markup in each link. This is a paradigm shift in dealing with costs. Most projects elect to cheapen the originally specified equipment to get a lower base factory price. However, this is not where the greatest markup in cost occurs. Hence, even cheap products might continue to cost the owner quite a bit more than the base factory price.

required on a given project). Obligations to the profession include not actively pursuing a commission on a project for which another IALD member has already been retained, and collaborating with other team members to develop optimal physical environments.

Designers who are part of an organization with potential conflicts of interest (e.g., selling or installing lighting equipment) should so state. A reasonable standard of conduct is to disclose in writing to the client the nature of the business in which the designer is engaged. Further, the designer should include sources of income (business or personal) that might affect design decisions or recommendations.

A code of ethics, however, is really only as good as the morals of the individual espousing such a code. Ultimately, it is incumbent on the client to make appropriate background checks. Even here, however, because of the litigious climate in America, it may not be possible to achieve a complete background check. Asking direct questions of prospective lighting designers may be the best method of establishing profiles. Is the prospective lighting designer an independent practitioner? Does the prospective lighting designer or his/her company have financial ties or familial ties to lighting manufacturing, installation contracting, electrical distributorships, procurement agencies, manufacturers' representatives' agencies, or other service or manufacturing outfits that the client feels may result in some undue, albeit perhaps unintended, influence on the designer's judgment? Such scrutiny also should be given to the selection of architects, engineers, interior designers, acousticians, audio–video consultants, landscape architects, and the like.

This is not to say that any design consultant with financial or familial ties to related businesses is not a good, competent designer. However, the designer

12.2.4 Construction

DN

Distributor Net pricing—the price at which a creditworthy electrical distributor or wholesale house should be able to purchase lighting equipment from manufacturers. Of course, distributors and some factories or their representatives would rather not have you or the client know DN pricing, thereby enabling the distributor to set whatever price at which he/she is willing to sell the lighting equipment to a contractor or directly to the client, owner, or end user. Further, some lighting representatives will quote different prices to different distributors, further confusing the situation. In other words, the lighting designer must be quite vigilant in obtaining this information.

has the obligation to fully disclose to the client these other interests, so that the client can then determine for himself/herself the overall value of the proposed relationship.

12.2.4 Designers as distributors and vice versa

Several shades of gray exist in this category where designers bill their activities foremost as lighting designers. Design fees may be comparatively small knowing that markups on the lighting equipment being specified and that also will be sold by the designer will more than cover the time necessary to design and specify the project. Arguably, this is ethical as long as the designer–as–distributor divulges such to the client prior to consummating an agreement. Even so, the client will likely never have benefit of a full design discussion outlining the multitude of lighting approaches and hardware that could be brought to bear on the project—because the designer–as–distributor will naturally work only with the palette of lighting equipment being distributed by his/her firm. For example, lighting consultant A, an independent designer and member of the IALD, proposes to charge a client US$10,000 in fees for a lighting design. Lighting consultant B, a designer with ties to an electrical distributorship (or wholesale house) and therefore not a member of the IALD, proposes to charge the client US$6000 in fees for a lighting design, with the goal of specifying lighting hardware that will be purchased through the electrical distributorship and, thus, setting up another stream of income for consultant B to help make up the difference in fees and likely result in a significant profit. Suppose consultant B gets the design commission. If US$100,000 **DN** of lighting hardware is specified by consultant B and purchased through consultant B's electrical distributor and if the electrical distributor's markup is 50 percent, there is now US$50,000 in profit that can be split between the electrical distributor and consultant B. Of course, consultant B is not likely to advise the client during budget discussions that the lighting equipment is going to be marked up 50 percent (if such came out, the client could shop to other electrical distributors for a more reasonable 10 to 20 percent markup—saving US$30,000 to US$40,000 on the distributor markup alone). Pricing information could have and likely would have been shared by consultant A with the client, and the client could have shopped for the most reasonable distributor markup! Caveat emptor.

12.2.5 Luminaire manufacturers

Application groups within manufacturers' operations are typically composed of qualified lighting engineers. These folks can offer layout and calculational support, but typically only if other team members provide the quantitative lighting criteria that need to be met. Of course, only layouts that use the respective manufacturers' goods are offered. Because these groups are typically responding to many requests, the results may not be well tailored to the specific project. For example, actual room surface reflectance values may not be used in calculations. Additionally, correct lamping, ballasting, and dirt and lamp depreciation values may not be considered in calculations. Finally, objects in space, such as open plan workstation partitions, may not be taken into account. All of these issues may result in serious overlighting or underlighting problems.

Image ©EyeWire, Inc.

Construction

12.2.6 Construction managers and contractors

Here, it is convenient for such criteria as cost and expedience to rise to the top of the lighting criteria priority list. Unfortunately, at this point, the client seems to forget that the project under design and/or construction is intended to be in place for many years to come and to offer good performance for the folks who will work and/or live there. Further, the client seems oblivious to the prospect that not all of the savings made available with cheaper lighting equipment are making their way to the client's bottom line (as discussed below and illustrated in Table 12.1).

12.2.7 Optional illusions

Pricing in the lighting business follows byzantine practices that can both confuse the client and provide extraordinary income to various parties of the construction team. Manufacturers sell lighting equipment through a network of representatives. These representatives then sell the lighting to electrical distributors, wholesalers, or other resellers. The distributors then sell the lighting equipment to contractors. Sometimes the contractors sell the lighting to the general contractor or at least provide a piece of the action by remitting a percentage value of the lighting to the general contractor and/or construction manager. Depending on market conditions and the number of parties through which the purchase progresses, the client may pay between 15 and 500 percent or more of the price the factory charges as the equipment goes out the factory door. Typically, anything more than 50 percent total markup from factory to the owner/client is considered exorbitant.

Follow the pea under the shell carefully! Table 12.1 outlines a possible pricing scenario for two different luminaires. Product A, as originally specified, is a recessed adjustable accent luminaire with locking swivel and tilt, as well as an accessory holder and a louver. Since the client and the rest of the design team had mocked up this particular luminaire and several others, all parties involved through the design development process realized that only one product met a host of variables, including the locking mechanisms, the accessory holder and louver, and the appearance of the luminaire. The client was informed that the DN price was about US$55 without the lamp and without installation. At this point, the client's desire should be to seek out a construction team that will clearly delineate all selling/purchasing agents involved in the purchasing and distribution chain and will outline agreed–upon margins for all involved. Indeed, the client's task should be to find the most cost–competitive construction team rather than the most shrewd construction team.

During the rush of construction and the pressure to keep the project on time and on budget, various parties on the project construction team attempt to offer "better value" options. For accent lighting, Product B is offered as an alternative to the client. Unfortunately, the client typically has no idea of the various selling/buying steps involved or of the vagaries of the changing margins from one product to another. This means that the client has absolutely no clout to negotiate with the respective construction team parties. Ultimately, the client loses confidence in the system, resulting in long–term disappointment and angst whenever construction projects must be undertaken. The client is left with a choice of simply saving US$6 per luminaire or not. No one informs the client that a luminaire with no locking devices (a result of choosing Product B) is likely to yield greater maintenance

12.2.8 Construction

costs (since the maintenance personnel will have to remain on the ladder a longer period of time attempting to re–direct or aim the luminaire back to its original position—a position about which no one has a clue unless the lighting effects are studied and memorized by maintenance personnel before a lamp burns out!). In an office setting, the lack of locking devices likely means that after the first relamping, lamps will no longer be aimed onto artwork, for example, that was used for visually distant focusing during "eye breaks" from computer work and/or that helped define a corporate image that, in turn, led to increased worker motivation. For a merchandiser, the lack of locking devices may mean accent lights are mis–aimed after the first relamping onto no merchandise whatsoever, and the sales effect of focal lighting is lost. If all of these pitfalls are known to the client, then the US$6 difference would be of little value, and the client would likely elect to proceed with the initially specified Product A.

Recognize that with the exception of the construction manager and/or general contractor (both presumed to be on fixed percentages), there is no incentive for any of the other parties involved in the distribution chain to promote the originally specified Product A. Every party will make more money on Product B because the margins are adjusted favorably to all parties involved. Indeed, if the client elects to proceed with Product A, all parties will still make a significant amount of money given the original margins—just not as much as with Product B!

Additionally, the client has no idea that if margins had remained fixed for all parties at the Product A margin rate, the client would actually be saving US$48 per luminaire with the substitution (which might provide a sufficient endowed fund for maintenance to take the time and effort to study the lighting effects and then carefully re-aim all lights when changing lamps in the cheaper Product B). Further, the client has no idea that margins are as great as they really are for most parties along the selling/purchasing chain. When these sorts of shenanigans are suspected of occurring, the client is best advised to seek out the actual factory price (or lacking this information, the distributor net price) for Product A and Product B and then to take relative ratios to determine that the alternative Product B should result in a savings of about US$48—and demand that the total savings be made available or that the originally specified Product A be offered at the same price originally quoted for Product B.

Pricing practices...........

- Know DN pricing
- Estimate fair markups
- Advise client on substitutions scams
- Hold the specification

12.2.8 Designer's role

It is incumbent upon the lighting designer to diligently address lighting criteria holistically. Further, diligence is necessary in understanding and reviewing budget information. The designer must be in a position to help the client fully appreciate the lighting criteria at stake and the attendant costs. Leading the charge on the users' issues—ergonomics (physiology of lighting) and psychology of lighting while simultaneously monitoring costs (both initial and operational). Further, reminding others of the purpose for the building project can yield greater appreciation for the need to adhere to original lighting criteria and original lighting design recommendations. To these ends, the designer must develop a good lighting specification and uphold it throughout the project duration.

12.2.9 Know your reps

The lighting representative can be the lighting designer's best friend or worst enemy. Good reps will keep the designer informed of new products, product

Image ©EyeWire, Inc.

Construction

Table 12.1 A Pricing Scenario for a Recessed Adjustable Accent Luminaire and a Proposed Substitute

Transaction Parties	Selling Price Product A (US$) as specified	Selling Price Product B (US$) as substituted	True First Cost Comparison (apply Product A Margins to Product B)	Client's Losses
Factory to rep	50	35	unknown	• Locking swivel • Locking tilt • Accessories for better light control
Rep to distributor	55	45	39	• Trust in system
Margin in US$ Margin of markup	5 10%	10 28%	4 10%	
Distributor to contractor	75	70	43	• Trust in system
Margin in US$ Margin of markup	20 36%	35 55%	15 36%	
Contractor to general contractor	105	100	60	• Trust in system
Margin in US$ Margin of markup	30 40%	30 43%	17 40%	
General contractor to construction manager	115	110	66	• None (fixed %)
Margin in US$ Margin of markup	10 10%	10 10%	7 10%	
Construction manager to client/owner	127	121	73	• None (fixed %)
Margin in US$ Margin of markup	12 10%	11 10%	7 10%	
Client savings in US$ Margin of savings	0 0%	6 5%	54 42%	US$48 and all above cited losses

technical or shipping problems, and product modifications. Good reps will have or be able to get, in short order, answers to technical, pricing, and leadtime questions, and be able to provide actual samples. The lighting designer should, if at all possible, view working samples of luminaires intended to be used in a specification. Graphic representations can be very misleading—not purposely, although this has been known to happen as well.

Lighting reps are very instrumental in helping the designer hold a specification. Alternatively, lighting reps can substitute a specification quite readily. Know the reps. Copy the reps with specifications for projects prior to any bidding. Include cover notes indicating that the rep is being copied with the specification as a courtesy (reps make commission only on those projects for which they "register" with the factory—your sending along a specification facilitates this registration process). Further, ask the rep for to review the specification and confirm your catalog numbers (perhaps you've transposed some numbers or letters, catalog numbers have changed recently, or the product has been discontinued, etc.), and to provide DN pricing and leadtime

12.2.10 Construction

for the specified equipment for which he/she is a rep. Advise the rep that you are not seeking any alternatives or substitutions (unless, of course, you are). Finally, advise the rep of the actual project location. Since reps have territories of coverage, your project may be outside of his/her territory. In this event, the rep must notify the rep responsible for the particular locale in which the project is located. Hopefully, your local rep will advise the distant rep that no substitutions are being sought. It is very easy for folks to get greedy. The distant rep may elect to try to get the whole lighting order! In this situation, he/she would have to substitute all of his/her products wherever you have specified another manufacturer's product. Clearly, the rep is now making design decisions and, ultimately, changing the legal aspects of the project's chain of responsible parties. This easily escalates into a situation where every other rep whose products are in the specification will also likely attempt to substitute the entire project with his/her specific brands. Ultimately, the client will likely end up "holding the bag," with lighting equipment that doesn't precisely meet the original design intent—perhaps missing some key programming requirements and/or design aspects that the team labored over for months.

This aspect of substitutions has become rampant over the past decade. Consolidation in the lighting industry has led to three or four conglomerates. Each conglomerate has commodified most lighting equipment and, thereby, believes that its products are as good or bad as those of the competition. To boost the bottom line, each conglomerate encourages its reps and distributors to "package" lighting projects—pull together a complete package of products that are, what the conglomerate believes to be, equal to the originally specified equipment. In reality, each conglomerate has strong products and weak products. By mixing and matching on any given project, the designer can put together a complete design specification that will meet most, if not all, of the client's needs most, if not all, of the time. Allowing substitutions will simply mean most of the criteria won't be met most of the time. The user ultimately suffers.

12.2.10 DN budget pricing

DN budget pricing should be sought for all projects. This is the budget pricing the manufacturers' lighting representatives propose for their respectively specified lighting equipment. Various scenarios have been proposed, most notably by lighting designer Randy Burkett.[1] The designer provides the various lighting representatives of the specified manufacturers with a copy of the specification and a request that the manufacturers' representatives review the specification of their particular products for accuracy and to establish DN budget pricing. Figure 12.2 shows a sample request to a manufacturer's rep. The reference to accuracy is important to ensure that the catalog numbering has not changed recently and/or that the designer has properly and accurately interpreted the catalog information. DN budget pricing is the price that the representative will likely quote to an electrical distributor for the kinds and quantities of equipment specified. Since the project is in a design phase and not yet ready for final bidding, this "budget price" is typically 10 to 15 percent higher than actual pricing at that point in time. Remember, inflation and/or simple raw material price costs may fluctuate by that much between this "budget pricing" phase and the actual purchase of the lighting hardware (which may be months away). **Advisory:** It is imperative to ask and receive DN pricing. Contractor pricing, distributor list

Construction

pricing, and consumer list pricing (also known as "list pricing") are all grossly inflated to cover the vagaries of industry markups and purchasing chain agents. Even the difference between the DN budget pricing and the final bid DN pricing can confound the designers and clients. It is crucial to seek clarity from reps about what quotes they are providing (DN pricing or DN budget pricing). For DN budget pricing, it is imperative to understand the percentage of "slop" involved.

12.2.11 Value engineering

Value engineering was introduced to the building design and construction process in the early 1970s. Initially, its noble goal was to offer the client a project with measurable value. At the time, a series of magazine articles on lighting warned of consequences if value engineering failed to account also for the more subjective (and immeasurable) qualitative aspects of building design.[2] Today, value engineering (VE) simply means cost cutting. There will be fancy arguments and spins on VE and "what it can do for the client." Since some VE arrangements offer the value engineer a percentage of the costs saved, there is extraordinary pressure to save costs at most any cost! Initial cost is reduced at the sacrifice of qualitative aspects and/or at the sacrifice of future operations' costs. Qualitative aspects include aesthetics, but more critically include subjective aspects, such as occupant attitude, well–being, and motivation. All of these elements drive productivity (in a work environment) and comfort (in a living environment) and, ultimately, should establish life cycle payback. Ironically, as energy criteria ratchet downward and if initial cost budgets also ratchet downward, clients often will be left with little more than a uniformly and dimly lighted drywall box. Not much of a value! The question is this: How can a partial team (value engineers) enter a project; spend little, if any, time on understanding the programming; have little, if any, interaction with the design team and client/owner and/or users during the design process; and propose effective solutions that will meet all of the same criteria and design issues as the proposed design? The answer: It can't!

12.3 Shop drawings

Shop drawings are issued during construction by the contractor if he/she wants the design team to confirm that he/she is procuring the correct equipment. It is also an opportunity to ensure that all of the specification information has been correctly interpreted by the contractor, distributor, and manufacturer. Finally, it is one last check to confirm that the specification was originally submitted with correct catalog designations.

It is the contractor's responsibility to determine if shop drawings will even be a part of the process and, if so, how, when, and to which team members they will be distributed. The contractor should distribute shop drawings to the registered professionals who, in turn, must decide if any of the project consultants will be asked to offer review comments. These review comments must then be considered by the registered professionals and either ignored or addressed accordingly.

Reputable contractors will use the shop drawing process to be certain that the specification was interpreted correctly, and that no technology, manufacturing, or cataloging changes have taken place since the original specification was written. Shop drawings also may help the contractor better understand installation or identify installation issues.

12.3 Construction

Less reputable contractors will "sit on the shop drawings" as a tactic to force the design team to accept substitutions. This is how this works (referring to Table 12.1). Product B substitution is disallowed early in the quotation process—the client agrees with the design team decision that was itself based on a laborious process. Product A is required. This decision may not sit well with some members of the purchasing chain. Hence, one way to attempt to force the purchase of Product B is to alert the design team that Product A takes ten weeks from time of shop drawing approval, but that Product B takes only four weeks from time of shop drawing approval. If the contractor holds the shop drawings to within five or six weeks of needing the lighting equipment on the job site, it will appear that the team has no choice but to permit the substitution of Product B (since Product A would show up after the date it is needed in order for the contractor to complete the project on time). However, if the specification has appropriate language in it (as illustrated in Specification Section 1.07.A in Chapter 11), then the contractor must provide the specified equipment (Product A in this case) at the cost he/she quoted and in the timeframe to which he/she committed.

To minimize the unnecessary hassle of incompetently made substitutions, the designer should qualify the specification to indicate that the contractor shall incur the cost of fees required for the design team to review, calculate, assess, and, if accepted as a substitute, revise plans. After all, the client hired a professional team for its professional expertise and opinions, and hired the contractor to execute those opinions.

Defensible design.........

- Establish criteria
- Comprehensive design
- Substantive analyses
- Systems integration
- Energy compliance
- Good specifications

The lighting designer, if given the opportunity, must review shop drawings carefully and quickly to assure correct and timely procurement. However, it is the contractor's responsibility to secure shop drawings from the manufacturers through the electrical distributor and then to submit these shop drawings to the registered professional architect or engineer on the project. The registered professional is responsible for final authority on shop drawing approval. The lighting designer's role is to confirm that the lighting equipment represented by the shop drawings will meet the lighting design intent—aesthetic appearance of the luminaire, aesthetic effect of the light from the luminaire, and light intensity from the luminaire. Typical disposition of shop drawings by the lighting designer includes: approved; approved as noted; approved as changed; not approved for reasons noted; or no substitutions accepted. Having indicated the recommended disposition of the shop drawings, the lighting designer should then sign and date them, and forward them to the registered professional(s).

A note of "approved" indicates that the lighting hardware shown on the shop drawing appears to meet the aesthetic qualities of the luminaire as specified, the aesthetic qualities of the lighting effect anticipated from the luminaire as specified, and the intensity requirements of the luminaire as specified. A note of "approved as noted" indicates that some notations have been made by the lighting designer. For example, if the luminaire was originally specified as "Polar White" in color, but the shop drawing indicates the color is "Winter White," a notation that the "Painted finish shall be Polar White as originally specified" would be appropriate. Another example, if a fluorescent striplight was specified with one lamp but the shop drawing shows two lamps, it would be reasonable to note that the "Luminaire shall use one (1) lamp in cross–section as originally specified."

Image ©EyeWire, Inc.

Construction

12.5

Sometimes some subtle (and hopefully simple) changes to lighting equipment are desired. For example, as construction progresses, the team may decide that the reflector cones on downlights will look better with the other hardware finishes if the cones are diffuse aluminum rather than specular aluminum. After confirming with the lighting rep that such a change would not affect the cost or leadtime of the luminaire, than an "approved as changed" note like, "Luminaire reflector shall be diffuse aluminum, with a catalog designation of XXX–XX" is appropriate (where XXX–XX is the actual catalog number for the now–desired diffuse aluminum reflector).

Where the shop drawing has significant errors, these errors should be cited along with a note of "not approved for reasons noted." This will typically result in resubmittal of lighting shop drawings so noted in order to confirm that the errors have been corrected.

If a shop drawing illustrates the wrong luminaire entirely or is a substitution attempt, then noting that "no substitutions accepted" will suffice. Shop drawing resubmittal will then occur with, hopefully, the as–specified luminaire shown.

A sample shop drawing is shown in Figure 12.3a and 12.3b. Typically, notations are in red ink, including the rubber stamp. This permits ready recognition of notes.

12.4 Construction assistance

Not to be taken literally, however, the lighting designer should be able to assist the team as questions arise from the field. This may even necessitate a few visits to the project site. There will be times when, regardless of the effort that went into the systems' integration and planning, one trade's work will interfere with another trade's work. Lighting is bound to be one of those trades. So, a luminaire may have to be moved 6" (150 mm) to avoid interference with a duct, sprinkler, structural element, or water line, etc. Conversely, lighting may need to influence the location of a duct, beam, or pipe, etc., if the luminaire's location is important for either the correct lighting effect, the correct symmetry of ceiling layout, or both. Clearly, this sort of effort must be team–based, because registered professionals need to assess the impact of any such interferences and resulting moves.

12.5 Lighting review and aiming observation

The lighting designer is not a qualified inspector of installation. However, the lighting designer should review lighting effects and luminaire finishes, fit, and alignment as they relate to the visual aesthetics of the lighting effects and the lighting hardware that is exposed to view. This constitutes a lighting review. Where luminaire finishes are marred or incorrect, these need to be corrected by the electrical and/or general contractor. Until the project is turned over to and accepted by the owner, the project is itself the contractors' responsibility. Excuses of "it was damaged in shipment" or "no one knows how it got that way" do not release the contractor from providing a complete and satisfactory project to the owner. Any lighting effects or luminaire finishes or layouts that are incorrect and/or damaged should be noted by the lighting designer and passed along to the registered professional(s) for his/ her (their) consideration as a punchlist item (a formal record of final work and

12.5 Construction

Figure 12.2
An example of a cover note used to distribute specification copies to local reps, and to request DN pricing. Fill in actual names, dates, cities, and states as appropriate for the actual project situation.

Ask the rep to review the catalog numbers for accuracy. Since manufacturers change catalog numbering systems from time to time, and since transposition errors are common, this step can serve as a very important check of the specification accuracy. Also, if any specification items are still unresolved, a note here is necessary to advise the rep not to make guesses about your intentions by filling in catalog numbers for you.

Let the rep know to which architect and/or engineer you will be submitting the specification and in which locale these firms are located. Reps typically must split commissions with reps from the AE issuing city and the city in which the project will be constructed.

Facsimile

Page 1 ©January 6, 2001

to:	**Local Lighting Rep**
number of pages:	19 (including this page)
from:	Gary Steffy
date:	January 6, 2001
subject:	Project Name DN Pricing
design phase:	Contract Documents
projected bid date:	Second Quarter 2001
original via:	Filed
project number:	16700

Please review the following excerpts from our lighting specification on the subject project located in City, State. Review for correctness and completeness as relates to those manufacturers' equipment which you represent and for which catalog numbers are given [NOTE: do not guess at our intentions—if no catalog numbers are given, please do not price said item at this time. We are still assessing this particular selection and we will make a determination in the next few months on exact manufacturers and products.] Please advise in writing ASAP of any discrepancies or if you believe an error has been made in the specification of this equipment for the cited use.

This specification will be submitted by us to Architect/Engineer in City, State for its use and subsequent disposition as part of its contract documents for the Project Name in City, State.

We are not seeking alternatives, so–called equals, or even substitutions, and ask that you and your manufacturer(s) and your

GarySteffyLightingDesign Inc.
2900 South State Street Suite 12
Ann Arbor, Michigan 48104
v/ 800 537 1230 & 734 747 6630
f/ 734 747 6629

Construction

12.5

Facsimile

Page 2 ©January 6, 2001

counterpart issuing–city and construction–city representative(s) respect the design process, the client, and us as designers by not offering same. This obviously means that we are not asking for "packaging" of the project. We copy you with this specification as a professional courtesy and so that you may assist us in preparing our cost magnitude for the client. This specification is copyrighted and may be used solely for your preparation of distributor net (DN) pricing on those items specified and for which you are the factory representative. Any other use is strictly prohibited.

Kindly advise us of DN pricing on a per–unit basis for each luminaire type where one of your lines has been specified. We have included a tabular summary of rough counts. We your DN pricing in our office by Month Day, Year, so that we may help the client establish a budget magnitude for the lighting.

There is no an assurance that this project will move forward nor that, if it does move forward, this will be the actual specification used for the Architect/Engineer contract documents.

You are encouraged to share this information, including DN pricing, with your counterparts in the issuing–city and the construction–city so that as requests are made in those/that locale(s), information is readily available. Please call me, email me or fax me with any questions. Thank you for your assistance.

file 00122801

GarySteffyLightingDesign Inc.
2900 South State Street Suite 12
Ann Arbor, Michigan 48104
v/ 800 537 1230 & 734 747 6630
f/ 734 747 6629

Clearly indicate that this is not a request for any sort of alternatives, equals, or substitutions. Further, indicate that the rep may not make copies of this specification material in order to assess substitutions (some reps will gladly forward a specification to one of his/her larger conglomerates in an attempt to have that conglomerate put together a package of so–called equals. This helps the rep "lock in" a complete package (the distributor and/or contractor are then unable to split apart and purchase only those luminaires that were originally specified).

Ask the rep for DN pricing. This may require clarification either in writing or during a phone conversation—you need the best DN price available, not "list DN" or "contractor net" or any other sort of similarly sounding, but inflated price. If DN pricing is unavailable or the rep is too dense to appreciate what is meant here, consider specifying other equipment or contacting the manufacturer directly.

Advise the rep to share this information with respective counterparts. This should help prevent misunderstandings as others involved in the project attempt to secure DN pricing.

Be sure to attach the relevant portions of the specification.

Construction

The lighting representative who is local to the electrical distributor's location has read the specification (see Specification Section 2.19 in Chapter 11) and elected to secure and submit this shop drawing (which is identical to the cutsheet shown in Figure 11.7). The lighting rep then hand–marked the key catalog items that he/she intends to order from the factory for the distributor. The distributor should then circulate this shop drawing to the electrical contractor who, in turn, will circulate it to the registered professional (architect or engineer) on the project, who, in turn, may elect to forward a copy to the lighting designer for review. Sometimes the contractor forwards the lighting shop drawings directly to the lighting designer. After review, in such a situation, the lighting designer could forward the reviewed shop drawing(s) back to the contractor with a note that all shop drawings require registered professional review and final disposition. Note: some shop drawings are even more detailed than this cutsheet and could include actual production drawings on large–sized prints.

TRIPLES-V 32/7

recessed compact fluorescent downlight/wallwasher

COMPACT FLUORESCENT 1-18

FEATURES

Triples-V 32/7 is a highly efficient 7″ aperture low brightness downlight designed for use with one 32-watt triple-tube compact fluorescent lamp of the 4-pin types made by GE, Osram/Sylvania or Philips. Triples-V 32/7 provides a shielding angle of 40°.

One housing allows interchangeable use of downlight and wallwash reflectors, permitting housings to be installed first and reflectors to be installed or changed at any time.

Triples-V 32/7 uses one 32-watt lamp providing 2400 lumens (nearly that of a 150-watt incandescent), a 10,000-hour life, a color rendering index (CRI) of 82, and color temperatures as warm as 2700°K (nearly duplicating the color qualities of incandescent).

Reflectors are available in clear (natural aluminum), semi-specular etch clear or champagne gold Alzak® with Color-Chek® anodizing, virtually eliminating iridescence. Wallwash reflectors available are: wallwash (120°), corner wallwash (210°), and double wallwash (2x120°).

Triples-V 32/7 includes a pair of mounting bars (³⁄₄″ x 27″ C channel). Specialty bars for wood joist and T-bar installations are also available.

APPLICATIONS

Fixture is suitable for downlighting or wallwashing in nearly all architectural environments, especially those spaces where non-directional luminaires are preferred over rectangular troffers. These include offices, stores, airports, schools, hotels, lobbies and public spaces.

Fixture is c(UL)us listed for Damp Location (may not be suitable for some outdoor environments). Fixture is union made IBEW and in compliance with the component based efficiency standards of the 1995 New York State Energy Conservation Code. Fixture is prewired with high power factor Class P electronic ballast and approved for ten #12 wire 75°C branch circuit pull-through wiring. Removal of the reflector allows access to the ballast and junction box.

Figure dimensions:
10 5/16″ (262mm)
1″ (25mm)
7″ (178mm) dia
8 1/4″ (210mm) dia
10″ x 15″ (254 x 38mm)
Requires ceiling opening of 7 ¹⁵⁄₁₆″ (202mm)

PRODUCT CODE

For complete product code, list basic unit and select one item from each following box.

✓ Basic Unit .... TRP 32/7

Reflector Type	
Downlight .... no suffix	Corner Wallwash .... CWW
Wallwash .... WW	Double Wallwash .... DWW

✓ Voltage
120 volt service 120   277 volt service............... 277

✓ Reflector and Flange Color — Overlap / Flush
Clear (Natural Aluminum) .... COL .... CFL
Champagne Gold .... GOL .... GFL
Semi-specular Etch Clear .... ECOL .... ECFL
Other reflector finishes are available on special order.

Standard reflector flange continues reflector finish. White painted flanges and custom painted flanges are available on special order. Add WF (white flange) or CCF (custom color flange).

OPTIONS

Specify by adding to the basic unit.

Dimmable. Not for outdoor application .... – DM

Emergency battery pack operates lamp in event of power outage. Not for outdoor application .... – EM

Return Air Plenum. Modified for maximum performance in air return ceiling plenums .... – RA

¹⁄₈″ (3mm) thick **clear acrylic shield**, spring-mounted within reflector .... – PS

▶ For combinations of the Options above, contact factory or Edison Price Lighting representative.

▶ An install-from-below version of this fixture, suitable for installation outside North America, is also available. Contact factory.

▶ Decorative reflector rings are available on special order. Contact factory.

EDISON PRICE LIGHTING
409 E 60 St, New York NY 10022, tel 212.521.6900 fax 212.888.7981 www.epl.com
©Copyright, Edison Price Lighting 2000   1:18

Cutsheet drawings courtesy of and ©Edison Price Lighting, Inc. Available online at http://www.epl.com

Construction

Type FCD1
Compact Fluorescent Downlight
file D1670001

 GarySteffyLightingDesign Inc.
2900 South State Street, Suite 12
Ann Arbor, Michigan 48104
v/800 537 1230
f/313–747–6629

☐ Approved

☒ Approved as noted

☐ Approved as changed

☐ Not approved for reasons noted

☐ No substitutions accepted

[signature]

Designer

August 5, 2000

Date

This indicates our review and subsequent suggestion(s) based on luminaires/lamps compliance with our proposed lighting design intent. WE ARE NOT REGISTERED PROFESSIONALS. Final disposition is subject to Electrical Engineering, Mechanical Engineering, Structural Engineering, Landscape Architecture, and Architectural review by registered professionals. It is incumbent on the purchaser to solicit registered professionals' direction.

1. Reflector and overlap flange finish shall be semi–specular etch clear (ECOI)
2. Clear acrylic shield (PS) option shall be included.

Figure 12.3b
Since the lighting rep mismarked several items, the shop drawing is annotated by the lighting designer. The shop drawing "stamp" may be relatively large and, even in red ink, may obscure information on the shop drawing. In these situations, it may be necessary to stamp the back of the shop drawing. If the shop drawing is reviewed by only the registered professional(s) on the project, then the caveat note at the bottom of the stamp may not apply— depending on the scope of the registered professional's work.

12.6 Construction

adjustments that the contractor needs to make prior to final owner acceptance of the installation). It is important to note that inspection of the physical installation aspects (e.g., how are lights mechanically secured, how are electrical connections made, is the circuit of sufficient size to handle the lighting loads, etc.) are not the responsibility of the lighting designer, but rather are part of the contractor's work, the registered professional(s) work, and the work of municipal building inspectors.

Wherever adjustable lights are specified, it is the contractor's responsibility to aim such lights according to the design team's direction. This may necessitate the architect, engineer, and/or lighting designer visiting the project site very near the time that the project is turned over to the owner and observing the contractor during aiming sessions. Where aiming is rather consistent, aiming observation may only require a few sample setups that the contractor then replicates. Other projects, with extensive accents aimed onto varying sized elements and details, may take days (and/or nights) of aiming observation. In any event, the contractor has the responsibility of providing all of the necessary equipment (lifts, ladders, and scaffolds), tools (for locking lights once aimed), and crews for the aiming.

12.6 System commissioning

Depending on the fee structure and scope of work agreed upon, as well as the degree of complexity of the lighting system and controls, commissioning of the installation may be appropriate. This typically involves the relevant team members, including the registered professional(s), the contractor, the lighting designer, possibly the lighting representatives, the client, and perhaps the users and/or the client's maintenance personnel. Commissioning is a "first run" of the lighting. Final aiming tweaks and/or control tweaks may be made at this stage. If motion sensors, photocontrols, timers, and/or other control mechanisms are used, this is the time to finalize their respective sensitive settings, output/input settings, and instruction to the client's authorized personnel on their operation and programming.

12.7 Post occupancy evaluation

This is a much–discussed, little–implemented phase of the work. It must be the last phase since it occurs after some period of facility occupancy. The intent, of course, is to understand how successful the project was at meeting the program criteria and how successful the program criteria were in establishing a comfortable, productive, and satisfactory environment. While some small, informal evaluation can be done by the design team, so many variables are involved in actual environments that a professional team of experts (typically researchers) need to be retained for meaningful results.

12.8 Endnotes

[1] Randy Burkett, "Building Quality Lighting Specifications," *Architectural Lighting*, April/May, 1999, 74–78.
[2] John Flynn, "The Psychology of Light, Article 8, The Scope of 'Value Engineering' in Lighting Design," *Electrical Consultant*, August, 1973, 20–25.

Image ©EyeWire, Inc.

Index

Index

Index

Index